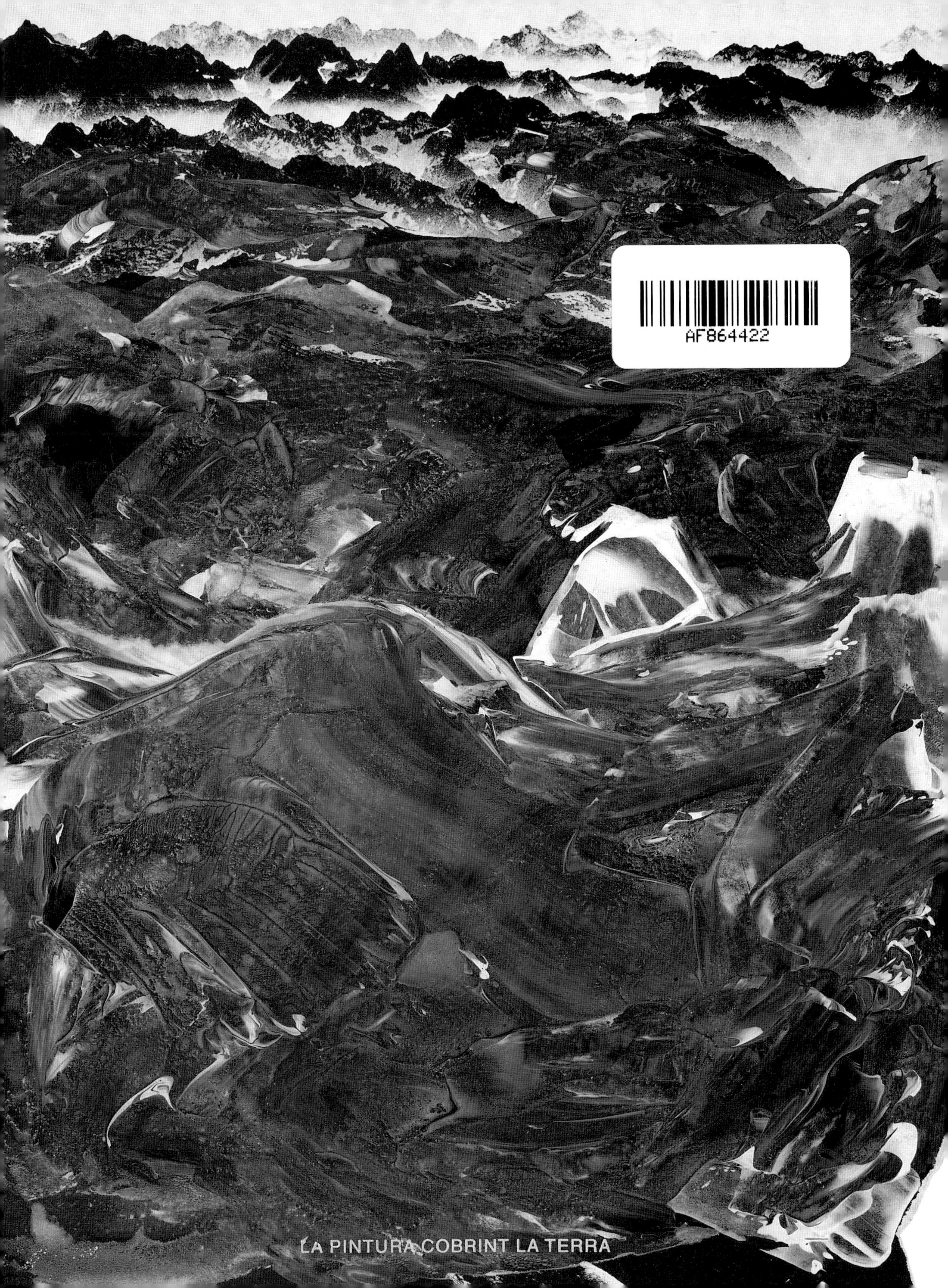
LA PINTURA COBRINT LA TERRA

Perejaume

DIS-EXHIBIT

EXHIBITION

Head Curators
Marcia Tucker, Carles Guerra

Curator
Glòria Picazo

Exhibit Coordination
Teresa Grandas

Assistant Coordinator
Inés Arderiu

General Coordination
Anna Borrell

Realization
Isabel Bachs; Mètode

Restoration
Sílvia Noguer, Xavier Rossell

Cultural Programs
Josep M. Muñoz

Activities
Anna Guarro, Yolanda Nicolás

Educational Services
Antònia M. Cerdà

Press
Nicola Wohlfarth

CATALOGUE

Idea and conception
Perejaume, Carles Guerra

Texts
Pere Gimferrer, Boris Groys,
Carles Guerra, Perejaume, Marcia Tucker

Coordination
Anna Jiménez Jorquera, Elisabet Surís

Graphic Design
Ramon Prat

Translations
Joan Gili, John Stone, Jeffrey Swartz

Corrections
Joquim Sala-Sanahuja, Tim Yonh,
Anna Tetas

Documentation
Marta Vega

Photography
Josep Armengol, Salvador del Carril,
Martín García, Martí Gasull, Jaume Maymó,
Wilfried Petzi, Rocco Ricci

Distribution
ACTAR
Roca i Batlle, 2-4
08023 Barcelona
Tel. +34 934 187 759
Fax + 34 934 186 707
arquitec@actar.es
www.actar.es

1a edició, Barcelona, abril de 1999

ISBN 84-95273-05-5
DL B 24326-99

ACKNOWLEDGMENTS

Vicenç Altaió, August Sander Archiv, Bellapart, Centre Cultural de la Mercè, Tomàs Biel, Erik Bullot, Pere Casanovas, Centro Galego de Arte Contemporánea, Leonardo Escoda, European Patent Office, Cesc Feixas, Manuel Guerrero, Josep de Ca l'Estrany, Aliki Kostaki, Xavier Mateu, Cristina Mendoza, Erik Mosel y Andrea Tschechow, Museu d'Art de Girona, Observatori de l'Ebre, Patrimoni-UB, Palma Dotze Galeria d'Art, Albert Roig, Marc Sarsanedes, Carme Sais, Joaquim Sala-Sanahuja, Tinglado Tarragona, Uniland, Universitat de Barcelona, Universitat Ramon Llull, Ernesto Ventós

Special thanks to Galeria Joan Prats: Joan de Muga, Gloria Pérez, Helena Tatay, and Núria Mateu

Loans
Ajuntament de Mont-roig del Camp, Vicenç Altaió, Miquel Barceló, Caja de Burgos, Col·lecció d'Art Contemporani Fundació "la Caixa" (Barcelona), Col·legi d'Arquitectes de Catalunya, Anna and Marc Domingo, Fundación Coca-Cola (Spain), Galeria Joan Prats, Galerie Mosel und Tschechow (Munich), Maria Guinart, Montse Jubany, Juan Luis Libano, Museu Nacional d'Art de Catalunya (Museu d'Art Modern, Barcelona), Museo Nacional Centro de Arte Reina Sofía (Madrid), Museu de Pintura Sant Pol de Mar, Gloria Pérez, Rosa M. Sardà, Michael Schmidt (Ulm), Staatsgalerie Stuttgart, Juan Uslé and Victoria Civera, Santi Viladrich

And all those lenders who have preferred to remain anonymous

Friends of MACBA
Fundación Andersen Consulting
Port de Barcelona
Carlos Duran

What We Must Be Drawing Through our Ways of Life

Night Itinerary, Ca l'Oller de la Cortada, Parc de Dones d'Aigua, Sant Iscle de Vallalta, 1978
Aerostatic Poem: Night Ball (Èczema), launching at Costabona Peak, 1980
Frames, 1986
Postcard Rack, 1984
In Image and Appearance, 1988
The Access, Josep M. Jujol, 1988
Lighted Frame, 1990
Hypsometry, 1992
Chauffeur-Piano, 1984 (Liliana Maffiotte and Benet Martorell painting)
Frames, 1986
Frames, 1986
Mirror of Crous, 1987
A Miró Painting at the Uja Plain, Escola Eina, Alta Garrotxa, 1991
A World Behind Words, 1989
Pyrenean I, 1990
Pyrenean II, 1990
Catenary, 1989
Hair, 1997
Chauffeur-piano, 1984 (Isabel Aragon)
Projections, 1987
Railway, 1980
Retable: Collection of the Sant Pol de Mar Museum of Painting, 1997
What We Must Be Drawing Through our Ways of Life, 1995

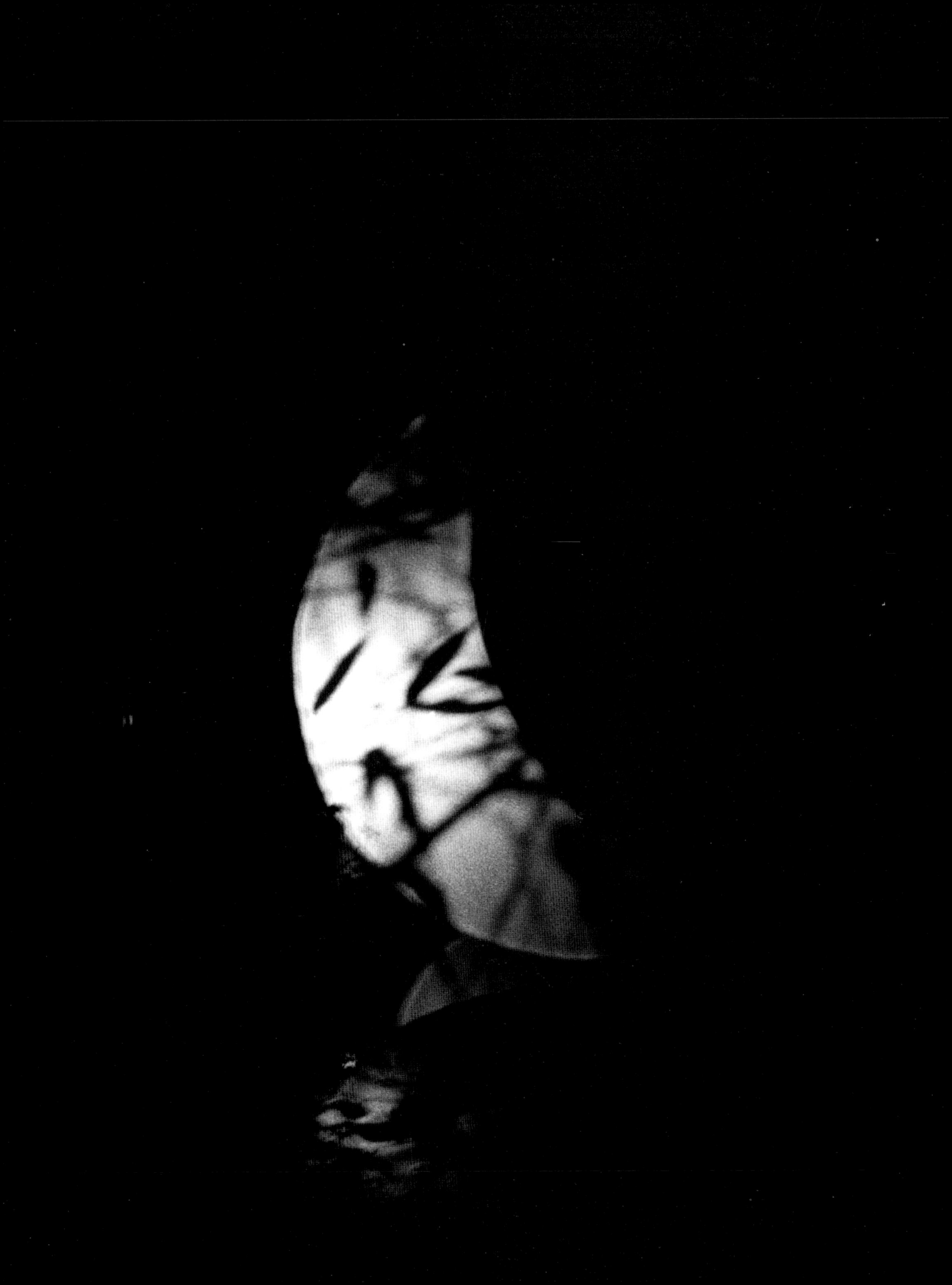

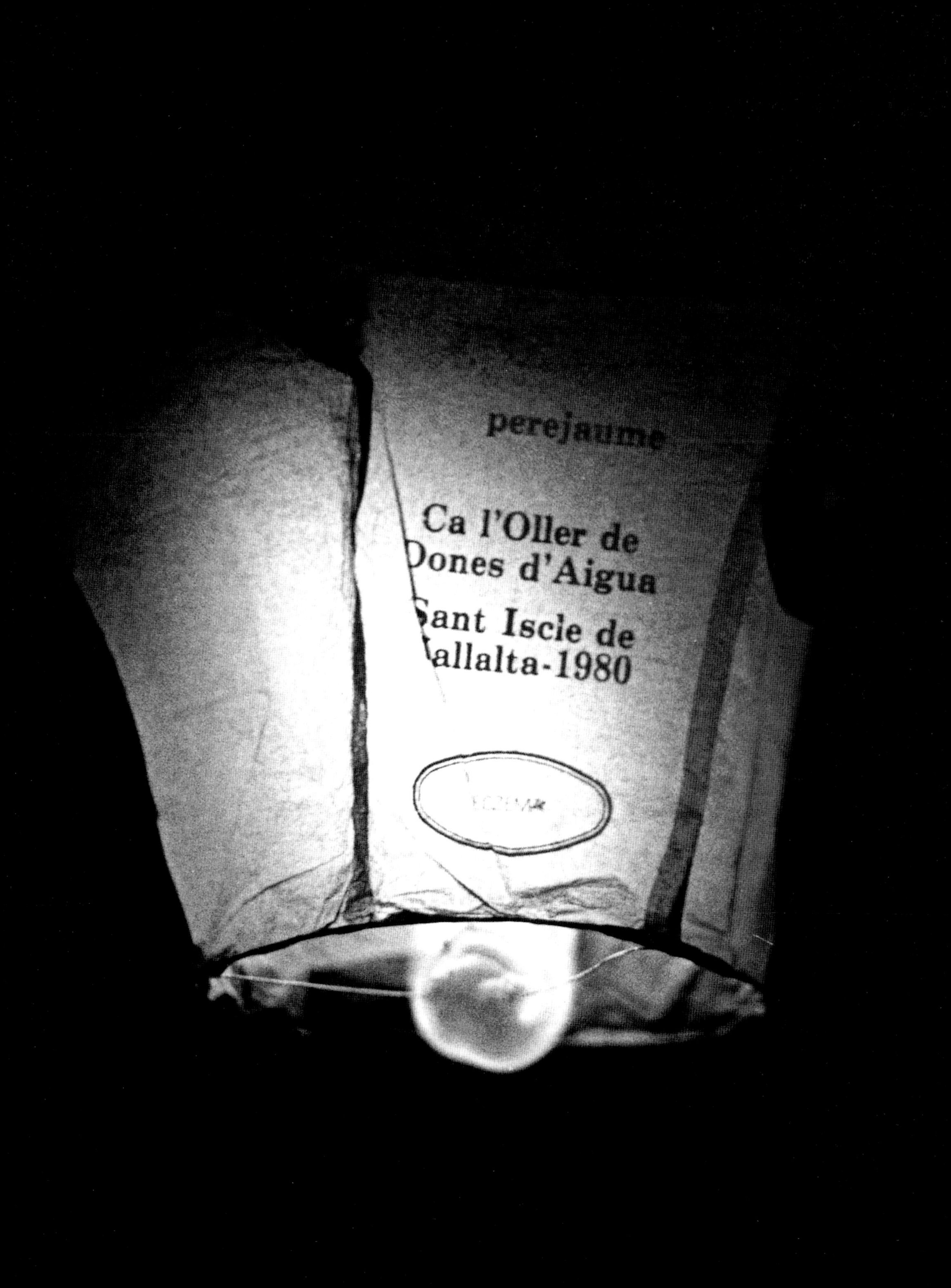
perejaume
Ca l'Oller de
Dones d'Aigua
Sant Iscle de
allalta-1980

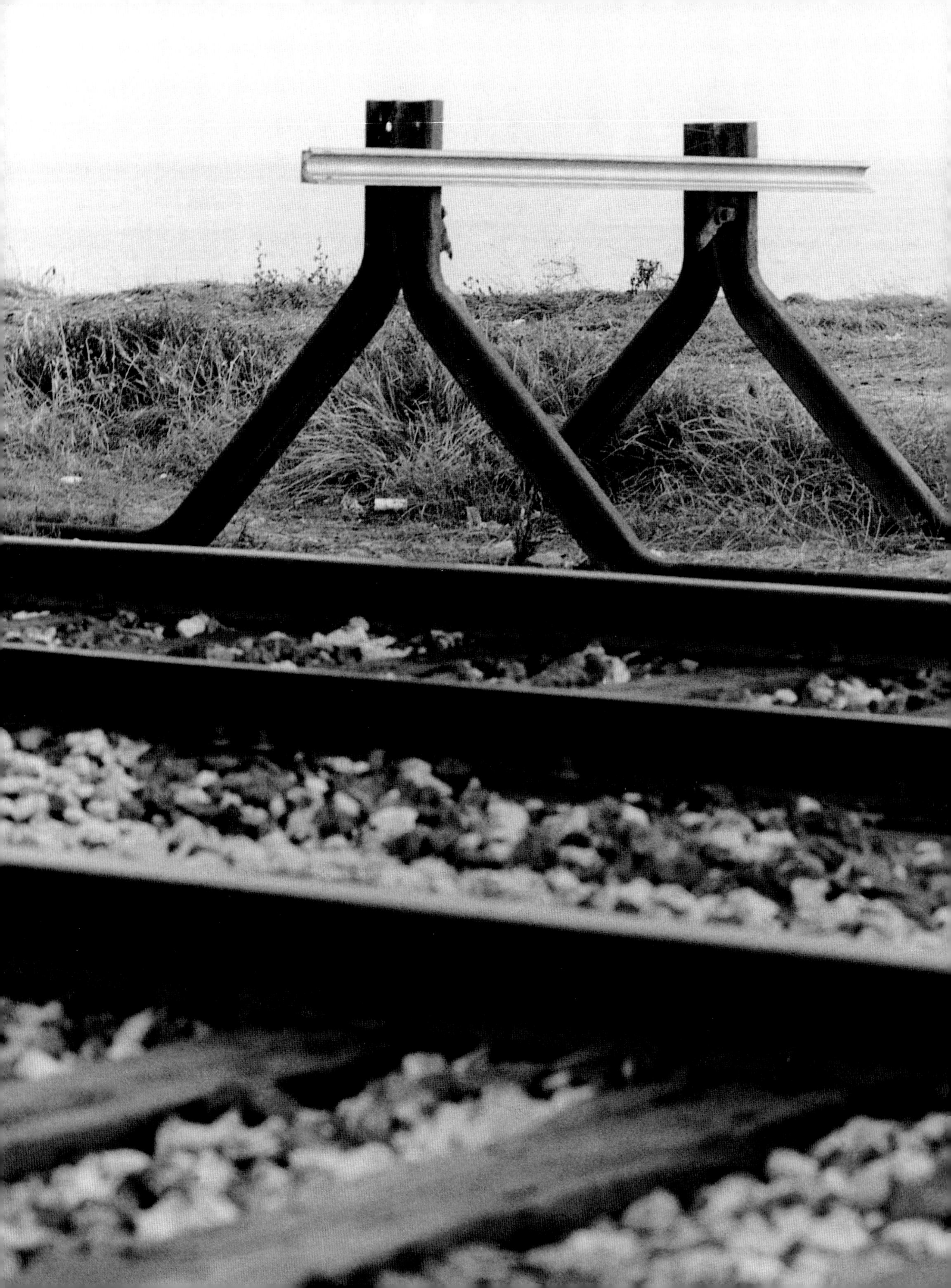

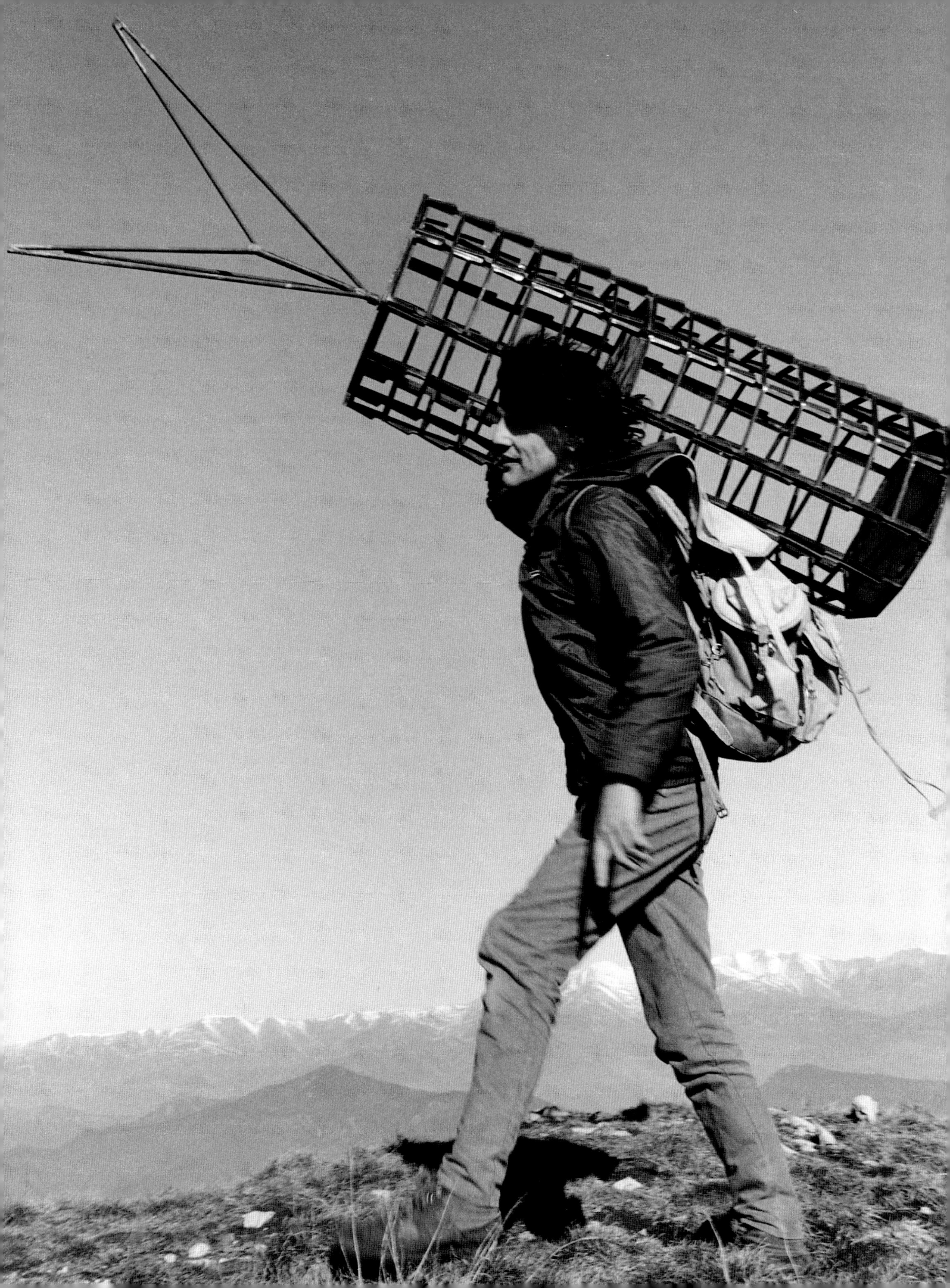

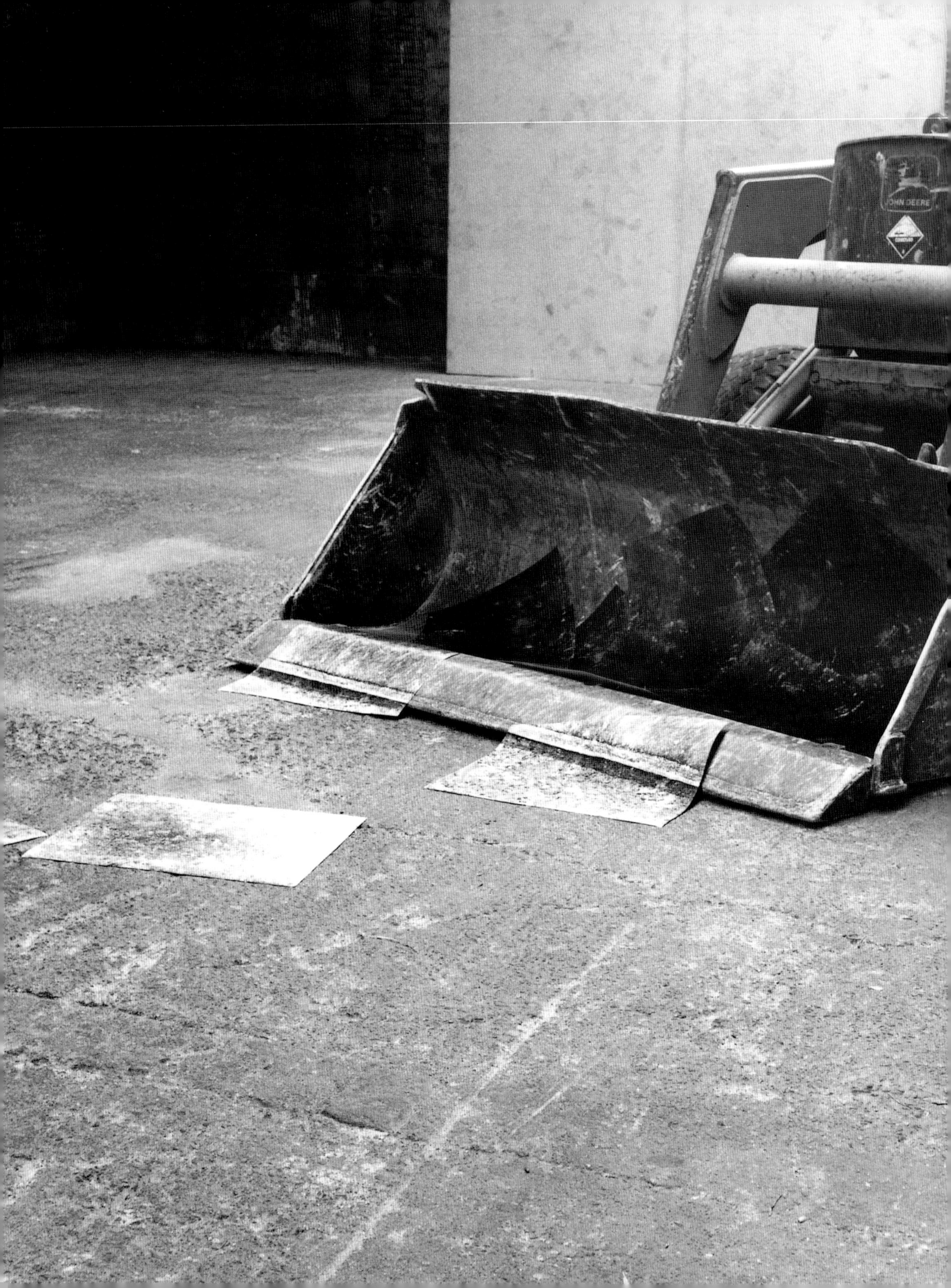
JOHN DEERE

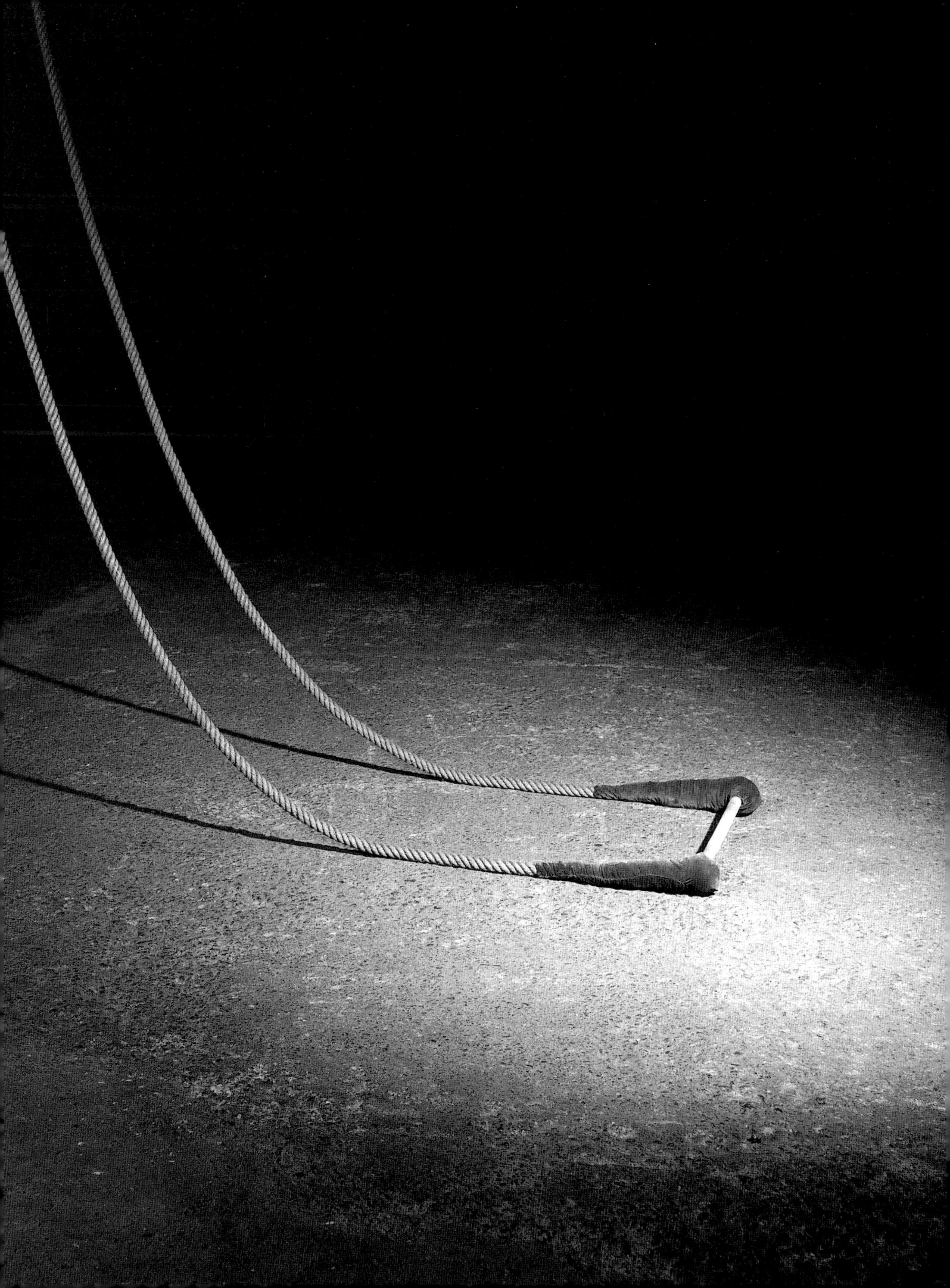

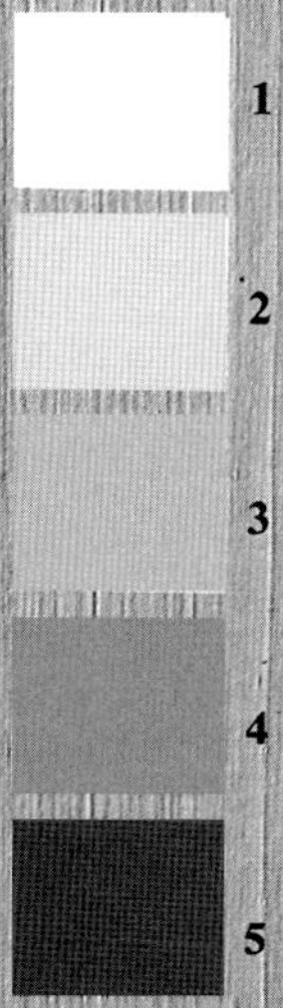

HIPSOMETRIA

1, de 0 a 200 m. de altitud; 2, de 200 a 500 m.; 3, de 500 a 1.000 m.; 4, de 1.000 a 2.000 m.; 5, más de 2.000 metros.

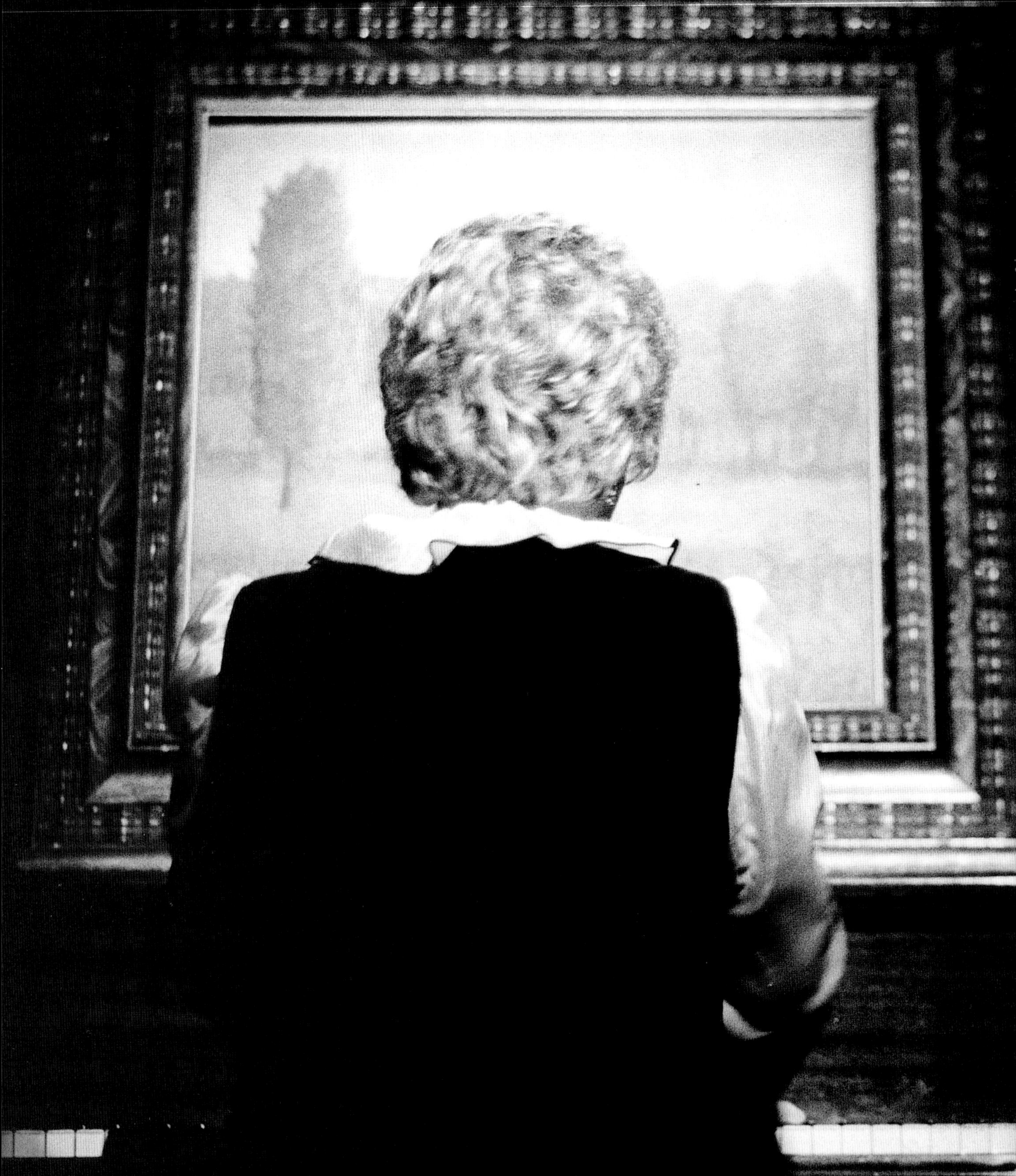

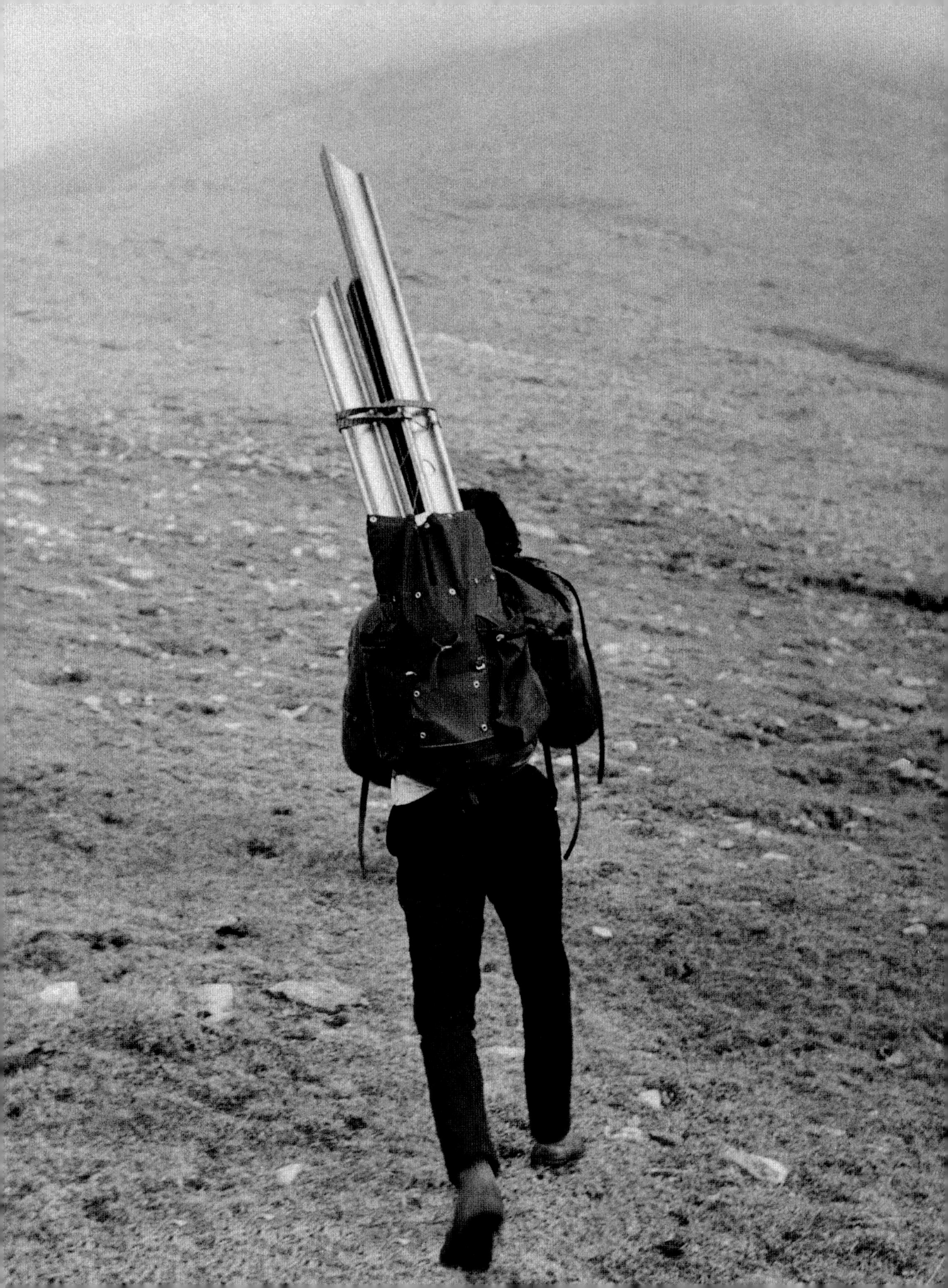

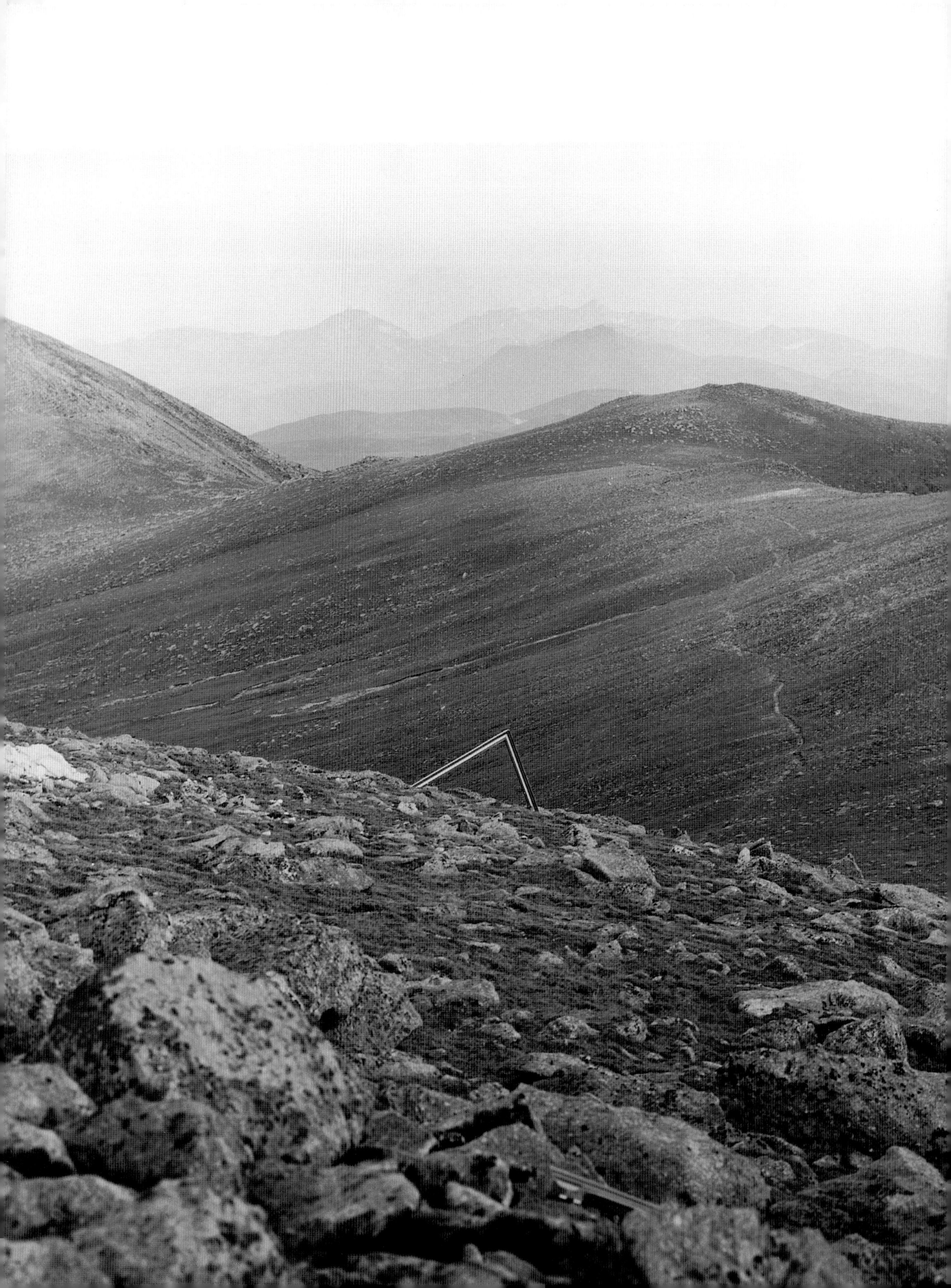

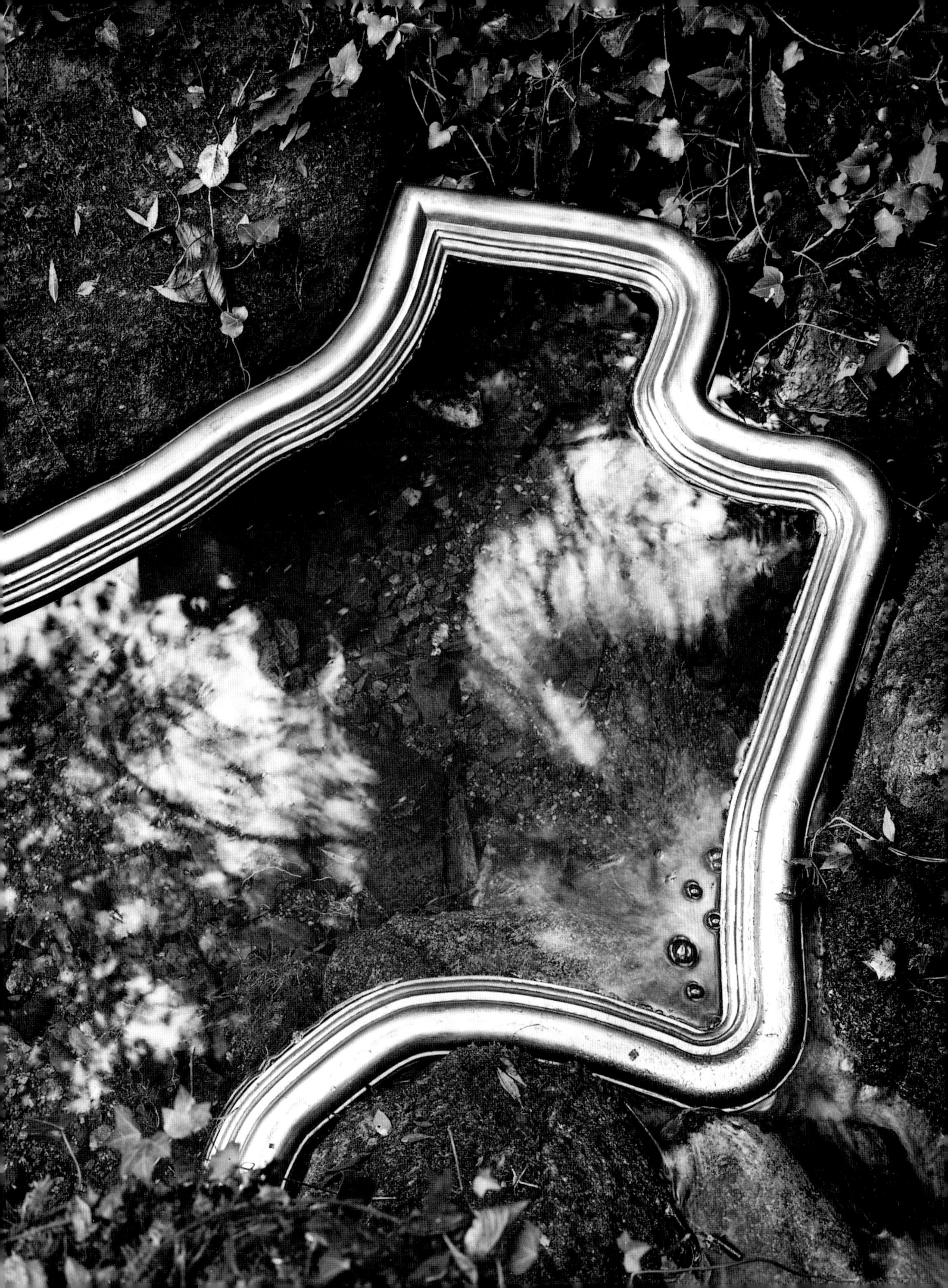

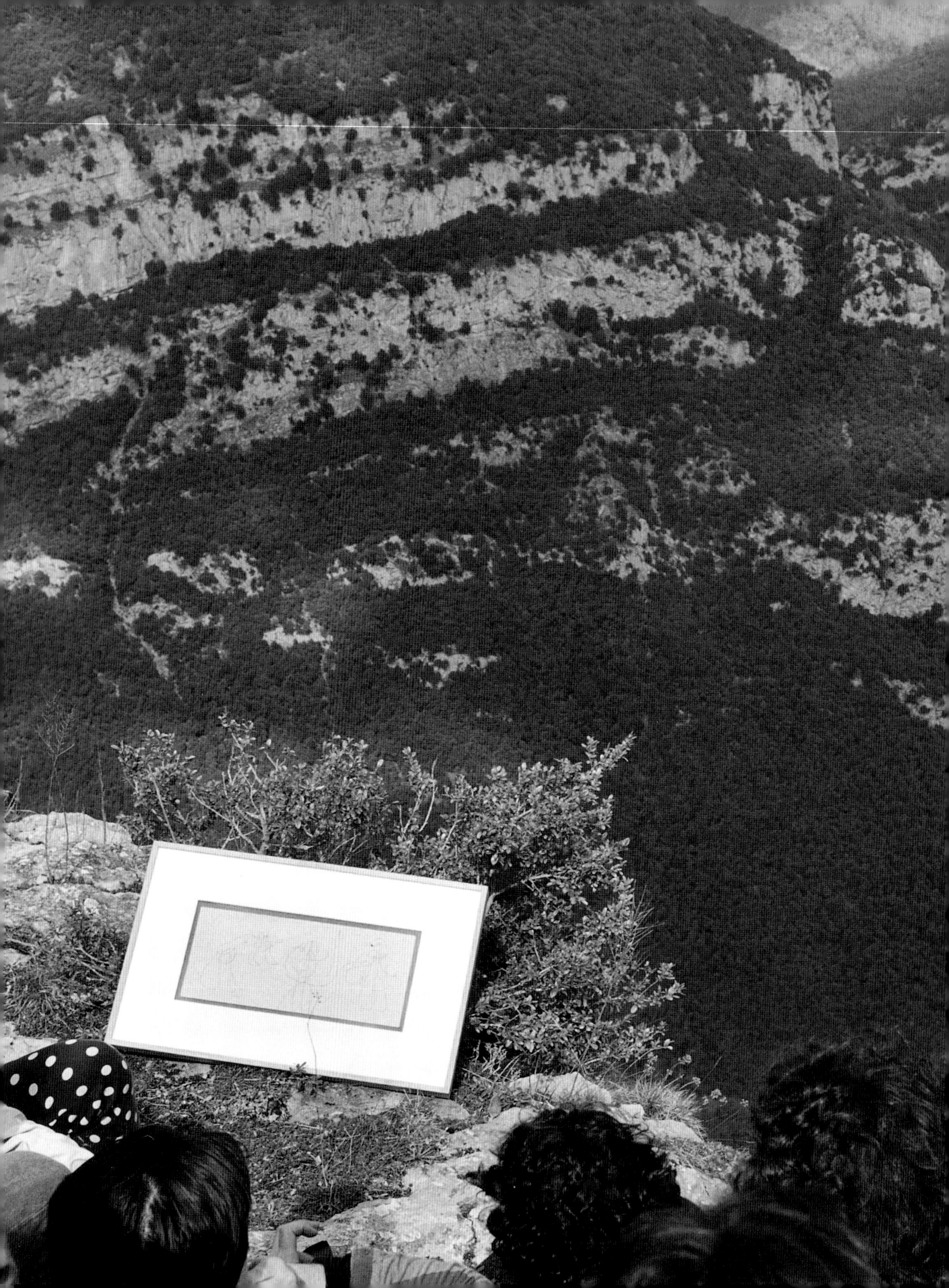

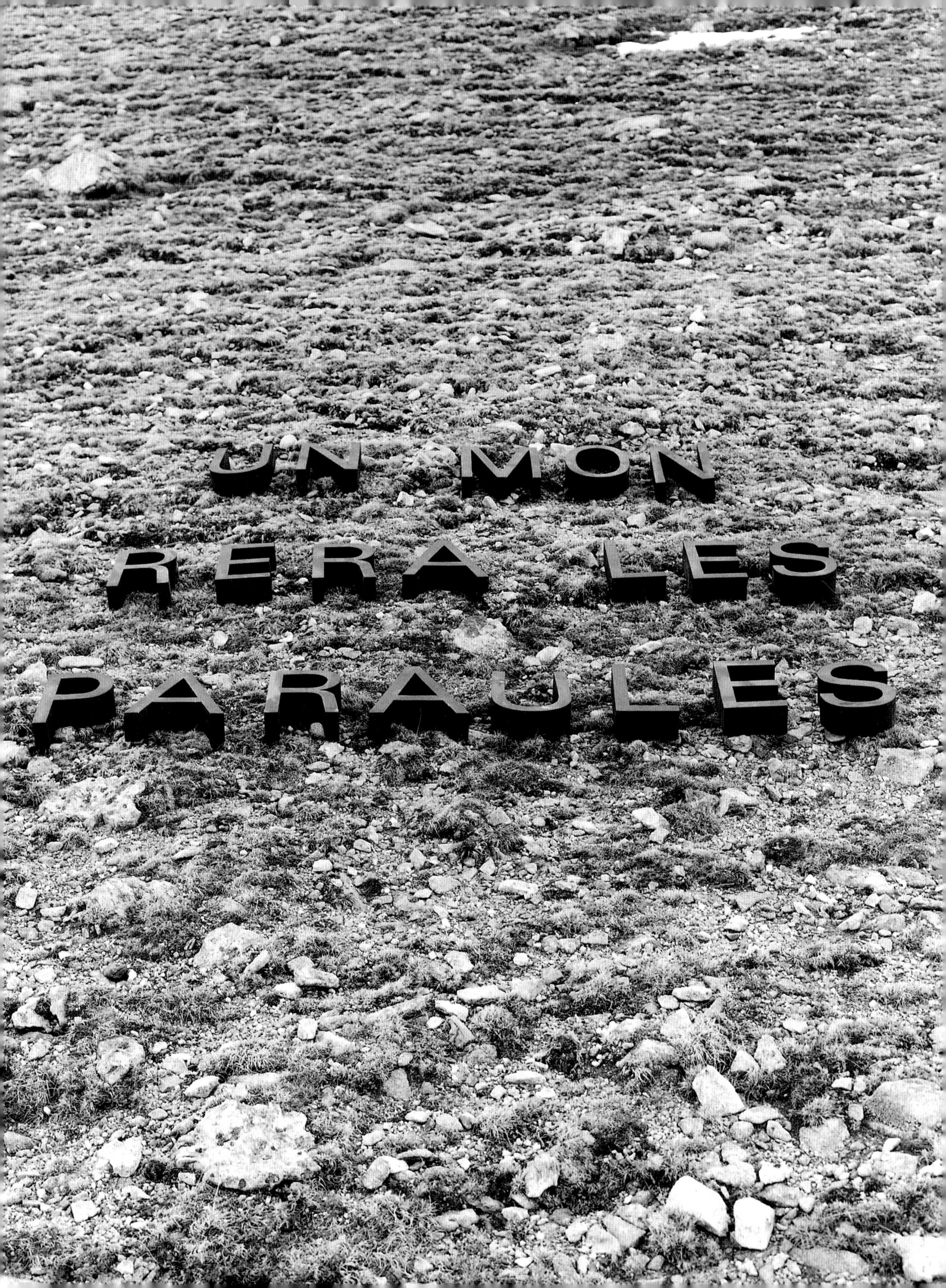
UN MON
RERA LES
PARAULES

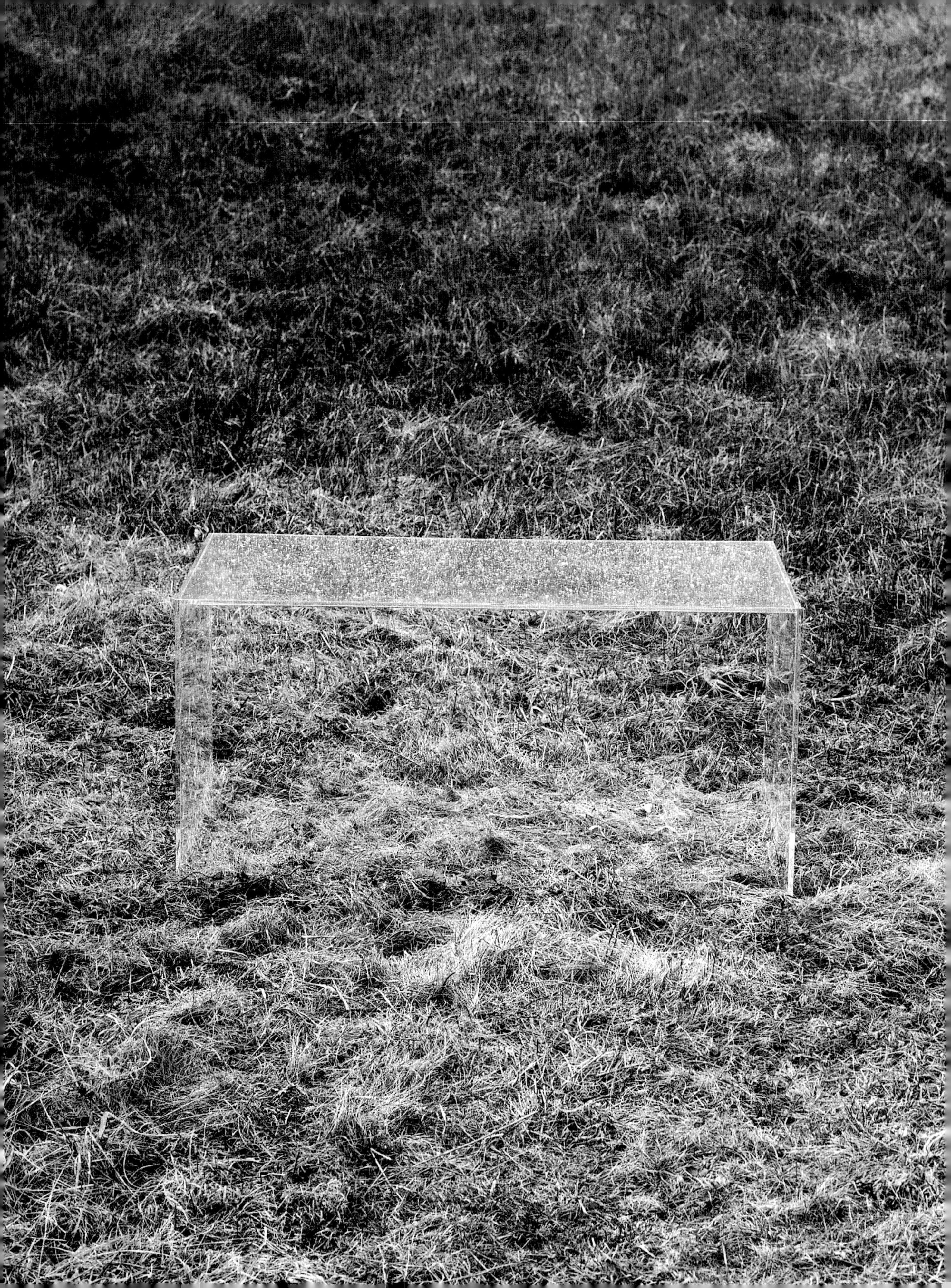

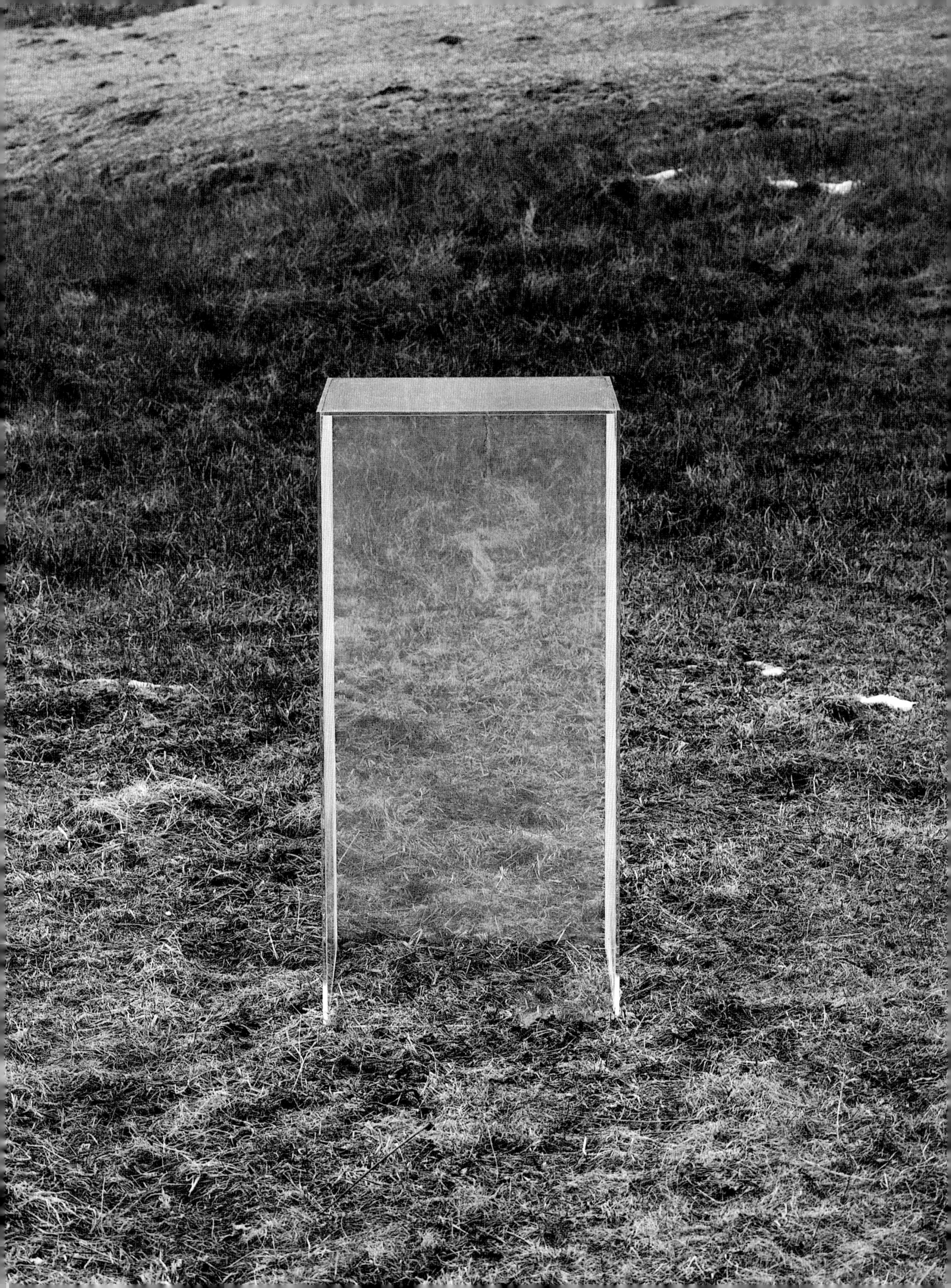

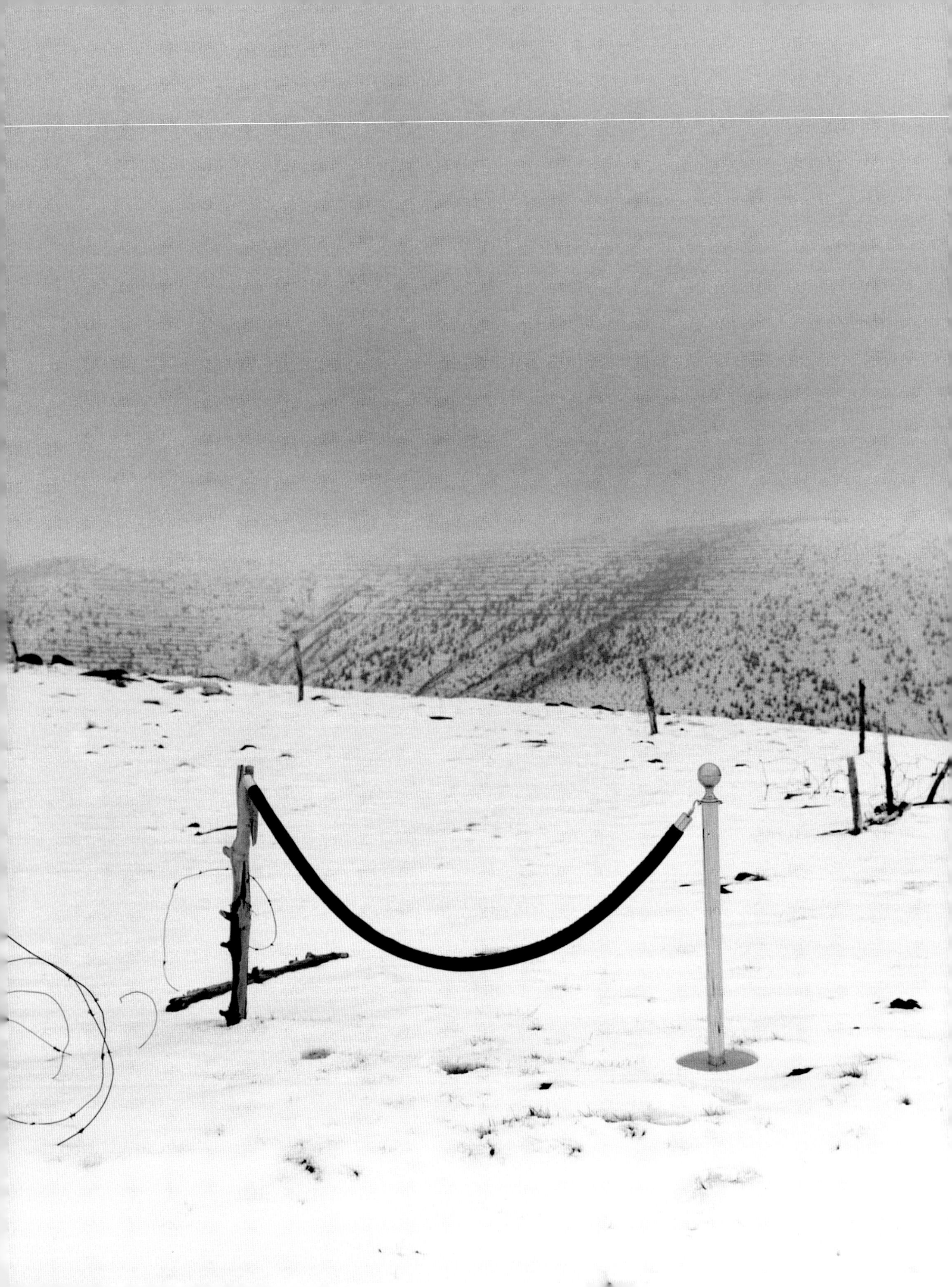

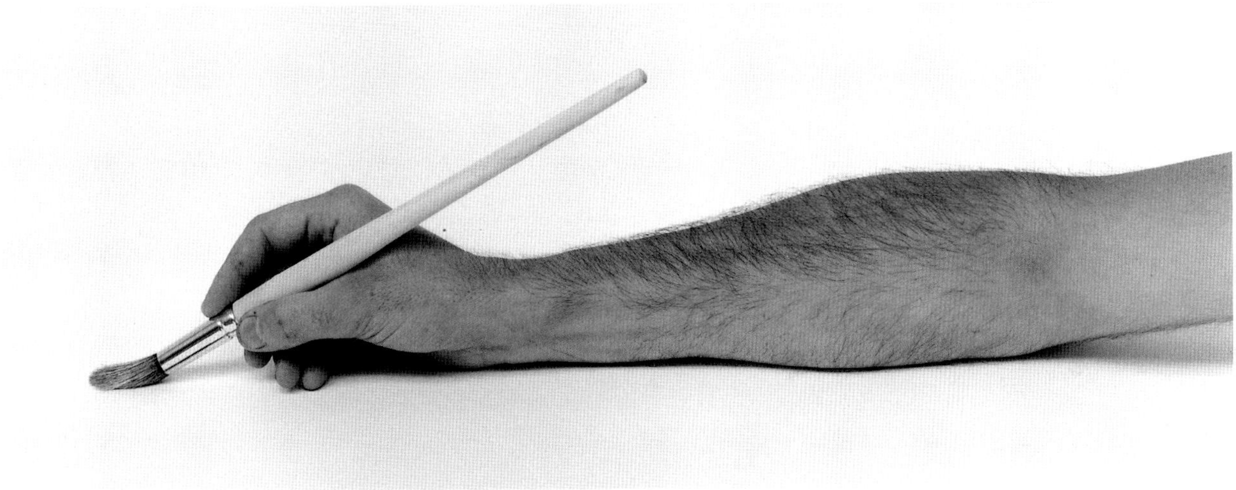

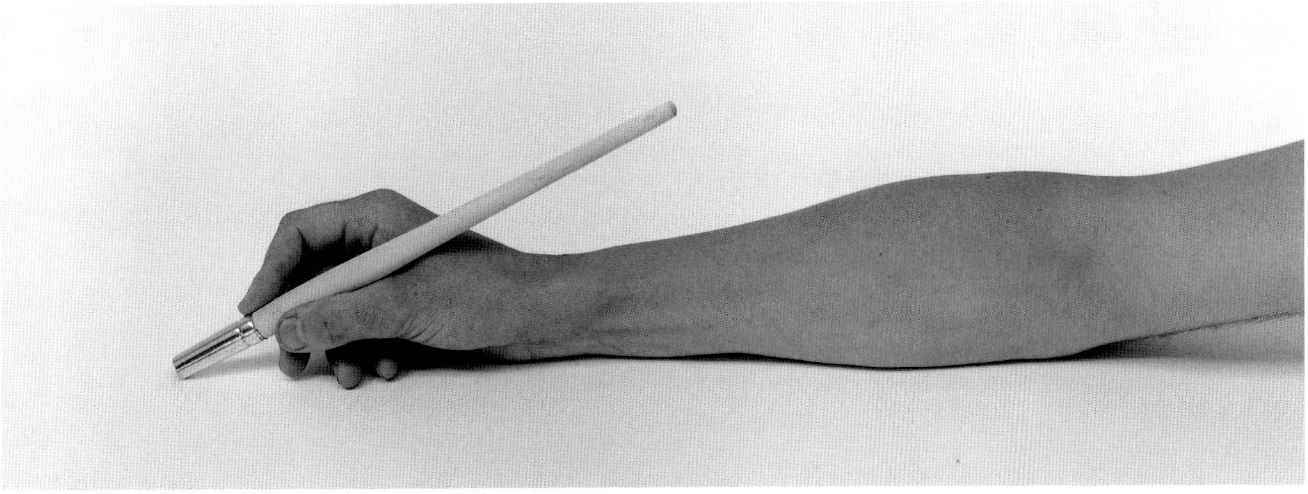

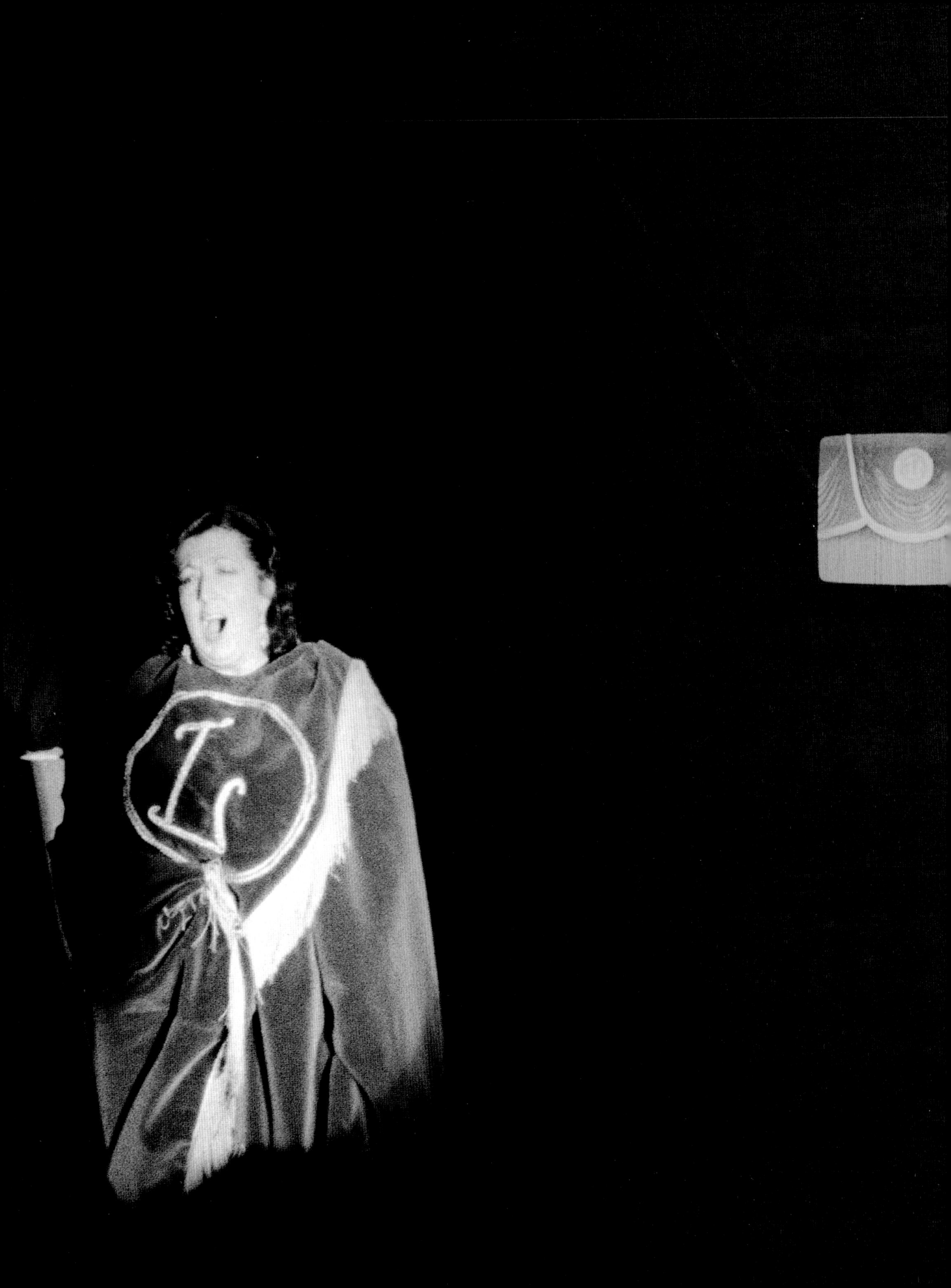

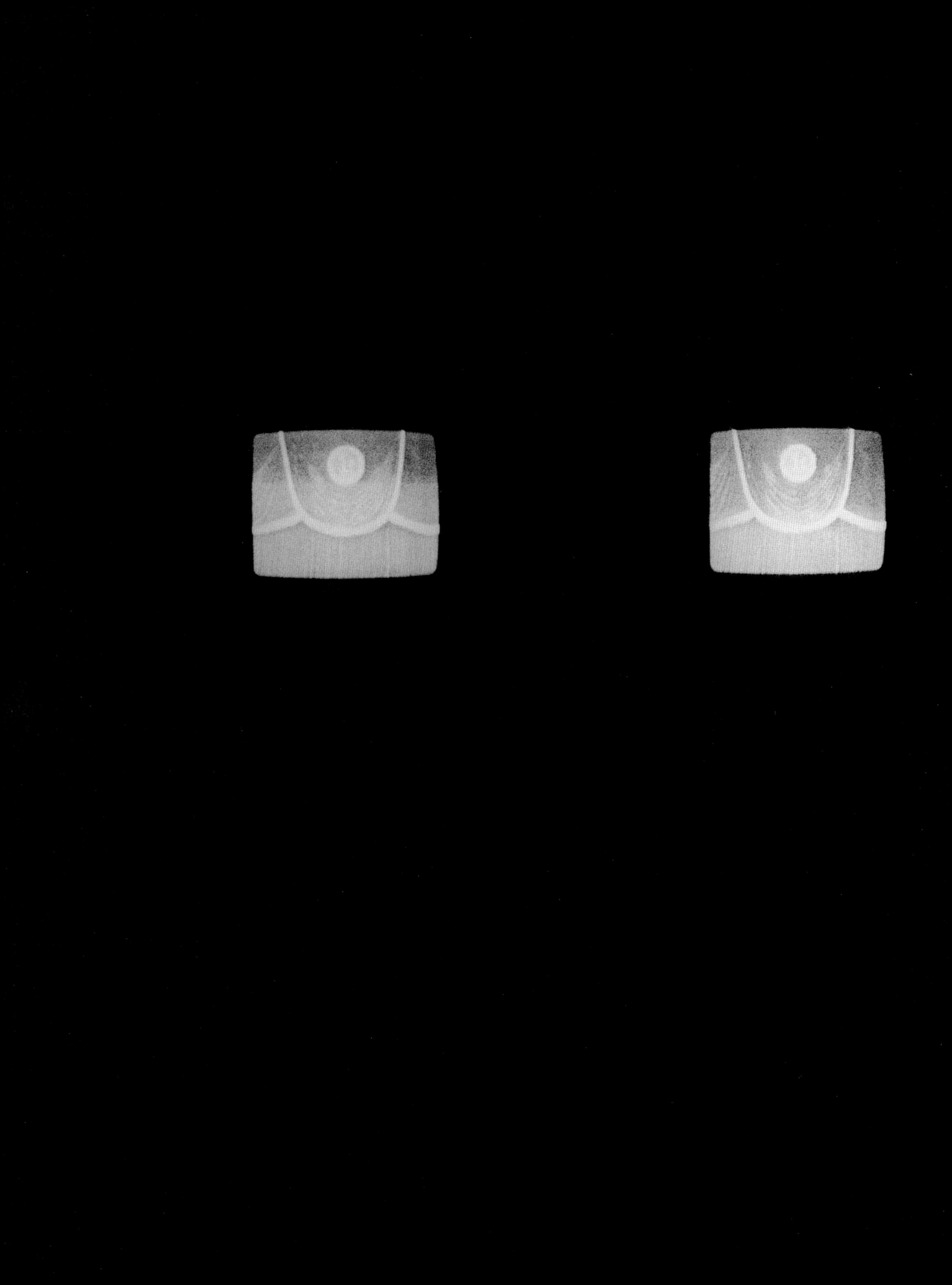

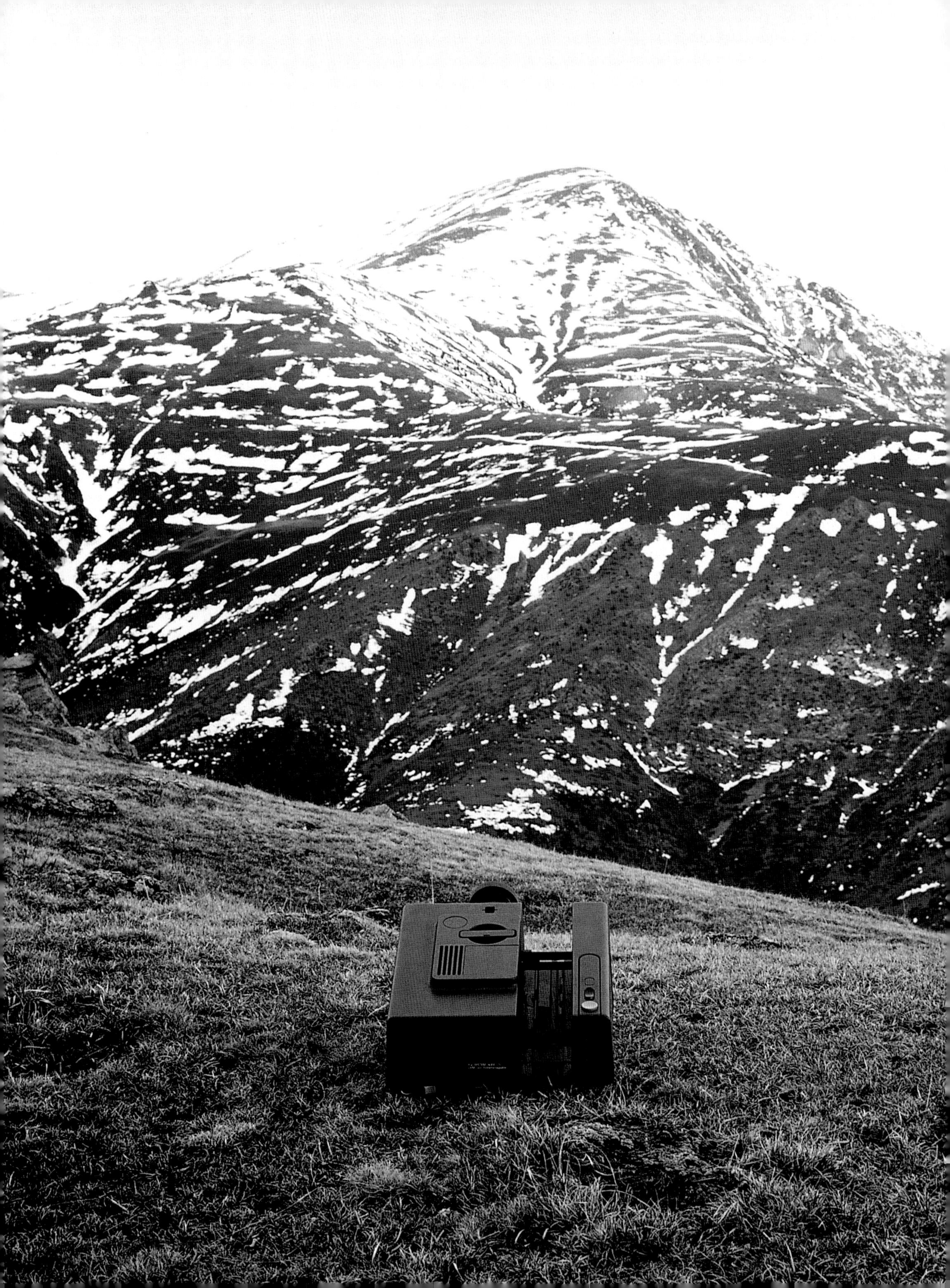

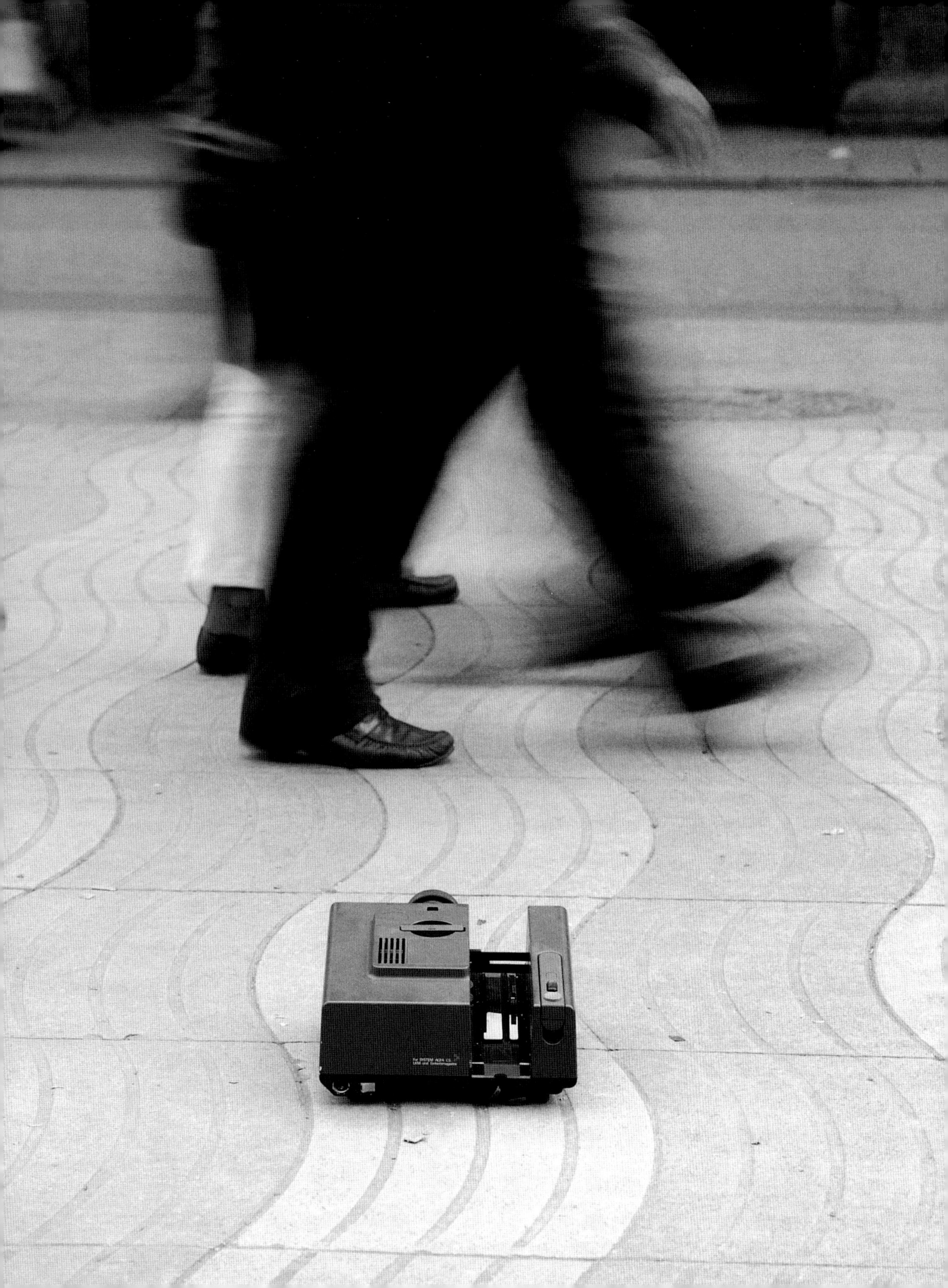

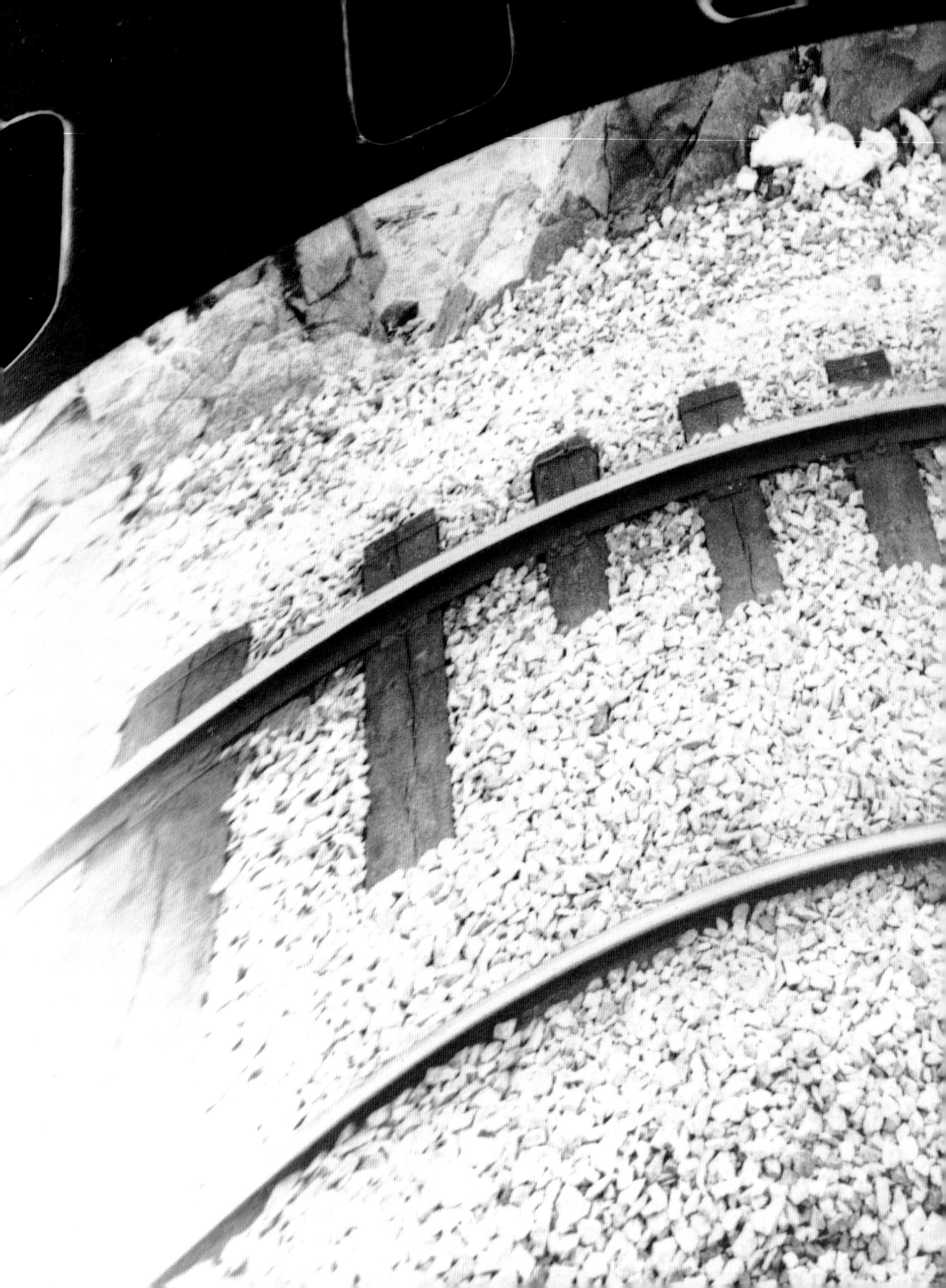

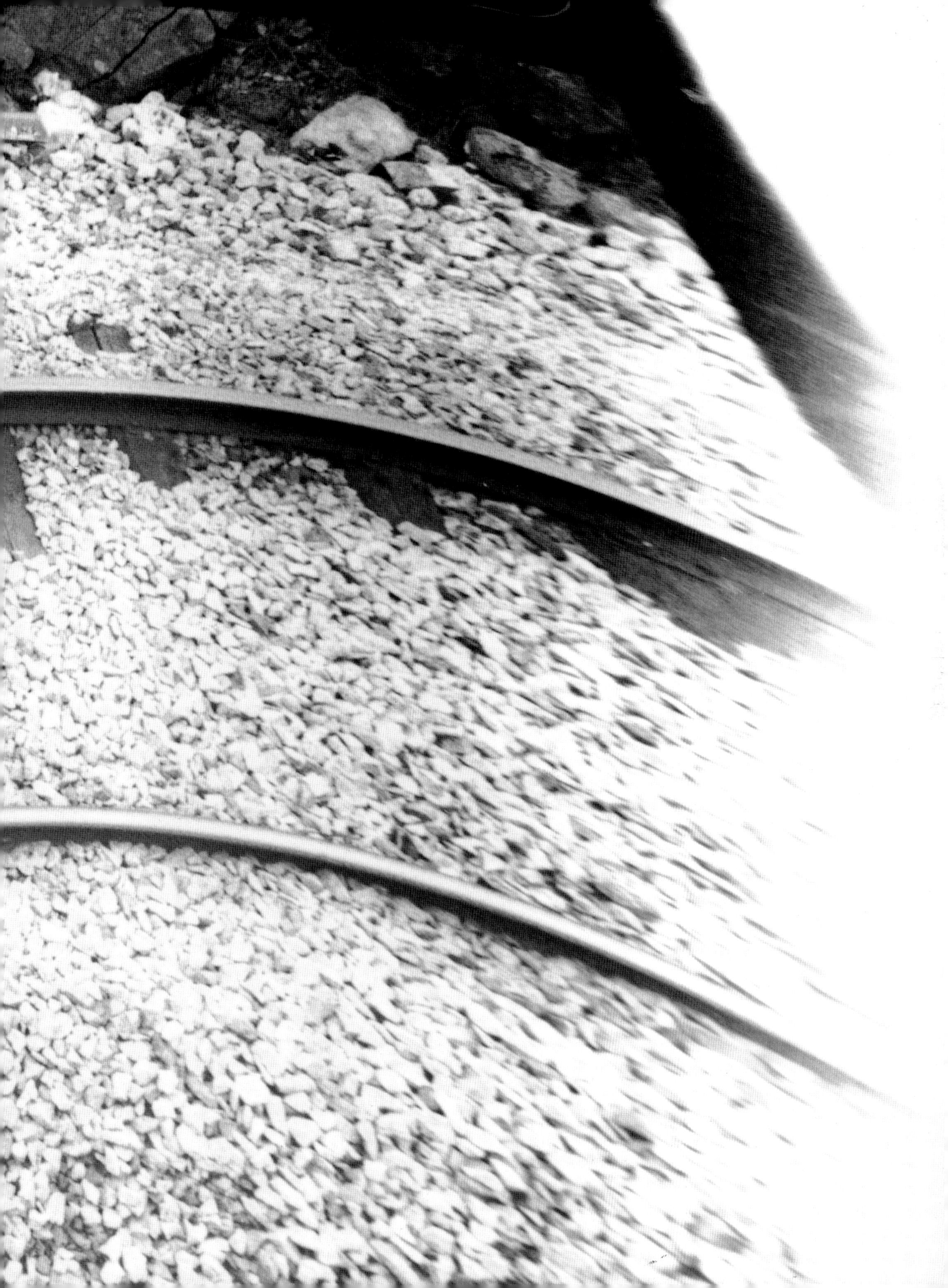

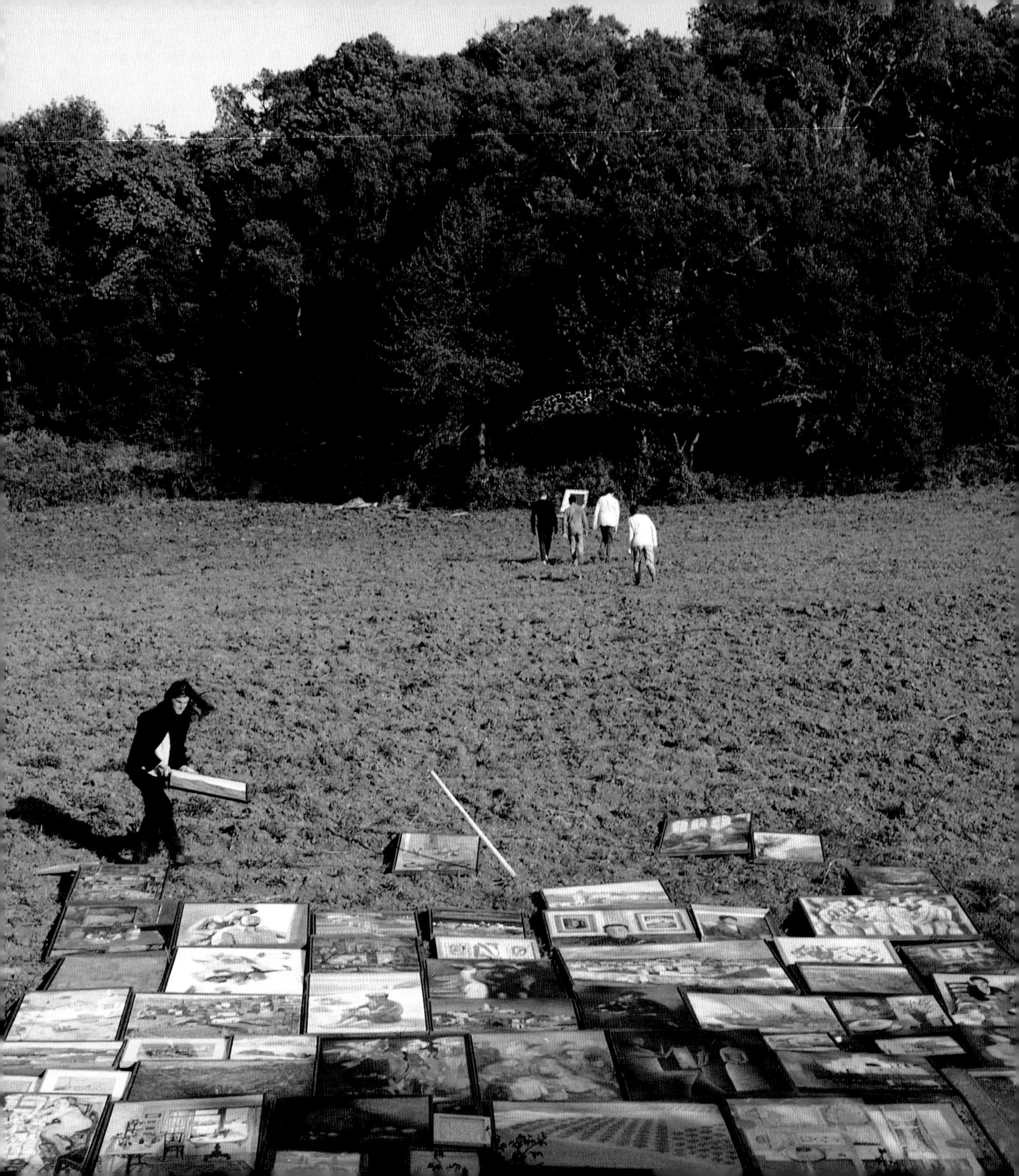

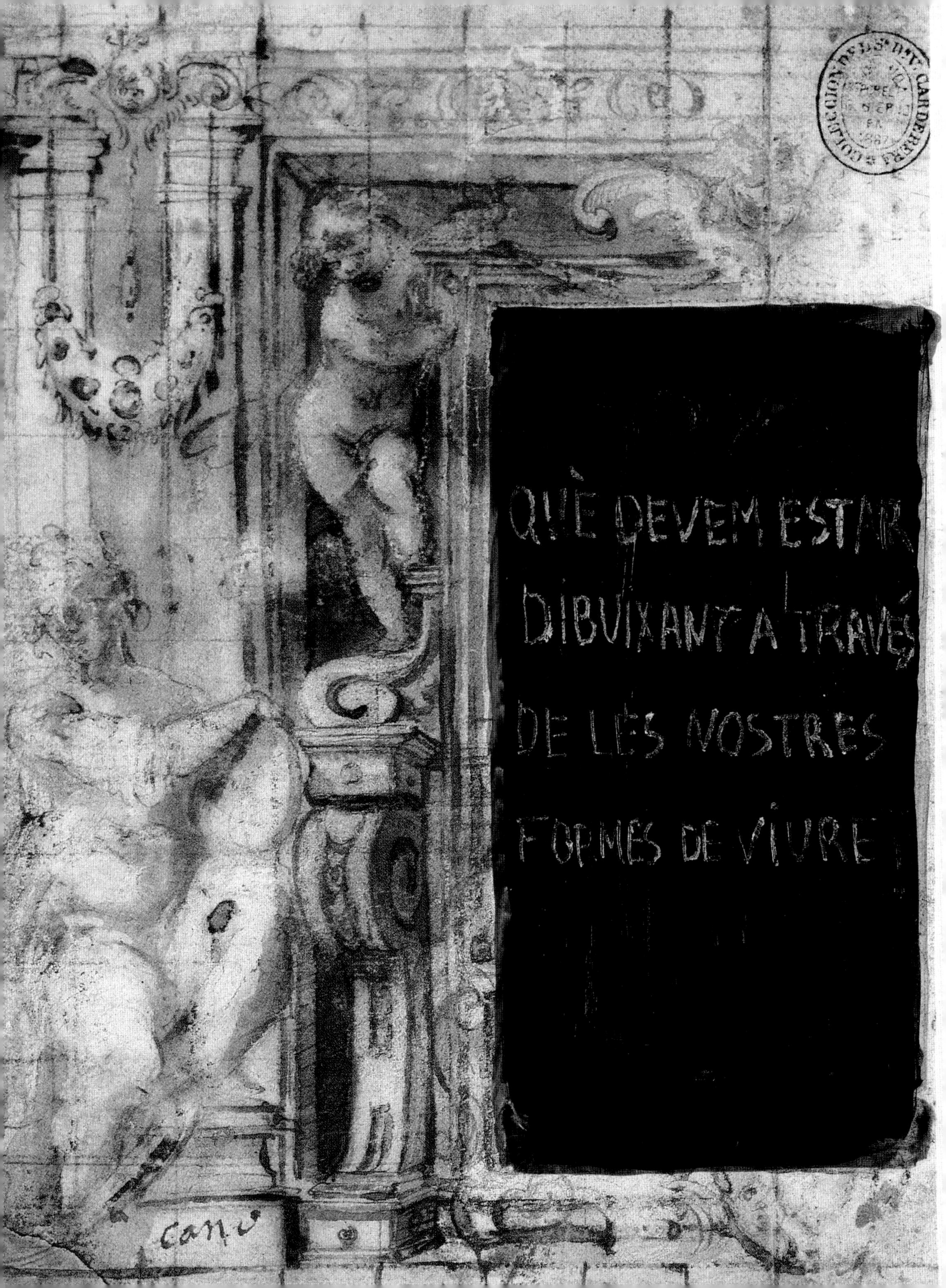
QUÈ DEVEM ESTAR
DIBUIXANT A TRAVÉS
DE LES NOSTRES
FORMES DE VIURE
cano

Topographic Works

Language is a cover. Our many writing exercises set out over a ground of reality have lead us to the opinion that such a ground does not exist, that the ground is nothing but our own projection. It is just as well true that it is obscured by the very works we try to see it with, made opaque, enveloped, as if sealed by a plaster coating.

In more general terms, amidst a more human presence, the idea that nature is nothing but a projection of men seems to impose itself. Such a view clearly excuses us from acting as landlords, required to make of the world all that seems necessary. Frankly, I find it hard to believe that we are everything, without there being any kind of alterity. Rather I believe –or think I believe– in the existence of a basis of reality that does not come from humans. An abrupt foundation that is not the creator that images it. A foundation of reality that, if it is indeed true that our works vainly try to grasp onto it, it is no less true that they express it accidentally, as a consequence of tumbling into it, a chance honing in. It is as if apart from our expression, the works too were an expression of that ground; yet not so much the works themselves but their traces: the forms of drawing that create the earth and the works themselves. It is then that, through the works, we might perceive this ground as a found obstacle, where the very impediment of seeing it would give it form, so that in the work of each creator the most genuine traces would be nothing but a rebound off the natural relief that marks its surface geography.

Perejaume

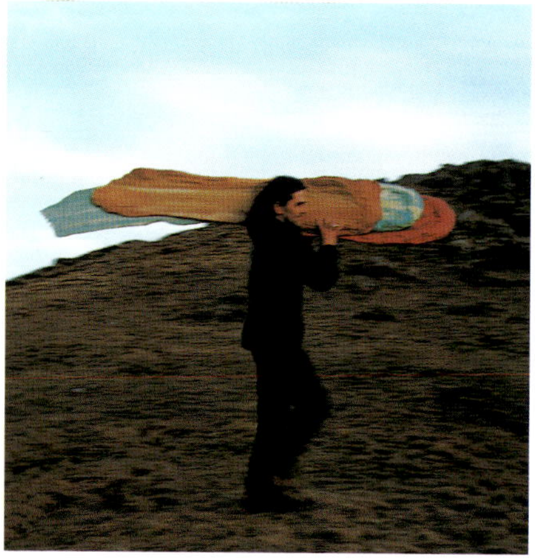

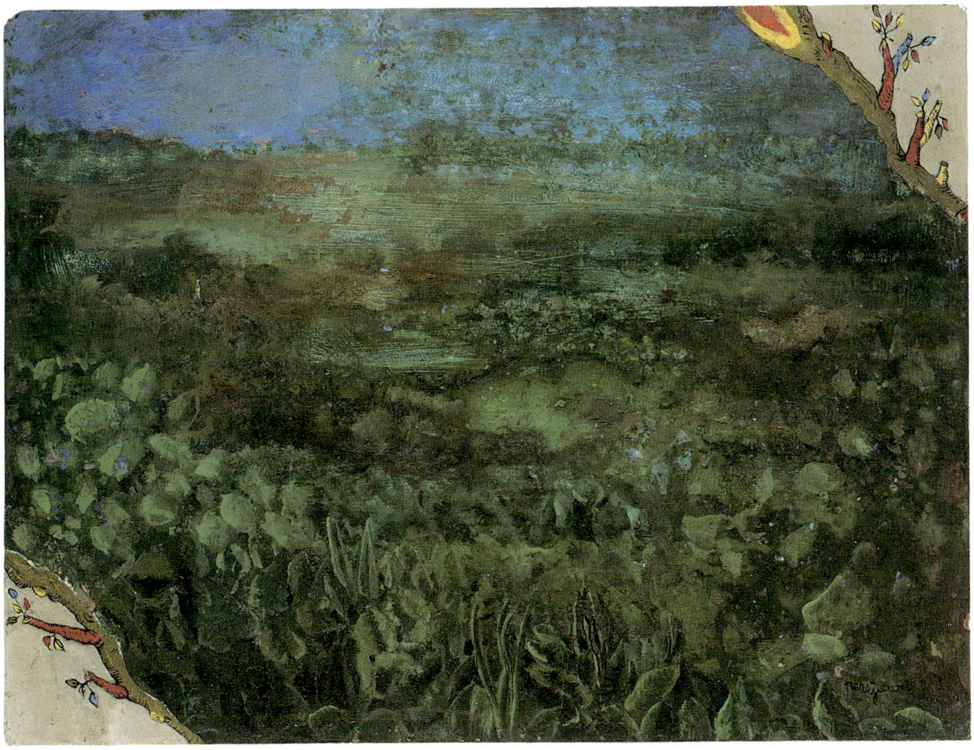

Bast paisatge per l'as 1977
(Great Landscape for the Ace)
Oil on wood. 26 x 35 cm.

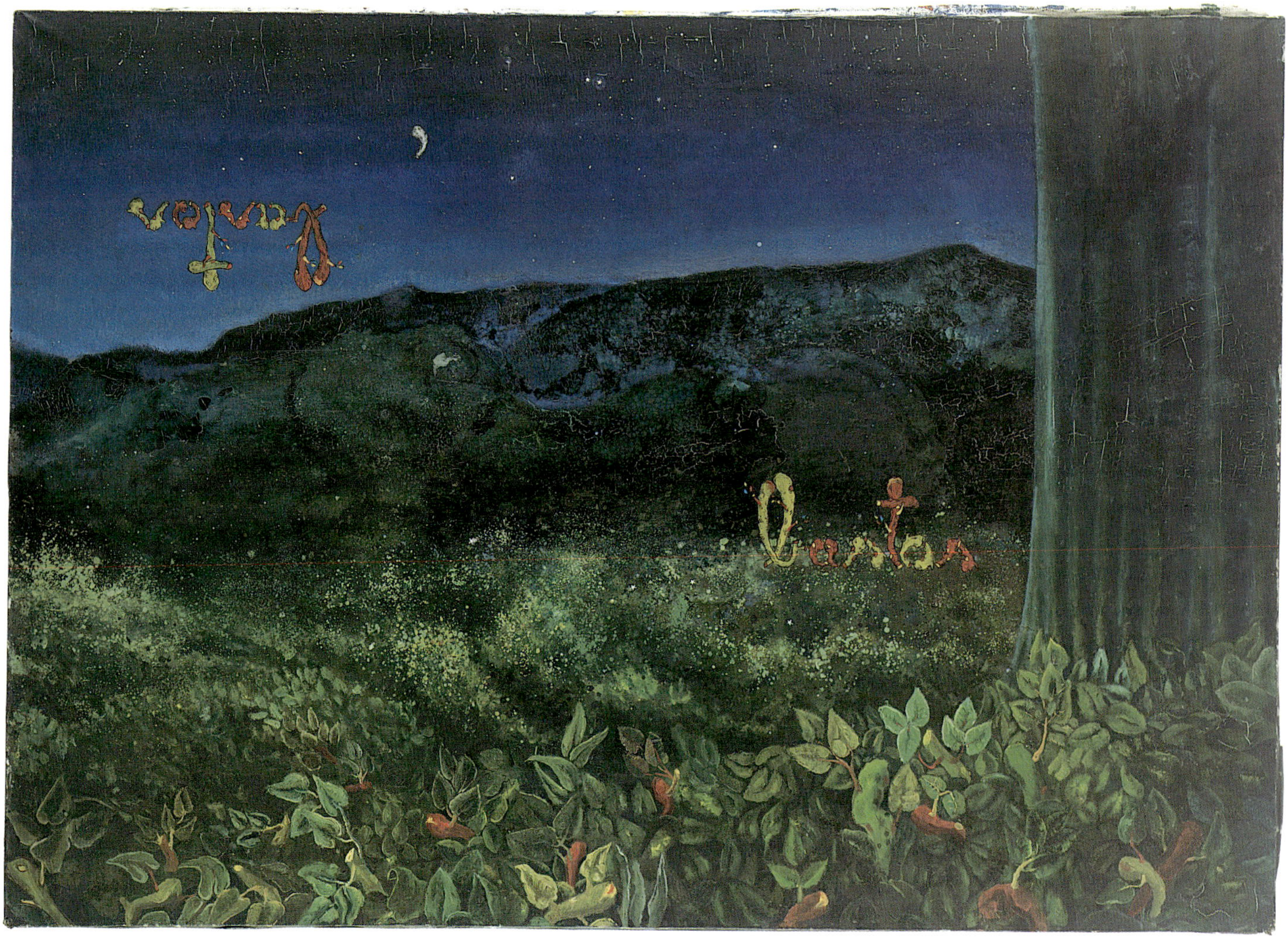

Montnegre 1976
Oil on canvas. 80 x 116 cm.

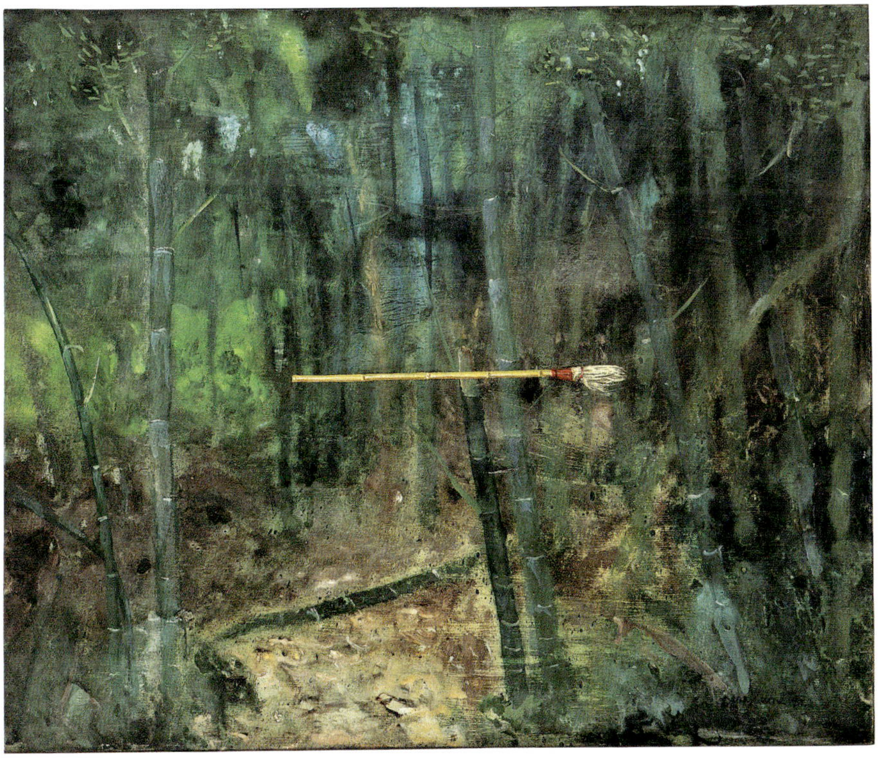

L'encanyadura tenora 1977
(Tenorous Reed)
Oil on canvas. 36.5 x 44.5 cm.

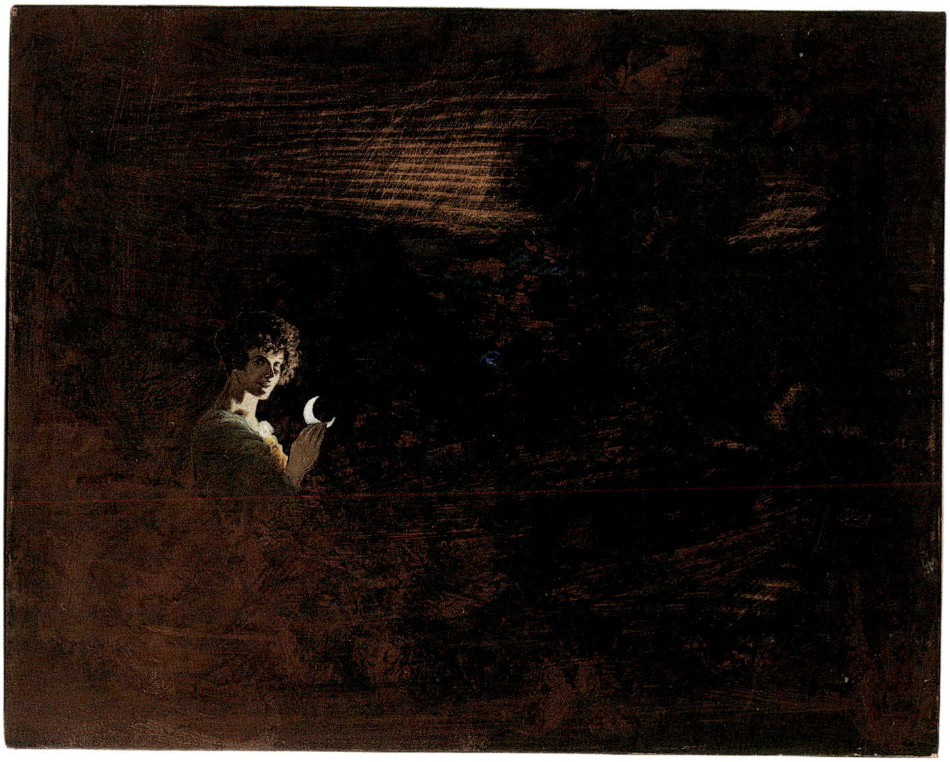

Els sorrals del fons del cel 1980
(Sands in the Depths of the Sky)
Oil on wood. 27 x 35 cm.

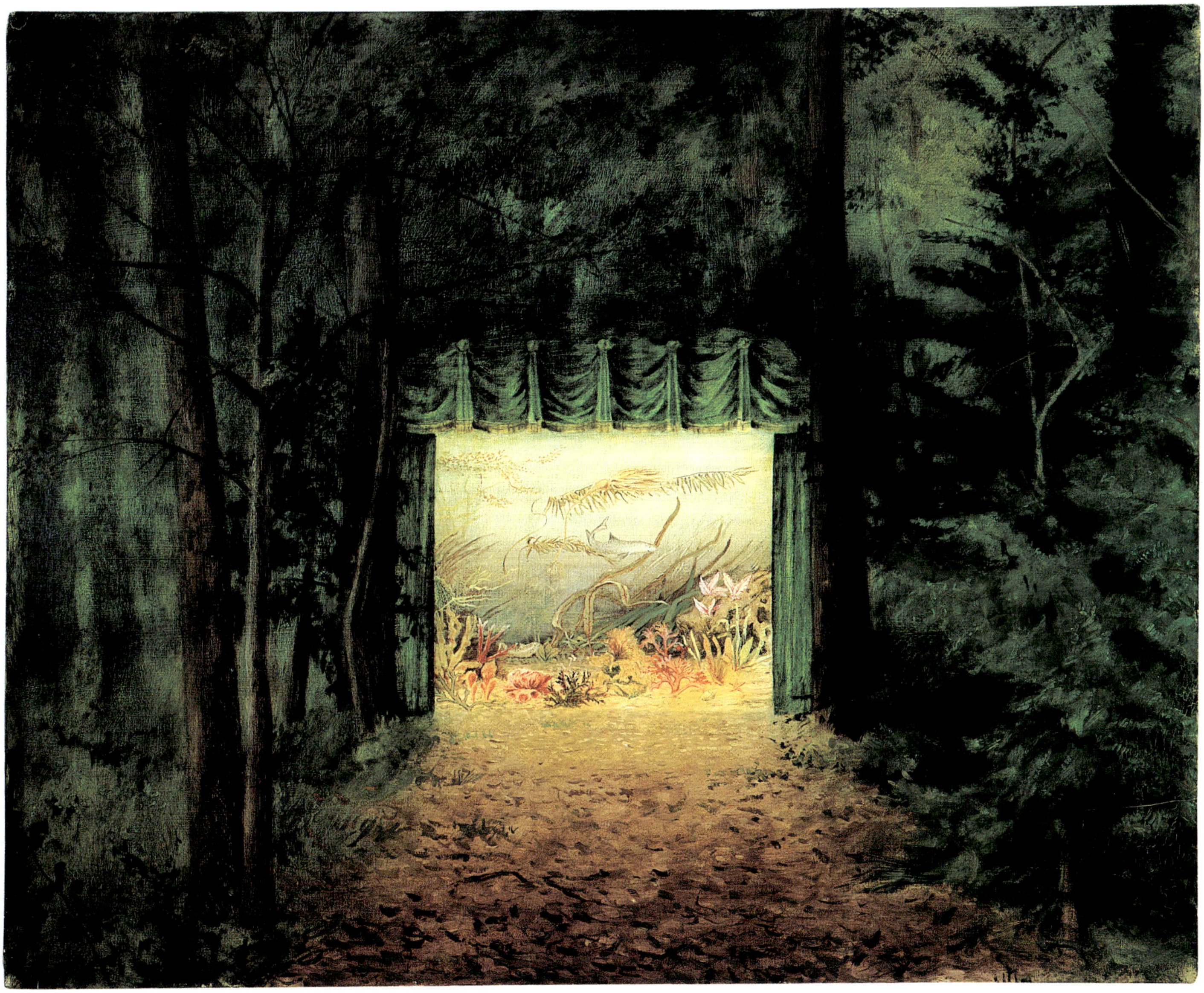

L'entrada del mar 1980
(Enter the Sea)
Oil on canvas. 73 x 92 cm.

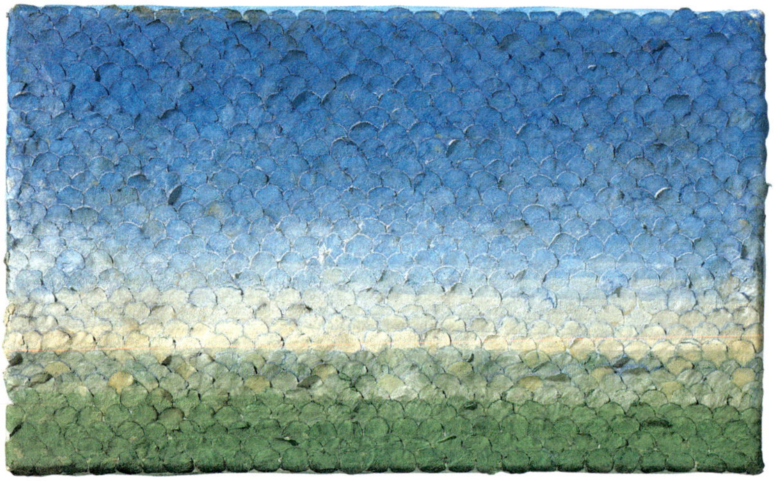

Paisatge d'escates 1981
(Landscape of Scales)
Confetti and watercolour on canvas. 16 x 27 cm.

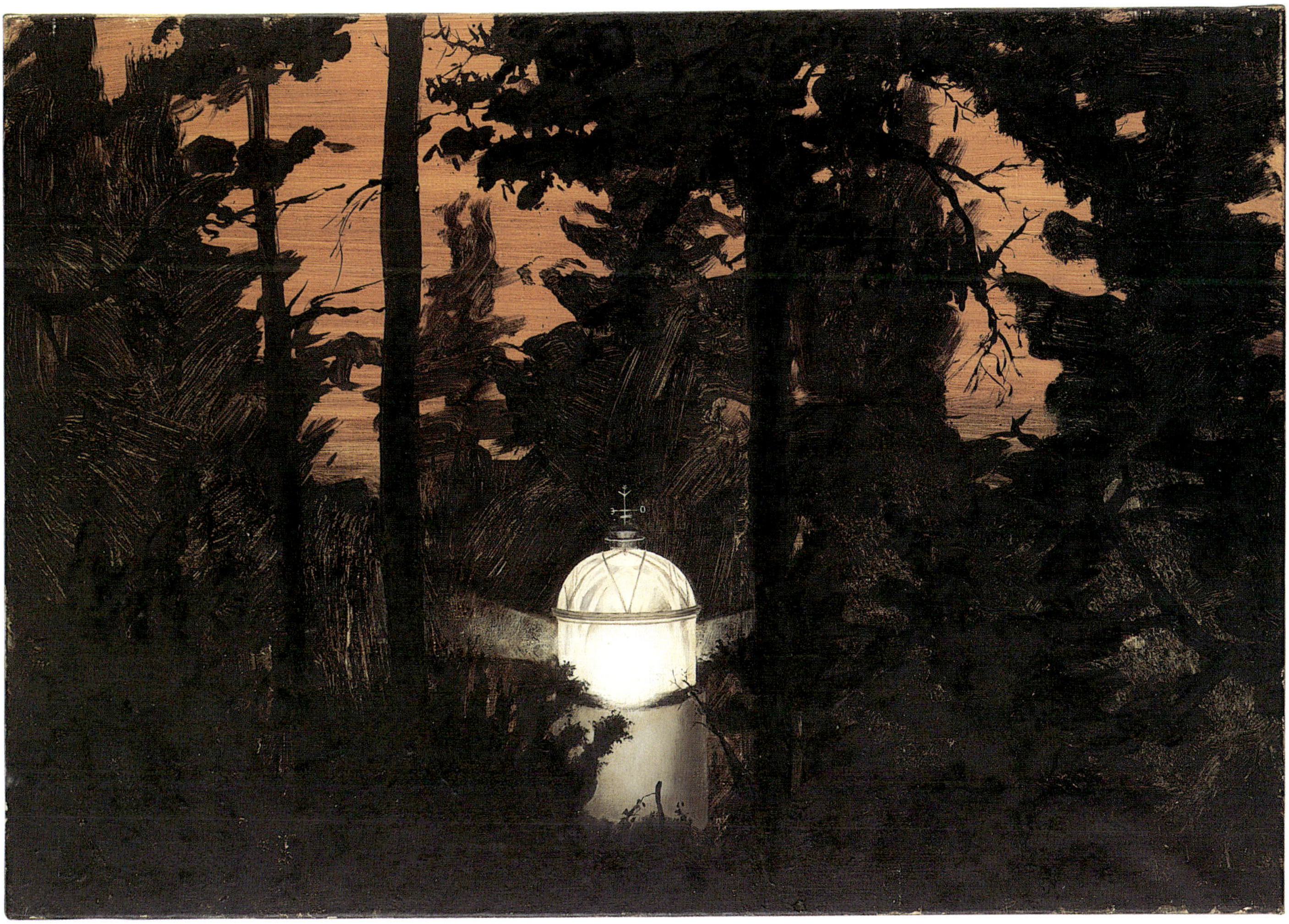

Far emboscat 1980
(Lighthouse in the Woods)
Oil on canvas. 50 x 74 cm.

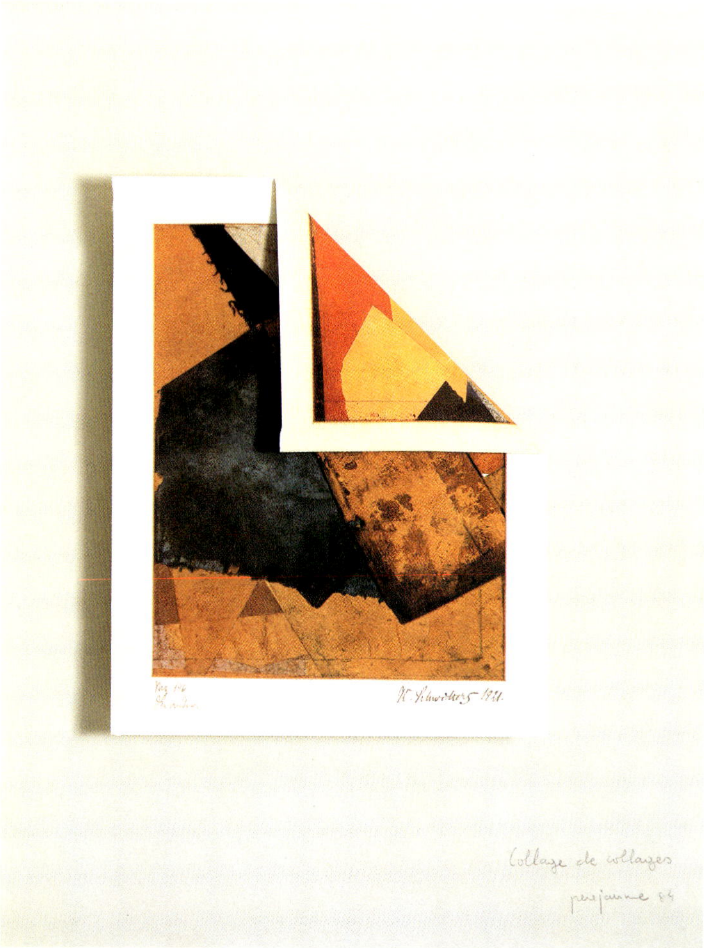

Collage de collages 1984
(Collage of Collages)
Collage. 32.5 x 28.5 cm.

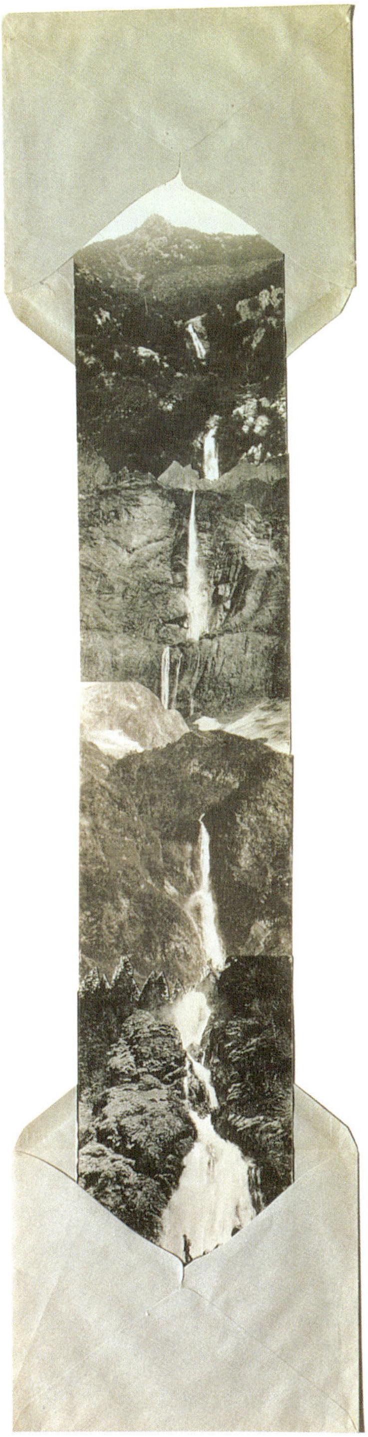

Cascada 1982
(Cascade)
Collage. 71 x 41 cm.

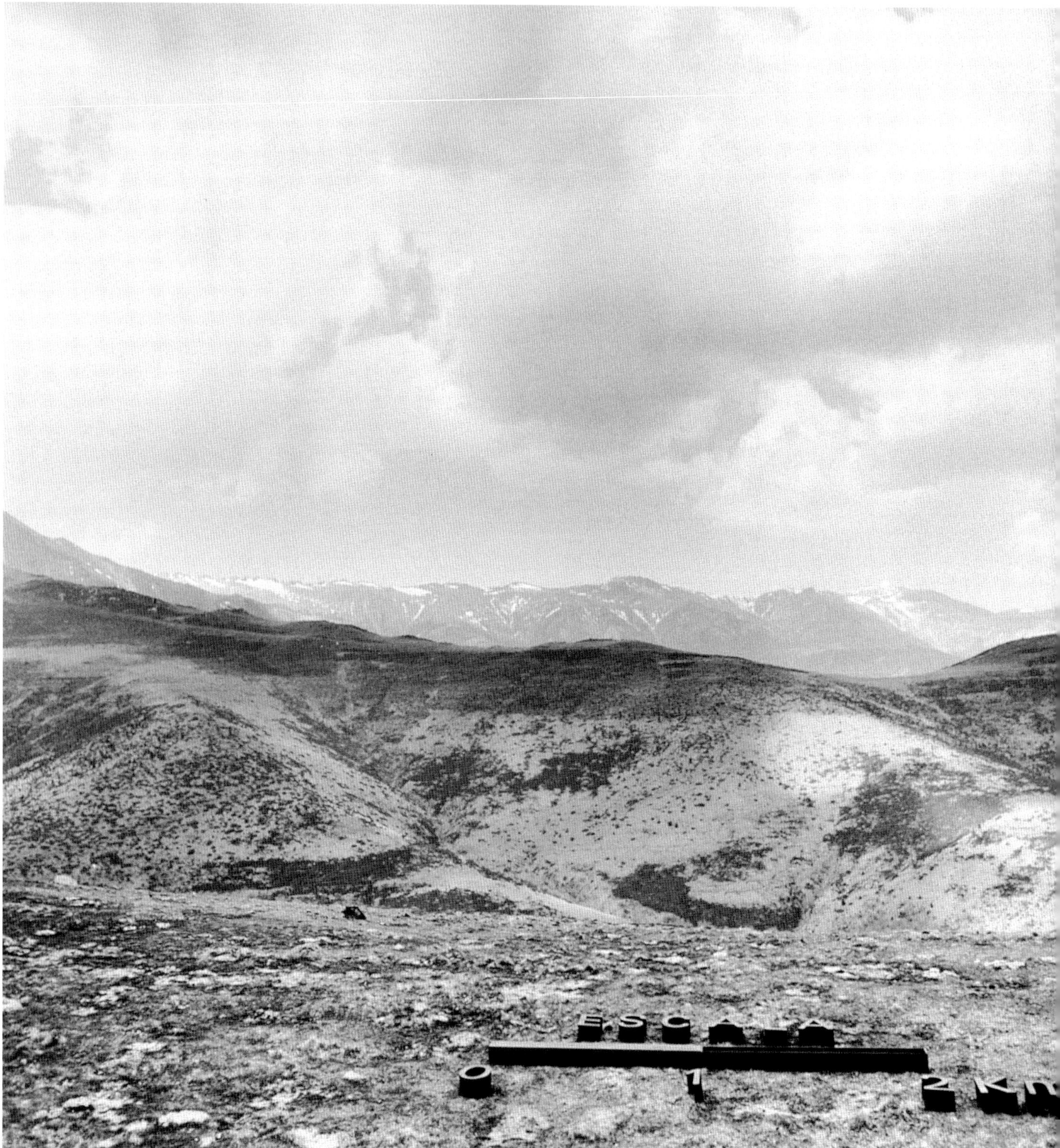
ESCALA
0
1
2 K

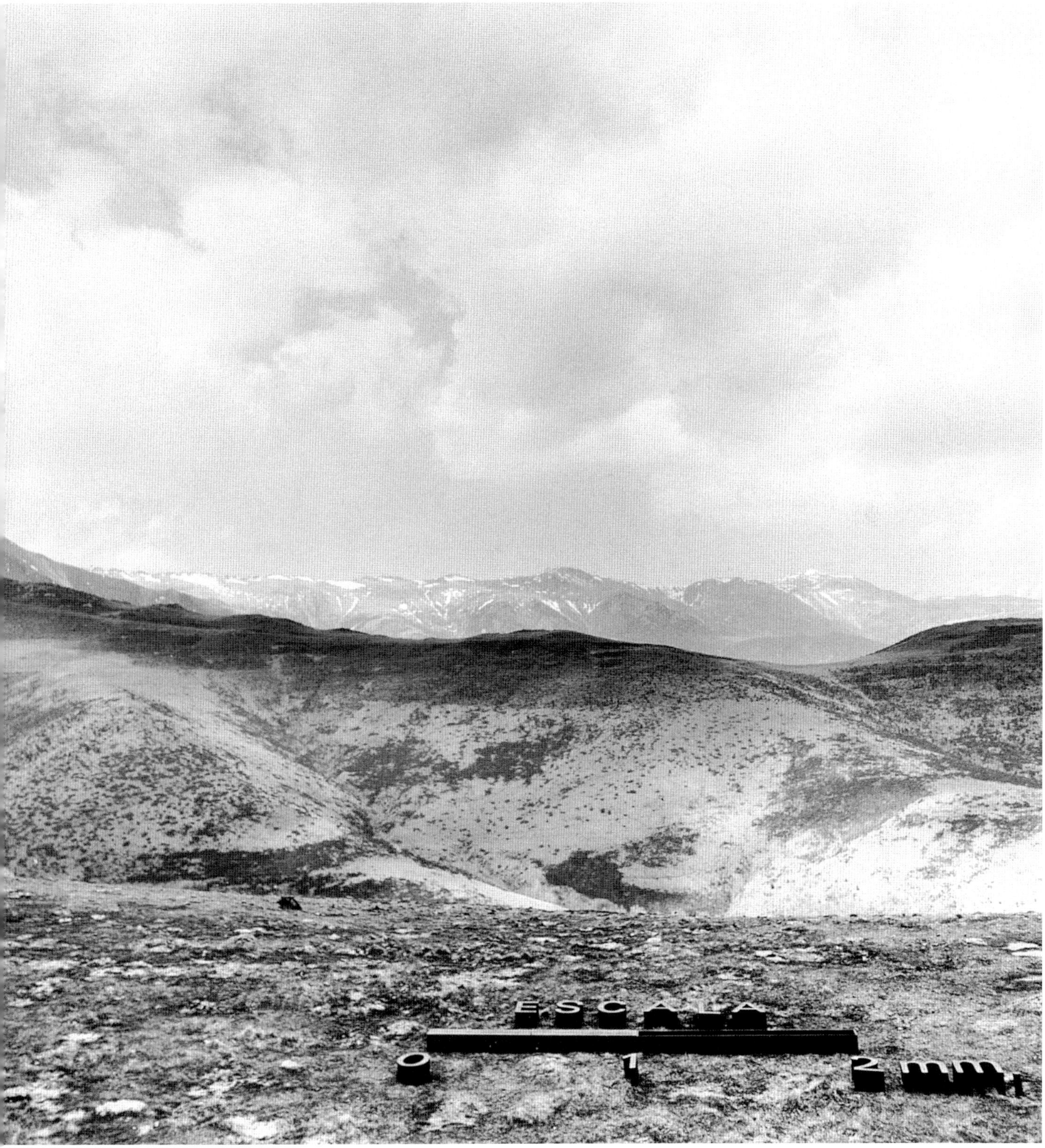

Escala 1988
(Scale)
Photograph. 37 x 65 cm.

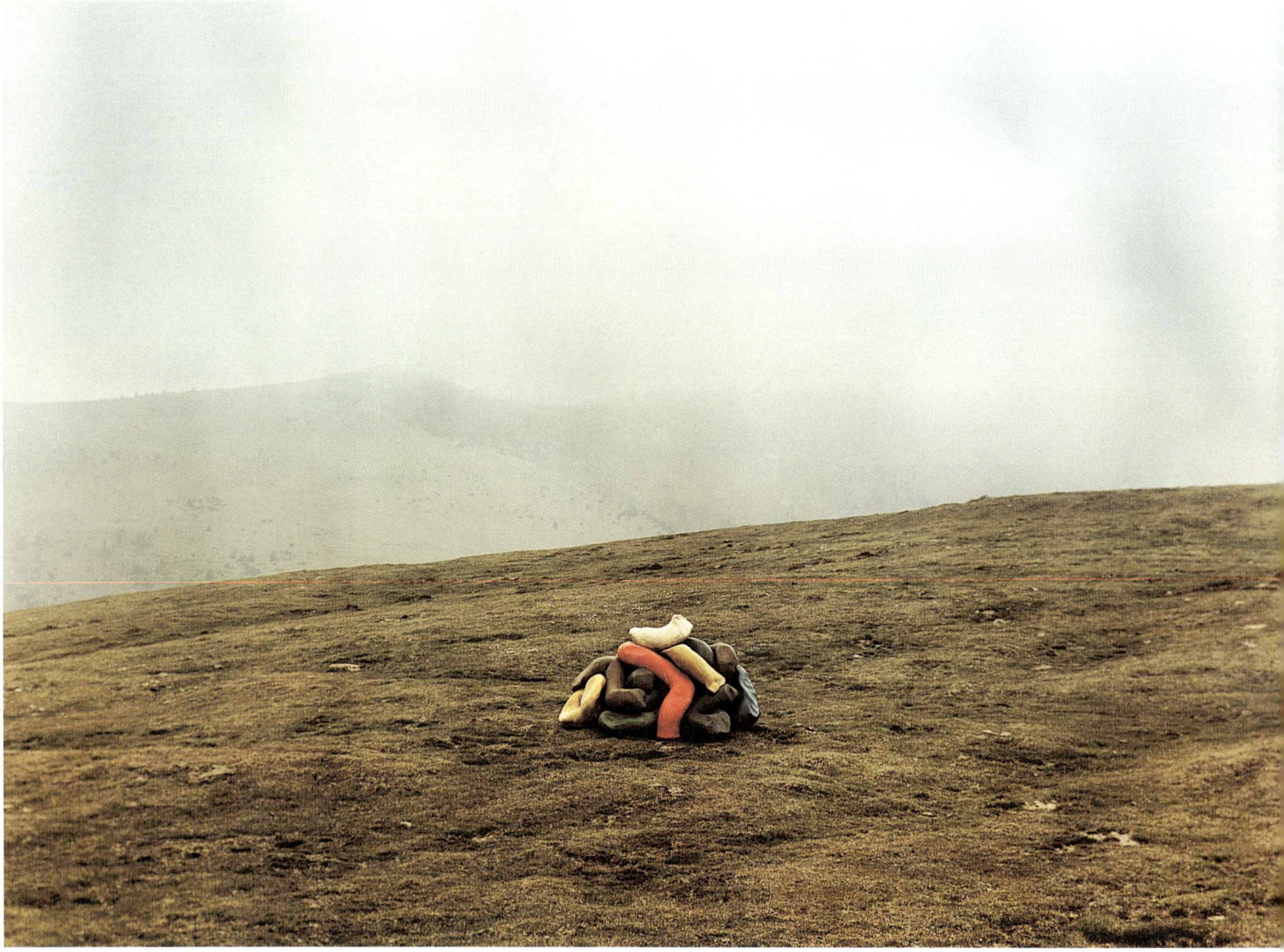

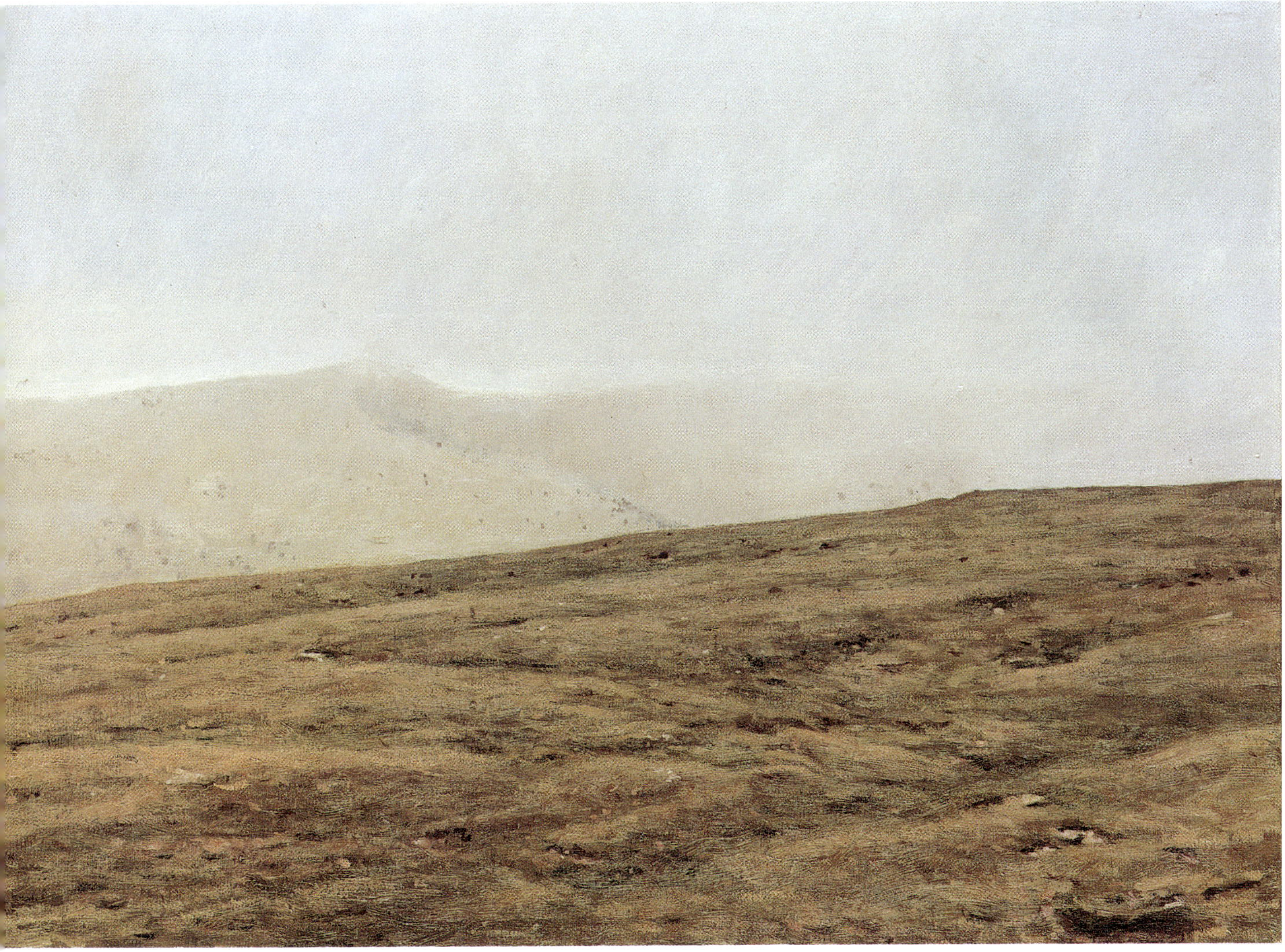

Le trompe-l'oeil du plein-air 1990
Photograph and oil on canvas. 58 x 138 cm.

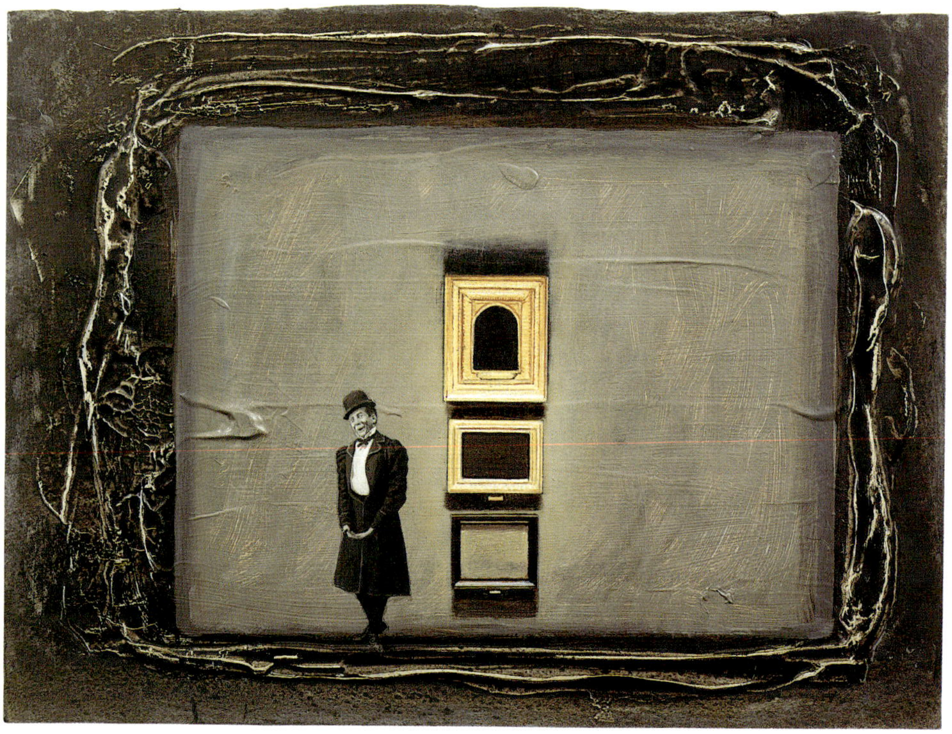

Quadrista 1990
(Picturist)
Oil on cardboard. 30 x 41 cm.

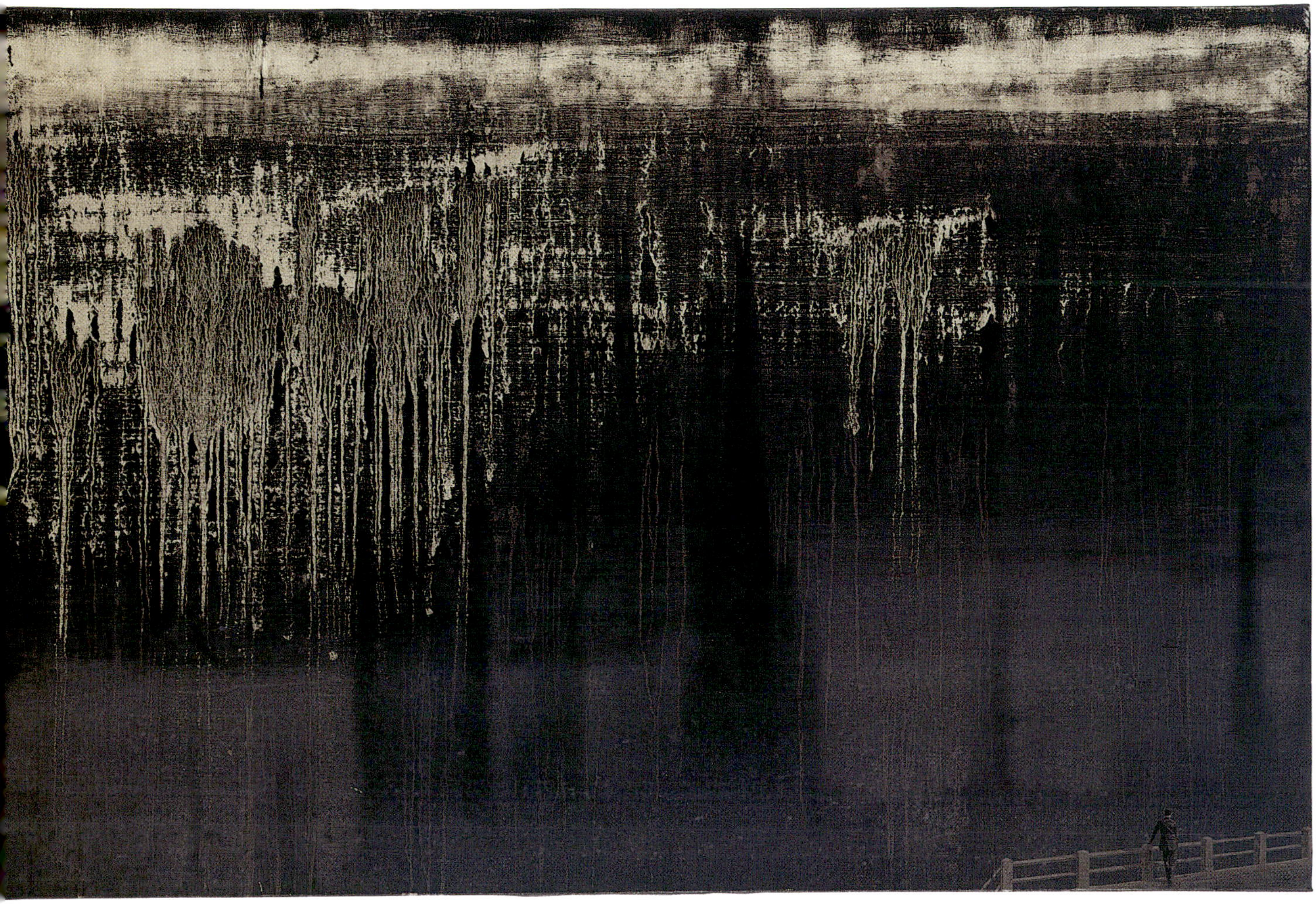

Personatge contemplant l'informalisme 1985
(Character Gazing upon Informalism)
Oil on canvas. 65 x 100 cm.

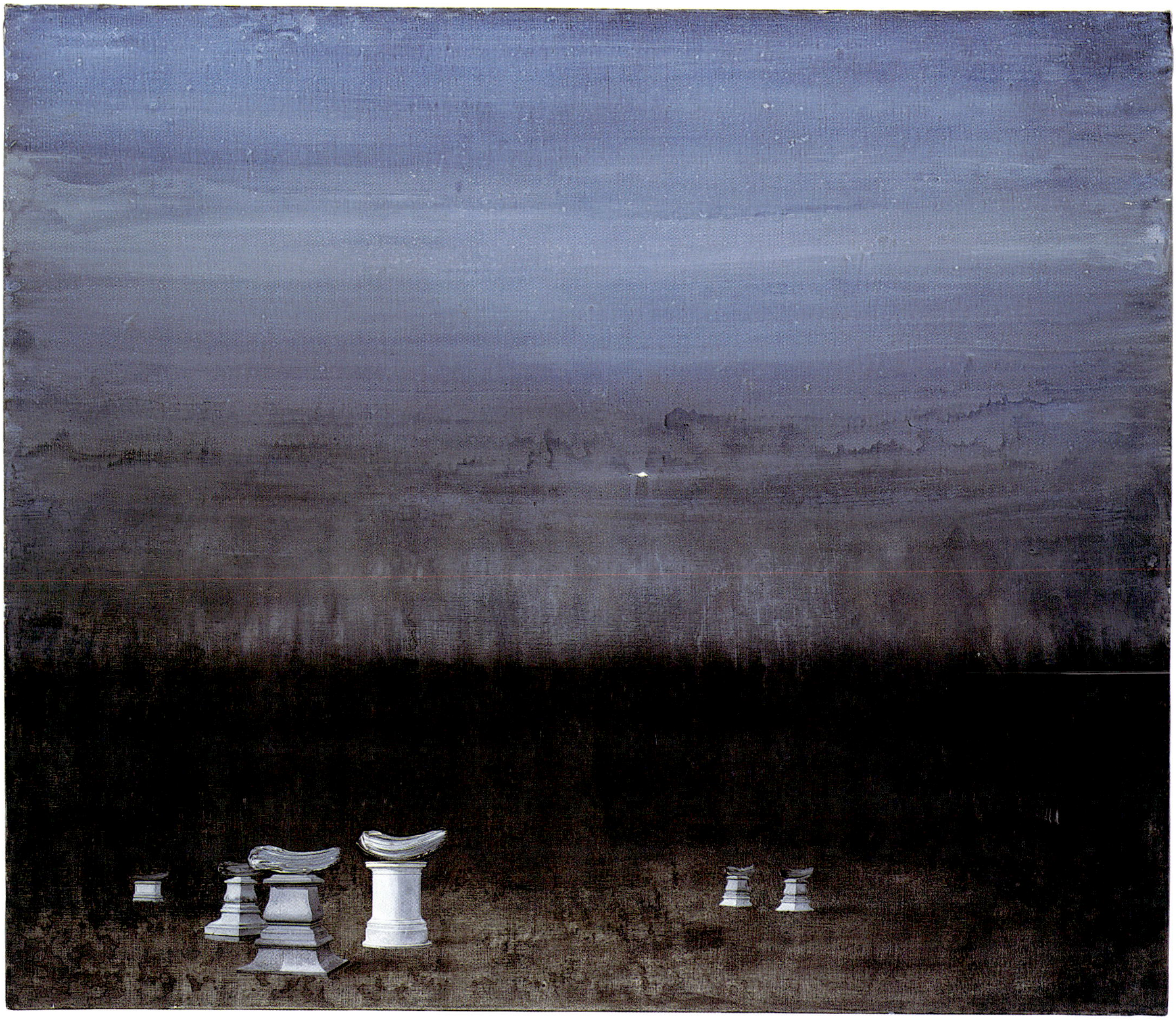

Pinzellades sobre peanya de monument 1994
(Brushstrokes on Monument Pedestal)
Oil on canvas. 97 x 116 cm.

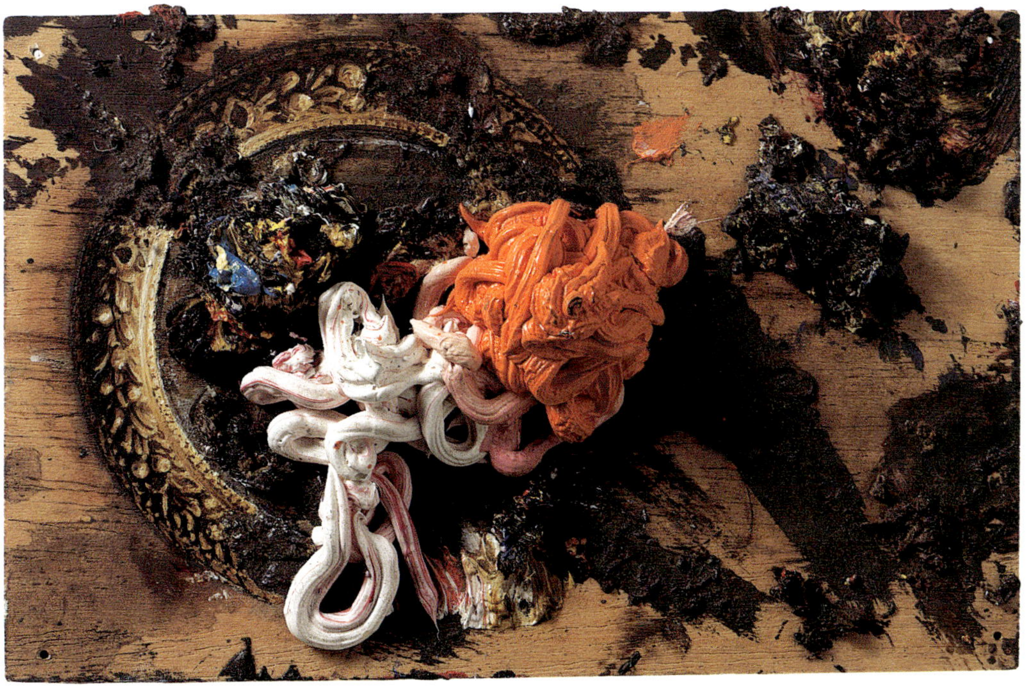

Marc i pintura 1996
(Frame and Paint)
Oil on wood. 21.5 x 13.5 x 3 cm.

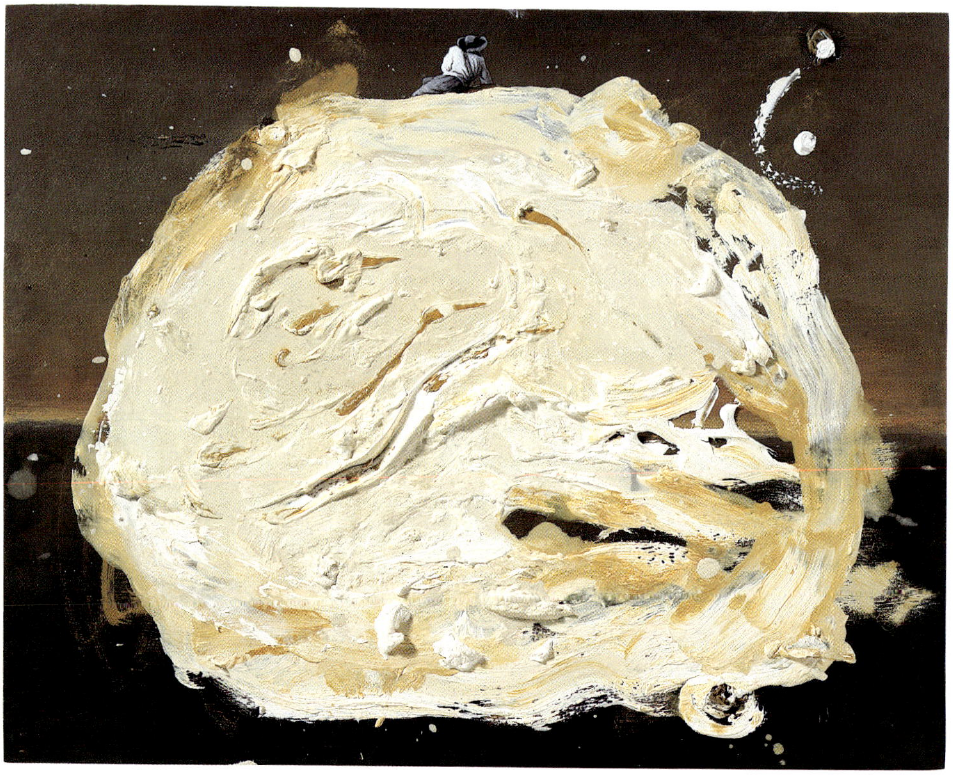

Personatge sobre un munt de pintura 1993
(Character on a Pile of Paint)
Oil on wood. 37 x 47.5 cm.

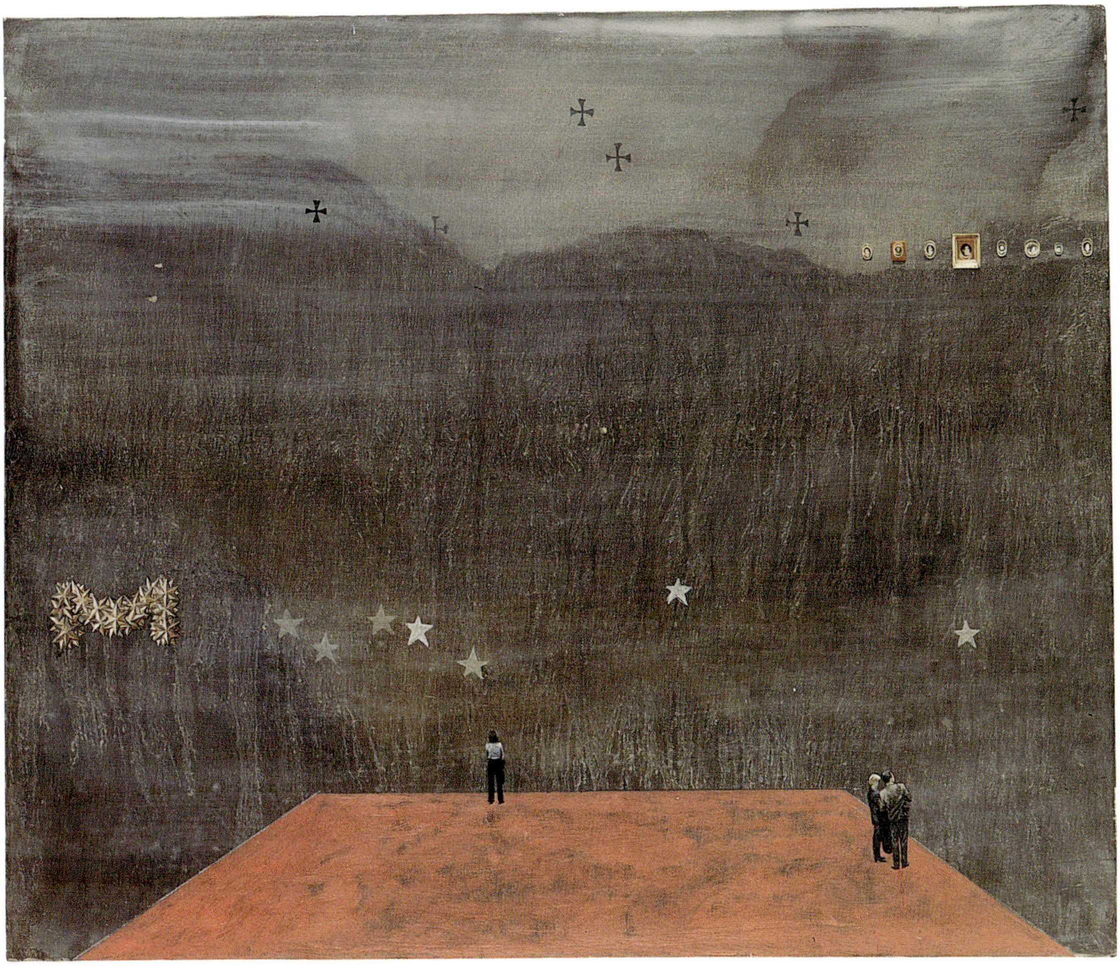

Olzinelles 1988
Oil on canvas. 56 x 64 cm.

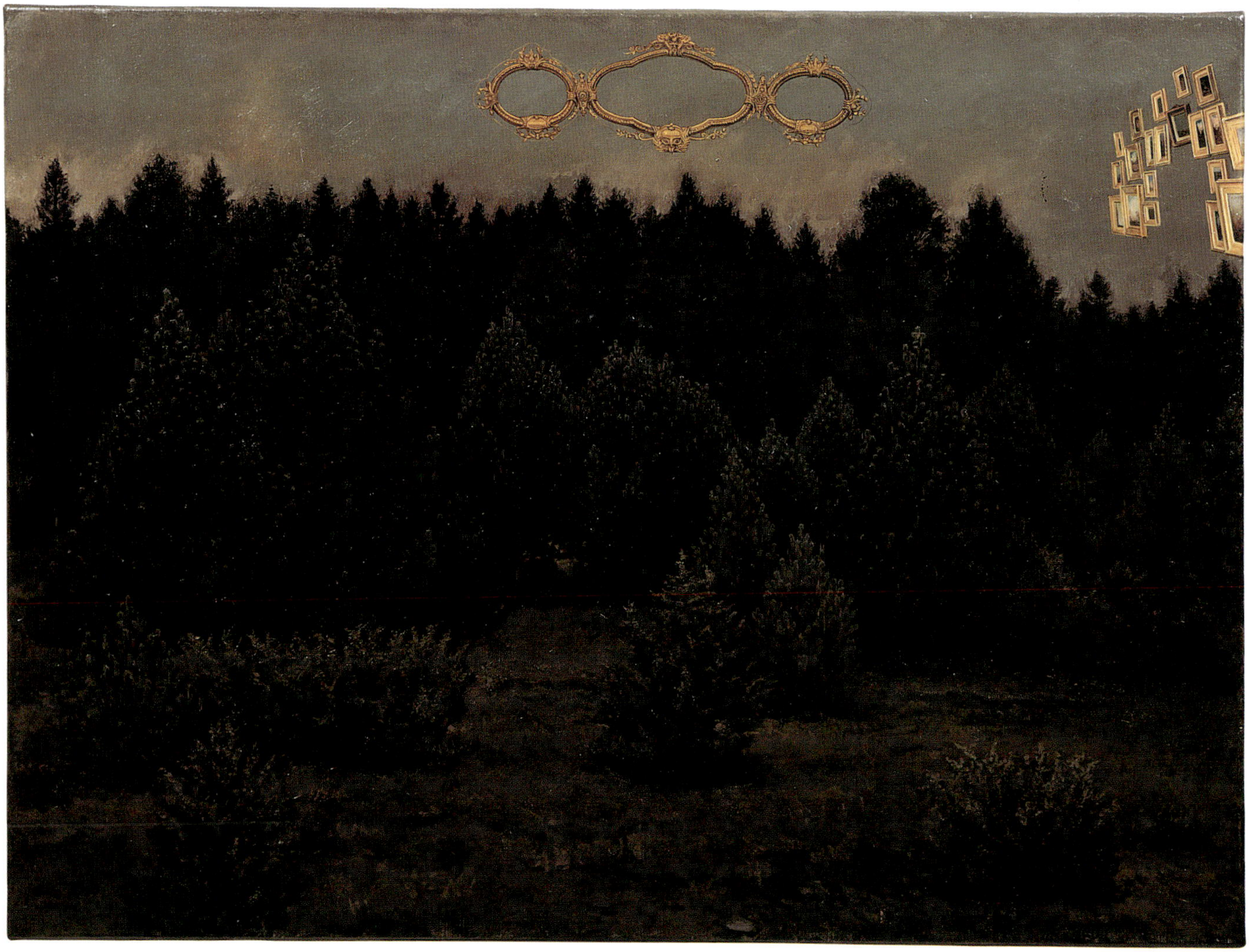

Costuix 1994
Oil on canvas. 73 x 100 cm.

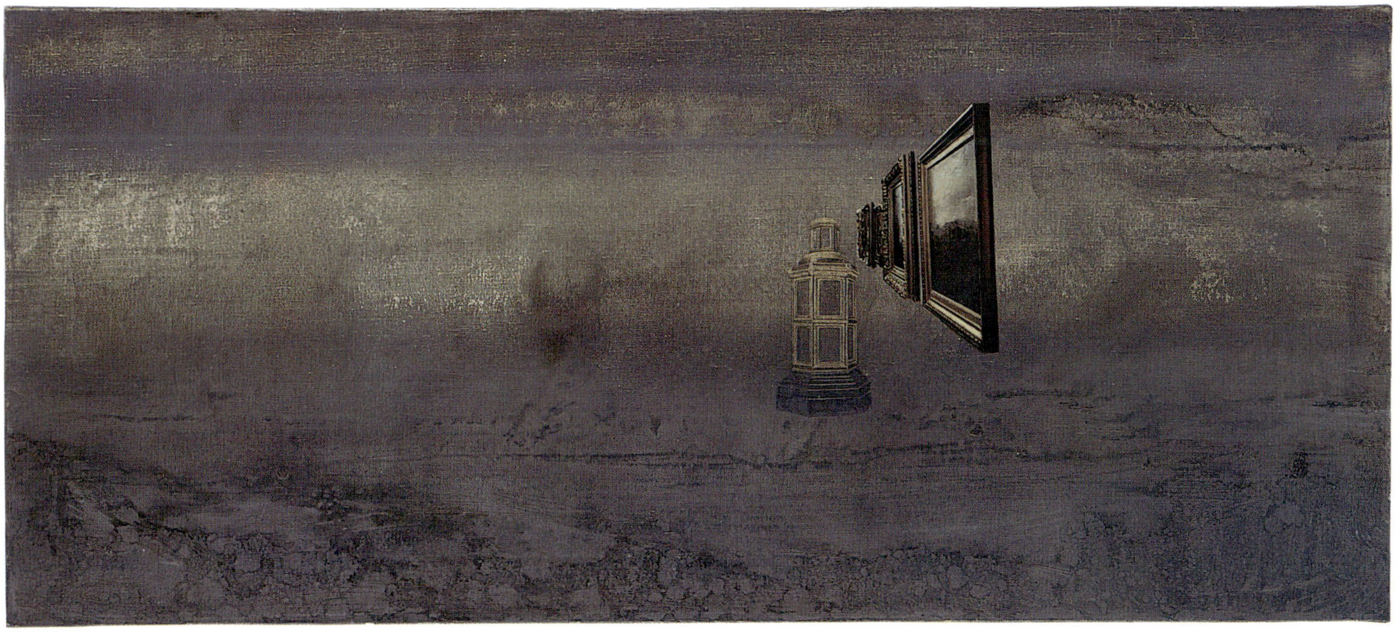

Far 1993
(Lighthouse)
Oil on canvas. 50 x 116 cm.

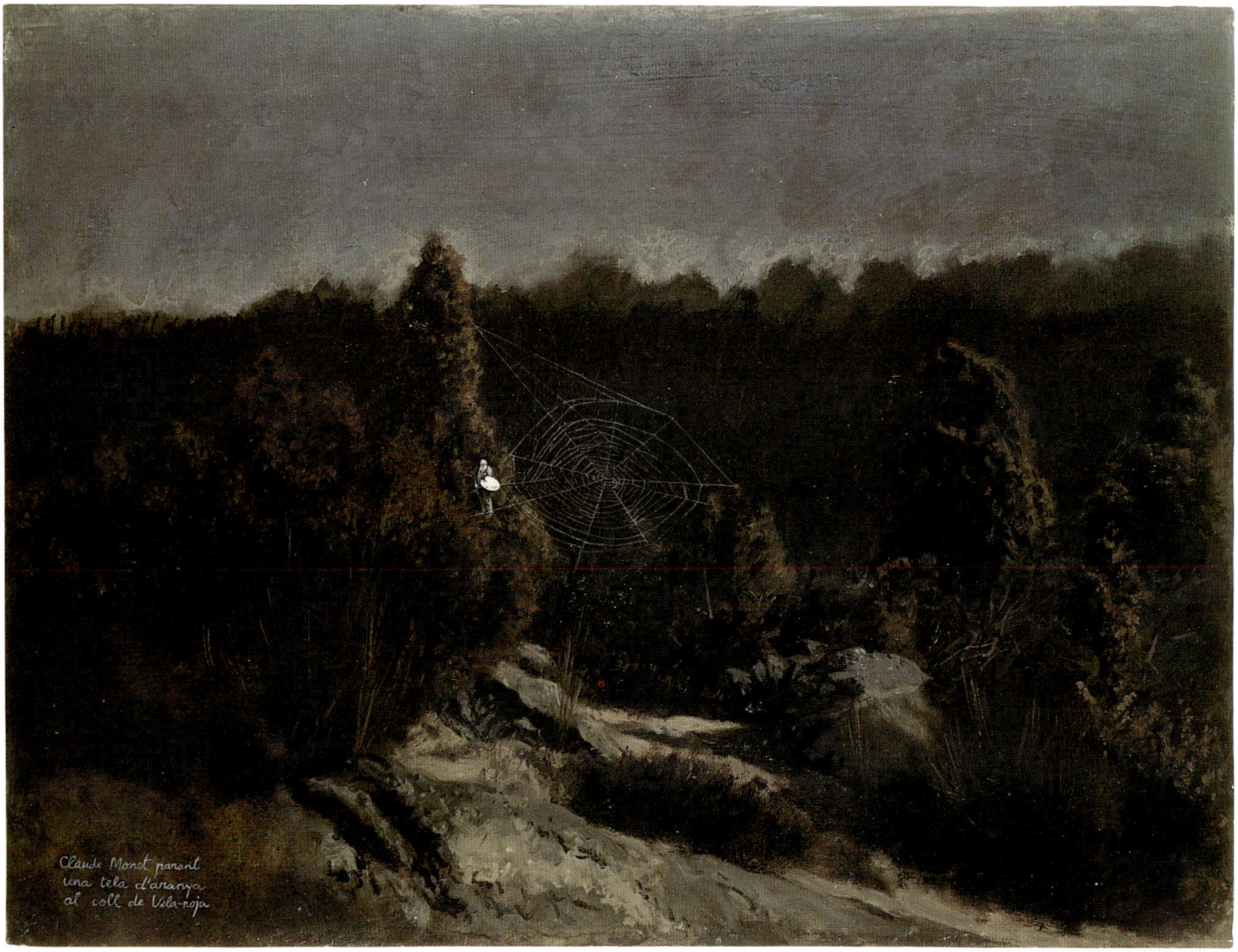

Claude Monet parant una tela d'aranya al Coll de Vila-roja 1993
(Claude Monet Placing a Cobweb at Vila-roja Pass)
Oil on canvas. 60.5 x 81 cm.

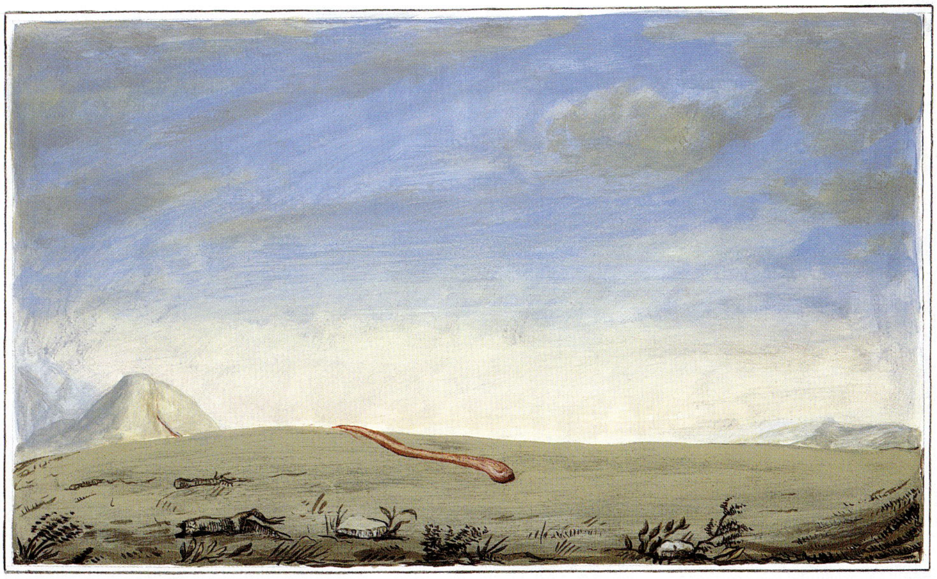

REGALIM DE PINTURA DE JACKSON POLLOCK, D'UNA MAGNITUD QUE ESBALAEIX

Regalim de pintura de Jackson Pollock d'una magnitud que esbalaeix 1996
(Jackson Pollock Paintdrop, Amazingly Long)
Gouache on paper. 30 x 42 cm.

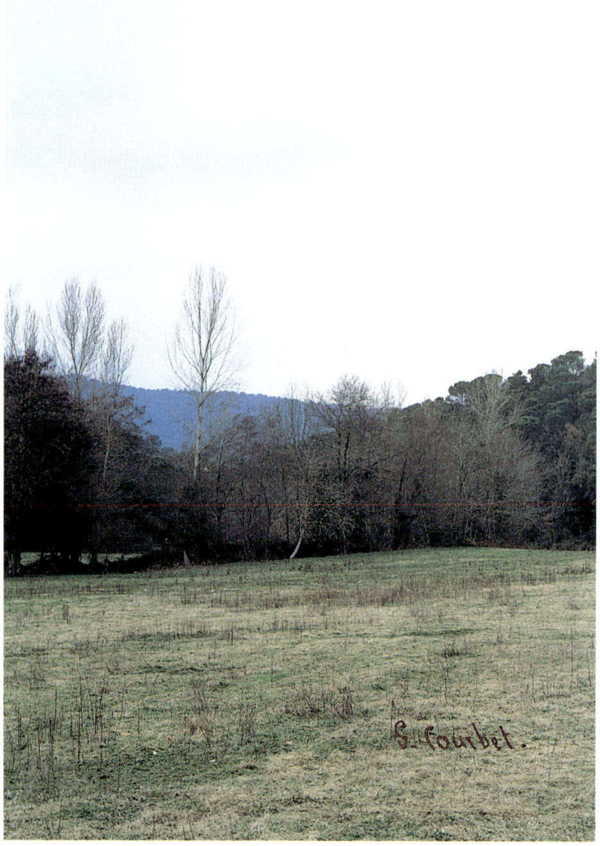
G. Courbet.

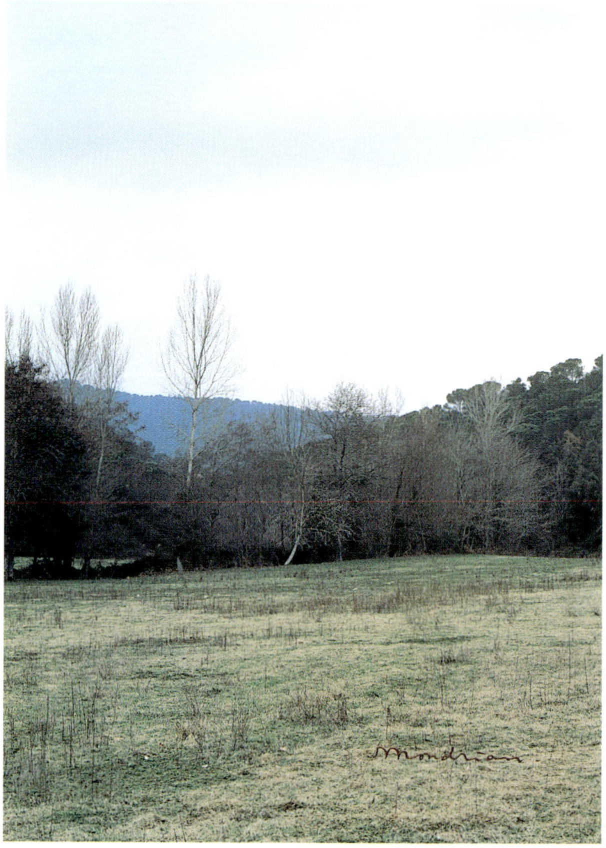
Mondrian

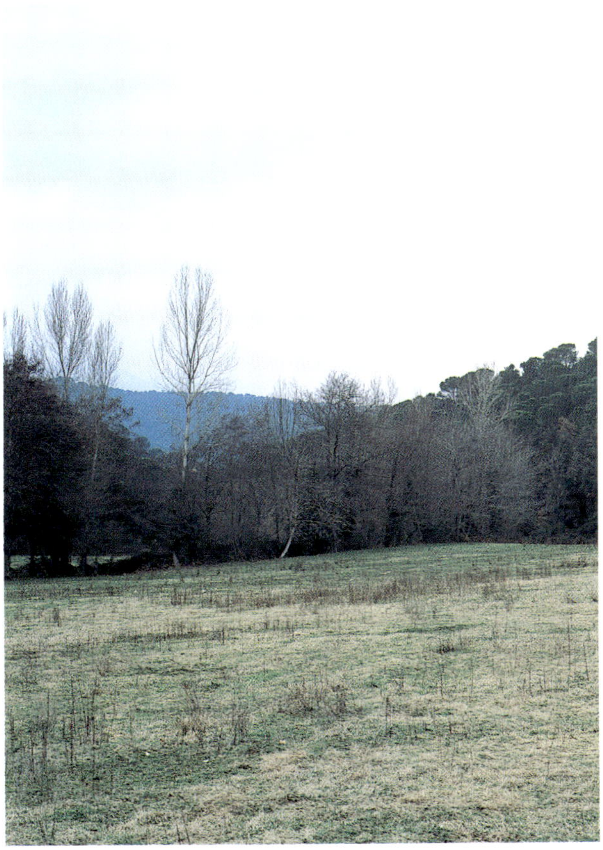

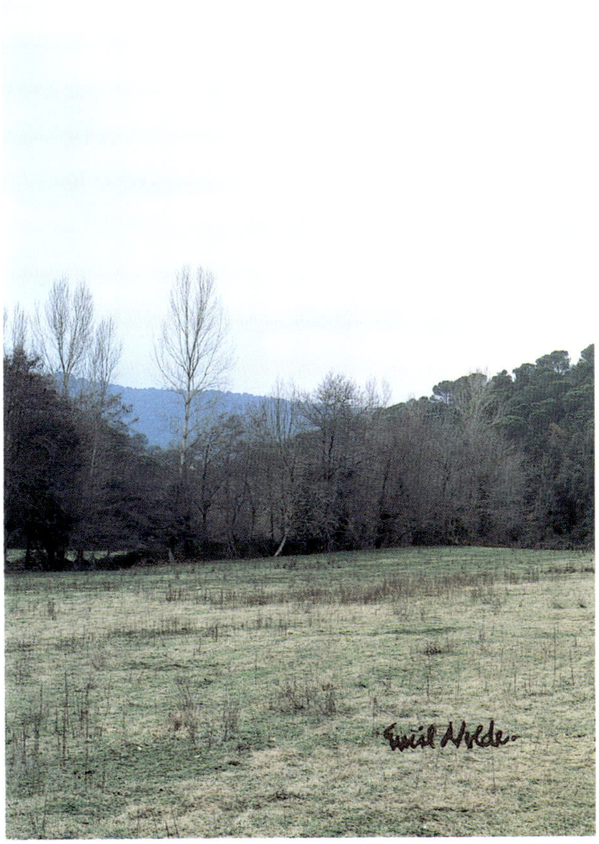

Autors 1990
(Authors)
Four photographs and golden frame. 150 x 120 cm. each

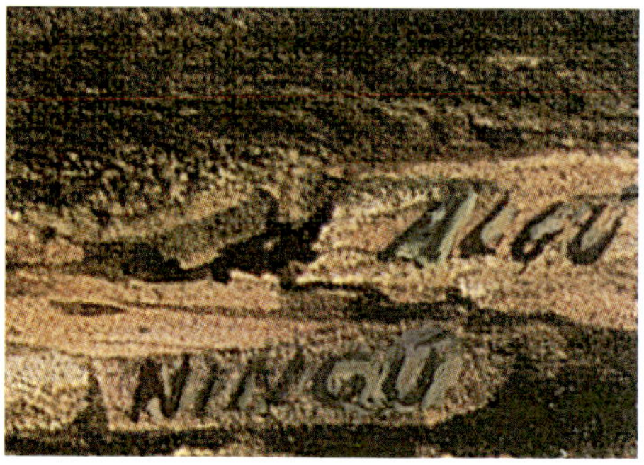

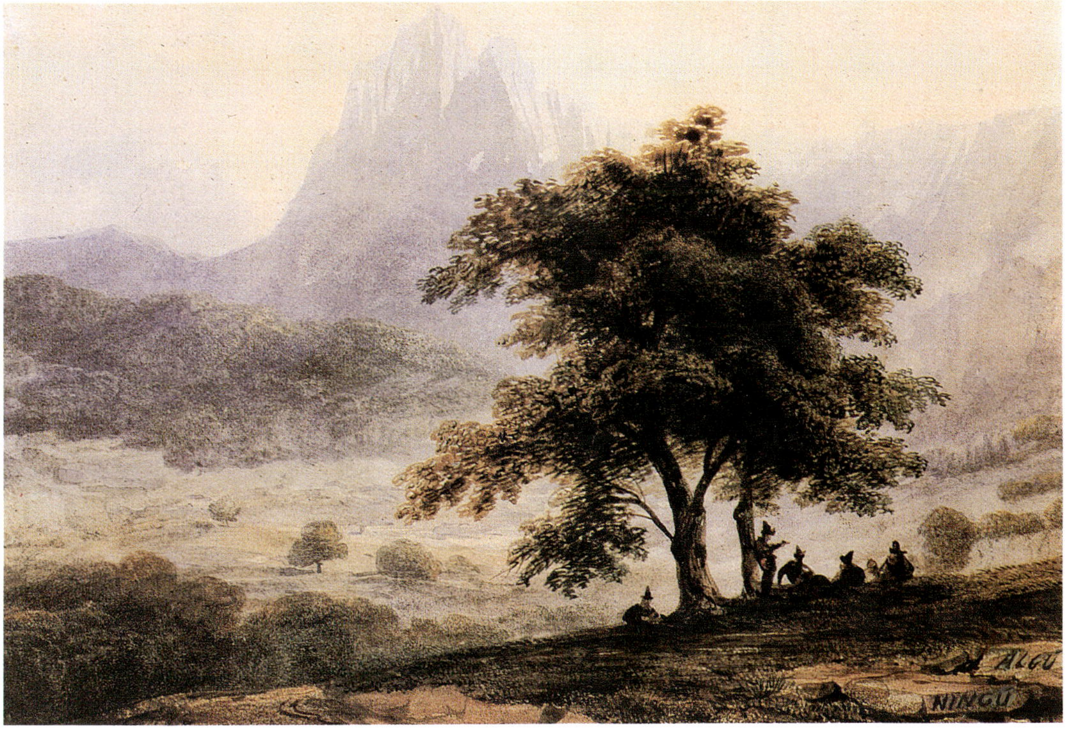

Algú ningú 1996
(Somebody, Nobody)
Mixed media on paper. 12 x 18 cm.

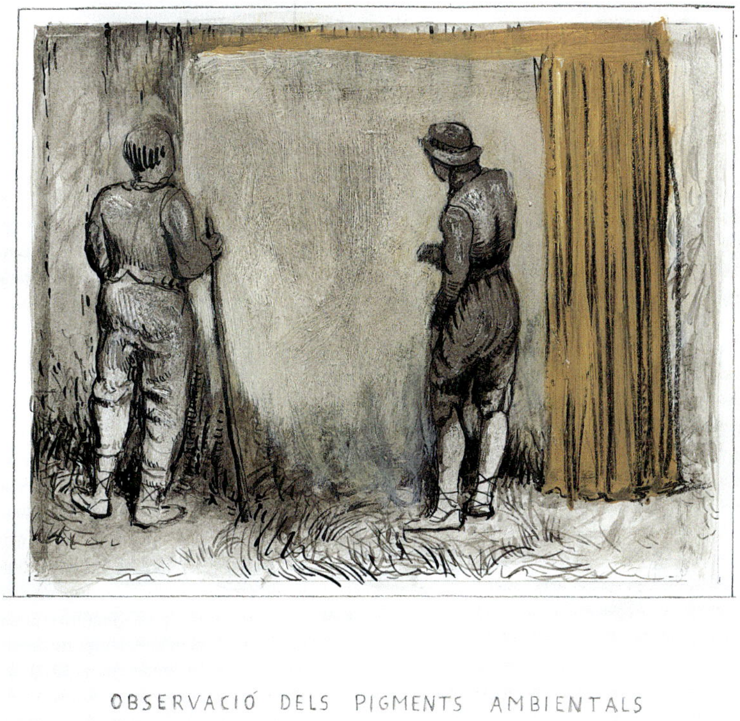

Observació dels pigments ambientals 1997
(Observation of Ambient Pigments)
Mixed media on paper 30 x 42 cm.

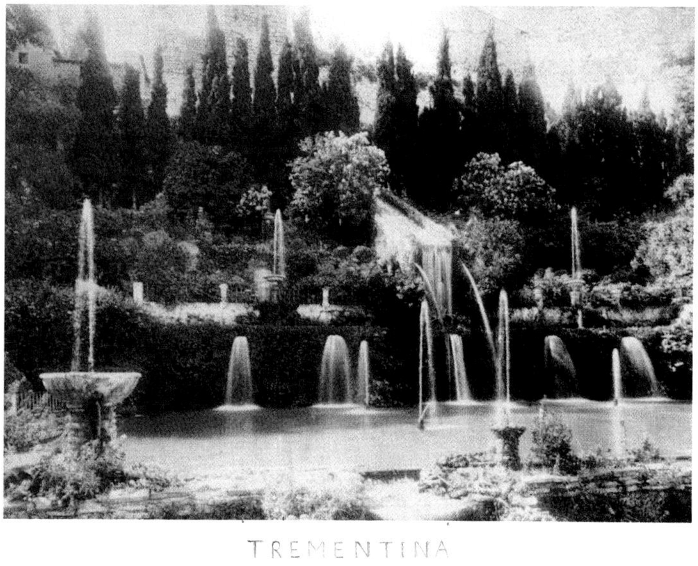

Trementina 1997
(Turpentine)
Mixed media on paper. 18 x 23.5 cm.

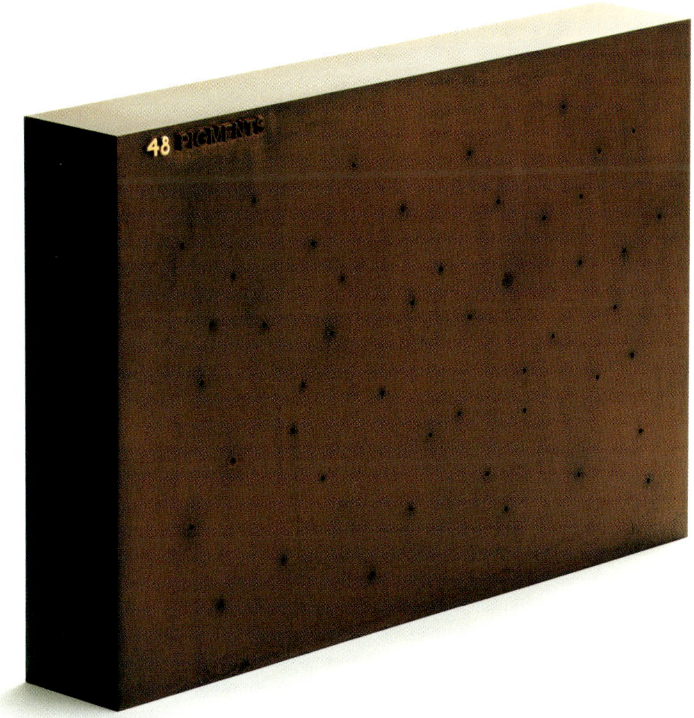

48 Pigments 1996
Iron and gold. 30 x 20 x 5 cm.

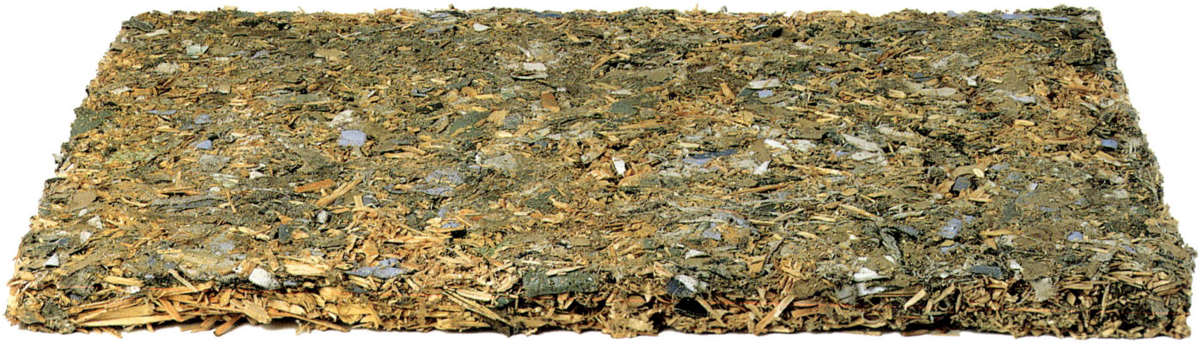

Compostatge de sis pintures 1994
(Six-painting Compost)
Oil, canvas and stretcher frame. 4 x 75.3 x 50 cm.

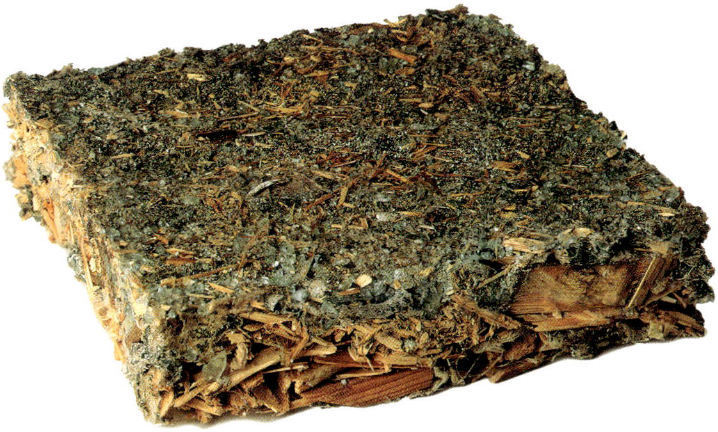

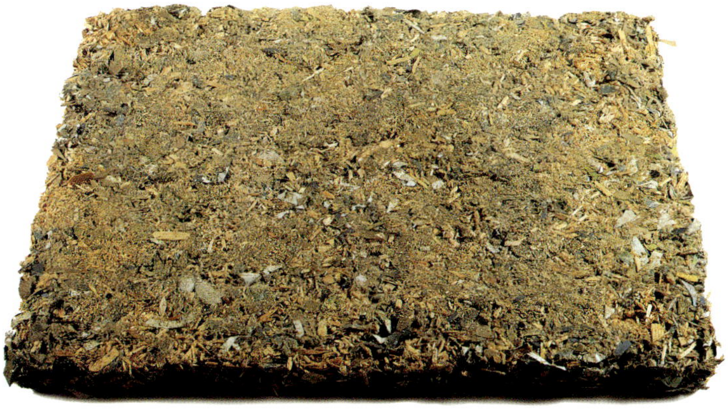

Compostatge d'una pintura amb marc i vidre 1994
(Painting Compost with Frame and Glass)
Oil, canvas, stretcher frame, frame and glass. 6 x 23 x 23 cm.

Compostatge de nou pintures 1994
(Nine-painting Compost)
Oil, canvas and stretcher frame. 3 x 52.4 x 44 cm.

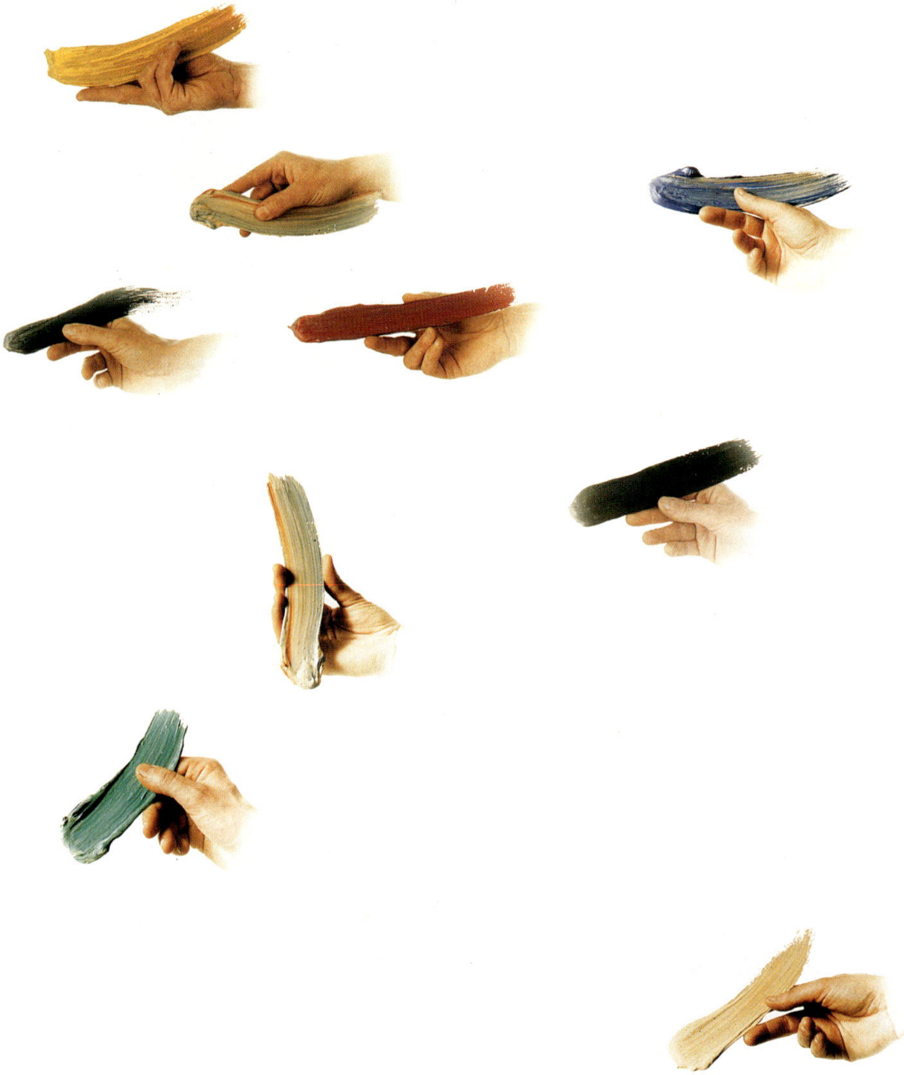

Pinzellades 1992
(Brushstrokes)
Photograph. 140 x 105 cm.

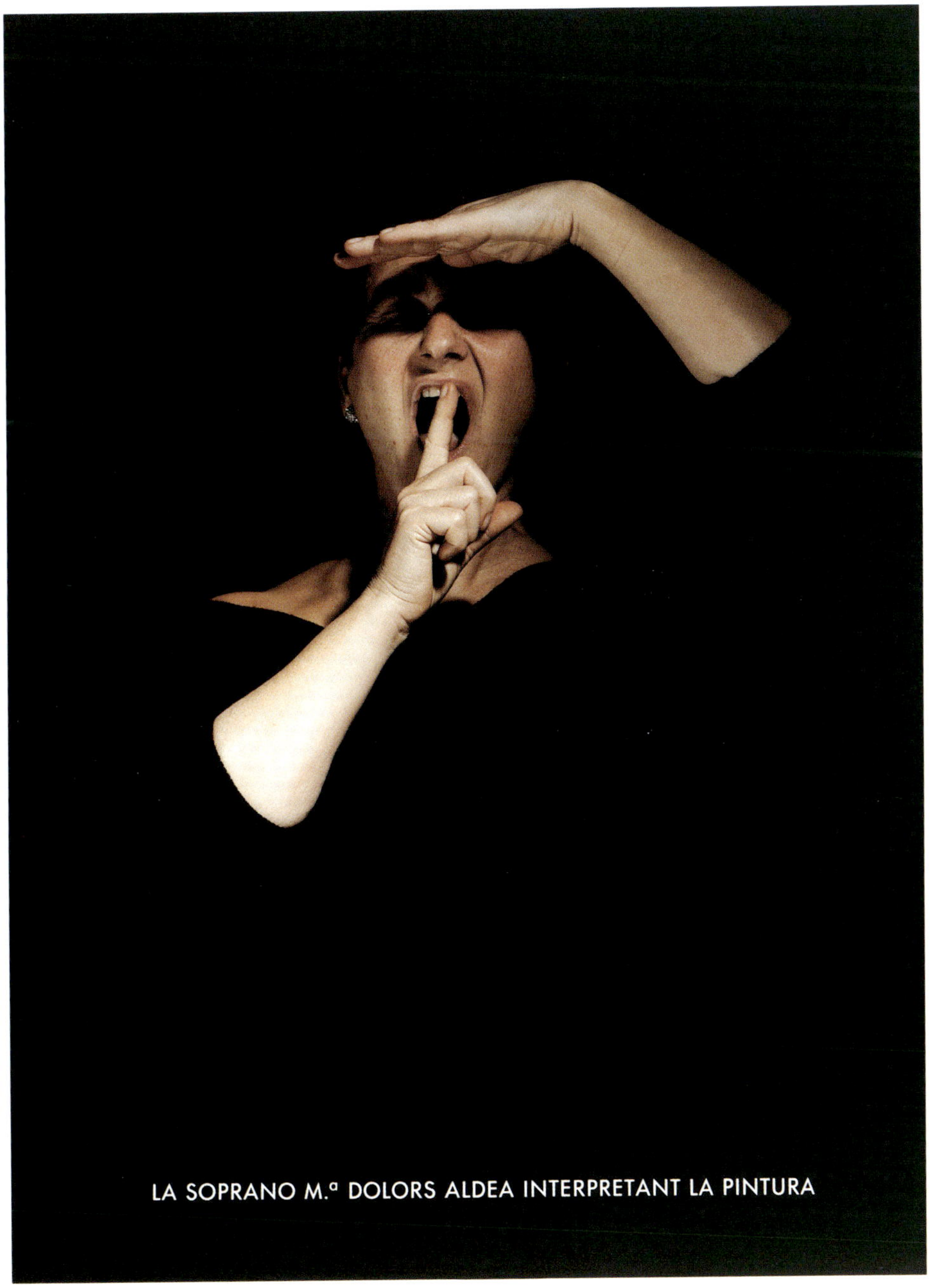

La soprano Maria Dolors Aldea interpretant la pintura 1994
(The Soprano Maria Dolors Aldea Performing Painting)
Photograph. 122 x 90 cm.

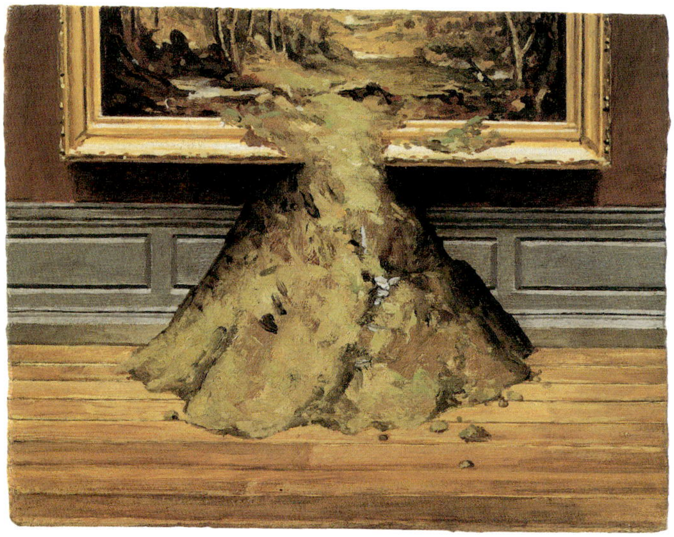

National Gallery 1998
Oil on wood. 12.2 x 16 cm.

Els boscos de Barbizon reclamen al pintor Théodore Rousseau que els torni les imatges 1995
(The Forests of Barbizon Demand Théodore Rousseau to Return the Images to Them)
Mixed media on paper. 39 x 49 cm.

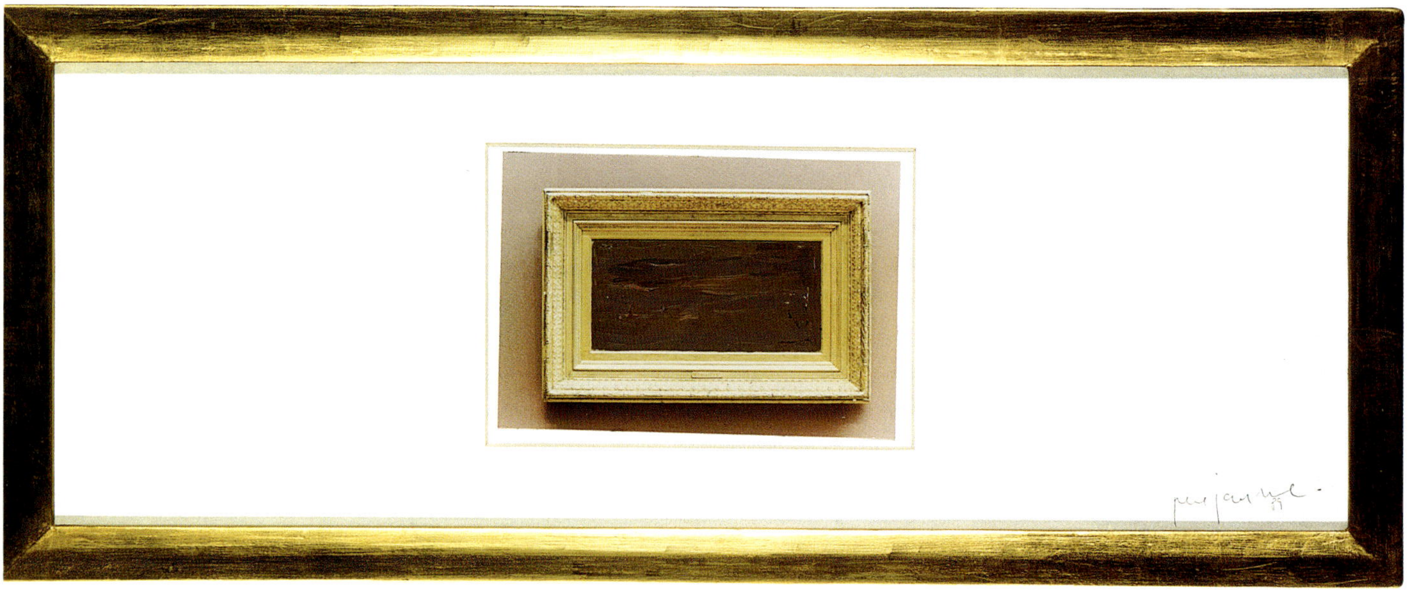

Pinacoteca 6 1989
(Picture Gallery 6)
Acrylic on photograph. 17 x 49 cm.

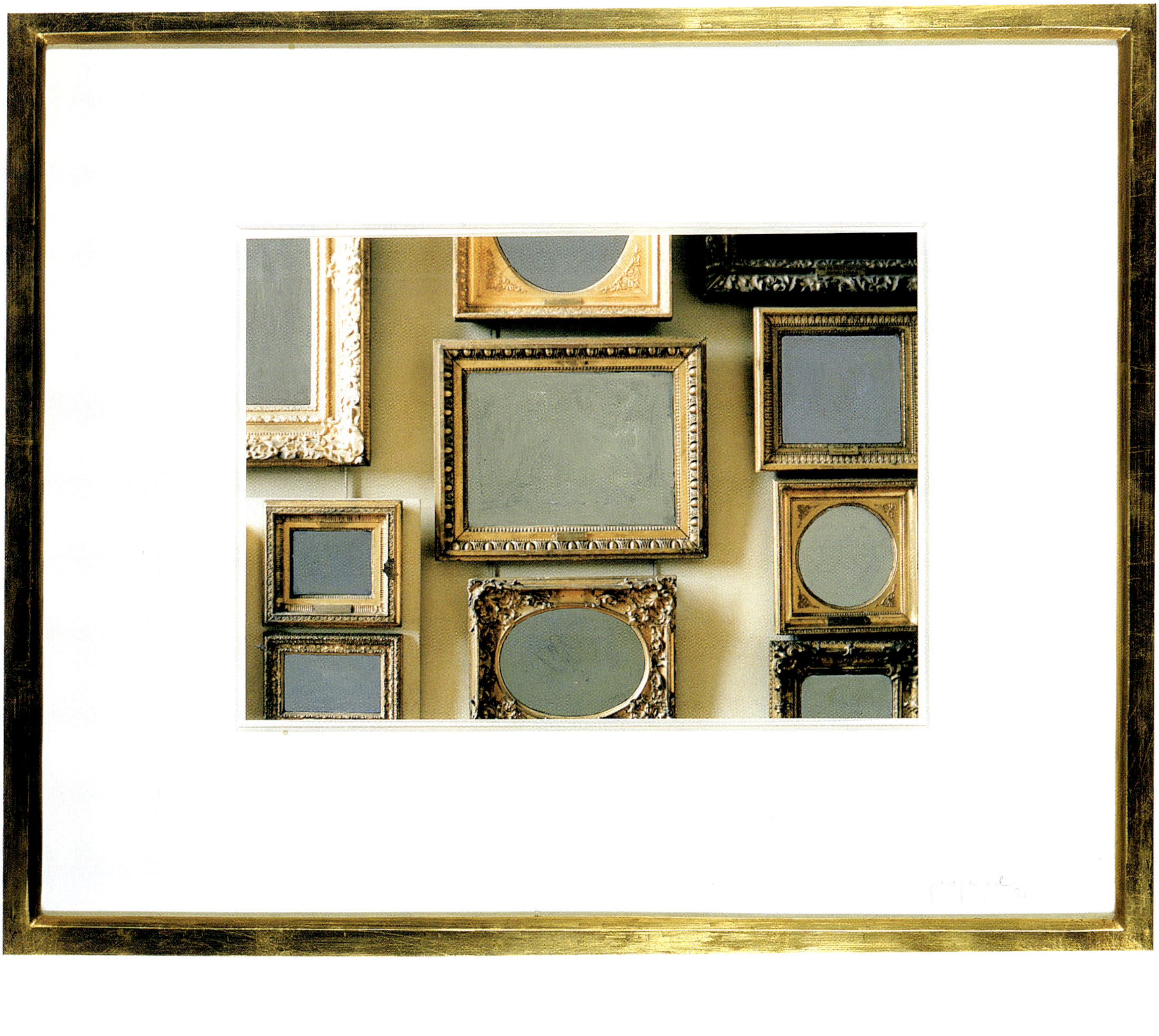

Pinacoteca 48 1991
(Picture Gallery 48)
Oil on photograph. 24 x 35.5 cm.

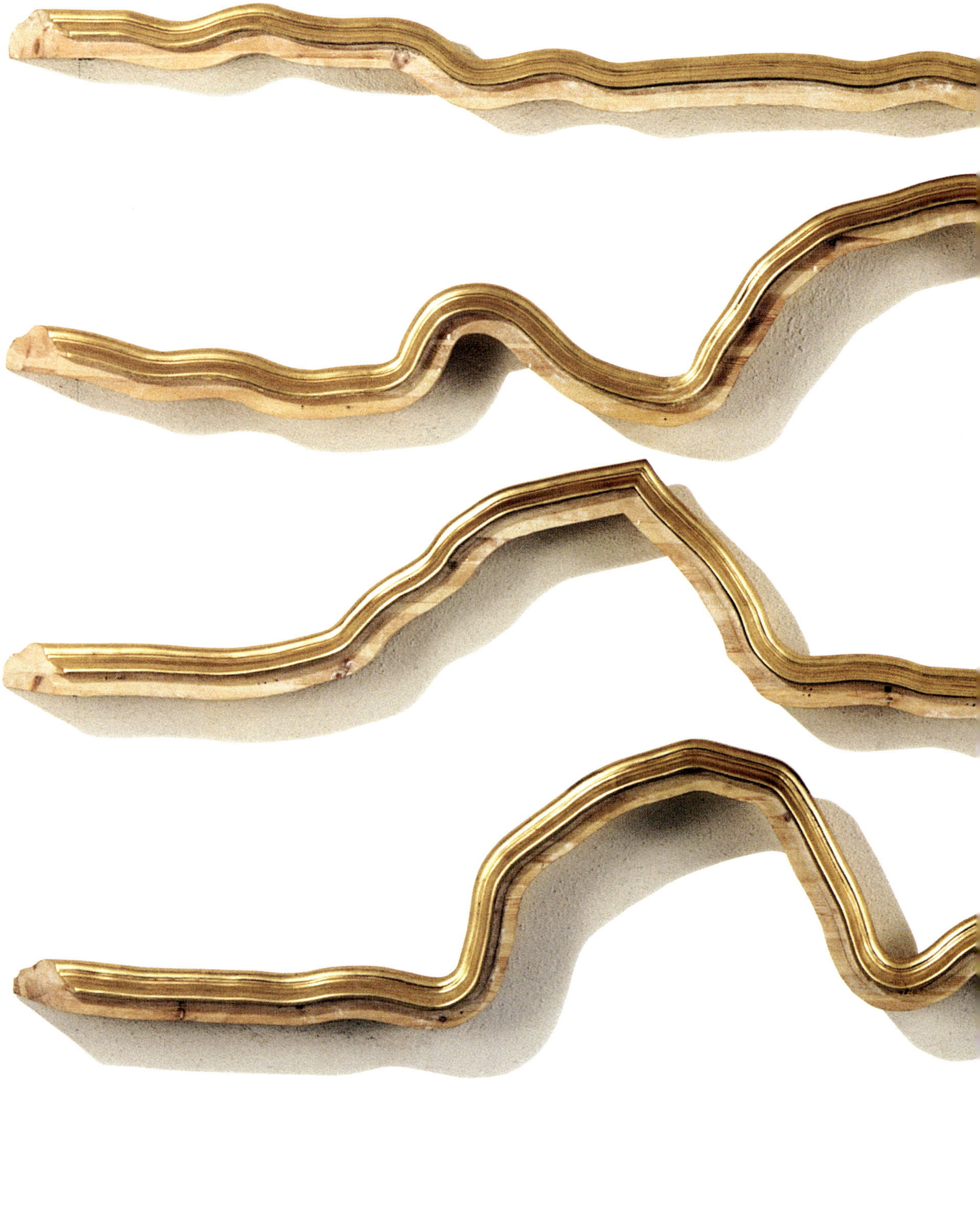

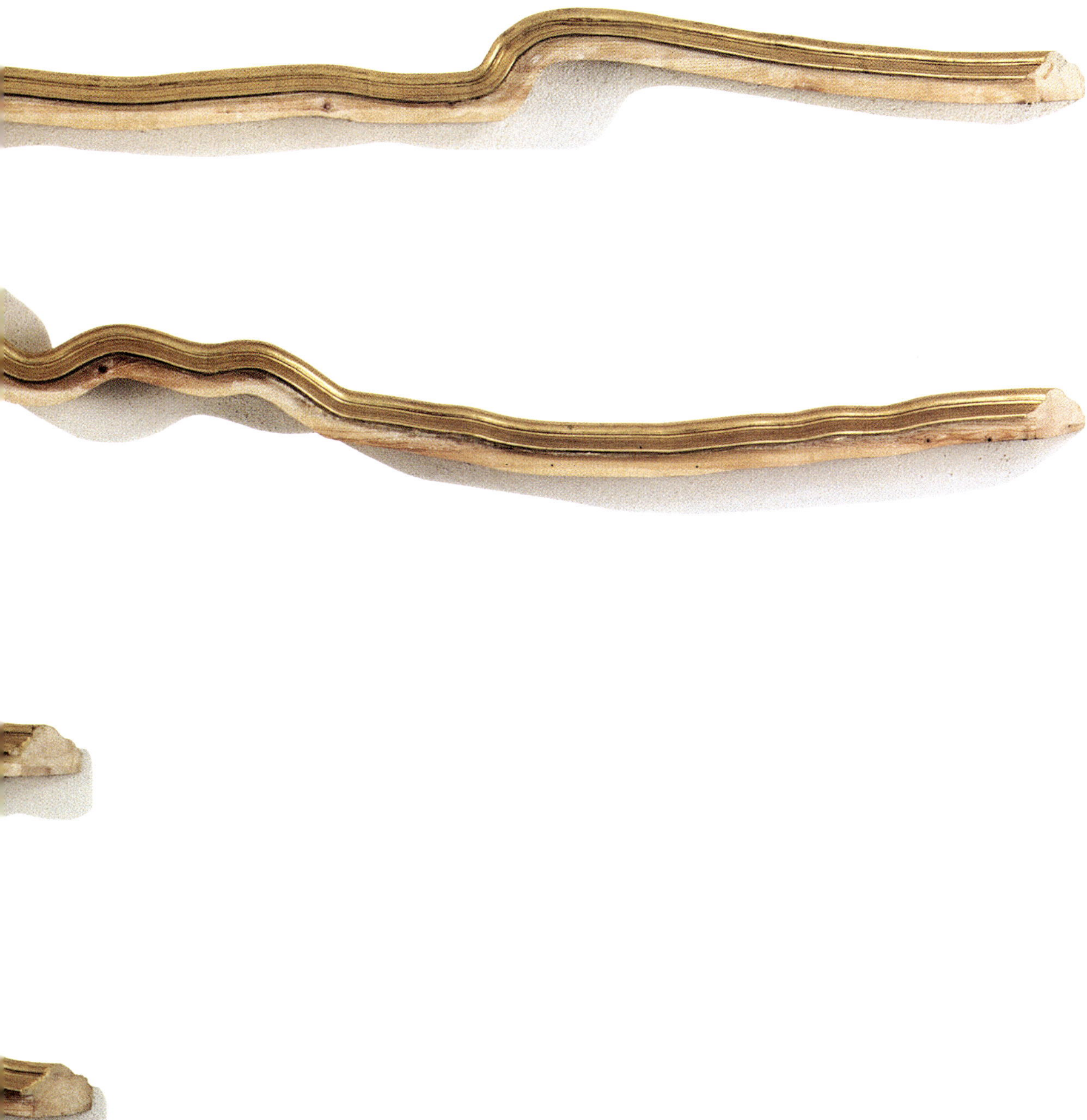

Els quatre horitzons 1991
(The Four Horizons)
Gilded frames. 180 x 370 cm.

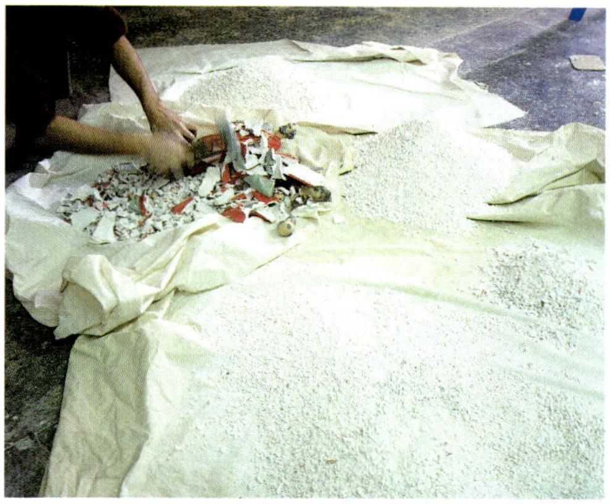

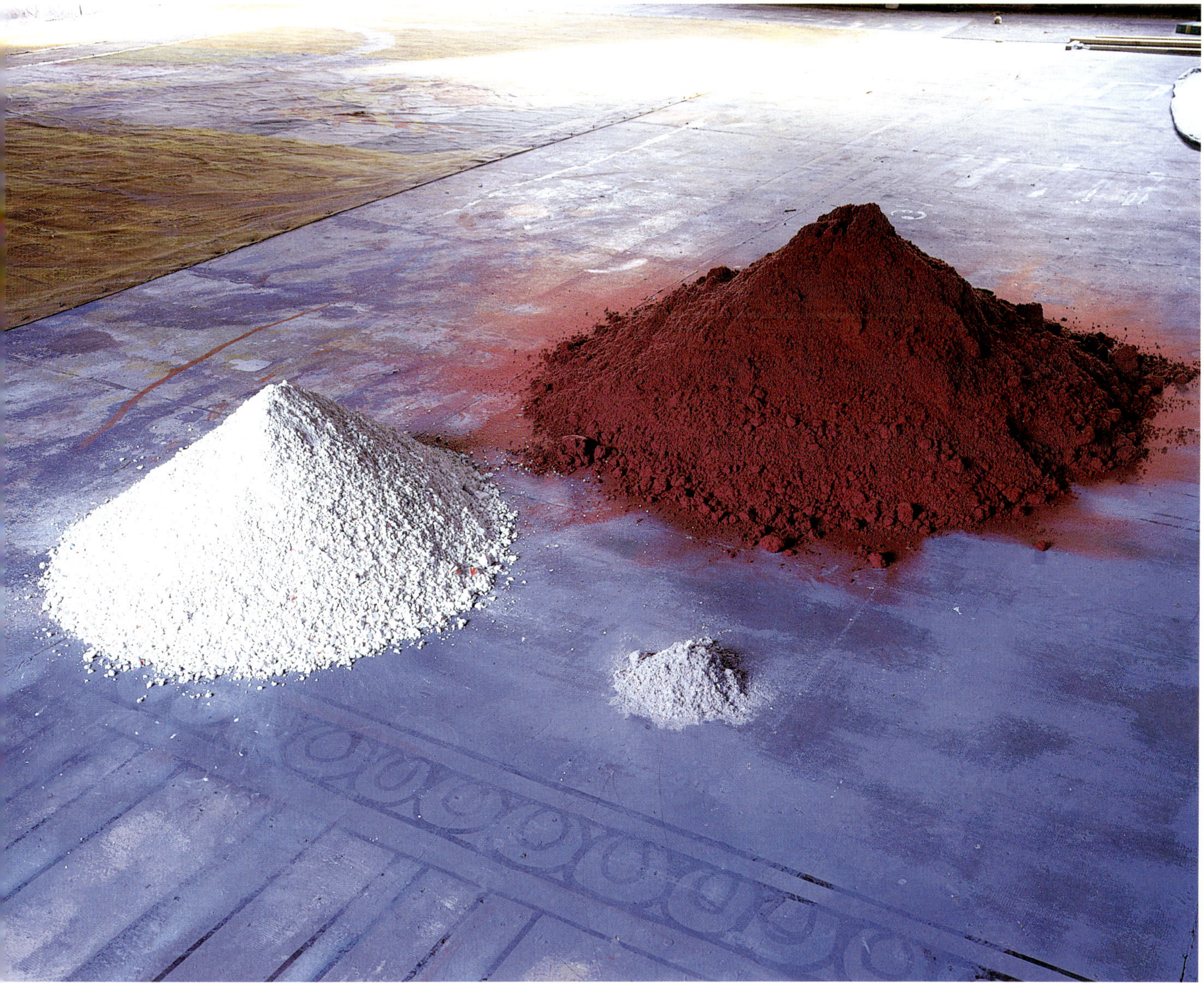

Tres pic-ments 1999
(Three Peak-ments)
23 m^2 of ground red velvet, 32 images of Saint Luke and a deck of cards

Perejaume, performed.*

Marcia Tucker

There are certain works of art that, once seen, remain indelible in the mind's eye. When I first saw a photograph by Perejaume of several rows of red velvet theater seats set up in a desert, the image stopped me in my tracks. My mind was suddenly filled with questions. Had the seats been thrown away? If so, why? They were in perfectly good condition. Were their occupants about to come back? What was something that clearly belonged inside doing outside? And why in such a desolate place? The piece made me both laugh and think. An audience, after all, would sit there for a purpose, assuming that something was going to be presented to it, and theater seats suggest a setting designed specifically for that purpose. But the desert is, of course, the opposite of a traditional theater hall with proscenium stage, and in this case, the audience hadn't arrived yet—if in fact it ever would.

In 1990, the New Museum of Contemporary Art invited Perejaume to do a site-specific piece for its Broadway Window. The resulting work, *Pintura i representació* (Painting and Representation; p. 82), which opened in May of 1991, delighted everyone. The piece consisted of two rows of blue velvet theater seats installed in the window, facing the street. A door was cut to provide access to the long, narrow space, and visitors could enter without having to pass the admissions desk. Those adventurous souls who climbed in and sat down were amused and beguiled by the spectacle of people and activity in the street, and often stayed put for a considerable length of time. Passers-by, in turn, were fascinated by the seated people inside who, while watching them, animatedly talked to each other, pointing and laughing at what they saw, and in general creating a spectacle of their own. In one simple, grand gesture, Perejaume rendered the museum permeable, its inside and its outside engaged in a literal dialogue with each other.

In addition to the work that first beguiled me, and the New Museum installation, there are a series of works by Perejaume, all of them with the same title, *Pintura i representació*. Seats from the Teatro Maria Guerrero were installed in the window of the Galeria Montenegro in Madrid in 1988; five rows from the Palau de la Música Catalana were placed on the steps of the Roman theater of Sagunto, near Valencia, and photographed (p. 82). Variations on these theater motifs have appeared in his work almost from the beginning. In the late 1970s, he painted surreal landscapes which included characters, like Pierrot, drawn from the traditional popular theater. Several paintings from the '80s contain images of empty theater seats or balconies, or of people looking out

1
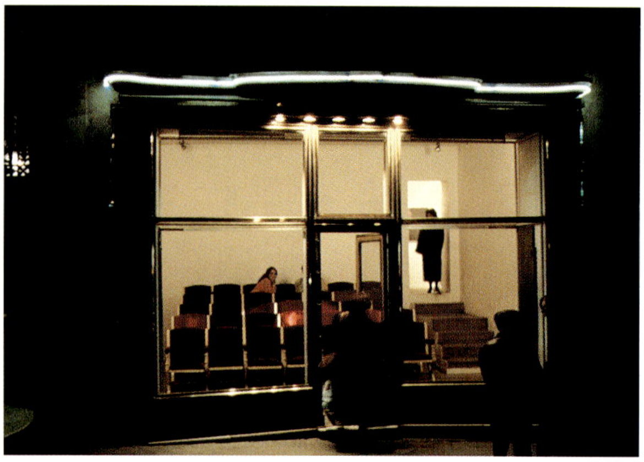

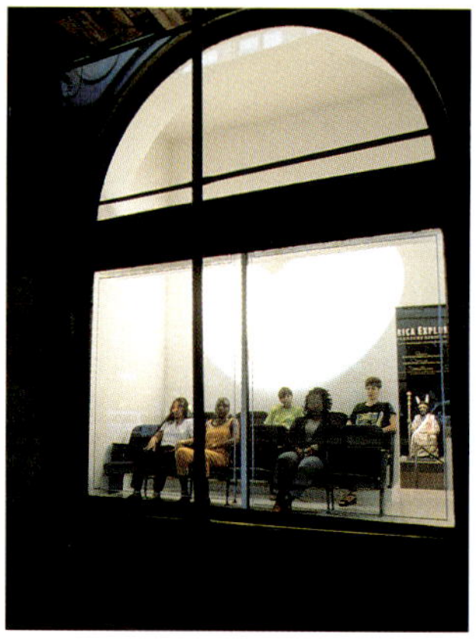
2

from them onto a vast landscape of abstract, painted canvas. By 1986, the idea of the painting and of nature itself as spectacle, and of the viewer as participant in a complex dialogue between illusion and representation, became central to his work.

As he treats concepts in all his work, Perejaume plays with the idea of theater by crisscrossing a variety of media and themes. In one of the tiny paintings of *Retaule* (Retable 1995; p. 84-87), we see the silhouettes of people from the rear, looking obliquely at an empty stage which occupies less than half the painting, while curtains occupy the other half. The image, despite its modest size, raises questions about the relationship between theatrical and painterly illusions. Are these simply two different kinds of representation? Is this a kind of conceptual doubling, wherein those of us who are looking at the painting are mimicking the spectators inside it who are looking at the theater? Where does meaning reside—in the viewer, in the work itself, or in the interstices between the two?

Another small painting of *Retaule* shows the top of a curtain, parted under an ornate entablature to reveal fragments of framed paintings behind it. Here, the implied spectacle is that of floor-to-ceiling paintings, and nothing more. Or should I say, "nothing less"? For, in terms of illusion, these "staged" paintings are plays within plays, plays on representation.

3
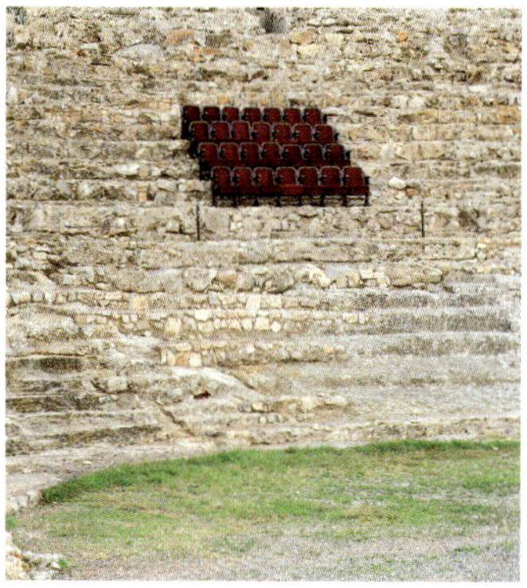

1 **Painting and Representation** 1988
Galería Montenegro, Madrid
(Seats from the Teatro María Guerrero)

2 **Painting and Representation** 1991
The New Museum of Contemporary Art, New York

3 **Painting and Representation** 1989
Roman theater of Sagunt
(Seats from the Palau de la Música Catalana)

4 **Painting and Representation** 1989
Ebro Delta
(Seats from the Palau de la Música Catalana)
Photograph. 135 x 122 cm.

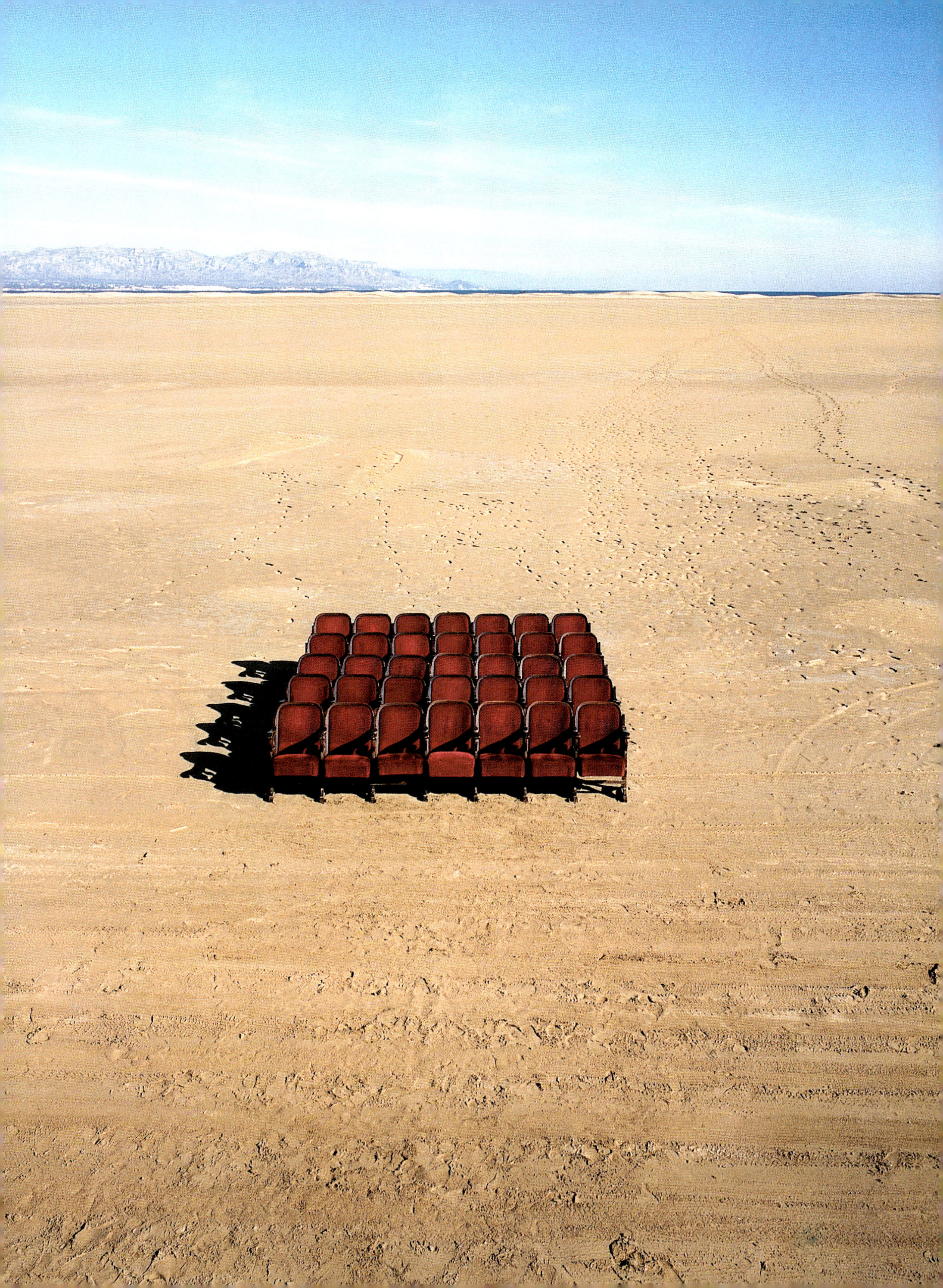

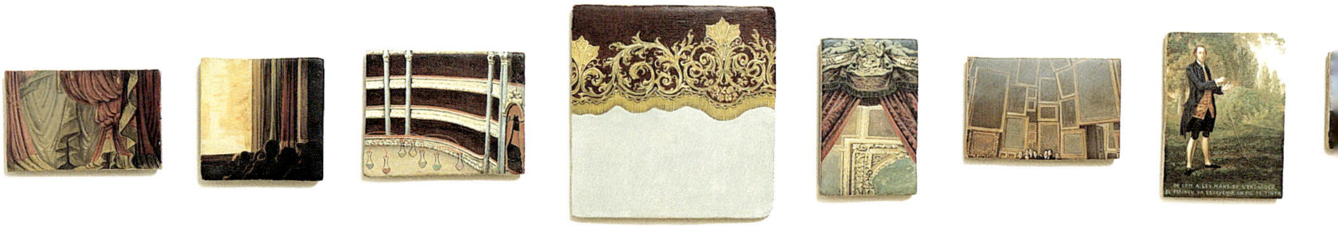

Retaule 1995
(Retable)
Oil on wood. 15 pieces

In fact, in yet another painting of *Retaule*, the heads of a group of spectators located at the very bottom stare up at the same floor-to-ceiling paintings, this time minus images. Typically, Perejaume also made a sculpture, entitled *Intempèrie I* (Open Air I, 1993; p. 224-228), a free-standing chamber composed of empty frames, gilded side in, providing, in effect, a room of imaginary paintings, whereby the viewer is privy only to his or her own envisioning.

In another work of 1988 a single ornate gilt frame "captures" a mountain top by configuring nature as a representation rather than a reality (p. 104). Perejaume's photograph shows us the top of a mountain range in which the landscape of its peak is literally framed by a gilded wooden frame which appears to have been melted in order to conform to the mountain's contours.

The same frame was also shown independent of the mountains, on a gallery floor, startling viewers by its peculiar, contorted shape and enormous size (3 m x 4 m x 50 cm). The audacious scale of a work like this relates to Perejaume's "pessebrisme", the use of small-scale fragments of nature as a stand-in for its life-sized counterpart through manipulation of the scale of objects which surround it. The Catalan term "pessebre" refers to the commonplace practice of using pieces of bark to represent mountain landscapes in homemade crêche scenes; Perejaume's gigantic frame, by taming, reconfiguring, and transforming a mountaintop into a painting, has created a pessebrism in reverse. A related work, *Teló* (Curtain 1992; p. 90), is a painting of an enormous red and gold theater curtain laid on the tops of the mountains, as if by the hand of a giant god. It brings together concepts of staging and transformation of scale as a way of locating and identifying aspects of nature as art. Thus it is linked to yet another series of photographic works in which a part of the ocean is isolated by a gold frame floating on its surface, or identified as an illustration by large iron letters spelling out "fig. 1" and "fig. 2", placed on the sand and photographed. These pieces exemplify the nonlinear and interconnected nature of Perejaume's thinking, by which every piece refers to an aspect of another piece, at once clarifying and complicating an individual work and the body of related works.

To my mind, Perejaume's most magical and extraordinary work is a recent one, part of a four-part

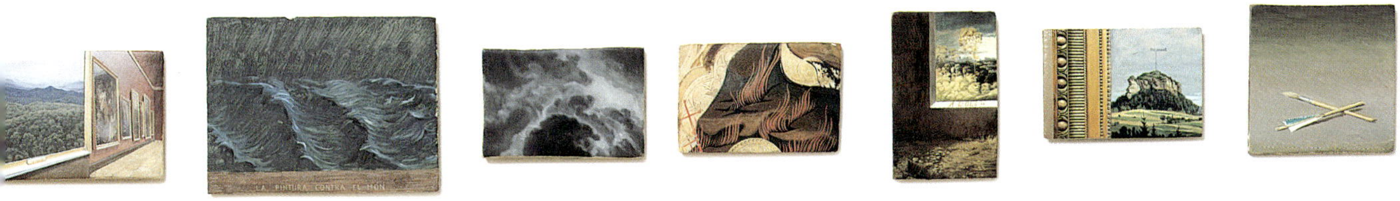

exhibition called *Girona, Sant Pol, Pineda, la Vall d'Oo*, done in the summer of 1997. Upon the empty stage of the ornate, late nineteenth-century municipal theater of Girona, Perejaume constructed a floor-to-ceiling multi-paneled sheet of glass where the curtain would ordinarily hang (p. 98-99). The theater was open to the public, as an art gallery would be, and the empty stage itself, separated from viewers by the glass, was the real spectacle. Across the street in a small space used normally for exhibitions, the word Pintors! (Painters!) was spelled out on the floor in large letters composed of alternating blocks of sugar and salt (p. 222). By using the gallery space in which to place the word "Pintors!" (interpretable both as an admonition and a rallying cry), Perejaume addresses absent painters, who will never—can never?—appear. For one thing, this is a venue in which individual painters haven't "painted" anything; for another, the "real" painter is a fiction, and the word "Pintors!" is nothing more than a linguistic representation posing as a sculpture, which in turn poses as a domestic conceit, consisting as it does of singularly unpainterly materials, i.e., sugar and salt.

In Sant Pol de Mar, Perejaume took paintings from the local museum and laid them out on a mountain site, entitling the resulting work *Retaule: fons del Museu de Pintura de Sant Pol de Mar* (Retable: collection of the Sant Pol de Mar Museum of Painting; p. 32). In the small town of Pineda, a local storefront displayed Perejaume's round photographs, taken looking down into the town's wells (p. 143); he named each image after the house where each well was. In Vall d'Oo, high in the mountains, particles of dust collected from the restoration of an altarpiece in Sant Martí de Llanera were burnt and, as a new altarpiece, were "restored" back into the air.

What kind of art work is this? Neither painting, sculpture, installation, nor theater, it defies categorization, suggesting a multi-layered, site-specific group of works closer in feeling to contemporary performance art practice. Unlike traditional theater, this practice isn't based on pre-existing characters—nor, for that matter, on characters at all—but on making the artist's process of seeing and thinking performative, and thereby available to others.

In the Girona *Retaule* the use of the theater space as a metaphysical spectacle alters its usual role,

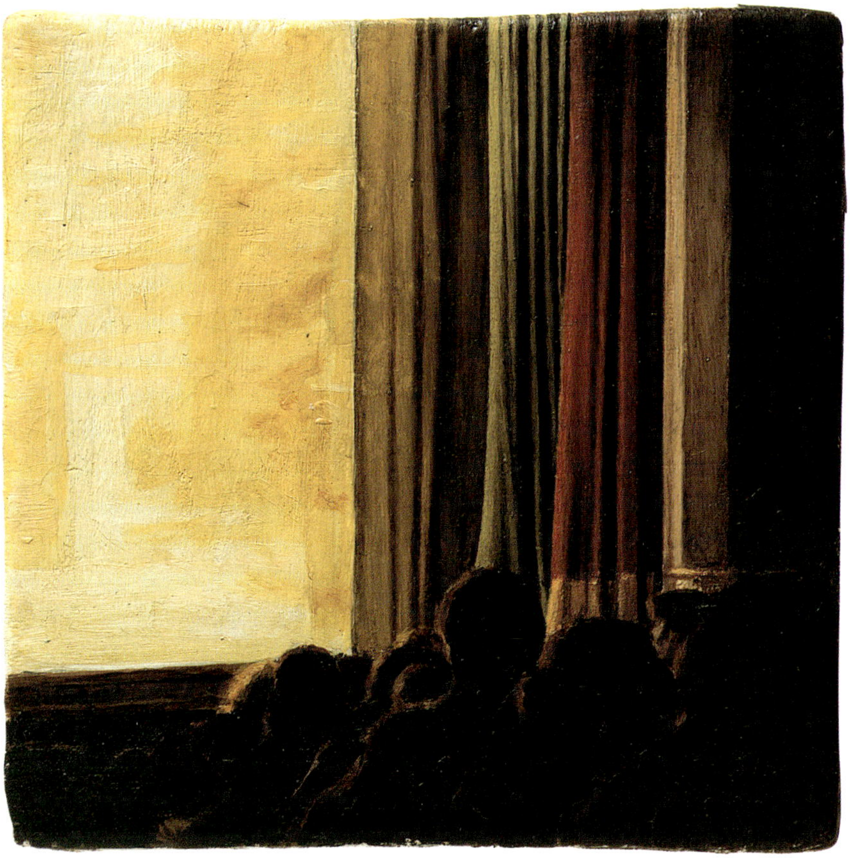

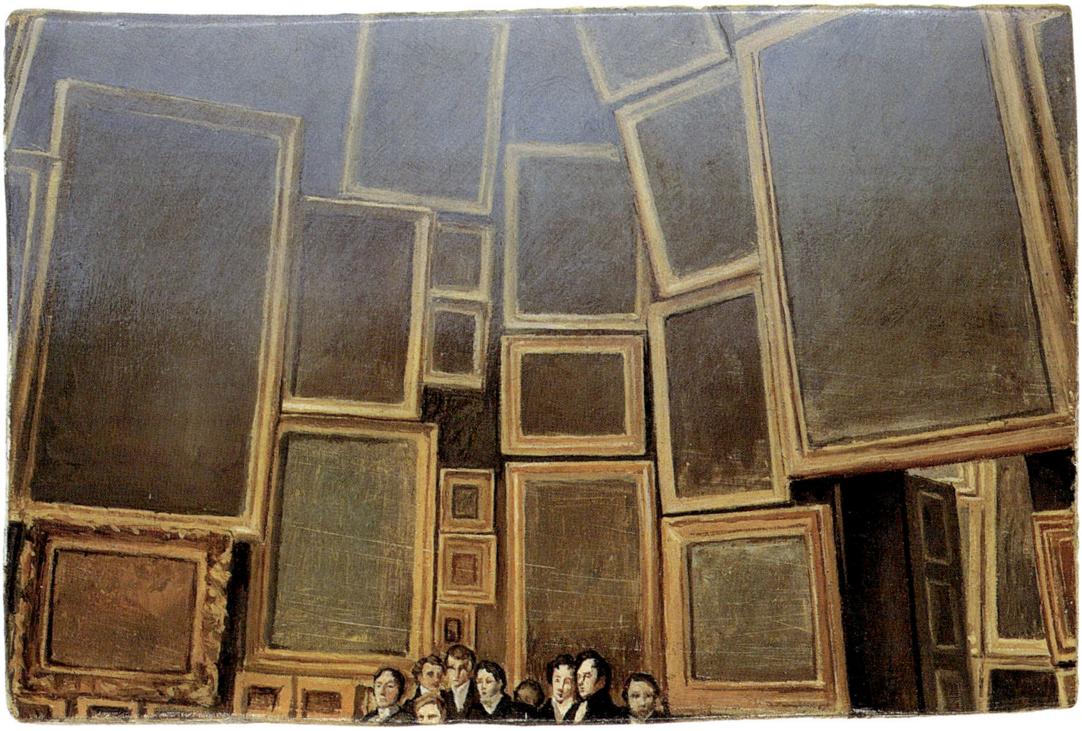

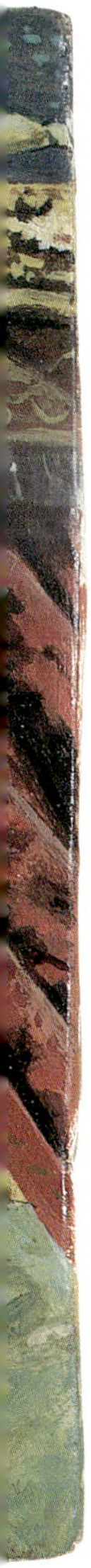

Retaule 1995
(Retable) Details
Oil on wood. 11.5 x 12 cm.
Oil on wood. 15 x 9,5 cm.
Oil on wood. 9.5 x 15 cm.

which is to present an illusion—a performed representation of "reality", constructed so as to suspend disbelief on the part of the audience—rather than to re-present the "real," or the everyday, the ordinary. People usually go to the theater to see a performance and interact with each other only minimally, e.g., laughing and applauding. Nevertheless if the function of theater is, as the critic Margaret Wilkerson recently defined it, to provide "an opportunity for a community to come together and reflect upon itself,"[1] then Perejaume's piece carries this out by transforming the space of the theater into a social space within which audience members—in this case visitors—become players as well as viewers. The audience for this complex conceptual work, at a site fairly remote from the usual art venues, was mostly townspeople, art-oriented visitors and some occasional tourists. As for the other locations, in Sant Pol, friends and neighbors of Perejaume were the "viewers"; at Pineda de Mar, the audience was made up almost exclusively of townspeople, many of whom were the owners of the wells depicted there. And in la Vall d'Oo, there were few, if any, spectators other than the artist himself.

The title of this exhibition, like several others by the artist, is a series of place names, whereas the titles of related works dealing with the specific imagery of the theater center on issues of painting and representation. But like all of Perejaume's works they share the characteristic interplay of images and words, in addition to temporal and spatial displacements, which confound the real, the illusory, the representational, and the pictorial.

Perejaume's "theater" pieces have neither actors nor audience in any traditional sense. With the exception of the New Museum's window and of the Galería Montenegro, the plush seats of the *Pintura i representació* works are always empty, eternally waiting to be filled or "performed". In *Sant Pol de Mar* (1990), the "actors" are books, a mound of bark, and the statue from a public fountain, introduced by a single photograph of the empty stage, then shown in paired photographs with the objects first *in situ*, then at center stage. Here the dialogue between public and private is such that interior, domestic objects are made to "perform" for an implied audience, while outdoor objects, accessible to all, are resituated as unwitting and solitary performers in an unnamed drama.[2] Such pieces turn the commonplace into art through displacement, making meaning accessible as part of everyday experience and emphasizing the importance of process over product. At the same time, Perejaume's work is playful, imbued with the imaginative, spontaneous, animated quality that characterizes the artist himself. His playfulness belongs more to the court jester than to the child, informed as it is by intelligence, wit, imagination, and mental agility rather than unselfconscious pleasure. On the other hand, Perejaume deflects any attribution of urbane cosmo-

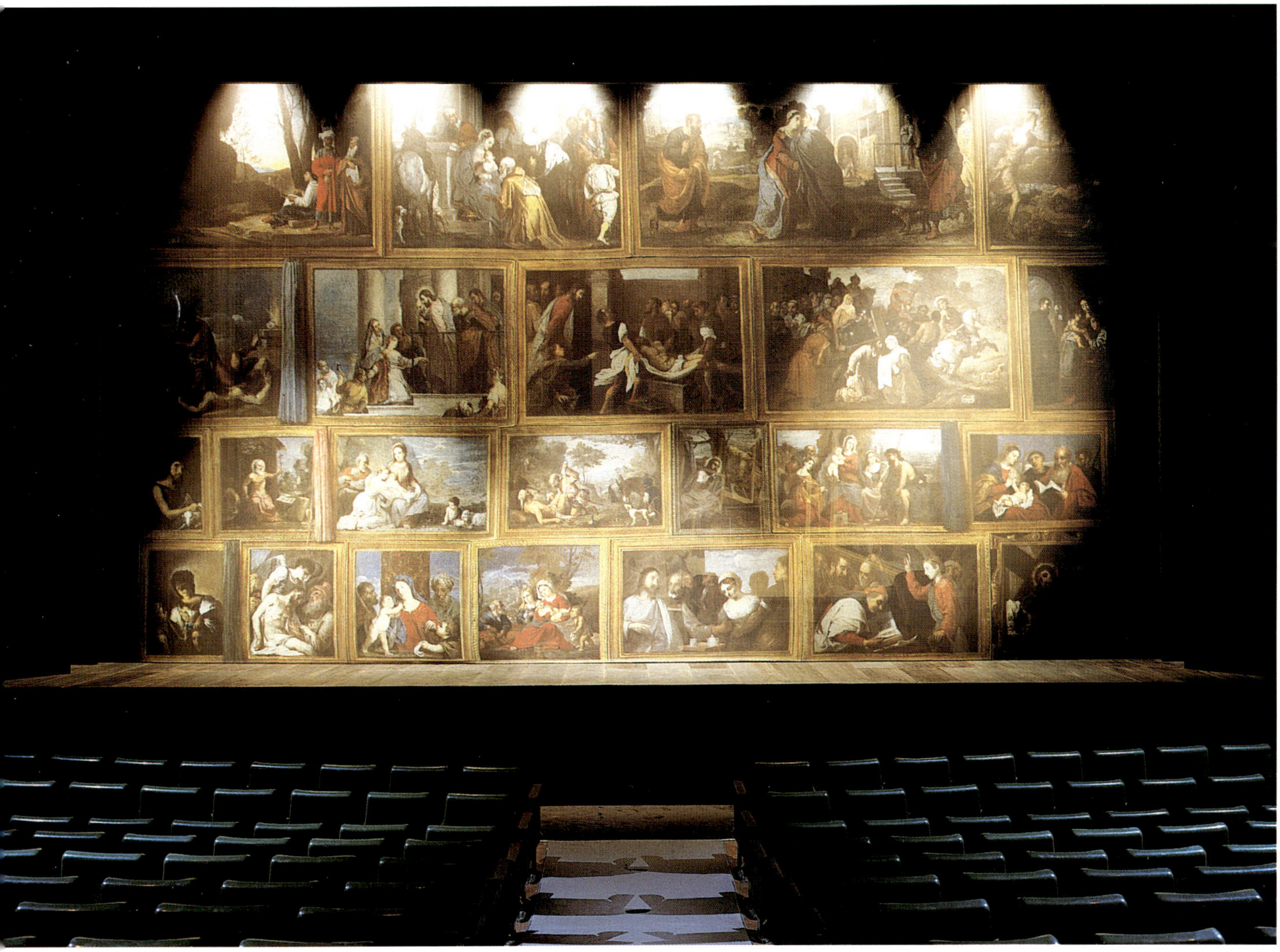

Scenery for El Visitant 1996
Teatre Poliorama

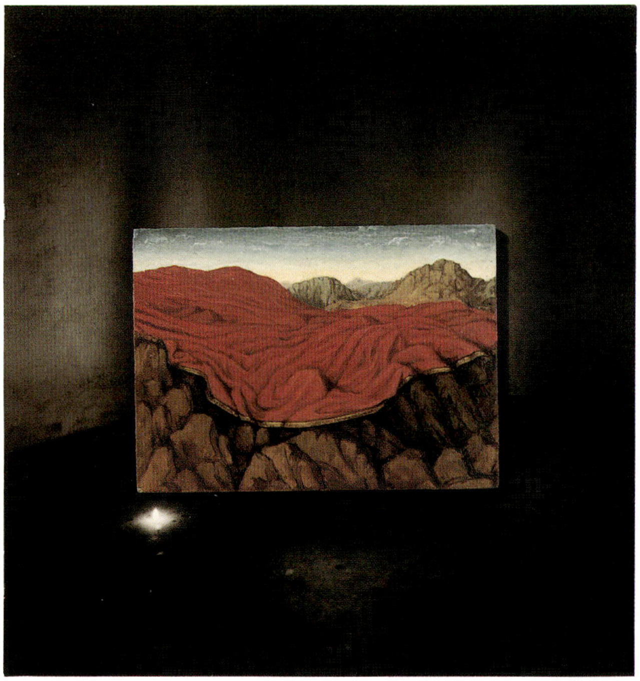

Teló 1992. (Curtain)
Oil on wood and on photography. 29.5 x 29 cm.

politanism to his character; instead he presents himself as a person deeply tied to local regions, people, and concerns, allied, in his own words, to the "peasant" class. If, as cultural critic Pierre Bordieu insists, "the primary business of culture is distinction, the stratification of tastes in such a way as to construct and reinforce differentiations of social status which correspond...to achieved or aspired-to class position", [3] then Perejaume has reclaimed culture in order to use it for exactly the opposite ends. His work instead deconstructs these kinds of hierarchies because it is created for a full spectrum of viewers ranging from local working class participants to art world professionals.

Perejaume's concern with showing work in non-art locales as well as in museums and galleries, his desire to engage audiences who have no experience with modern, conceptual, or any art at all for that matter, is inherently political, addressing questions of elitism, access, and class.

His activism literally pertains to the *polis*, the social relations and politics of everyday life. Since he is deeply involved with the customs, history, structures, and habits of wherever he goes, Perejaume's activities mark him as a citizen and as an "artist".

At the same time, for Perejaume the entire history of art, theater, literature, poetry, philosophy, and of history itself is his artistic meat and potatoes; his works are filled with references to both

Catalan and international artists, writers, political figures, and their texts. Perejaume is at once a visual artist, a poet, a filmmaker, an essayist, philosopher, performer, and historian. And he takes the traditions of *plenairisme*[4] and pessebrism both seriously and literally.

Perejaume crosses the mountains with his students, carrying a drawing by Miró as a visual reference to nature (p. 20). He builds a wheelbarrow-like contraption (p. 93), a chair with a curved wooden screen into which a window is cut, which can be wheeled and placed anywhere so that its operator can frame and contemplate any part of the landscape. He builds actual theater sets consisting of floor-to-ceiling copies of old master paintings in gilt frames (p. 89). Commissioned to paint the ceiling frescoes of the newly restored opera house in Barcelona, he fills the circular panels overhead with images of row upon row of the same red velvet seats and parterres that have been rebuilt within the opera house. This is a *tour de force*, the creation of a meta-language, a play within a play within a play of images.

What Perejaume offers us is not an ordinary, or even art-related peformance, but rather a "dialogical" performance, one which brings together "different voices, world views, value systems, and beliefs so that they can have a conversation with one another".[5] And what his work "performs" is a nonlinear, multidimensional, open-ended network of visual and linguistic narratives which are also social transactions. The result is an ongoing process of interrogation and exchange that resists conclusion and entices everyone to enjoy and fully engage with it.

*

Monòleg del poeta i el pintor 1988
(Monologue of the Poet and the Painter)
Oil, charcoal and canvas. 33 x 90 cm.

1 See Marvin Carlson. *Performance: A Critical Introduction*. London and New York: Routledge, 1996, p. 196.
2 In the United States, the use of objects as performers is perhaps best known through the early work of Scott Burton, a New York-based sculptor who, in the late 1960s, did a series of performances featuring domestic furnishings. Between each "act", the curtains were closed so that a chair, for instance, could be rearranged in another position and then re-opened, creating a kind of theatrical, real-time flip book of anthropomorphic gestures.
3 Pierre Bordieu, quoted in John Frow. *Cultural Studies and Cultural Value*. Oxford, England: Clarendon Press, 1995, p. 85.
4 The French term for painting directly from nature, also used to refer to its widespread use in late 19th century Europe.
5 Carlson, p. 31.

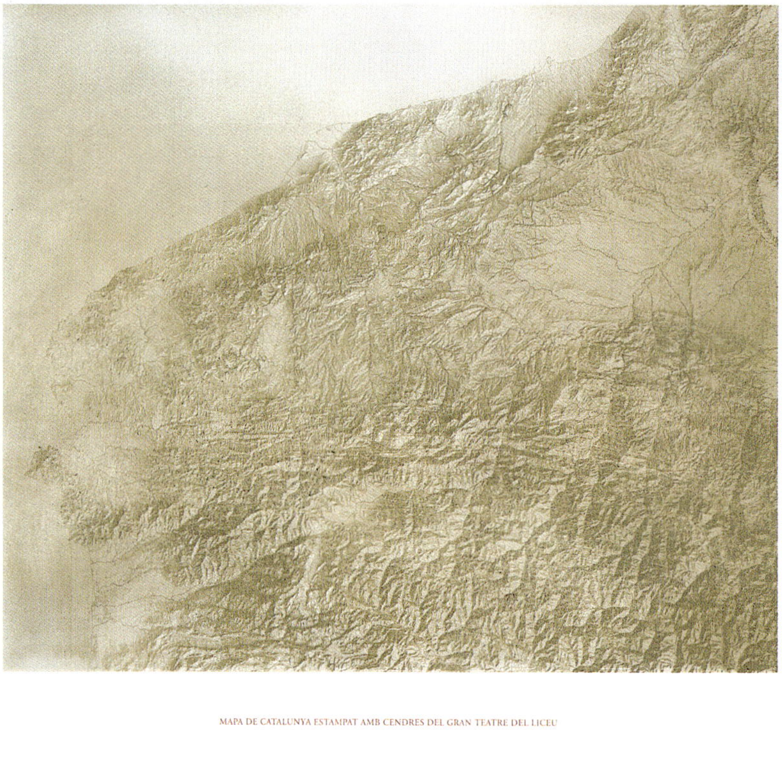

Mapa de Catalunya estampat amb cendres del Gran Teatre del Liceu 1995
(Map of Catalunya Printed with Ashes of the Gran Teatre del Liceu)
Silkscreen. 70 x 80 cm.

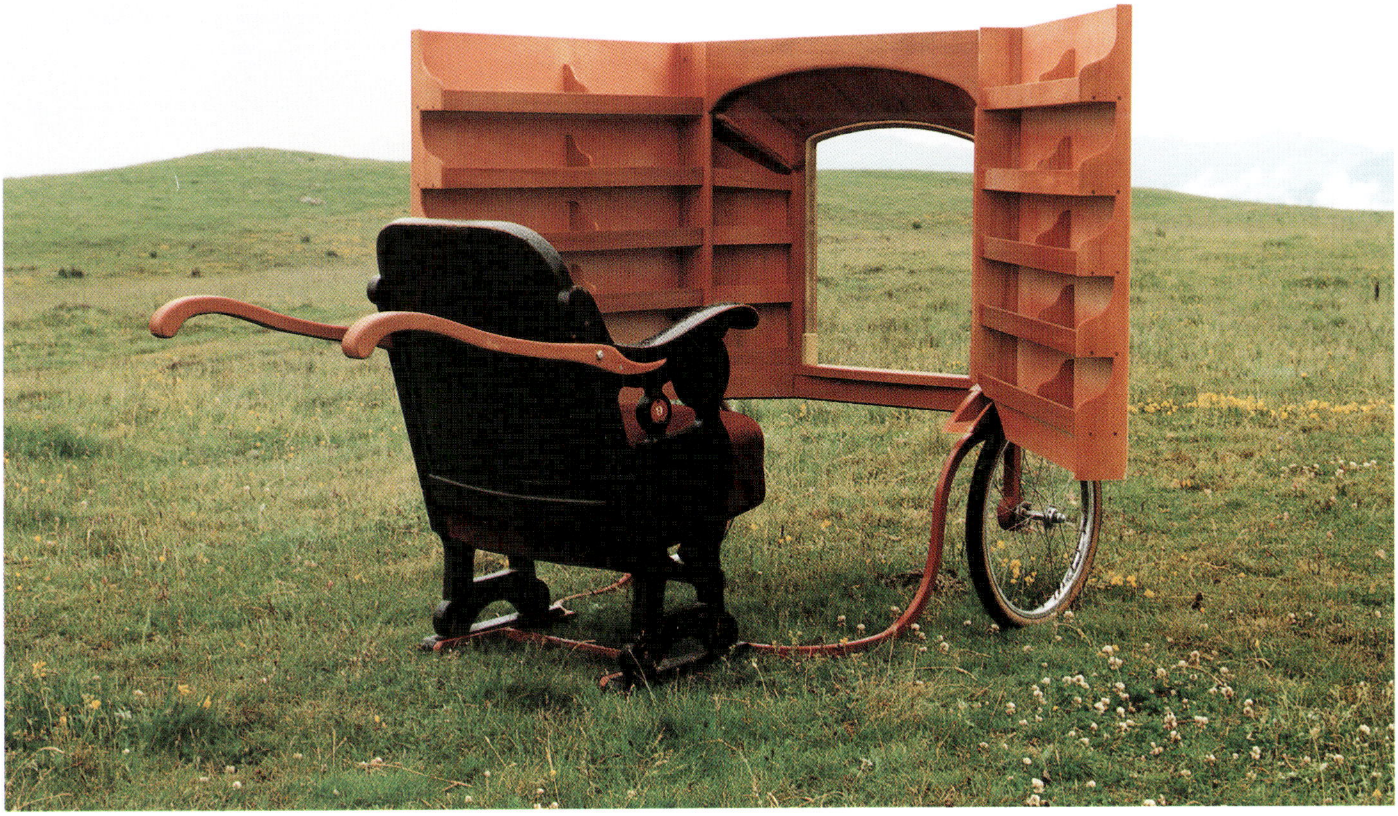

Rambla 61 1993
Seat and structure. 120 x 190 x 105 cm.

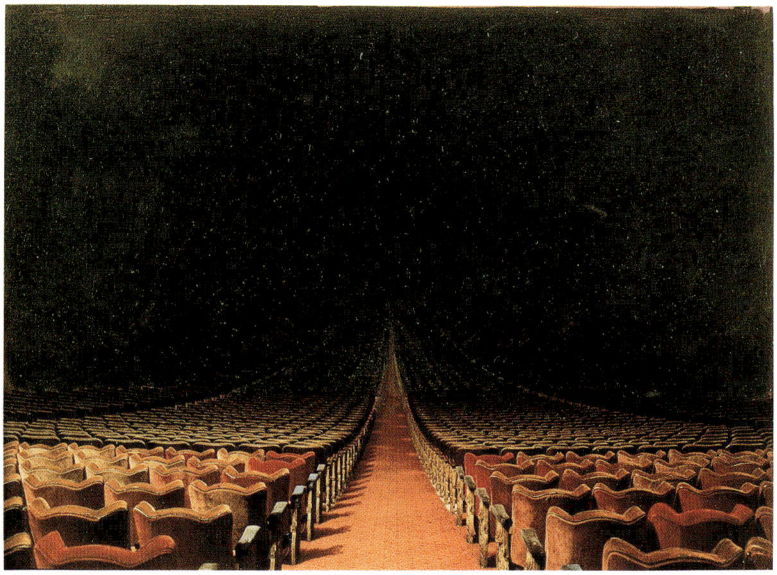

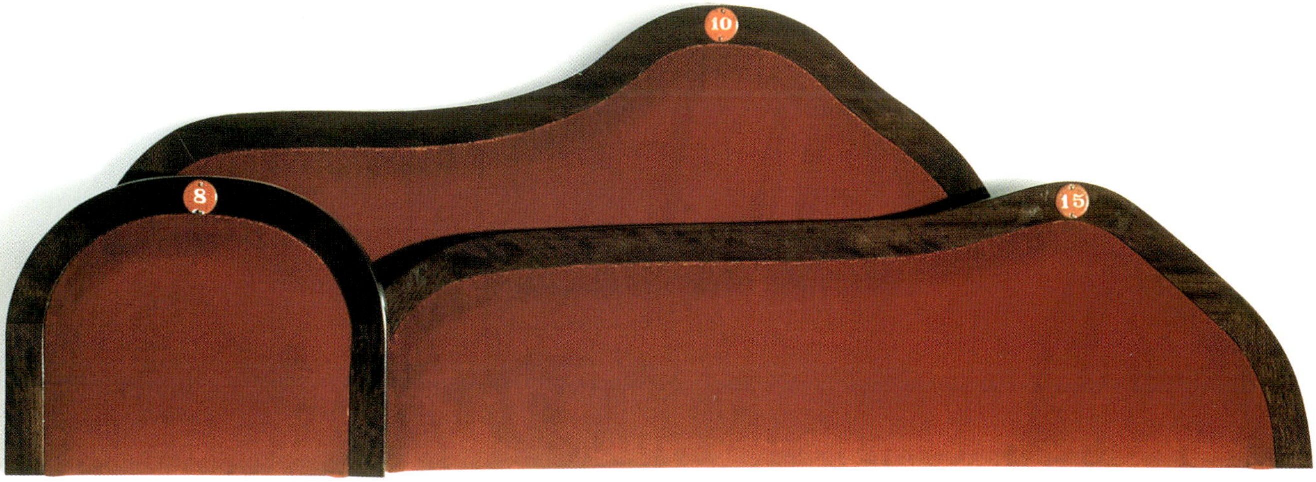

Llocs i localitats 1991
(Sites and Places)
Oil on printed image. 12.5 x 18 cm.
Wood and velvet. 66 x 180 x 20 cm.

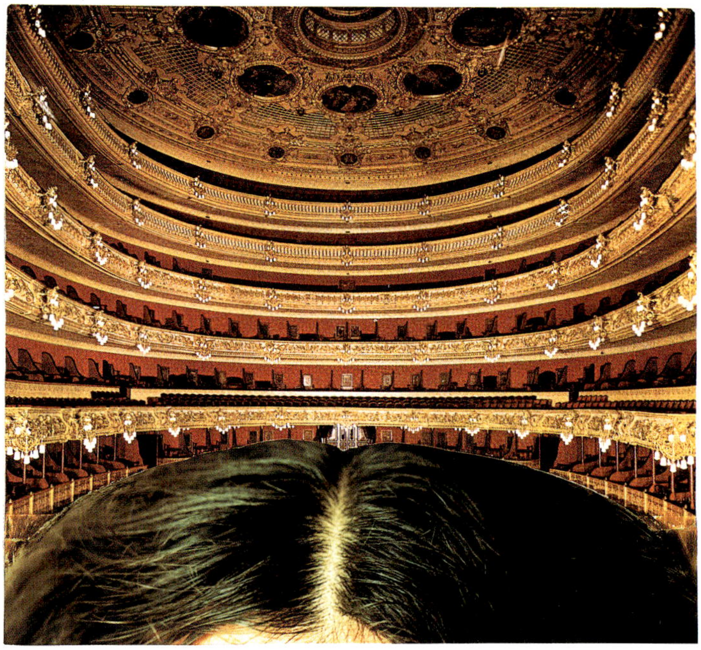

Corona 1989
(Crown)
Photograph. 17 x 18 cm.

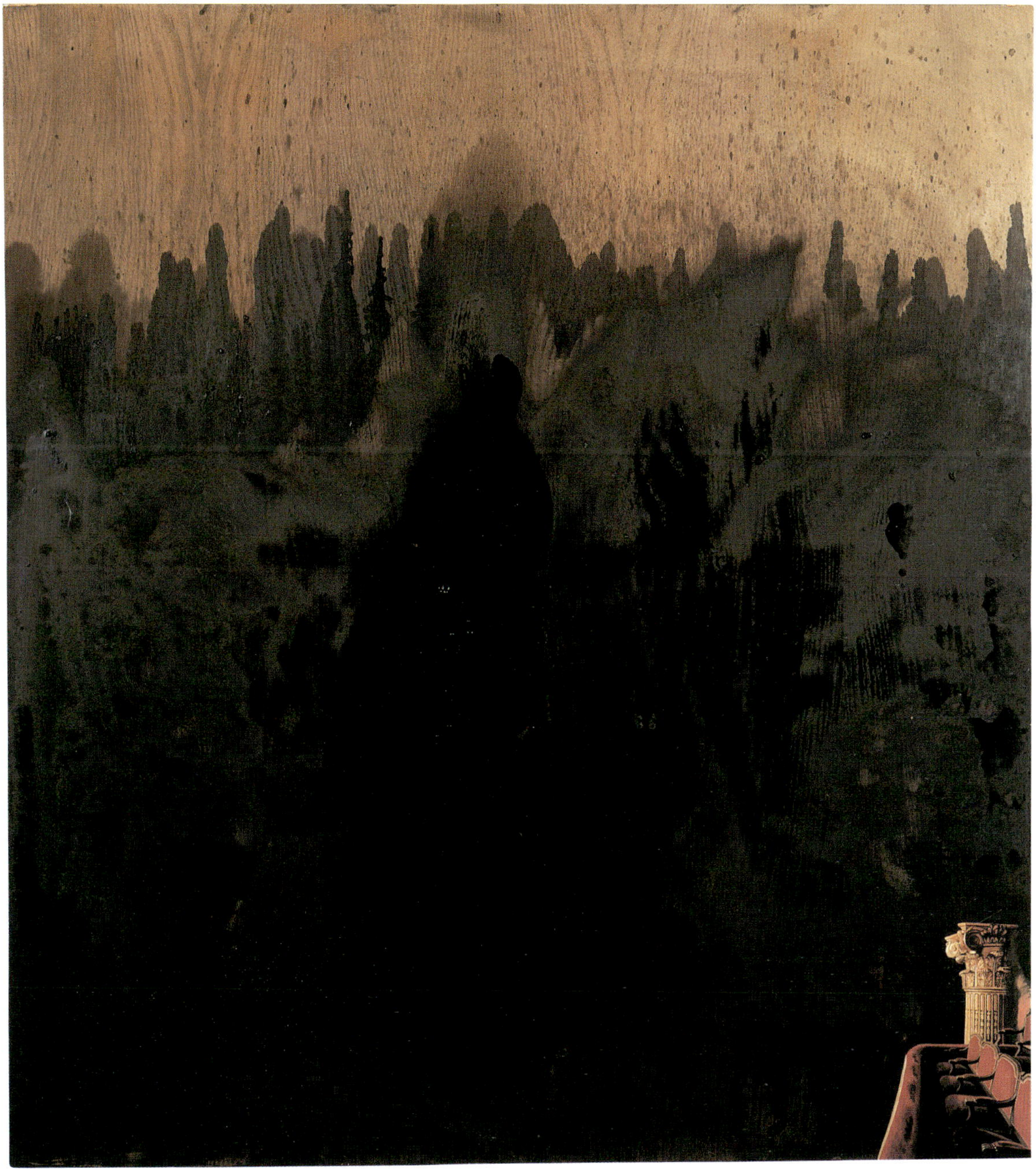

Butaques i taques 1987
(Seats and Stains)
Oil on wood. 135 x 123 cm.

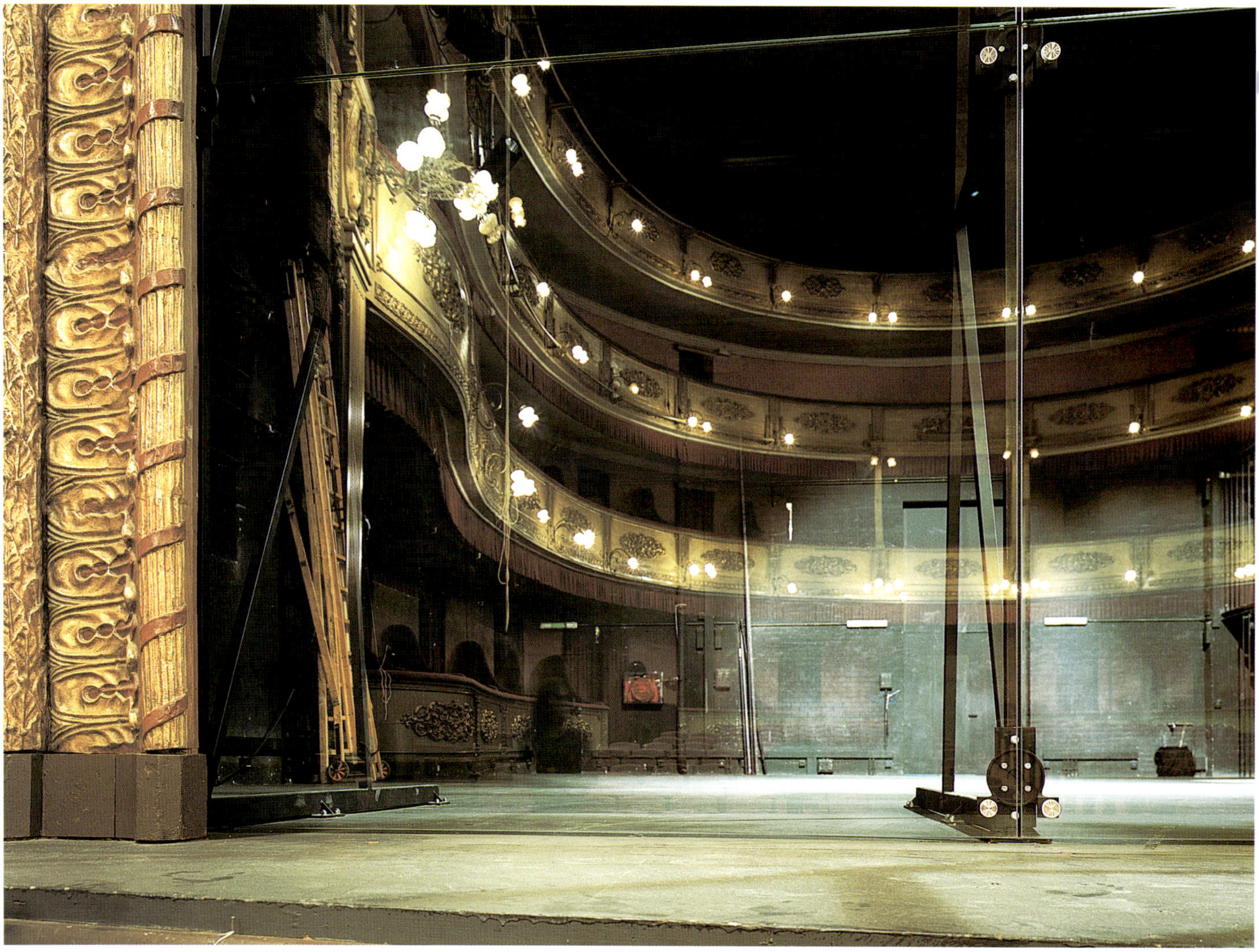

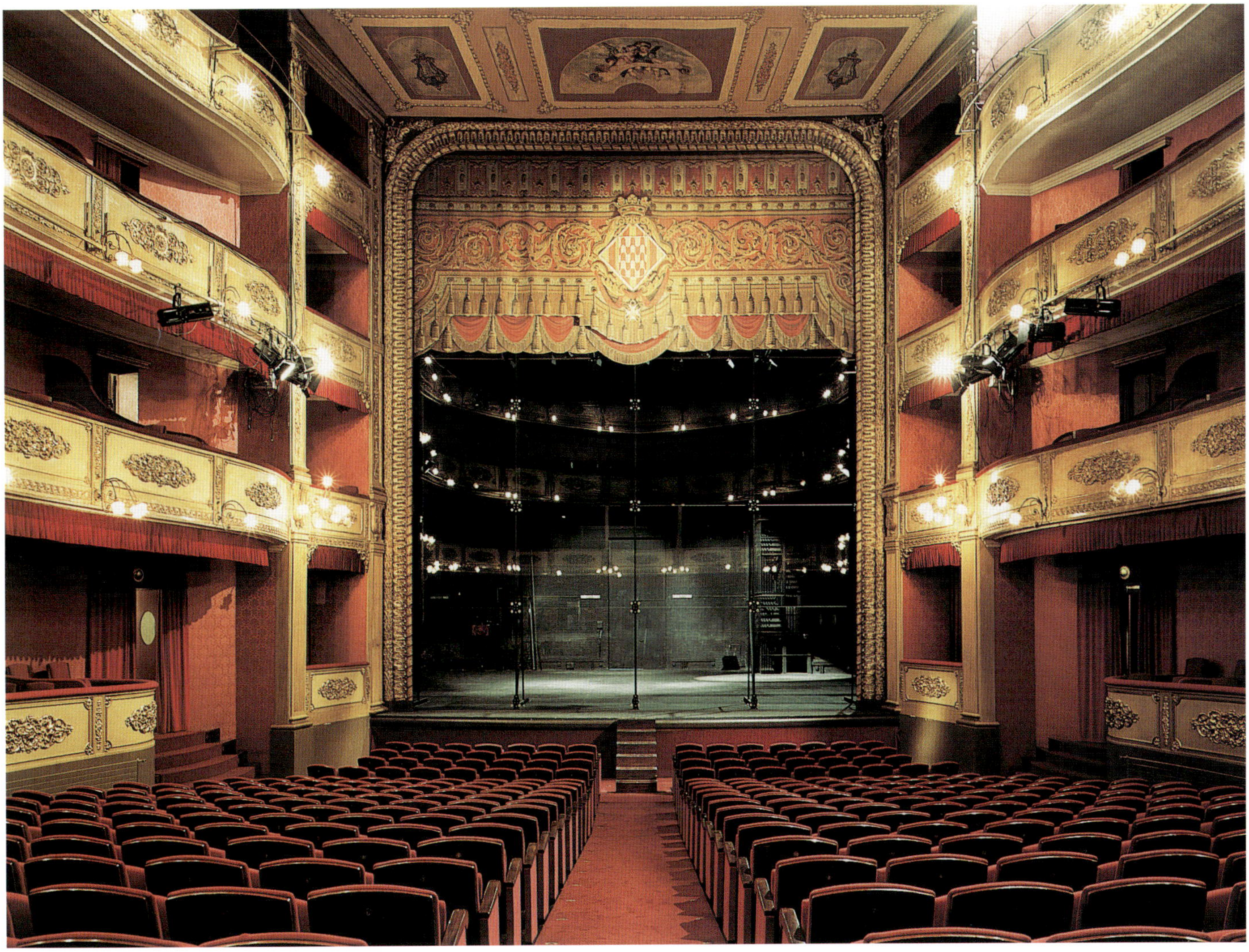

Retaule: Teatre Municipal de Girona 1997
(Retable: Girona Municipal Theatre.
How to Put Glass on a Stage Proscenium)
800 x 800 cm.

Sublime Readymades

Boris Groys

When I received a letter suggesting that I write a catalogue essay contextualizing Perejaume's work "by talking about the present artistic situation within a global perspective," I felt a bit perplexed at first. How could I presume access to a global perspective in which to contextualize an individual body of work? And moreover, how could a single, mortal being, whose conceptual horizons are necessarily quite limited, possibly be seen as the representative of such a global gaze? Only later, after I had given Perejaume's work fuller consideration, did it become clear to me that the request was actually on target, since the question of a global perspective —its horizons of possibility, its constitution— lies at the very center of Perejaume's work. For a long time now we have been hearing about the Death of the Author. But it is more and more the case that what is missing from contemporary art is actually the viewer. And so artists are increasingly beginning to envision and invent their own kind of viewers, ideal viewers to whom they would eagerly present their work, and with whom a real viewer might identify. According to Perejaume's designs, the figure of such a global spectator is perhaps one of the most sublime —and therefore also one of the most ironic.

1. The globalized gaze

Today it seems that those involved in the market, politics, and especially in art derive particular pleasure from discussing the process of globalization. That one make one's work accessible to a global gaze is expected of every single active member of the art world, be he an artist, curator, or critic. Two things are assumed: that every individual work has to be judged in the global context, and that this judgment has decisive significance in terms of the Author's future destiny. As a result, each art world member's heart fills with hope as well as anxiety. In order to anticipate the global judgment of his own work —and perhaps even to correct it— each individual tries to gain a global perspective as quickly as possible. But that clearly does not work, nor could it ever, since no one can actually imagine who, after all, could represent an ostensibly global perspective, not to mention the criteria by which this viewer would pass judgment. We know we are observed, but we do not know by whom. We feel ourselves seized by the gaze of the Other, but this Other remains invisible, absent. Even if the Other is taken to be the international art institutions, these institutions still elude conceptualization and description. The global art world remains a vague, albeit plausible, concept, which lacks any immediate evidence. Multiple aspirations, suspicions and anxieties are bound up in this concept; they manifest themselves in the many conspiracy theories which spawn and proliferate in the art milieu.

Pessebrism of the Monochromes 1993
White, Blonde and Black at la Roca. La Roca, Mont-roig del Camp

Perhaps the main reason why an artist would pin his hopes to one of the art institutions active at the global level is that affiliation with such an organization can serve as a kind of escape hatch from the tastes and sensibilities which predominate in his local circles. Thanks to advances in communication, an artist need no longer trouble himself with changing the cultural orientation of neighbors who might not appreciate his work; instead he can pointcast like-minded individuals from far and wide, and thereby obviate the kind of urgent emigration which artists like Picasso, Kandinsky, and Buñuel could not avoid. Incidentally, this explains the sense of depoliticization in contemporary art, which many perceive. Earlier, the artist who found little favor within his home community had no choice but to project his hopes on the future: he would try to change the thinking of those around him and, in so doing, conjure forth a new viewer, a new man of tomorrow, bringing to life a whole new society, and, when necessary, entering into the forceful currents created by political movements who were striving to effect social transformation.

In the contemporary moment, however, these avant-garde, utopian impulses have exhausted themselves; alliances are no longer sought in the future, but rather beyond the geographic limits of the political and cultural spheres into which one was born. The utopian imagination has changed direction; now it projects itself into space instead of time. In place of the temporal utopia imagined by the Modernists, there has emerged a new spatial utopia: the Global. Today we look to the processes of globalization for redemption, investing in them the kind of aspirations which were once pinned onto the future. Following this point, it would seem that the anxieties about the depoliticization of art have no grounding; instead of an avant-garde politics of the future, today the artist engages with the politics of globalization. Indeed, finding renown outside of one's locale can actually add leverage to an artist's influence at home and even work transformative effects on local institutions. Aware of such potentials, the global artist or intellectual can devise strategies to influence the situation back at home.

But where there is utopian hope, there lurks also the fear that this hope will not be fulfilled, that utopia will devolve into dystopia, that the foreign, globalized perspective might augur condemnation instead of redemption. After all, future expectation is fueled much less by utopian hope than it is by dread of an imminent apocalypse. Moreover, the global spectator's gaze must not necessarily be a benevolent one: it could very likely pass a negative judgment over an artist's or intellectual's work, and then, following this verdict, sentence it to historical oblivion. Contemporary mass culture preys on just such insecurities with films like *Independence Day* o *Mars Attacks*, in which aliens, posing as global spectators from outer space, find little fascination with all things human. The most desirable global gaze which one could imagine would not only have to telescope out to encompass the entire universe, it would also have to be compassionately humane yet secular. One would hope for an affable and enlightened space tourist as the possessor of this gaze, a being who would look down upon us and affirm our world.

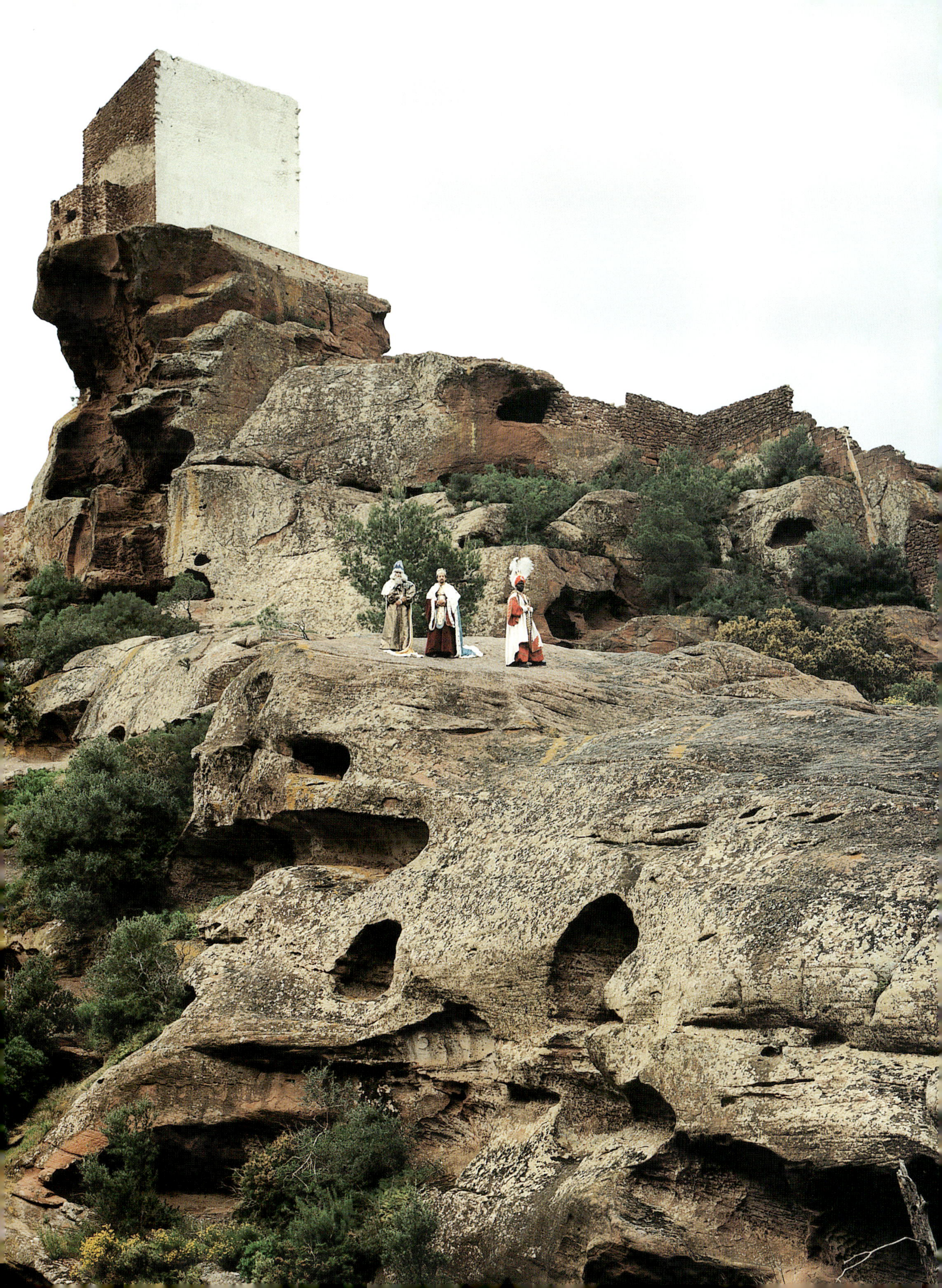

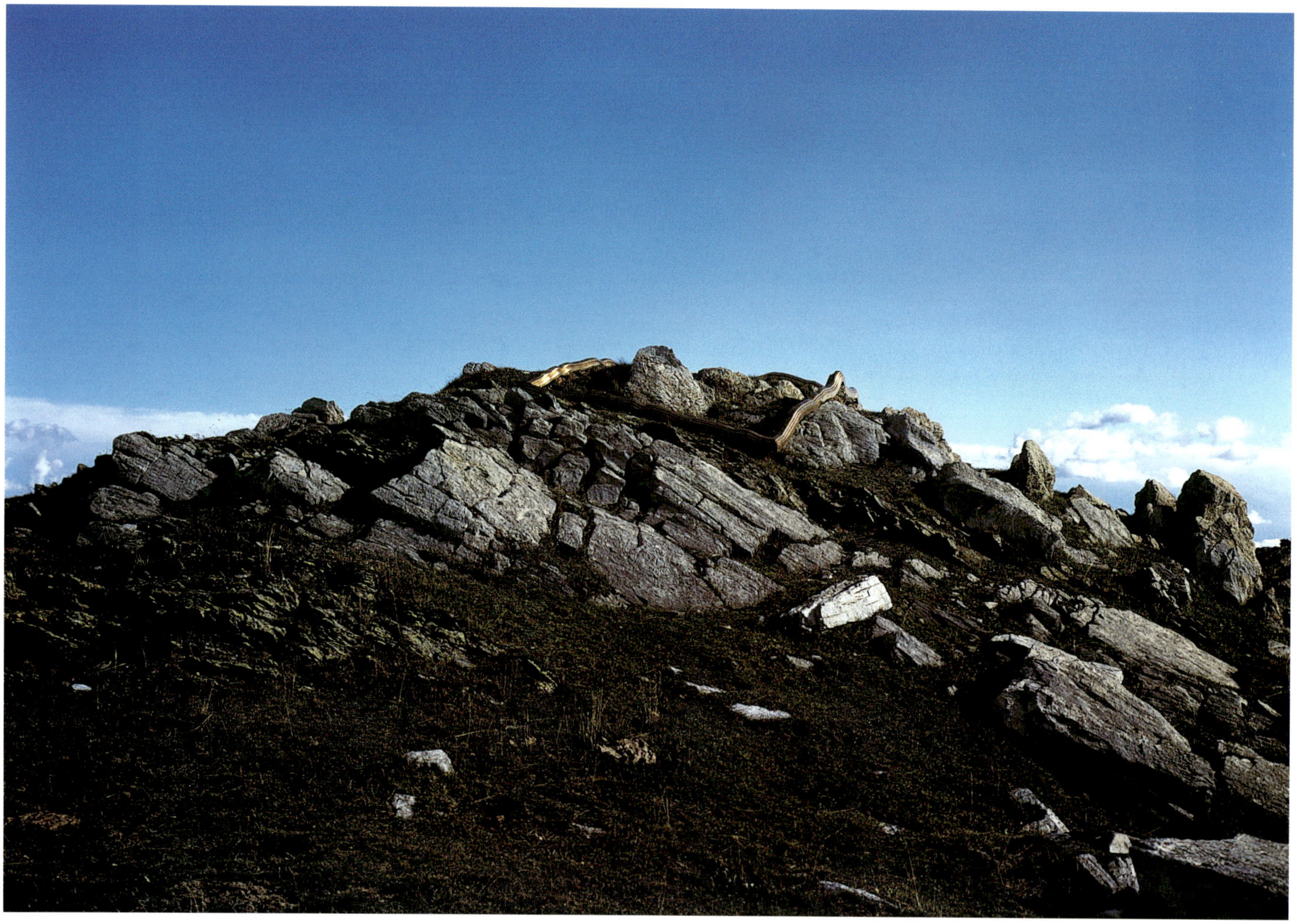

Cim de Catiu d'Or 1988
(Catiu d'Or Peak)
Gilded frame and photograph. 300 x 400 x 50 cm.

It is no accident that Perejaume's writings and works harken back to Romanticism with such frequency, for this cultural moment marked the advent of the global spectator who was secular, benevolent, and capable of viewing all the cultures of the world with the same intense enthusiasm and compassion, a representative, in fact, of Hegel's Absolute Spirit, who could reconcile human perspectives with those of the global and sacred. The significance of this reconciliation is accurately registered in a passage from *The Aesthetics of Ugliness* by Karl Rosenkranz, a student of Hegel's: "If we took our planet as an example, in order to be considered a beautiful celestial body, she would have to be shaped like a perfect sphere. But she is not. She is flattened at the poles and swollen at the equator, furthermore her surface is marred by the greatest dissymetries of elevation. A profile view of the earth's crust shows us, when viewed stereometrically, the oddest confusion of heights and depths in its intractable contours. Similarly, we could never say of the moon's surface that its disorderly proportions of elevation were beautiful, etc." [1] When Rosenkranz published these remarks, humankind was hardly capable of exploring outer space. Nevertheless Hegel's student characterizes the global viewer as a kind of sci-fi extraterrestrial who jets into our atmosphere on his flying saucer and judges the aesthetic merits of our solar system. Rosenkranz implies that, since this creature from outer space shares the same Classicist tastes of the author, he must therefore come to the same conclusion in his examination: planet Earth and its surroundings do not look good. The alterations necessitated by an attempt to correct the Earth's unseemly proportions, however, would prove unpleasant for Earthlings. It could be argued, then, that Rosenkranz anchors his arguments squarely within the aesthetic principles of ugliness in order to placate any potential global spectator who might make his presence known to us in the future. Without intending to, the Hegelian judge of global aesthetics reveals again and again his comic side. Soon after his appearance, this figure would be mercilessly satirized by Kierkegaard. Yet the contemporary international art system —with its implicit (and at times explicit) claims towards a global aesthetic— continues to feed off of the Hegelian promise of reconciliation between the global and the local. So criticizing, satirizing, or negating these aesthetic claims actually seems less interesting than investigating the technological means with which such claims are formulated and asserted. It is precisely this type of investigation which Perejaume undertakes in his artwork.

2. Pessebrism: Globalization through minimization

If Rosenkranz speaks about the shape of the Earth in this way, it is because, for him, the Earth resembles the big blue marble depicted in astronomy books; indeed he seems to base his reflections on the gaze (that is, the actively globalizing gaze as well as the one which has been passively globalized) on this type of illustration. Rather than inquire into the institutional, political, or economic conditions of globalization (a move which others have already made), Perejaume investigates the precisely these formal and technical conditions of the global gaze. Perejaume calls this technique "pessebrism", deriving it from the Catalan "pessebre", the genre of miniature sculptural representations of Bible stories (such as nativity scenes), in which scenes from distant times and places can be viewed in miniature scale. Fittingly, Perejaume mentions Noah's ark as a primary example of pessebrism: here the global can be viewed only once it has gone through a process of diminution and domestication. For Perejaume, the universal and global spectator, as described by Romantic philosophy, always depends upon techniques of miniaturization —such as those engaged by painting as well as the Internet— which disseminate "pessebristic" images of the world to him. The illusion of a universal or global gaze, the notion of enlarging perspectives, and the broadening of knowledge, among other phenomena are the effects of these reductionist techniques. Pessebrism functions for Perejaume as the other, opaque, unreflected side of globalization, since we only gain purchase on a global overview by mechanically reducing the world. In order to understand the nature of the global gaze, then, we must first grasp the mechanisms of pessebrism, that is, the minimization which specularizes the world. In his work Perejaume does just that, with no small degree of irony: he not only tests the techniques used to reduce and render the world into an aesthetic object, but he also suggests how problematic the constitution of a global gaze actually is, given that it defines itself according to those same operations of minimization.

Mimesis is the classical technique of reduction; when an artist paints a landscape he necessarily reduces it, rendering it fully accessible to the viewer. The labor involved in these procedures of reducing and trivializing is most evident in the instance of the mountain landscape, a genre which the Romantics considered especially magnificent and sublime. That mountainscapes are also one of the favorite subjects of Catalan pessebre artists has not escaped Perejaume's attention —but he himself seems transfixed by the manner in which the sublime in such a geological formation resists both reduction and mimetic translation. Problems of mimesis do not seem to be of great concern in contemporary art; Modernists already did that job earlier in the century, relentlessly interrogating and subverting mimetic operations, and ultimately negating them. Still, Perejaume's reflections on the pessebre prompt him to link the Modernist problematic of mimesis to the investigations of the readymade which are so prevalent today. The sort of readymades ubiquitous in contemporary museums can be easily interpreted as mimetic representations of things found outside the museum environment; but since the standard technique for producing readymades does not demand that the artist reduce the size of the object, the readymades cited in or imported into the gallery from "the real world" usually maintain their original dimensions.

Perejaume focuses his artistic strategies on this point. The sheer size of a given object determines whether it can function as a readymade in the museum space. What happens with the objects which are too large to fit through the museum's portals? What of the objects which obsessed the Romantics —not only mountains, seas, and forests, but also the very Earth and moon? They only fit into the museum in their diminutive versions. Perejaume selects the same objects which inspired the Romantics, and attempts to bring them into the exhibition space under the strict condition of reduction. His work *Cim de Catiu d'Or* (Catiu d'Or Peak, 1988; p. 104) is a case in point. It consists of a distorted golden picture frame, which reveals the damage which would be inflicted were such a frame to be multiply enlarged, then forced to fit around a real mountain, and then finally reduced to original size to fit into the gallery. This is pessebrism at its most paradigmatic: a structure resembling a conventional readymade reduces and depicts the outlines of a mountain which would be impossible to frame. Perejaume works within the systems of equivalence and proportion inherent to classical mimesis, foregoing the perhaps more convenient option of playing against them, which has become so popular of late. But for Perejaume these equivalences are impossible, and thus sublime; that is why he is drawn to them. Perejaume's works are sublime readymades in the Kantian sense: they propel the imagination in the direction of the mathematically infinite. Following the footsteps of Romantic philosophers from Kant to Nietzsche, Perejaume wanders along his mountain passes in search of the mathematical sublime, in search of something which cannot be inserted as a readymade into the space of the contemporary art system. In his work he appears to satirize the kind of globetrotting art spectator who would expect an artist to reduce the world to the point that it could be captured in a single glance. That which exceeds measurement in the mountain remains hidden from the spectator precisely because he is looking for such a measurement. Perejaume's type of irony is highly ambivalent, however; Kant himself noted that even a mountain range is too small to represent either the infinite or the unmeasurable. Whatever sense of the sublime we can experience testifies to an idea of the infinite which can only exist in our imagination. The role of phenomenal reality in all this is only one of stimulation. The sense of the sublime which flashes up within us is not an effect of nature —in order to recognize it we would require the kind of cultural formation which would enable us to wrest our gaze away from the sight of the tremendous, but finite creation of nature and direct it towards the idea of the Infinite. A peasant who lives in the mountains, Kant holds, cannot recognize the sublime amongst their peaks. To this extent Perejaume assumes the stance of a Romantic spectator. Instead of presenting his own work to the global viewer, Perejaume redirects the viewer's attention towards the beauty of nature. The game which Perejaume plays with the spectator's gaze, like that played by many of his contemporaries, is, thus, a rather manipulative one. Instead of offering his own work up for the viewer to assess, he deflects his audience's gaze onto the fields, onto the mountains, onto the sea. And who, after all, is so insensitive and unsentimental that he could refuse to admire fields, mountains, and the sea? Any possibility of negative critique is therefore excluded in advance.

3. Manipulating the viewer's gaze

Perhaps Perejaume plays with the gaze of the global spectator for no other reason than that it appears so easy to manipulate. Indeed the readymade technique suits itself well for the kind of ironic charge that he wants to create. Any need for an unmediated, physical elaboration of the image is thoroughly eliminated by this technique; instead it is replaced by a series of conscious decisions which are both strategic and verifiable. By exposing his process of selection, Perejaume not only formalizes and strategically deploys his production techniques, he also enables their future repetition, a gesture which dispenses with any claims that the work could stand as an unmediated, unreflected manifestation of the artist's inner nature. This is not the work of Romantic genius in the traditional sense. Since the viewer's gaze is directed toward external nature, the artist's body no longer stands in the way of any repetition of his authorial gaze. The artist's perspective is "disembodied": it becomes a pure gaze, one which does not actively work per se, but rather merely passes evaluation, selects, and combines. This gaze can also be "embodied" once again, in the event that anyone felt moved to either think through the process which the artist has laid bare, or to retrace his series of specular choices. Such a strategy suits the change in the function of the museum. No longer the place where history is displayed in all its uniterable singularity, the museum now runs like an archive in which different ways of seeing are collected and catalogued for retrieval and future use.

Historically, the interest in representations of the world was internally split, since no one could determine if the source of a work's interest was derived from the actual object depicted or if the artist's nature was so extraordinary, that it alone conferred to the image its particular degree of attractiveness. Consequently, ingenious, artistic individuality became a rarity, a collector's item. This development made it impossible to distinguish between the immanent interest in an individual object and in the mode of its representation. Both counted as products of nature. To a great extent, in earlier art collections the lines which would separate artefacts of natural history and examples of industrial design from their depicted representations were only loosely drawn, if at all.

Along with the obsolescence of the notion of genius, today the artist has been transformed from collectible to collector. The artist is no longer equated with the laborer (even a privileged laborer), rather he begins to observe the world through the same lens as an aristocrat with a penchant for collecting. This transformation discloses itself most markedly in the temporal economy of the gaze and the changing status of the artist within it. In the traditional dynamic between art production and consumption, the artist's investment of labor, time, and power was inordinately greater than that of the viewer; after the artist's lengthy and arduous process of making the work, the viewer had only to happen upon it in the gallery in order to effortlessly consume it with a single glance. Hence the assumed superiority of the consumer, the viewer, and the collector over and against the artist as image-supplier,

who produced his works through meticulous, physical labor. The artist would first stand on common ground with the collector when he presented himself as a producer of photographs or readymades, since, as such, he made images with the same quasi-instantaneity with which the viewer consumed them. In taking up the position of a pure spectator or absolute consumer, the artist compensates for one of the most severe traumas of modernity, namely the disappearance of the aristocracy. This is a theme central to Perejaume's *Fragments of Monarchy*. Today one frequents a large exhibition or art installation in the same way that aristocratic palaces were once visited. The viewer is admitted to enter before the art, but he is not its actual consumer. Whereas many once sought to affect aristocratic lifestyles displayed in palatial settings, now the contemporary art viewer tailors his consumption according to the things he sees in the art space. The viewer no longer merely consumes the artist's products —like an artist, he invests his own labor into the process of consuming the world.
Possessed of a sovereign gaze, Perejaume takes on the airs of a *flâneur* who regards the world, finds it lovely, and directs the attention of others to that which he has noticed. He turns the spectator's gaze away from himself and his own work, conducting it onwards, to culture, to the outside world, to nature. In a certain sense the artist wants to surveil unseen, unnoticed; he does not want to stand in the spectator's field of vision, but rather desires to impel the viewer further ahead by making his gaze an offer which it cannot refuse— that of mountains, seas, and nature. As a result, the artwork begins to function as a device for specular manipulation; its potency in relation to the viewer's gaze is maximized the longer it stays in the dark, the further it withdraws into the shadows. But Perejaume's readymades do something else as well: they also leave open the possibility that the spectator might choose to shift his gaze to the actual artwork in order to observe its inner working. His readymades reveal the processes of reduction and depiction, mechanisms which, as Kant maintains, outfit the gaze with a pair of cultural spectacles —the very ones which allow him to apprehend the sublime in nature.

4. The sublime spectator

Even if the international institutions of modern art assume the power to display images of our planet in reduced versions for the visual pleasure of the global spectator, these institutions still remain nothing more than small parts of the same world they want to depict. As long as pessebrism is understood to be the one-way depiction of nature in the exhibition space, it would not adequately address questions about the kind of gaze which could view both the world as a whole and all of the art which is produced in it. In order to cover this conceptual ground, Perejaume also practices a kind of inverse pessebrism: he brings art into nature, installing it in the wilds, where, we might suppose, no one will see it. This is the case in his *Pessebrisme dels monocroms* (Pessebrism of the Monochromes 1993; p.103), where he integrates three colors of Malevich's suprematism –black, and red– into the

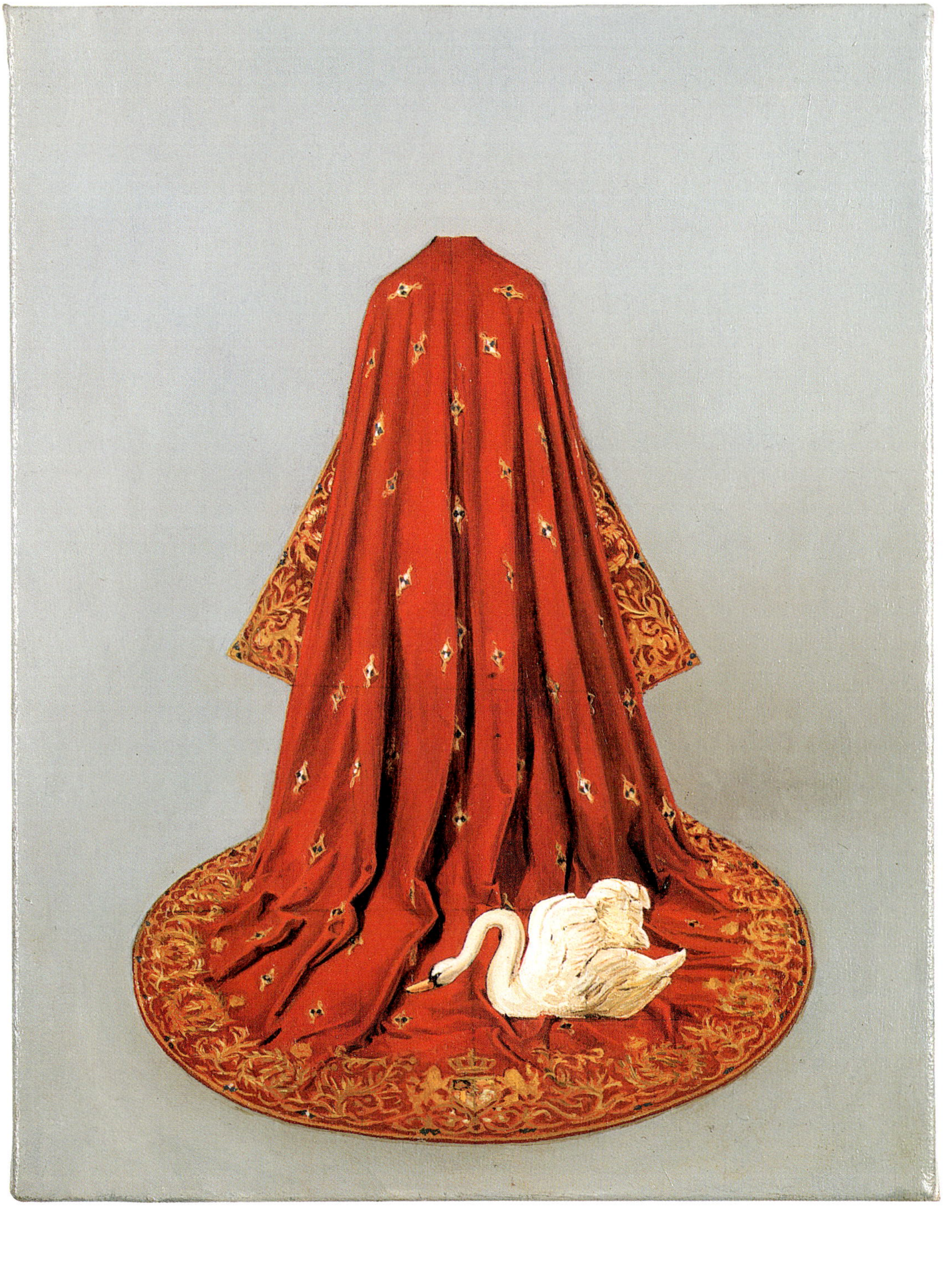

El paó i el cigne 1989
(The Peacock and the Swan)
Oil on canvas. 30 x 24 cm.

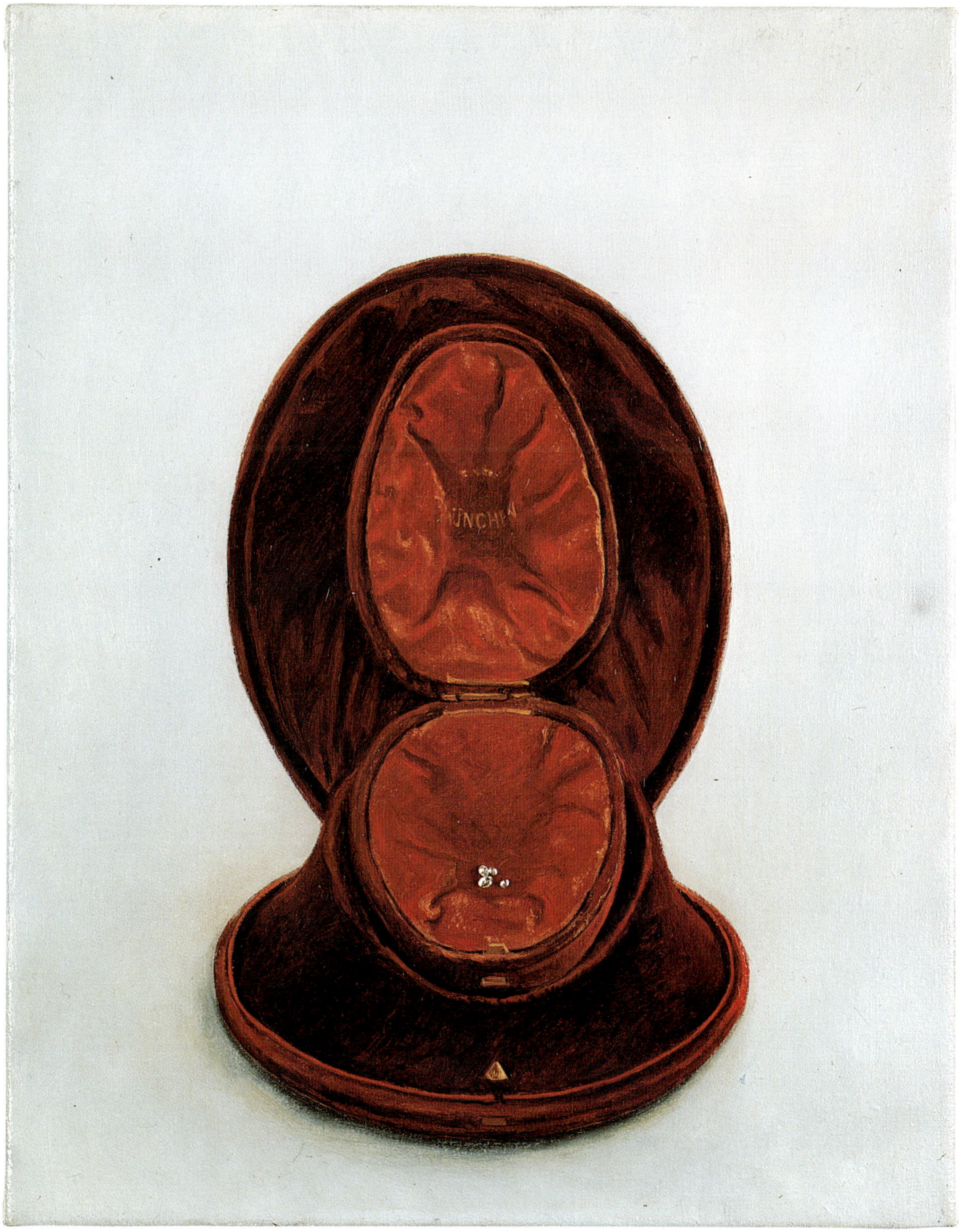

Tenebrari 1989
(Tenebrous)
Oil and gems on canvas. 30 x 24 cm.

folkloric scenery of Catalonia. Here nature is no longer miniaturized and made viewable for the gallery visitor; instead, the art is removed from view and taken off to the mountains. Similarly, in his *Fragments of Monarchy* Perejaume inverts the pessebre and, as a result, makes plain his admiration for the power and might of King Ludwig II of Bavaria (p. 110-111). The king himself engaged in a proto-readymade process, imposing palaces on the grand order of Versailles as well as their accompanying manicured landscapes into secluded sites where they would have scant practical function and where only God and the select few could be able to see them. This Perejaume's move could be seen as a kind of castling —the museum and nature trade places; nature becomes an exhibition space set free of the museum's spatial constraints.

At first it seems that the inversion of the conventional relationship between the museum and nature is possible only from a theological perspective. In order to imagine a global viewer who does not need to reduce the world, we must believe in God. Yet Lacan, in his renowned analysis of the gaze, has already shown that not only God can serve as a vantage point from which the global gaze is lowered; we can also be seen by a sardine tin floating on the sea and reflecting bright spots of sunlight.[2] We tend to imagine the sources of light which illuminate the world as points from which we could be observed. The visibility of the world as a whole owes itself to this light whose white-hot source ultimately escapes our sight. Because no one can control the light which catches us in its rays, rendering us visible, the artist, too, is nothing more than another detail of the big picture, an image whose magnitude exceeds his powers of surveillance. Even when Perejaume installs an artwork in the most remote spot, it still loses nothing of its exhibited nature; as long as it remains in light, it continues to be beheld.

In this sense Perejaume's gesture of inverting the pessebre is most apt, since it sustains the expectation that there exists a global viewer who would do more than just represent the international art milieu. Such an expectation lends itself to a social psychological interpretation, one which would diagnose it as the effect of the artist's internal division, a split which was cleaved into the artist as a result of his double-identification with Catalan culture and the international art scene. Lacking the ability to recognize and evaluate the codes, references, and problematics discernible by an art world insider, a local viewer cannot properly assess Perejaume's art. The international art *flâneur*, on the other hand, is impervious to the myriad details and associations which refer back to Catalan culture. In a certain sense, every contemporary artist, Perejaume included, inhabits a no man's land between his own culture and the international art scene; many who find themselves in this predicament sorely want for an audience of receptive viewers. So it makes sense that the artist should expectantly await a spectator who is absolute, messianic, if you will —one who can close up the gap between the local and the global with his all-encompassing gaze— even if this spectator is nothing more than a Lacanian sardine tin, whose subjectless light bleeds out all cultural contrasts. Nevertheless

Perejaume no more harbors the illusion that light, including the sun's rays, could function as the ideal global viewer of his art, than he does the illusion that art could function within the wilderness or, further, that there could exist an image of nature so supremely comprehensive as to subordinate all the secondary images which are derived from it.

In his work Perejaume surveys precisely the no man's land between "local nature" and the international art industry, the dark places where contemporary artists lie in wait. As Perejaume writes, "The healing and corrective power of a work of art derives more from the intermediate place that it occupies than from any deliberate intention on its part to fulfill such a role. Capable of opening up gaps and breaches, fundamentally intermediary, art is a lapse, a no-man's land, situated between nature and signature." [3] And further, "We are in the dark orchestra pit of pessebrism[,] convinced that there is a geography that exists previous to both nature and signature, with real landscape and painted landscape set up in front of us to give us some sense of equivalence".[4] It seems that the sites where art is made and consumed form a whole geography which must remain out of sight. Visibility can only be achieved after art has established its systems of equivalences through enlargement and reduction, as well as through various modes of depiction.

But even when, as a result of this, we define the relationship between nature and culture as pessebristic, there remain dark recesses within the intermediate rifts, places which cannot be illuminated. Using the same figure of thought as Kant does in his third Critique, one could say that the sublime viewer, whose omnivoyant judgment we could only fear, is just a byproduct of our reason. The artist works with an ideal viewer in mind, who, in reality is merely a figment of his own imagination. But since the conceptual horizons of any actual spectator are necessarily limited, such a spectator can only partially represent the sublime viewer of infinite capacities whom the artist wistfully envisions. Nevertheless, the more deliberately and intelligibly the artist discloses his technical processes, the better the actual viewer can play his role as a sublime viewer. Indeed identifying with the global spectator which Perejaume conceives holds a certain charm for the normal, mortal viewer. Without contending with the traditions of mimesis, Perejaume manages to expose its internal mechanisms, and, at the same time, offers up to our gaze views of his beautiful country, places where we would gladly let our gaze linger a while.

1 Karl Rosenkranz, *Ästhetik des Häßlichen*, 1853, p. 15.

2 Jacques Lacan, *Le Séminaire*, book XI. Paris: Éditions du Seuil, 1973, p. 88 ff.

3 Perejaume, "Two geographies" in *El grado de verdad de las representaciones.* Madrid: Galería Soledad Lorenzo, 1991, p. 46.

4 Perejaume, "Nature and signature" in *El grado de verdad de las representaciones.* Madrid: Galería Soledad Lorenzo, 1991, p. 49.

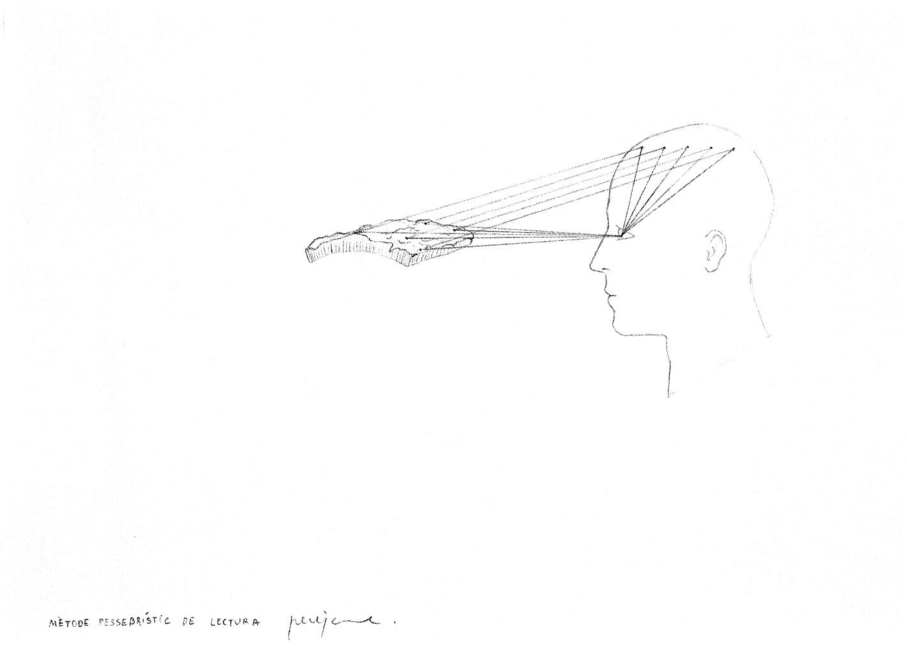

Mètode pessebrístic de lectura 1990
(Reading the Pessebristic Way)
Pencil on paper. 21.5 x 31.5 cm.

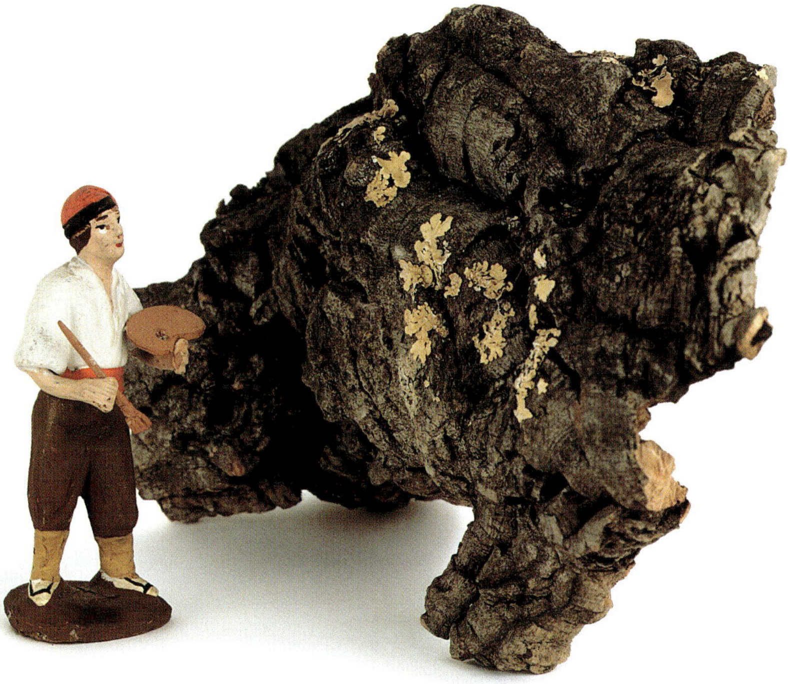

Plenairista 1992
(Plenairist)
Figure and cork bark. 12 x 15 x 21 cm.

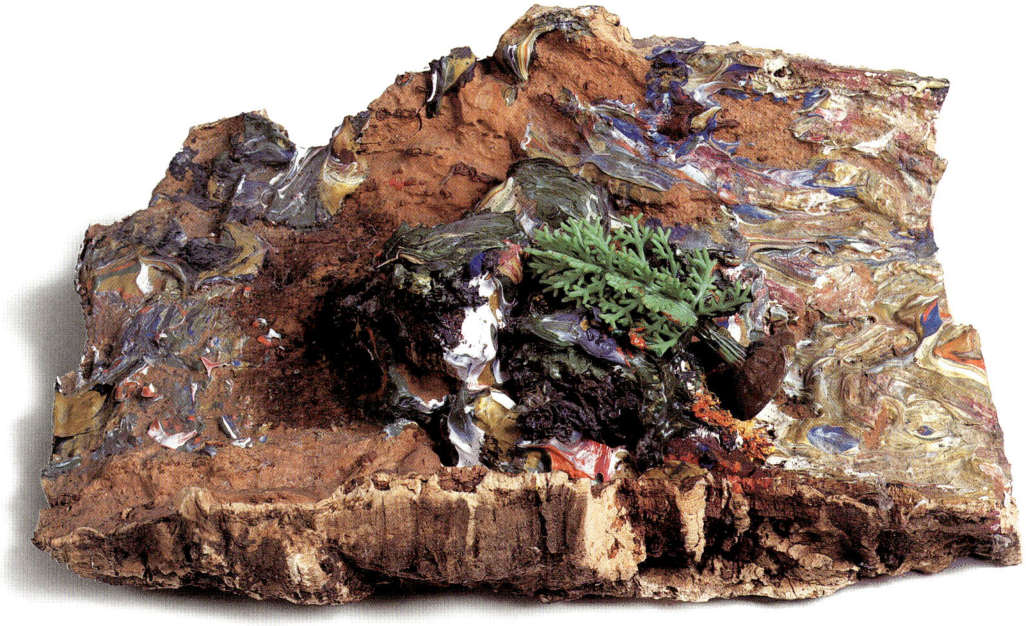

Pessebre 1997
Cork bark and paint. 11 x 19 x 27.5 cm.

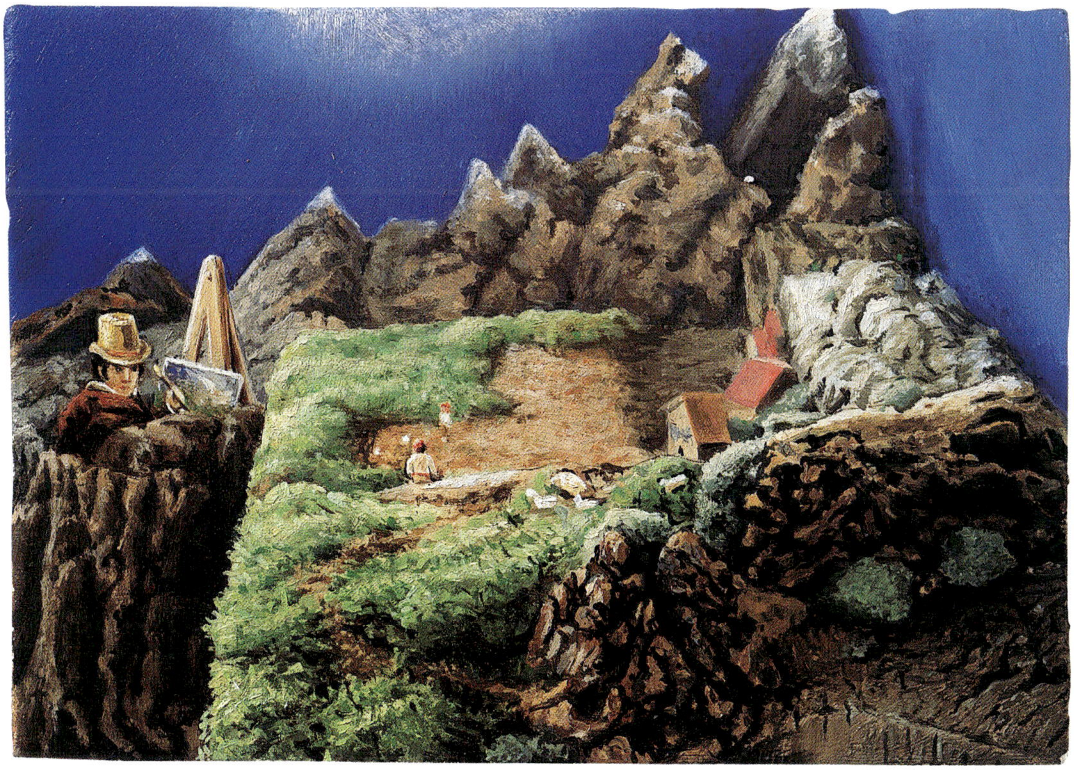

Plenairista 1998
(Plenairist)
Oil on wood. 11.7 x 17 cm.

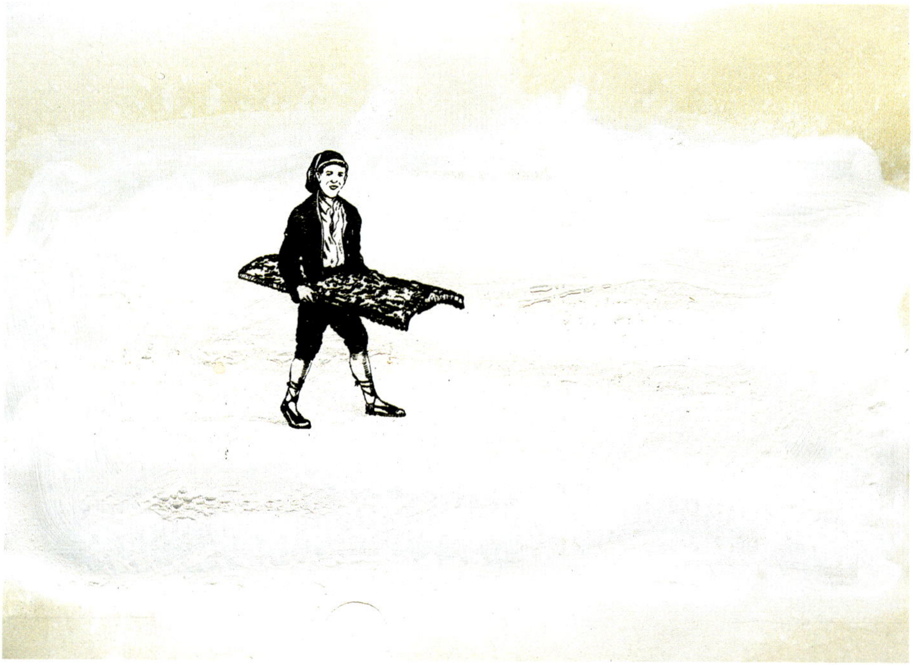

Metòde pessebrístic de lectura II 1997
(Reading the Pessebristic Way II)
Mixed media on paper. 29.5 x 42 cm.

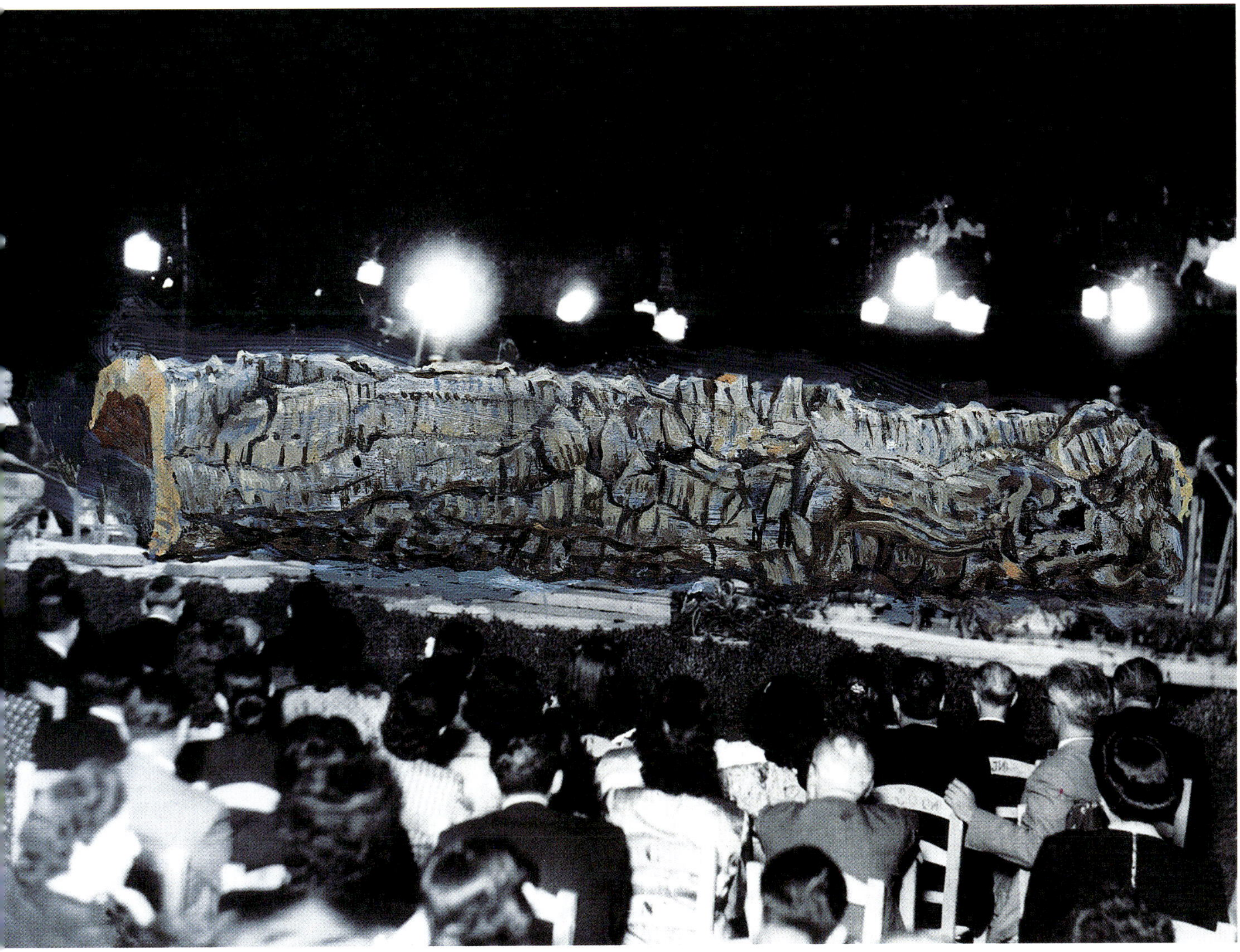

El suro de Sils 1998
(The Sils Cork)
Mixed media on paper. 17.8 x 23.5 cm.

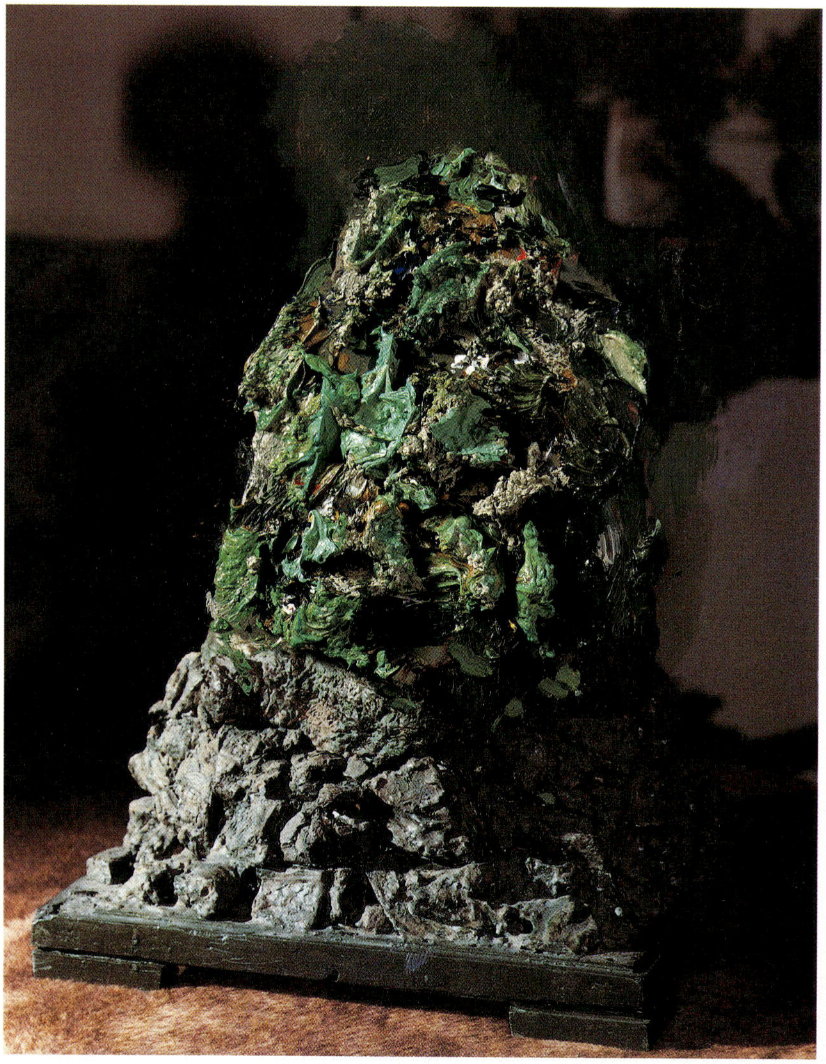

Pinacoteca 59 1998
(Picture Gallery 59)
Mixed media on paper. 27.5 x 20.5 cm.

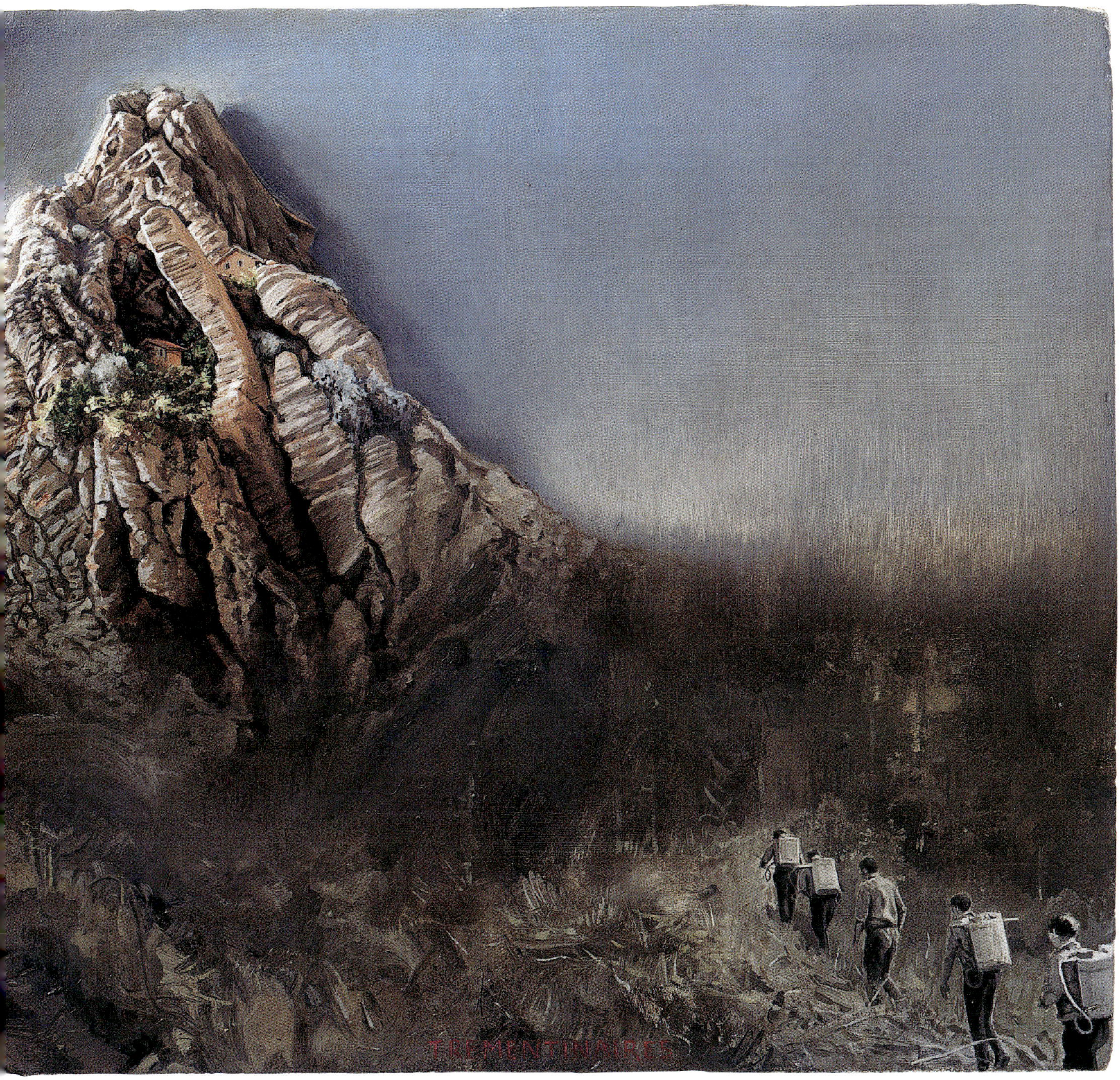

Trementinaires 1997
(Turpentiners)
Oil on wood. 27.7 x 30.5 cm.

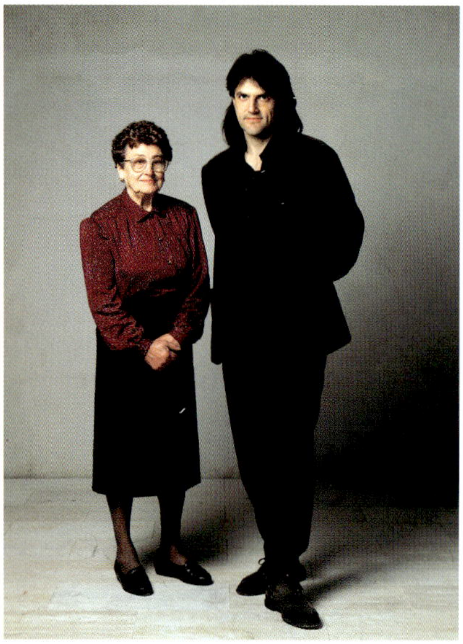

Els tossals 1993.
(The Hillocks). Photograph

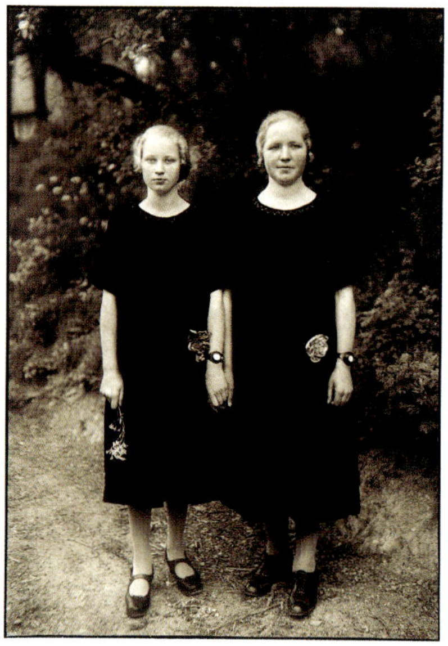

August Sander **Farm Girls** ca. 1928.
August Sander Archiv (Cologne)

The Painter with his Back Turned

Carles Guerra

1. An Agreed-to Position

In *El Pirineu de baix* (1997), among the most recently published collections of Perejaume's work, there appears, isolated from the book's main sequence of images, a photograph: a portrait of the artist and an old woman, both of whom are standing. This photograph has been placed where one might expect to find an epilogue, beside the list of works catalogued in *El Pirineu de baix*. It serves more than one purpose, functioning as a work in, a commentary on, a frame for, and a conclusion to the volume.[1]

This image is a fitting marker of the place taken up by all of Perejaume's works. The difference between what does and does not form part of his body of work is worked out at the edge of the frame. Perhaps for this reason, Perejaume's work features a wide range of frames: emptied frames, frames stranded on a mountainside, buried frames, frames dragged, burnt and consumed, painted, projected, lifted and hung, deformed, curled, cut, open and closed, smashed and destroyed.

Yet the photograph in question also destroys an intangible frame. Perejaume's meeting with Consol Boquera — who posed, early in life, for Joan Miró's painting, *Retrat d'una vaileta* (Portrait of a Young Girl, 1918) — seems to erase the line between representation and referent. It is well known that the distance between representation and referent constitutes a taboo. Nonetheless, the meeting portrayed in this photograph has a hint of the impossible to it: it evokes the lost moment in which Miró himself stood before the young Consol Boquera.

The order which spills forth from this serene portrait — this image of an elderly woman squeezing hands that rest below her waist, the artist towering over her — is comparable to the images of mountains which appear so often in Perejaume's oeuvre. As so often happens in his works, anything may become a mountain. Even questions of cultural order seem to be absorbed by those of natural order.

The title of this photograph — *Els tossals* (The Hillocks, 1993; p. 122) — confirms this mirage. The title renders the image new, making it one of the artist who adds his body to the presence of a woman's body, grown pleasantly old. What had been a commentary, an addition, has become a work, just as these bodies have become mountains.

The photograph's documentary tone, in the style of August Sander (p. 122), effectively demonstrates this subversion of chronology. By coming so near Consol Boquera's body, Perejaume has freed her from the confinement to which Joan Miró's painting had subjected her. The law of physical proximity overcomes any other kind of bond. Nonetheless, the price paid for having let the original go is that of a new attribution of

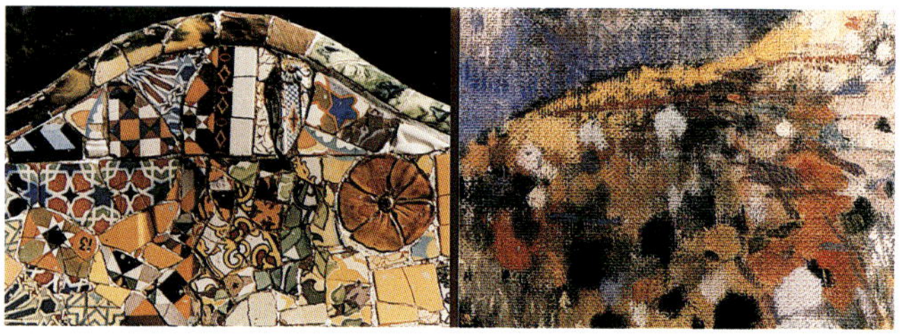

Trencadís català 1993.
(Catalan Mosaic). Photographs

authorship. Perejaume has now taken this function upon himself because he stands closest, as it were. As a result of this synchronisation between the artist's time and Miró's model's, between Perejaume's time and Consol Boquera's, there appears a space of fiction. Kinship, which was more or less implicit in the typology of portraits of two people posing together, has then to be understood in photographic space. By dint of this kinship, Perejaume is placed in the sphere of Joan Miró. In this sense, then, this photograph provides a place in history. However, this is not a matter of stylistic continuity, nor of the kind of sequencing one finds in art history. Rather, it will show that to construe art in historical terms is to depend on a framework of causality which serves to determine what may be placed beside what and what may and may not be compared. Our placing of this portrait of the artist with Miró's model in history is, to get to the point, an example of a policy of encounters.

This kind of encounter, which owes something to the surrealists' policy of image production, has taken on an extraordinary dimension in Perejaume's work. The homely setting for this surrealist meeting ("the chance encounter, on a dissecting table, between a sewing machine and an umbrella") is extended by Perejaume to historical, cultural, and geographical levels. These unsuspected connections play an important role here: in order to re-make the explanation of reality, one must first modify causality. It is for this reason that the move into the realm of fiction seems unavoidable; there, politics become once again poetical.

In Perejaume's case, the most visible model for this course of action is to be found in the first of his books to be published. In *Ludwig-Jujol. Què és el collage, sinó acostar soledats?* (1989), this alteration in the logic of history was intended to make the rhetoric of formal history into fiction. Throughout the text, geography contracts, bringing intersections into being, yoking newly paired elements. Territories, place names, architectures, cultures, periods, and scenographies overlap in a shared space. The universes of King Ludwig II of Bavaria (1845-1886) and the Catalan architect Josep Maria Jujol (1879-1949) come together through a range of varied connections. All the same, the quality of these connections cannot be verified. The logic of space having been suspended, one has to trust in poetic fluidity. As Perejaume wrote, "We shall allow a shady stream to flow from Bavaria's melting snows to a washing basin in the countryside around Tarragona."[2]

These connections are capricious, acting as they do against the flow of what seems to be natural. Yet nothing is more loaded, ideologically, than that which shuns comparison with alternatives. Perejaume consequently sets about inventing kinship by creating series of juxtaposed images, as in *Trencadís català* (Catalan Mosaic, 1988; p. 124). The simulation of continuity which he achieves is intended to erase differences.

Yet when he places Leonardo's *Virgen of the Rocks* beside Caspar David Friedrich's *Promeneur au dessus des nuages*, the kind of fiction one encounters is composed by a sequence of images. [3] The transition between one image and the next evokes a rational de-composition of the encounter.

These relationships are to be followed by a space given over to explanation. In this space, a rationality of a sort will reappear in support of such juxtapositions, thus generating the conceptual site in which Perejaume works. Just as the photograph which concludes *El Pirineu de baix* functions in relation to the other works contained in the volume, other elements of Perejaume's output do not enjoy the sort of autonomy which is characteristic of the objects of modern art. The supplementary character which we had anticipated is now confirmed and shown to be an illustrative function. More specifically, these works require the presence of an object, another body; it is only by reference to such an object that they can be explained. Otherwise, what would they 'cling' to? This explains the eagerness to 'be placed' — whether historically, spatially, culturally, or aesthetically — to which these works are subjected.

As for the scene in which Perejaume and Consol Boquera appear together, it merely makes a negotiated, historical 'placement' in time visible. In order to make the coincidence of Perejaume and Consol Boquera in a single image meaningful, one must understand that the same image viewed from a conventional historical perspective would be 'placed' very distinctly. In fact, in staging this photograph Perejaume has prepared a contradiction which leaves his own position as an artist unresolved. [4]

2. Scattered Paintings

It should now seem evident that the question of Perejaume's 'place' cannot be answered in completely straightforward terms. Both the photograph and the text which situate him in history give rise to a dialectic which renders it impossible to pin him down. In the case of this artist, the sense of movement in history is answered by the geographical path which Perejaume has followed.

Some of the writers who have tried to trace the path of Perejaume's work have offered an inventory of places where the artist has worked. In 1980 the art critic and historian Alexandre Cirici Pellicer visited Perejaume's studio. The result, a text written for the catalogue of Perejaume's first individual exhibition, at the Joan Prats Gallery in Barcelona, evoked a number of places associated with nineteenth-century culture. [5] Ca l'Oller de la Cortada, where Perejaume was then working, became for Cirici "a Gustave Doré engraving", "a shadowy world of kitsch, of Ludwig II of Bavaria's Neuschwantsein", with "an evaporated Wagnerian perfume", as well as "an atmosphere halfway between Japanese lacquer and Millais' Ophelia". He ends by stating that "everything is nineteenth-century" and that everything to be seen in the artist's studio gives one the impression that "one is looking at realist canvases painted in 1870". Eight years later, Vicenç Altaió furthered this effort to make an inventory: "Can Riera, in Fuirosos; Ca l'Oller de la Cortada, in the Dones d'Aigua park; Can Maresme; the Torre dels Focs and Can Rocosa, on the slopes of Montnegre; the bell-tower of the Church of Saint Sebastian, in Santa Eulàlia de Riuprimer; Sant Martí d'Ogassa..." [6]

Now, rather than bringing this list up to date, rather than adding to it, the task at hand is that of inquir-

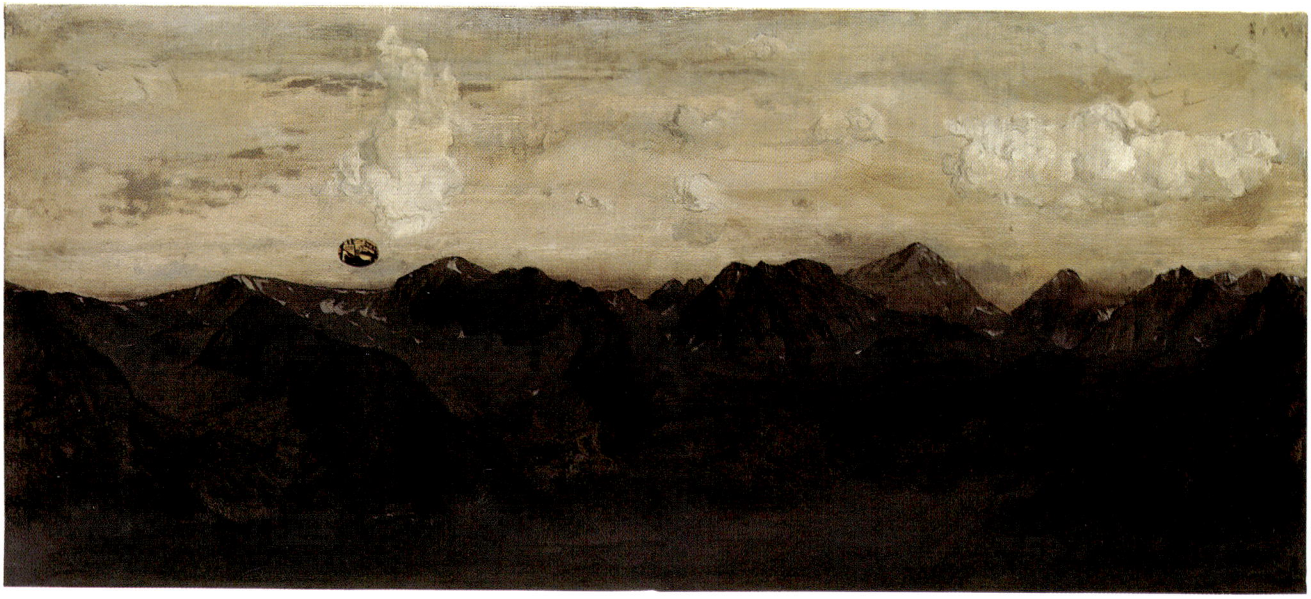

Braque a Costuix 1992
(Braque at Costuix)
Oil on canvas. 50.5 x 116 cm.

ing after the underlying economy to be found in this list of places that are both real and imaginary, after the meanings of these passages from place to place.

In many of Perejaume's paintings one finds representations of other displacements of paintings, often of nineteenth-century paintings. This displacement parodies the growing exchange of works between museums. Yet the nineteenth-century paraphernalia signals a shift not in movement, but of mover: it is no longer museum-goers who travel, but the museum itself which ventures beyond the confines of its premises. These roving works become comparable to the movement of consumer goods. In such a situation, the frame seems to propel the canvas through the air, as the museum walls had melted into nothingness. The institutional apparatus surrounding representations is largely gone, leaving behind the canvas and its gilded frame. From this point on, the frame seems all the more to function as protection for the painting, covering the edge of the canvas and shielding the work from new interpretations.

The sense of strangeness which we sense on seeing, in some of these works, paintings flying in formation across the sky, is heightened by the muteness of the trees. We know, from the titles of Perejaume's paintings, that the places portrayed are quite specific: the sky in *Costuix* (1994; p.56) is seen through empty frames and groups of paintings; in another painting, *Braque a Costuix* (Braque at Costuix, 1992; p.126), cubism is flying over the mountains in Vall Ferrera; in *Cal Peraire* (1993; p. 219), the corner of a picture gallery alights in a field; and in *La llotja dels Crous* (The Crous' Box, 1991), the painting hovers before a group of theatre stalls. These precise place names stand in the way of the universality extolled by high culture. Notwithstanding this sensation, the opposition at play may be inverted, and the presence of paintings may give the place depicted a sheen of exoticness. It is not very likely that frequent museum-goers will recognize the places which the titles designate. The geography of culture may well be imprecise, yet it is better known and closer at hand than are real places found but a short distance from us.

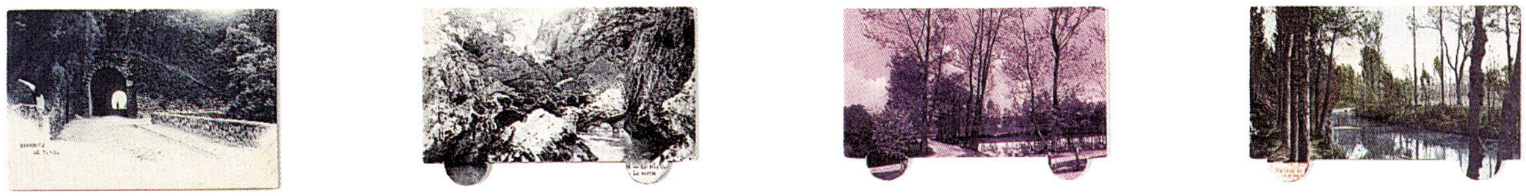

Tren de postals 1981. (Postcard Train). Four postcards on paper. 29 x 98 cm.

3. A Silent Occupation of Space

Tren de postals (Postcard Train, 1981; p. 127) is an early manifestation of the ubiquitousness. A symbol of the industrial revolution, the train stands for all manner of potential connections — among them, connections, transmissions, and distributions of images. Rails, like frames, have functioned for Perejaume as metonyms of the propagation of representations. Indeed, given the overlap between rails and frames, one could sustain that frames sometimes take the place of rails, and rails of frames (*Marcs* [Frames], 1986; p. 10 and *Paysages de l'Europe. Gare d'Orsay*, 1996; p. 166).

The flow arising in these scattered works cannot be plotted on any map. It is uncontrollable flooding which bears a most striking similarity to this flow. All in all, the common objectives these paintings share is that of making a map through the route of representations. Landscape is thus, as a genre, reconceptualized at the great nineteenth-century drive to create means of transport.

Yet a more contemporary formulation of this problem would have to refer to an exchange of signs. When representations adopt fully capitalist means of distribution and consumption, they have entered the market place, however immaterial they may be. It is then that the virtual quality of representations seems to seek out materialist objectivity, thus bringing this compulsive movement to a standstill. All in all, this will lead to quite extravagant creations which allow for glimpses of their movement and their status as objects. The interruption of their movement, far from being a block, makes their identification possible.

This is because, in order to interrupt movement, one must first detect it. The visual portrayal of movement makes movement's invisible and silent occupation of space evident, although we consider this an illusion in the end. This suggests that representations may also be subject to economic and political control. Perejaume does not set out to provide a definitive account of the manner in which images and representations are propagated. It suffices to see the kind of tools which he puts in his works: *Claude Monet parant una tela d'aranya al coll de Vila-roja* (Claude Monet Placing a Cobweb at Vila-roja Pass, 1993; p. 58) commemorates the Impressionists' desire to capture the landscape and 'take it captive'; *El motiu* (The Motif, 1994; pp. 128 and 129) shows an image pinned in the sand with four thumbtacks, the image of a place which will change, inevitably, as a consequence of environmental change. This desire to ascertain and later store is expressed in every work by Perejaume discussed so far. Yet that which evades its own visibility is likewise impossible to label and shelve. A work such as *Postaler* (Postcard Rack, 1984; p. 131) had already posed this two-faceted problem in Perejaume's development. The metallic structure intended as a commercial display of postcards is instead a display of mirrors, carried by the artist's back from place to place in a peripatetic action documented in a series of photographs. The presence of many atmospheres rendered *Postaler* a changing painting, visible from all angles.

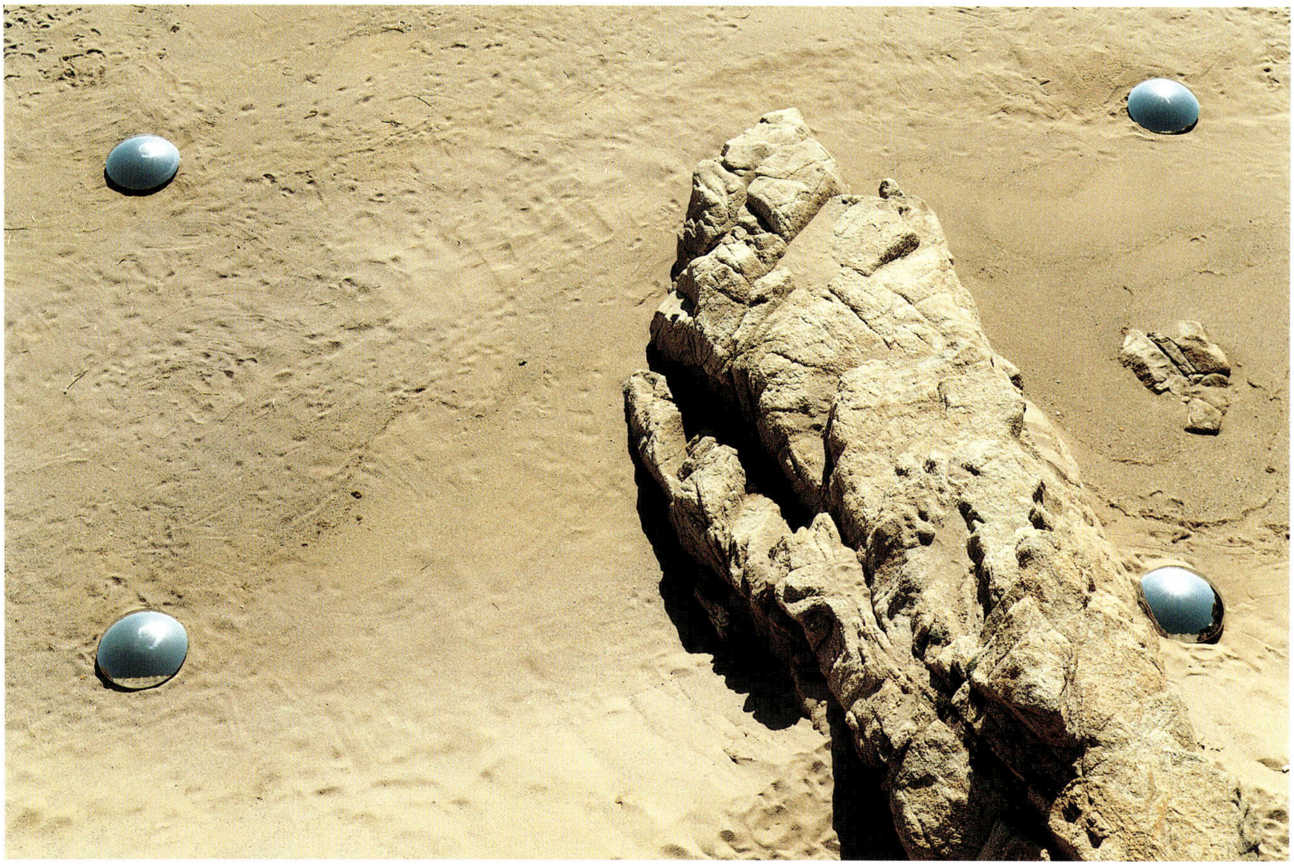

El motiu 1994
(The Motif)
Four stainless steel thumbtacks and photograph of the thumbtacks in the sand
ø 120 cm. each thumbtack

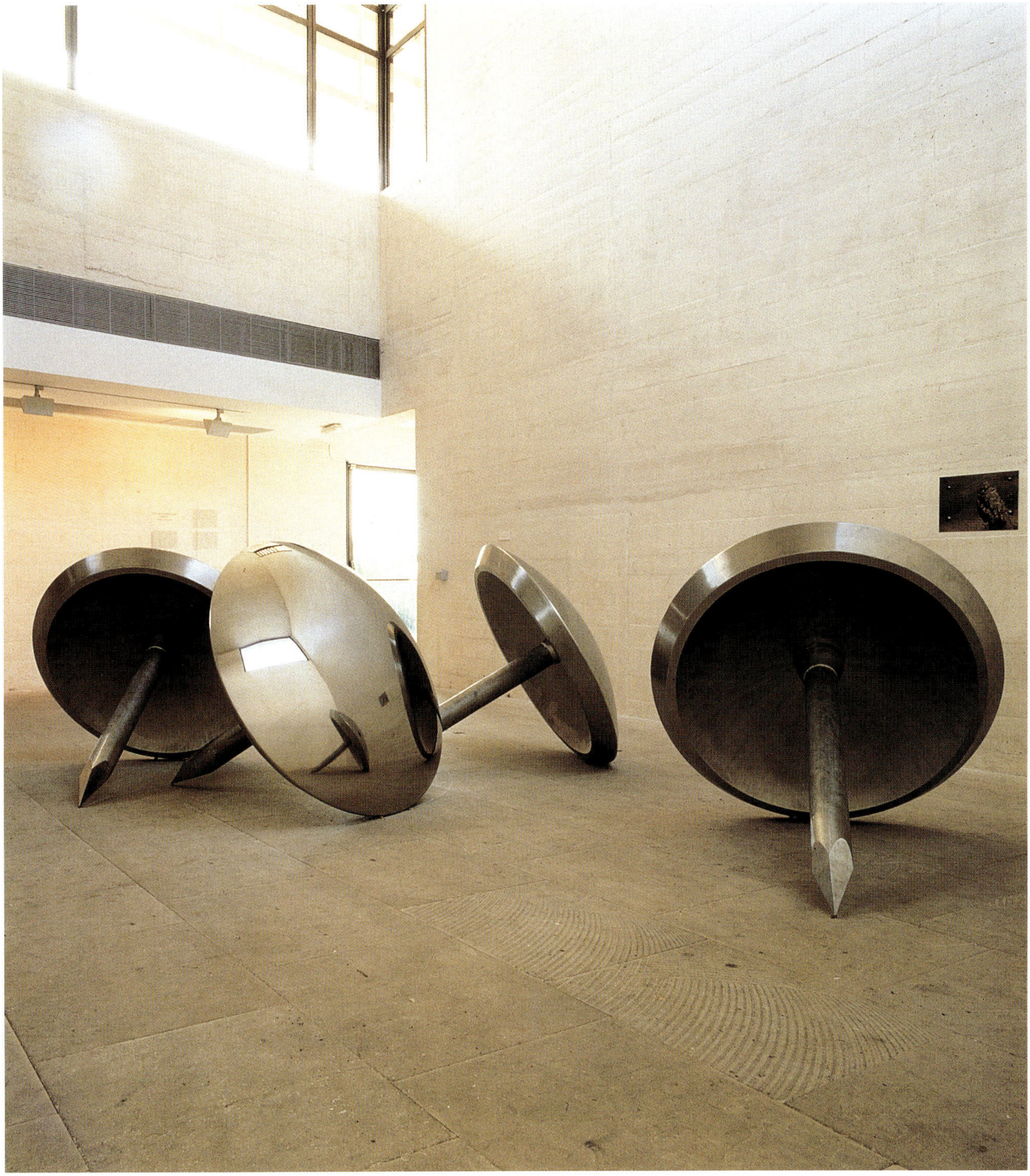

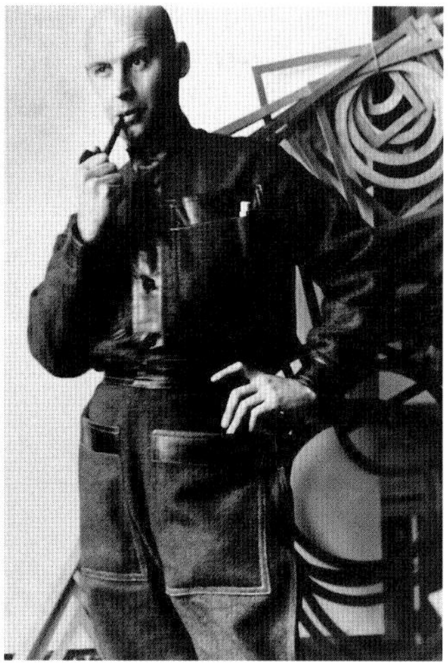

1

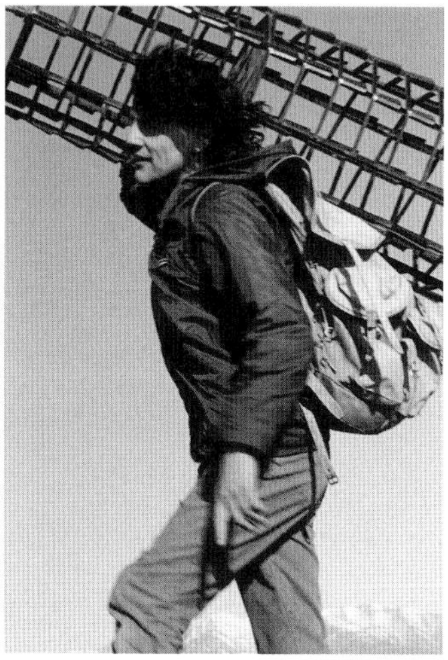

2

4. Resisting the Archive

It may thus seem that *Postaler* is comparable to Robert Smithson's and Robert Morris' undertakings with displaced mirrors in the late 1960s and early 1970s. Yet it is significant that *Postaler*'s most remarkable aspect is its influence on notions of the exhibition and the archive. In historical terms, the mingling of the notion of a work and the format of an archive has its roots in a work by Aleksandr Rodchenko (1891-1956), one of the leading Russian artists in the period following the Revolution of October 1917: *Spatial Constructions* (1922). Both Perejaume's *Postaler* and Rodchenko's disassembled ovals are affected directly by the idea of a museum as a place to store representations. The conclusion to be drawn from an encounter with these two works together is that museums must, by virtue of their institutional character, take works apart (both literally and metaphorically) in order to be able to safeguard them.

The full meaning of this comparison is not borne out unless one places a well-known portrait of Rodchenko standing before dismantled elements of his *Spatial Constructions* (p. 130), beside a photograph of Perejaume carrying the postcard rack on his back (p. 130). These two images represent that which the museum would consider an unproductive moment, given that unassembled works cannot communicate what they do when they are placed in their pigeon-holes. This comparison is interesting inasmuch as it portrays the incorporation of the taking apart of a work in the process of production. This moment, which is incompatible with public exhibition, traditionally belongs to the archive. The archive is more than a place where works are stored and looked after; it is also an act which hides representation. It is for this reason that in *Postaler*, a framework which is the archive par excellence, there are no images left.

1 Rodchenko standing before dismantled hanging constructions, 1922
Photograph: M. Kaufman. Georges Costakis Collection

2 Perejaume carrying the postcard rack

3 **Postaler** 1984
(Postcard Rack)
Postcard rack, mirrors. 197 x 56 x 50 cm.
Photographs. 29.5 x 138.5 cm.

3

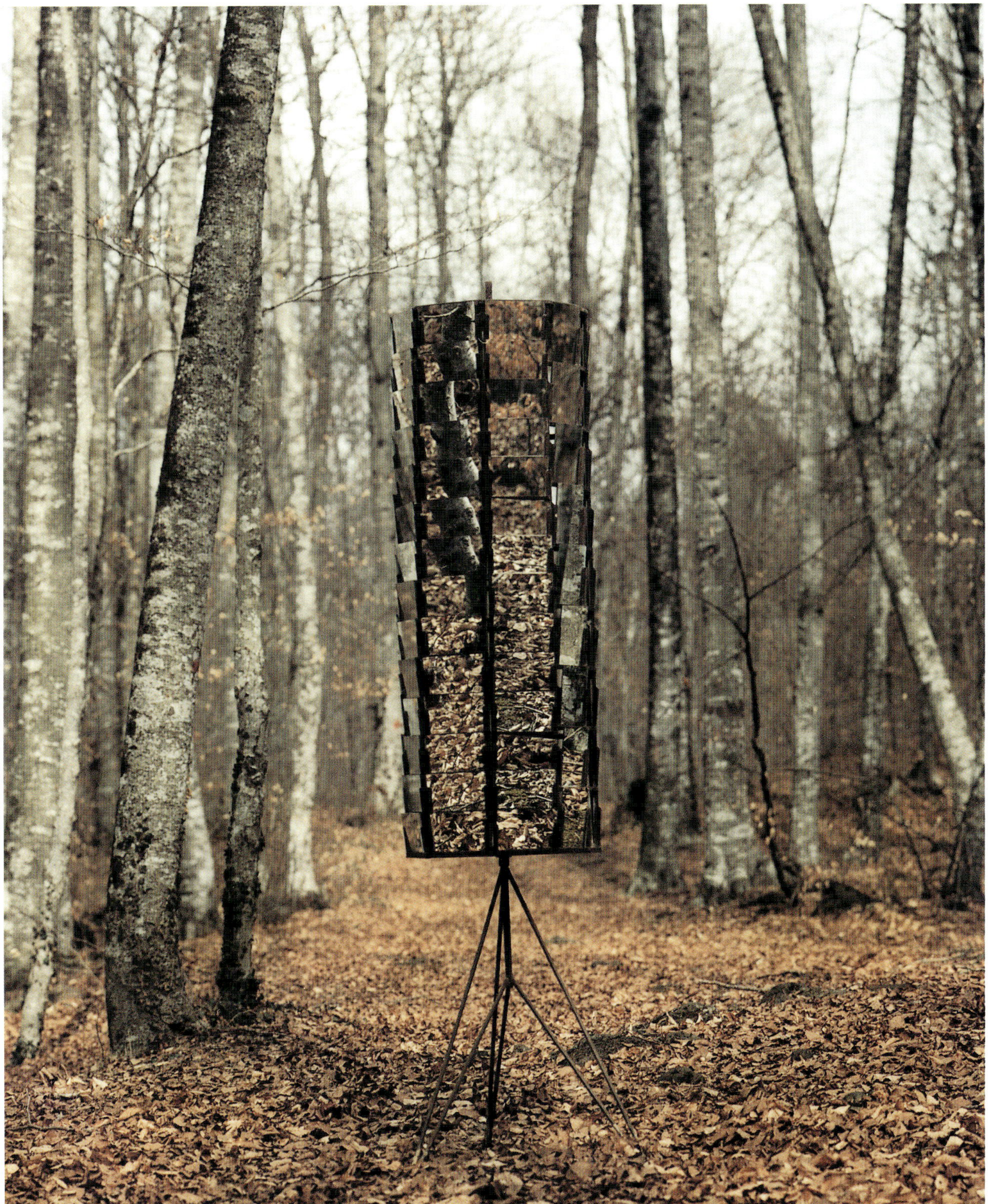

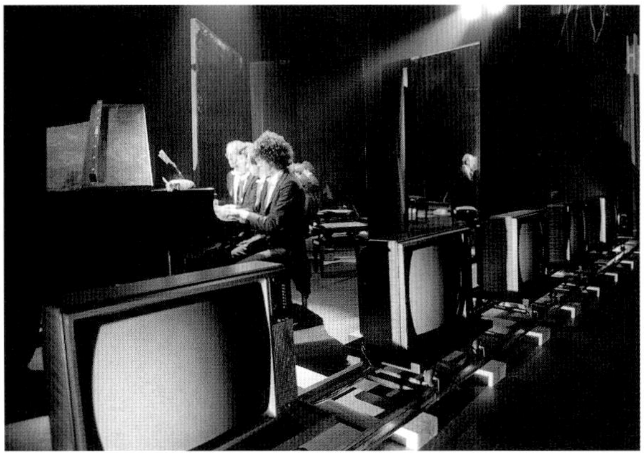

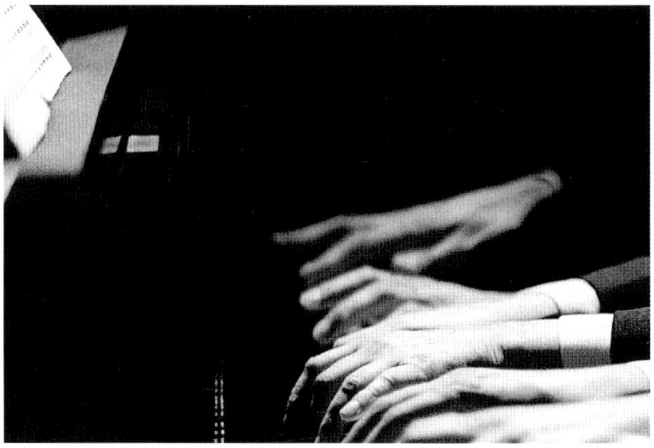

1

1 **Piano-xofer** 1984
(Chauffeur-piano)

2 **Postaler II** 1984
(Postcard Rack II)
Photograph. 93 x 167 cm.

Postaler is also in some sense the outcome of a show Perejaume staged with the musician Josep M. Mestres Quadreny. *Piano-xofer* (Chauffeur-piano, 1984; p. 132) consists of a series of staged scenes furnished with a number of the devices which are often found in Perejaume's work: a postcard rack; the curtain from Barcelona's Liceu opera house; mirrors; video monitors, and the piano on which four pianists play, both mounted on rails for the sake of mobility. The moment in *Piano-xofer* which I would like to highlight, is that in which a battery of video monitors rolls down the rails together. In the same moment, all four pianists are playing, eight hands are on the keyboard, and this image is multiplied by mirrors. Both the placement of the monitors in an assembly line-like setting and the accumulation of piano-playing hands evoke images of early twentieth-century mass production techniques, of Henry Ford's factories, images which lay behind Rodchenko's productivist approach in the early 1920s. The technique used in staging *Piano-xofer* is thus an extension of *Postaler*.

At the same time, the video images which appear both in *Piano-xofer* and in the original exhibition of *Postaler* suggest a context of interpretation in which the piece is displaced into the field of electronic images. The function of *Postaler* is thus faced with a paradox: it both stops and files trade in images.

This paradox may only be neutralized by providing an ontological definition for these images, fleetingly and yet incessantly caught and reflected by mirrors on whose surfaces they leave no trace.

Postaler, then, is an appeal for ontological precariousness and for a constantly changing position; yet neither of these qualities is suited to the museum's task of pinning works down. It follows, therefore, that *Postaler* stands in opposition to the institution of the museum: this is because it does not seek to retain representations, by virtue of which the meaning of artistic production is widened. The institution which Rodchenko himself had run in the early Soviet period, the Museum of Painterly Culture (MZhK), was not conceived of as a place to store unique objects, but rather as an archive.[7] In this way, the museum had sidestepped the problem of representations. Rather, it became an institution designed to control the assembly and disassembly of works, which process we may also associate with production.

2

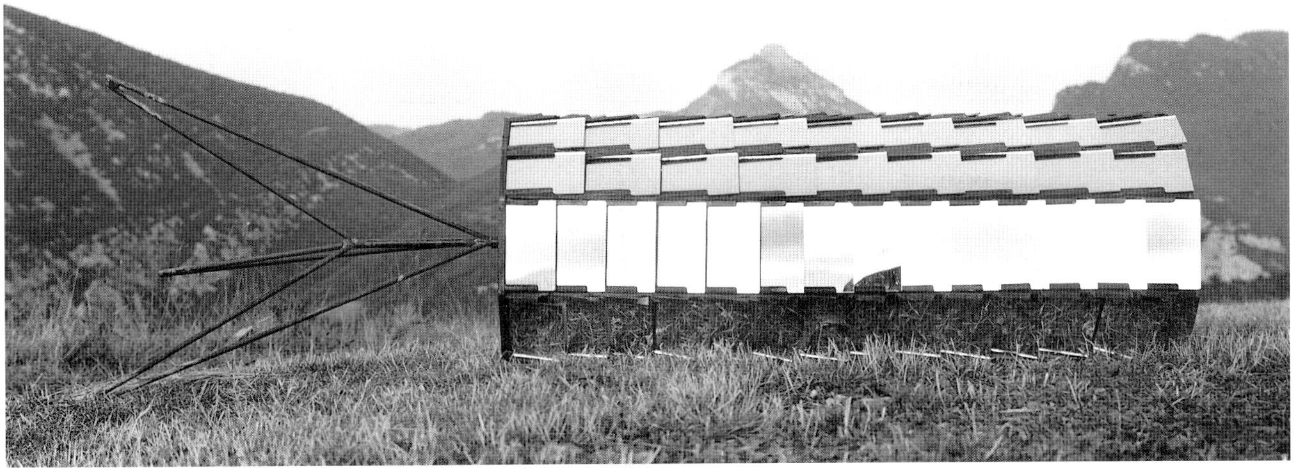

5. The Laid-down *Postaler*

Apart from rhetoric about process, there is one moment in the development of Postaler which helps to explain Perejaume's work. The moment in question has been recorded in a photograph which shows the metallic structure of the postcard rack full of mirrors. What makes this image different is the placement of the rack, which is lying on the ground in such a way that its perpendicular axis coincides with the horizon (p. 133). Apparently, this operation reproduces an image which occurs frequently among Perejaume's works: that of a landscape within a landscape. In this case, given the presence of mirrors, two horizons are superimposed on one another. It may be possible to see a precedent for this use of landscape in *L'entrada del mar* (Enter the Sea, 1980; p. 41), in which the landscape acts as a curtain which, pulled back, reveals another landscape. Indeed, as Cirici Pellicer remarked in his text, "[In Perejaume's works] landscape is often treated as though it were the painted landscape of a theatrical backdrop."[8]

In addition to the advantage of providing us with a retrospective vision, this laying-down of *Postaler* acquires a meaning that goes beyond the model of a landscape within a landscape. Postaler's change from a vertical to a horizontal position has implications which we would do well to explore. In Perejaume's evolution, this kind of displacement between one axis and the other has become a methodological reference.[9] If to our encounter with this horizontal *Postaler* we were to add a series of works such as *Cim de Catiu d'Or* (Catiu d'Or Peak, 1988; p. 104), *Ombra de la motllura d'un quadre de Nicolau Raurich a la paret del Museu d'Art Modern de Barcelona* (Shadow of the Frame of a Nicolau Raurich Painting in Barcelona's Museum of Modern Art, 1988; p. 134) and *Pessebrisme del Quadrat Negre* (Pessebrism of the Black Square, 1993; p. 135)[10], we would find the resulting collection quite heterogeneous. Yet this apparent diversity masks a similarity of movement. In the three latter pieces, a work transported at a 90-degree angle is transformed and read as though it were a deformed reflex of itself. Freud's writings speak of the acquisition of culture as representing a kind of forgetting which occurs when we incorporate the vertical; if so, in this laying down we can perceive a memory. This relationship between one moment and the other maintains a causal link. Accordingly, in the third of the above-

1

1 **Ombra de la motllura d'un quadre de Nicolau Raurich a la paret del Museu d'Art Modern de Barcelona** 1988
(Shadow of the Frame of a Nicolau Raurich Painting in Barcelona's Museum of Modern Art). Photograph. 17 x 24 cm.

2 **Pessebrisme del Quadrat Negre** 1993
(Pessebrism of the Black Square)
Iron and photocopy of Malevich's painting
The Black Square 1915. Variable dimensions

mentioned works— *Ombra de la motllura d'un quadre de Nicolau Raurich...* — we find the result of a projection, just as the title indicates. The shadow, a mechanical reproduction of the frame's moulding on the wall, imposes a change of meaning. The positivism which is evident in this procedure seems to have been betrayed by the result. The projection of the frame on the wall sketches a series of protrusions. Once again, everything has become a mountain. This brings us to the great, twisted moulding that is the *Cim de Catiu d'Or* (p. 104), in which the projection of the frame on the rock prevents the frame from keeping to the angle at which, by all rights, it should be set. The relationship of causality becomes here both a force for deformation and a source of information. By separating the frame from the rock which gives it shape, the woodwork and gilding recover their autonomy. Though the frame may seem empty to us, as others to be found in Perejaume's works seem empty, it is here filled by means of this process. The frame, then, works as index, as portable mark. The ornamental quality of this frame-index adds meaning to it. On seeing *Pessebrisme del Quadrat Negre*, we realise that the cracks in the canvas dilate and become labyrinthine when they reach the ground. This drawing of time begins with the negative (on the surface of the painting) only to reach the positive (on the ground). The black rectangle in itself loses importance, which is ceded to these unpredictable lines. Supreme abstraction is tattered amidst complex flourishes. The repressed ornamentation of Suprematism reappears by chance, naturally and by an organic process. And the ideal of the tabula rasa, which the avant-gardes associated with the autonomous communicative power of colour and form — and exemplified by landmark works such as the Russian artist Kazimir Malevich's *Black Square* (1915) — reappears here in the 'laying-down' of that same painting. Virtually, when the painting reaches the horizontal line, it dissolves in natural space in such a way that the cultural and historical are condensed geologically.

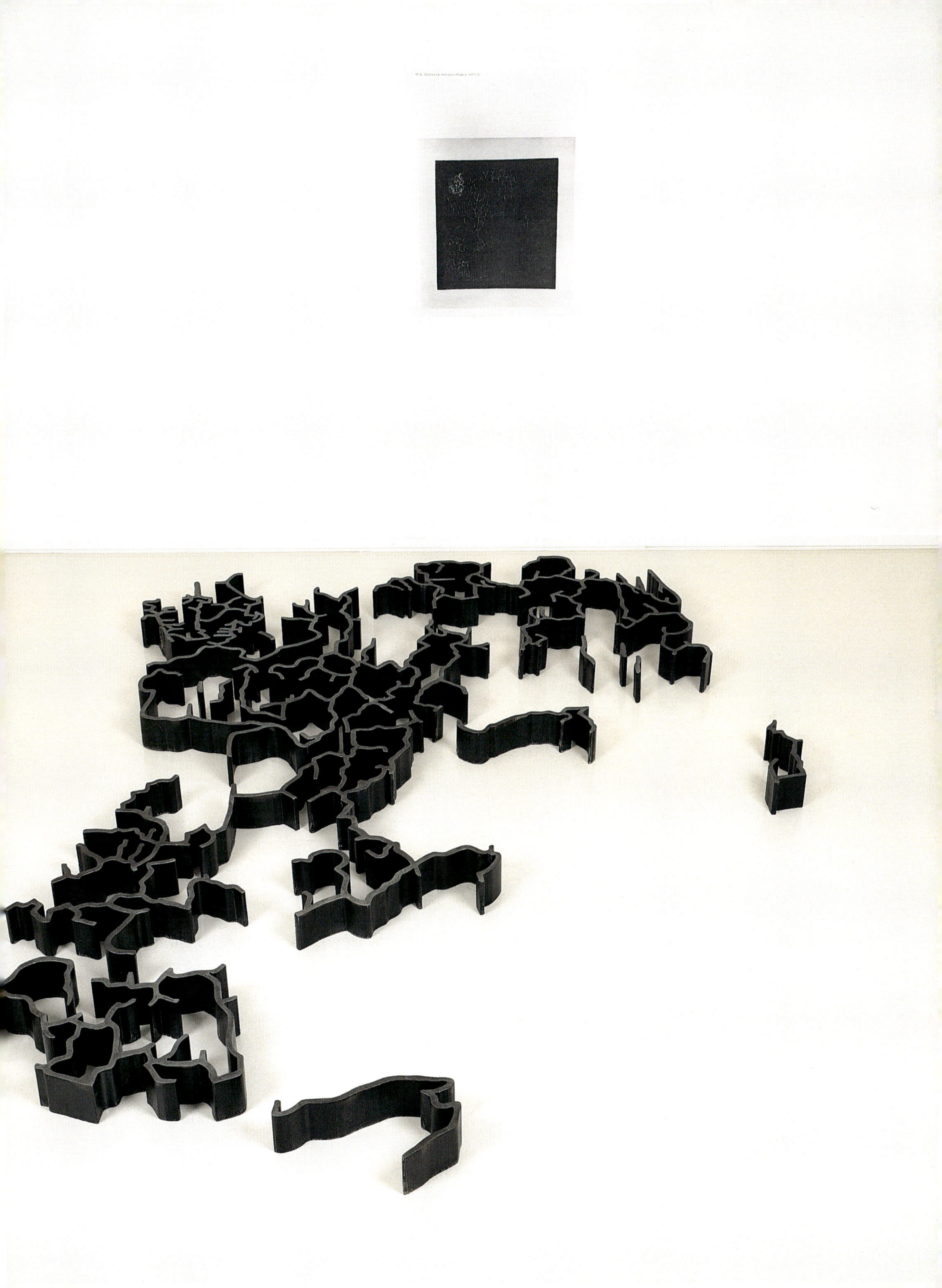

6. Facing Culture, Turning One's Back to Nature

These laying-downs, projections and displacements absorb one another. The authority of the original is relegated by the authoritarianism of the process. Artists, works, frame, territory, and viewers speak during this process by means of an exchange of positions. For example, in *Metamorfosi* (p. 136), a book created together with the writer Pere Gimferrer, Perejaume replaced the poet's name with his own. The poem entitled *Signe*, originally signed by Pere Gimferrer, re-appears on the next page.

In this movement, the copied poem loses the name of its author and acquires Perejaume's signature, printed in the same blue ink as the rest of the poem. In this exercise of apparent mimesis, and of illustration, Perejaume has left the poem's authorship untouched while changing its signed attribution. This paradox may be explained if one allows that mimesis, or duplication, makes for a weakening of the singular, individual quality of that which has been copied. In this sense, Perejaume has seen fit to interrupt the mimesis which would undermine the poem with his own name, if necessary. He thus saves Pere Gimferrer's name. In fact, this operation is already familiar to us. It is not very different from Perejaume's having replaced Miró's name with his own body in order to save the model in *La vaileta* from being frozen in painting.

Beyond resemblance, mimesis disorients — it causes one to lose one's co-ordinates, the frame of reference which allows one to place something as natural or original. In *Natura i signatura* (Nature and Signature, 1990; p. 157), the title of the work as reproduced both in the exhibition and in its catalogue poses this very problem. *Natura i signatura* contains both a stone and its exact copy. The copy, which appears on the left, takes on an ordinal priority which contaminates its status as cardinal: it seems to move towards be-

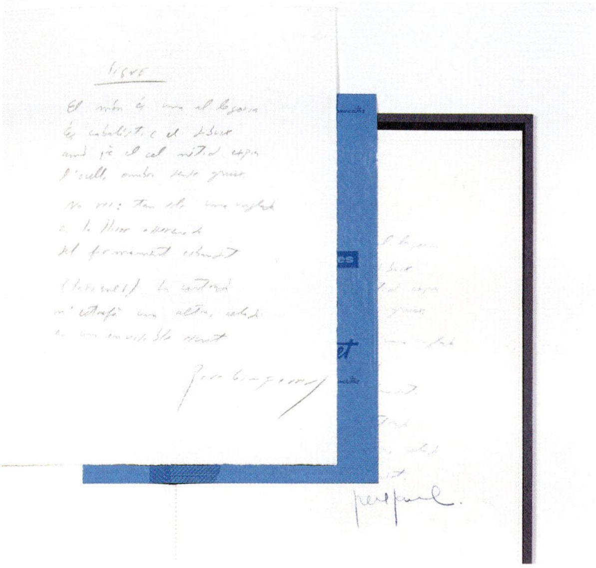

Metamorfosi 1988
Artist book by Pere Gimferrer and Perejaume

ing read in terms of the axis of nature, perhaps because it is seen almost as though it were writing. The true stone, which is the second to be read because it appears on the right, seems to belong to the axis of culture. Whether or not this placement is accidental, however haphazard my interpretation may seem, what is speaking through me — as Roland Barthes would say — is the shaping force of culture. The very order of the title, *Natura i signatura*, is a mirror image of the order of the work itself, an image in which the natural and the cultural have been inverted. And this process of inversion could go on infinitely. In this spiral of substitutions, the signature establishes signs of culture's ownership of the realm of the natural. By the same token, *Gabinet fantàstic* (Fantastic Cabinet, 1985-1988; p. 138), far from appearing as a mere accumulation of copies, produces an equally disorienting effect with its signatures superimposed on a cityscape of Granada originally painted by the nineteenth-century Catalan artist Marià Fortuny.

Fortuny's painting, *Landscape of Granada* (1870-1872), is in all probabilty the referent for Édouard Manet's *Landscape at Oloron-St. Marie* (1871), which forms part of the collection of the Stuttgart Gallerie. In this case, Manet's copy recovers a plausible referent by acquiring a new place name. Just as the frame fell onto and moulded itself along the peak of Catiu d'Or, the image of Granada lands on that of Oloron-St. Marie. The effect of this adaptation widens the format of Manet's canvas slightly, stretching the landscape. Yet the change is not merely one of formal proportions. The corrected proportions are those of a greater closeness to nature. Thus, to legitimate itself in history, Manet's painting must evoke a first-hand relationship with landscape. Perejaume has not undertaken an essentialist recovery of this relationship with the natural; rather, he has made it into the stuff of fiction. It is thus very probable that these 'layings-down' and projections, which are presented as ostensible returns to natural values, do not in fact lead to a rediscovery of the co-ordinates of nature. When the vector of culture drops to the co-ordinate of the natural, it becomes yet another moment in culture.

In a short text by Perejaume, *Em giro a mirar* (I Turn to Gaze, 1986), this effect by dint of which almost everything has become a product of culture is dramatiszd as a bodily gesture which, in another variation on the theme of 'laying-down', turns around completely, just as the title suggests:

"Past the mouldings of the grove, by a twist in the path, there comes into view an late-coming landscape, behind a dark and musty glaze. The hills and vales have something Romantic about them, as though they had been pessebrated by Lluís Rigalt or Francesc Xavier Parcerisa. The sky, however, is newer, seemingly drawn from an afternoon of Francesc Gimeno's as clouded over for Joaquim Mur in his youth. Where the fading sunlight is strongest at dusk, one can make out saffron-tinted brushstrokes at the foot of the gilded relief of the western sky. As it grows darker, the lights of farmhouses, half-hidden behind the oak trees, are doubtless the work Nicolau Raurich." [11]

Here, painting is projected on reality. Yet Perejaume, when he turns, does not see landscape or even painting but literature. What is more, by means of this gesture, he is facing culture, and perhaps turning his back on nature. That which cannot be seen, which lies outside his field of vision, is nature by virtue of lying outside the frame of culture. Yet this 'outside' is relative: were we to read this passage from a Foucaultian perspective, the landscape would break up into cell-like fragments, each respresented by an author, and if we were to leave any of them we would inevitably enter another. In this sense, what this text reveals is more than cultural contamination; rather, it is what Freud in *Civilization and Its Discontents* called the guiltiness of the gaze — of the educated gaze.

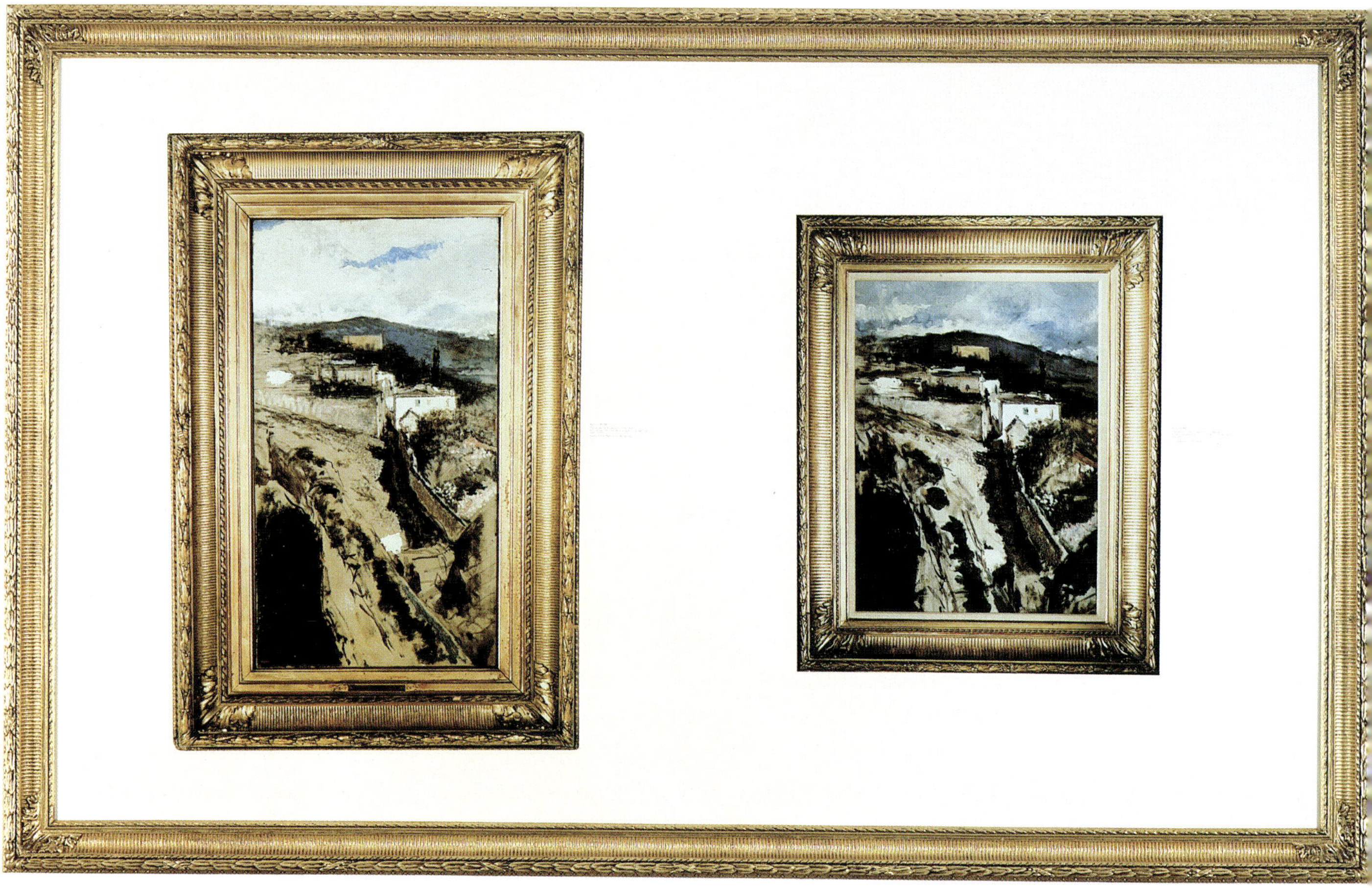

Gabinet fantàstic 1985-1988
(Fantastic Cabinet)
Photograph and golden frame. 158.5 x 258.5 cm.

7. The Value of the Word "Pessebrated"

Nonetheless, the key to this procedure is to be found in the word "pessebrated", which appears in the quotation from *Em giro a mirar*. Perejaume himself has coined this derivation, which is practically a neologism. A widening of the semantic field of pessebrated might well help us to discover the value of the use of this word. The fragment below, extracted from a longer text by Perejaume, provides a further example of this procedure which, beginning with the horizontal *Postaler*, I have discussed in terms of 'layings-down', transpositions, displacements, mimeses, substitutions, turnings, and so on:

"Let us turn to another *pessebration*. In 1908, Ferdinand Hodler met Valentine. In 1914, Valentine *fell ill* and went to a clinic in Laussane for treatment. Holder then began a series of sketches of the *bed-ridden* Valentine, each of which is dated. The realism is striking; the formats tend progressively towards that of *landscapes*. As Valentine lay slowly dying — she died on Jan 26, 1915 — Holder alternated between these portraits and views of Lake Léman *at dusk* from the window of Valentine's room. The range of hills looming over the lake and Valentine, *lying* in bed, come to be less and less distinguishable from one another. Valentine's body is increasingly *hill-like*, and the *mountains come to be depicted on a human scale*. Her face and hands, the pillows and the folds in the sheets, become a tucking-in of the landscape; and the real hills and foggy valleys, an echo of a human figure, a portrait. In the last portrait, Valentine's hands are clasped on her belly, her face still and hardened: she is *lying* on the bed, *stretched out*, wearing a green dress." [12]

Perejaume identifies each italicized word with this notion of pessebrism. Yet pessebrism involves more than just 'layings-down'; it also involves raising, enlargement, extolling. Here and there we find examples of monumentalization (p. 52). The monument's pedestal thus serves to separate and to raise. A brushstroke may be raised, literally, along a cultural axis, i.e. brought closer to our axis of vision. Thus, if the 'redemption' which followed upon the abandonment of the vertical line has not entailed a recovery of nature, this is because pessebrism also serves to sublimate. By this I mean that the very act of trying to identify with nature creates further distance from nature. The result of such an action is rather a further projection of culture, where the recovery of nature had been desired. Therefore, pessebrism — to refine this concept further — mixes both the falls and the ascents of these two axes. As Perejaume says, "Valentine's body is increasingly hill-like, and [at the same time] the mountains come to be depicted on a human scale." The sense of a single direction grows correspondingly weaker. Yet the delay in the appearance of this sought-after image of nature does not mean that it has been forgotten. Both 'laying-down' and sublimation serve as an approach to the same point, whether they come closer or nearer, and brand ideology onto the land. Perejaume's work has, therefore, both material and, if you prefer, natural achievements.

'Layings-down' and sublimations never entail rescue. It is therefore incumbent upon us to speak of a second nature, of a nature which is superimposed on an unreachable nature. The second nature is that which offers itself to our beholding as a product of vision.

8. Status of Method

Perejaume presents pessebrism as something which aspires to the status of method. In this representation of his own praxis, there appears a series of works whose task it is to explain, systematize and visualize it. Drawings and objects form part of this effort to make method clear. Thus, *Mètode pessebrístic de lectura* (Reading the Pessebristic Way, 1990; p. 114) explains the relationship between chunks of cork, the eye, and the mind by means of a three-figured diagram. *Plenairista* (Plenairist, 1992; p. 115), on the other hand, presents pessebrism as a method of observation by placing a small clay figure which represents an artist before a piece of cork bark. The traditional materials of the nativity scene are thus extrapolated for pseudoscientific use. Works, visualizations, and texts also reproduce a triangular relationship which strips the method of any essential truth. Each vertex refers us on to the rest in a circular fashion. The result is accordingly one of a constant shifting exemplification of the method itself, rather than a clarification.

Pessebrism is thus founded upon references to other authors, and unfolds by means of these references. Alexander Cozens, an eighteenth-century English painter, and Fuxier, a character drawn from the novel *Impressions d'Afrique* by Raymond Roussel, are superimposed in a sequence of quotations appearing in Perejaume's *La pintura i la boca*, a book by Perejaume published in 1993. Two elements are brought together: Cozen's method of basing the composition of imaginary landscapes on a series of ink stains; and the fantastic stories of a sculptor named Fuxier, who possesses the secret of coloured tablets which fleetingly catalyse figurations. Together, they add a pseudohistorical value to the method of pessebrism. This obsessive paraphrasing, which seems intended to reinforce the method, has the eventual effect of producing derivations from pessebrism. In fact, this method should by all rights be included in a geneology which would place it after a series of former manifestations associated with the paintings Perejaume produced in the late 1970s and early 1980s. These sudden appearances in the landscape of elements or characters which seem to have been imposed on the artist by the very places he depicts (pp. 39-40) constitute a more primitive, somewhat surrealist formulation of the methods which were to be put into practice later in collage (discussed above as a policy of encounters), unpainting, and oism. None of these methods entails any hiding of its artificial quality. The noise which they generate in practice unmasks the silent occupation of space by images and representations. By regulating the production of images, these methods tend to become methods of figuration. It would seem impossible to introduce some degree of control in this space if it were not true that communication is mastered by exercising control in ways which entail an utter lack of transparency. Perejaume's methods constitute a critical reflection on and of this situation. The forms of his imagination, as represented and interpreted by him, do not constitute working guidelines for Perejaume alone. Rather, they engage in an ironic dialogic with an image-saturated public space.

The dematerialization which characterises Conceptual Art and monochrome paintings would seem to be the fitting forerunners of this attitude, were it not for the fact that Perejaume himself evaluates these achievements in literary terms. Far from being monuments to the insubstantial quality of modern culture, they form the last layer of language. As Robert Smithson remarked, language "covers" rather than "discovers". [14] In taking up this point, Perejaume has disclosed the weight of dematerialization. By the same token, Lawrence Weiner's explanations of his first 'statements' serves to confirm that painting, like sculpture, had become literature because of the effect and the predominance of modern criticism ("Total literature!").[15]

For Perejaume, the turn to language is not a mere metaphor. Rather, by accumulating discourse in a geological volume, the turn suggested is a literal one. By this I mean that this turn entails distrust in the metaphorical quality of modern art, submitting metaphors to an absurd quantification (*Set mirades* [Seven Gazes], 1992). Perejaume thus brings about a situation in which positivism comes to be confronted directly by its own uses.

9. Unpainting

In practice, these methods are valuable inasmuch as they interrupt. This discontinuity consequently produces a duplication of Perejaume's work. In this way, he creates works which, once unfolded and self-duplicated, criticize themselves. The method of unpainting, which is manifest as well in undrawing and unsculpting, assumes the interruption of this incessant activity of representing. Unpainting, then, is Perejaume's means of lamenting the excess of images which characterizes the contemporary world. As though echoing Smithson's words, Perejaume goes on to make the practice of art serve the "discovery" of the layers which together make up the world.

Following this, unpainting appears on the line of the vertical axis, along which various strata which are both geological and cultural may be detected. Once this aim has been assumed, the various layers which have shaped the landscape may be recovered by means of an archaeological introspection. There are works of Perejaume's, such as *Pintura: Clisson* (Painting: Clisson, 1989; p. 142) and *Pintura: Fuirosos* (Painting: Fuirosos, 1990; p. 142) which both take part in this fiction and illustrate it. The excavations which these two works stage represent a desire to demonstrate what the method of pessebrism had foreseen as a hypothesis.

The yearning which this verification entails highlights a relationship with Salvador Dalí's 1963 text *El mito trágico del "Angelus" de Millet* in which Dalí demanded that Millet's "Angelus" be X-rayed to check if, as he had been told, there might be detected under the surface of the painting the concealed image of a dead child lying in a coffin between the feet of the couple portrayed. This crazed desire of Dalí's is not very different from that which drives Perejaume. As Dalí wrote in one of the latter passages of *El mito trágico*:

1 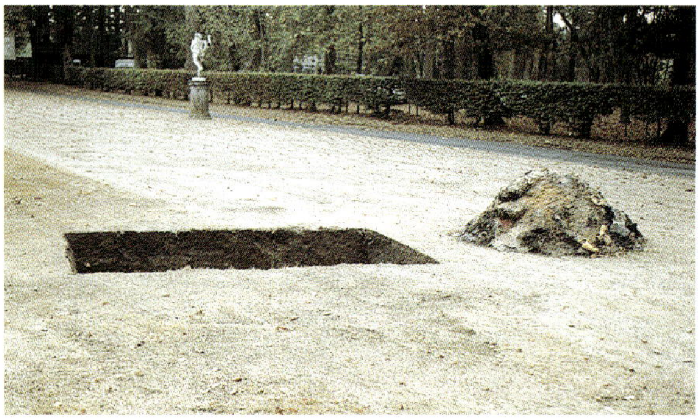

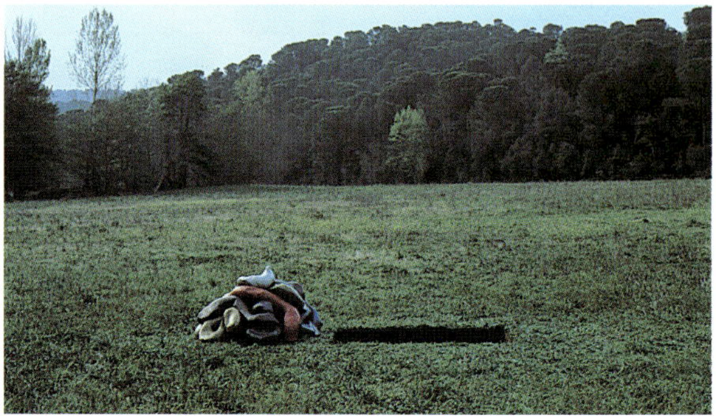

"It appears from certain letters that a friend of Millet's who was then living in Paris informed the painter of changes in Parisian taste and the growing feeling against excessively melodramatic effects. Millet very probably took this to heart and hid the dead child under a layer of paint representing the ground." [16]

That which Dalí was able to extract from this final phrase ("...and hid the dead child under a layer of paint representing the ground.") in psychoanalytical terms is comparable to that which Perejaume, in narrative terms, is able to extract in his own work from this layer of paint which settles on and represents the ground. Both Perejaume and Dalí consider painting as a means of forgetting which constitutes a kind of moral and physical blocking and masking.

These layers — which may also be read as accumulated interpretations of landscape — function structurally as hermeneutic circles which may only be broken by a pragmatic approach. Thus, while the rhetoric of Romanticism had been able to generate and bring forth landscape by means of poetic exaltation, in a re-incarnation of the vertical axis, we may observe the placing of the cross-section — the frame of geological perception — in radical opposition to this. The 90-degree difference which has manifested itself between the axes in Perejaume's 'layings-down' comes now to generate different ways of talking about landscape. The resulting dialectic besieges modern aesthetic reception. [17]

Dalí himself, having X-rayed Millet's "Angelus", closed his prologue to text E*l mito trágico del "Angelus" de Millet* with an allusion to this conflict:

"After this had happened, Gala told me 'If this result constituted proof, that would be marvellous; but if the whole book were nothing but a pure spiritual construct, that would be sublime!'" [18]

1 **Pintura: Clisson** 1989
(Painting: Clisson)

2 **Pintura: Fuirosos** 1990
(Painting: Fuirosos)

3 **Terra sobre mirall: Pineda de Mar** 1997
(Earth on Mirror: Pineda de Mar)
Well at Can Jaume Comas
Well at Can Rossell
Well at Can Benjumea

This opposition between the empiricism which requires proof and an outburst of spirit serves to deactivate, as it were, the Romantic rhetoric to which many spectators submit Perejaume's works, and which many of his works seem to demand. It reproduces, in a way, the oppositions and compensations between poetry and public rhetoric which characterized the eighteenth century.[19] The pragmatism of geological discourse seems to drive off sensuality. The products of the spirit are confronted with examples of a rationality which is as simple or as complex as the first term of comparison.
In Perejaume's praxis, vision is not omitted from this confrontation. As vision is no longer disinterested, it becomes an accomplice. It thus recovers its dependence on text. Consider, for example, another series of works, *Terra sobre mirall: Pineda de Mar* (Earth On Mirror: Pineda de Mar, 1997; p. 143), in which wells are privileged ways into the aquifer.
The water at the bottom of these wells becomes a mirror. If we should choose to play around with this identification, it must follow that there is an immense underground mirror which can be seen now and then, here and there. In this exercise in illustration, the commonplace of depth is at once represented and dismantled. The overlap with the fictional text devised by Perejaume would now seem irreversible. Smaller-format works such as *La pintura cobrint la terra* (Painting Covering the Earth, 1995; p. 1) consequently take on the value of a mythological episode. Vision thus strengthens its optical sense as an illustration of the world.
When all is said and done, methods such as pessebrism add to the narrative structure of this myth, while unpainting is responsible for its own unravelling. This doing and undoing erodes certainty about the starting point of this whole story. As Lautrément said in one of his aphorisms, "fundamental principles must be excluded from discussion". [20] In this sense, the fact that the starting point can be neither returned to nor recovered strengthens myth as a foundation narration. Writing and reading thus become absolutely necessary activities if this narration is to be maintained. Vision, by way of contrast, becomes a secondary instrument of exegesis.

3

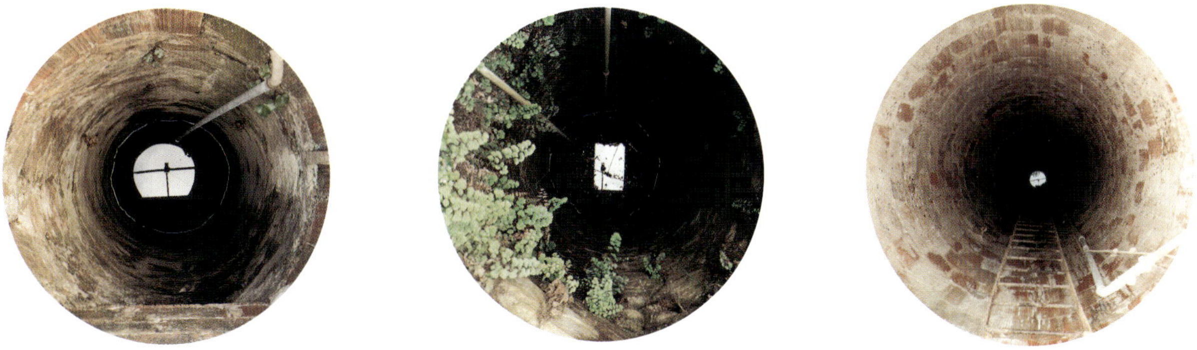

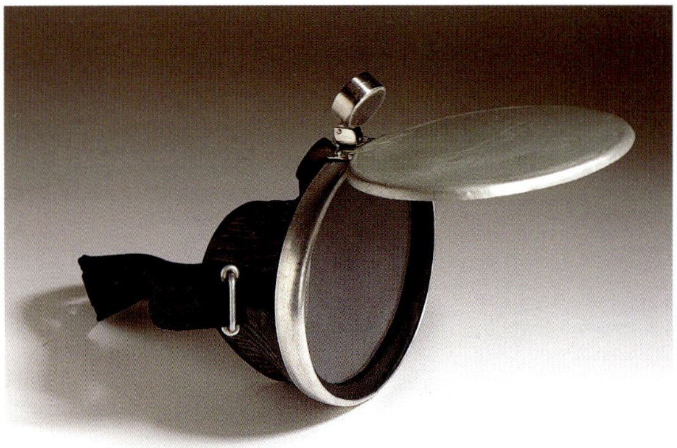

Brugaters i algòlegs 1980
(In the Undergrowth, in the Algae)
Underwater goggles. 14 x 15 x 16 cm.
Action in which the artist dove into the sea with the mask on to observe the algae and, before leaving the water, flipped down the cover. Accompanied by a friend, the artist was driven to a dense and humid forest in the heart of Montnegre with his eyes covered. Once there, he flipped up the cover to look at the vegetation, as if the underwater greenery and the forest undergrowth were connected realities.

10. The Painting Recorded on The Body

In this process of instrumentalization, there are works which appear to be tools whose function is imprecise. These tools may be considered technical prostheses of vision. The textual metaphors which appear throughout Perejaume's writings are very often sustained empirically by virtue of these prostheses.
Brugaters i algòlegs (In the Undergrowth, in the Algae, 1980; p. 144) is nothing more than a diver's face mask that has been tampered with and which is worn in a series of settings ranging from the seabed to the mountains, all of them characteristic of Perejaume's output in the late 1970s. These immersions and transitions in the landscape, accomplished by literary means in the poems *Oli damunt paper* (Oil on Paper, 1978-1981), complement one another in the space of demonstration. Without there being a user's manual handy, this object invites us to make a series of hypotheses in order that we might accord it value in terms of its function, rather that an aesthetic value. Covered by a visor that blocks forward vision, it seems likely that this mask was used by someone to experience a contiguous vision of the seabed and of wooded ravines. That much is suggested, at least, by another painting from the same period in which a lighthouse emerges from among the shade trees (*Far emboscat* [Lighthouse in the Woods], 1980; p. 43). The mask's visor darkens the field of vision, and this manipulation of vision thus serves to disorient the user, disrupting his or her sense of place.[21] In the same period, Perejaume wrote verses such as the following: "Visc en el mar, però d'un aigua tan/antiga, que fingeix plans i pujols" ("I live in the sea, but the water is so/old that it feigns plains and hills").[22]
In some sense, this kind of darkening may be associated with a highly unorthodox pictorial technique: that of telepathic painting, which Michelangelo Pistoletto describes in his book *L'uomo nero* (1970). Pistoletto explains his experiences of telepathic painting, and how he would invite visitors to his exhibition to lie on a mattress on the floor of the gallery. Together, visitors and artist closed their eyes. Pistoletto then spoke the following words:

"Now the transmission of telepathic painting will begin. Close your eyes, everyone, and I'll create ecstatic, kinetic paintings — colours, lights, and drawings against the blackened backdrop of my closed eyes. You will see my works against the screens of your closed eyes."[23]

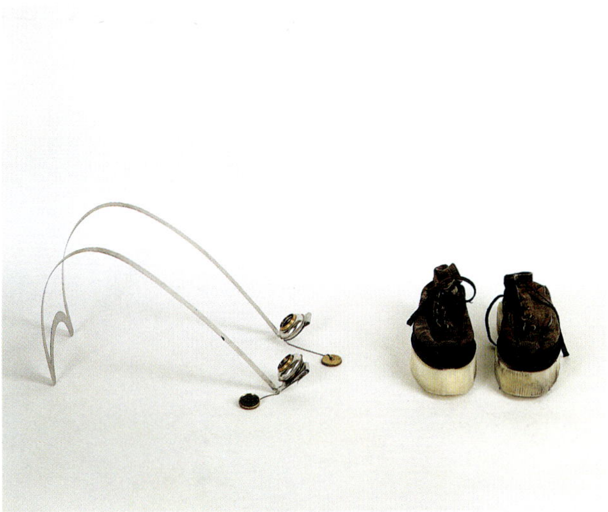

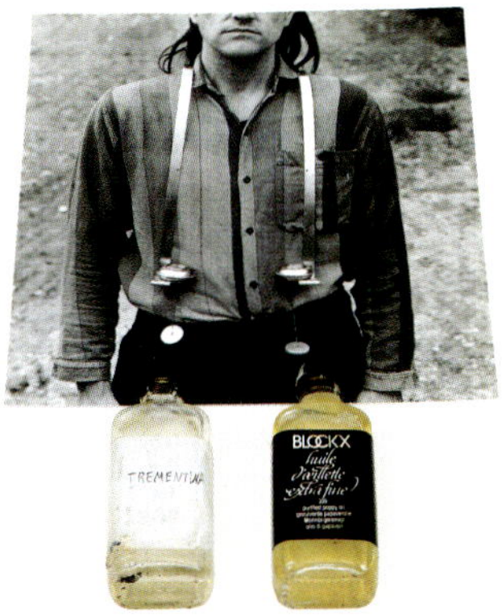

Simulador de pintura 1993
(Painting Simulator)
Cruets to be worn while walking in order to smell turpentine and linseed oil. Foam rubber-soled boots which give the sensation of treading on paint-like ground.

Actions of this kind, which Pistoletto often performed in collaboration with his troupe “Lo Zoo”, enable us to speak of a return to painting that has nothing to do with the return to painting which took place in the 1980s. Furthermore, these examples of Perejaume's and Pistoletto's enable vision and performance to discern painting. Dismantled as a genre and later reconstructed, painting will never be the same.

The performance sought by such tools as the mask mentioned above turns the body into the locus of a process of phenomenological proof. The last proof consists in causing the senses to believe in the fiction which Perejaume's works build up. *Simulador de pintura* (Painting Simulator, 1993; p. 145) — like the mask, an example of play with tools — modifies one's interpretation of reality. As the *Simulador*'s subtitle states, “cruets to be worn while walking in order to smell turpentine and linseed oil” and “foam rubber-soled boots which give the sensation of treading on paint-like ground”. This jump from stating method to performance does not undo the spell under which the artist willingly works: rather, it seals it. The soundness of this pictorial vision of reality depends on perception. From this point of view, the illusion of autonomy which painting appeared to have achieved was, in fact, a contamination of the autonomy of the landscape.

In light of this, it is the fate of painting to be recorded on the body. The repertory of gestures which denote painting — hand shading eyes, the gesture of silence, or the gesture which holds painting (*Pinzellades* [Brushstrokes], 1992; p. 70) constitutes a gestural inscription, just as abstract expressionist painting came down to the transcendental enacting of gestures. The performance depicted in the photograph entitled *La soprano Maria Dolors Aldea interpretant la pintura* (The Soprano Maria

Gran emmarcatge (Aureolació ocular) 1998
(Great Framing (Ocular Aureola))
Gold. ø 4 cm.

Dolors Aldea Performing Painting, 1994; p. 71) presents a repertory of gestures which evoke its reception, as had been the case in the *Simulador de pintura*. The body repeats painting as a series of grimaces until painting comes to be fixed ergonomically. In this aspect, therefore, in addition to the unfolding in territory discussed above, there also takes place a re-folding.

The last of these possible re-foldings was consummated in the form of two golden receptacles for vision. It is thus that, at either end of a line of similar tools, we find the mask of *Brugaters i algòlegs* and we have the framed eyes of *Gran emmarcatge* (Great Framing, 1998; p. 147). These two framed eyeballs de-territorialize vision and separate it from the body. As Jonathan Crary says, "[visual experience] is given an unprecedented mobility and exchangeability, abstracted from any founding site or referent." [24]

But this apparent reductionism conceals the vastest of spaces in order that the distance between these two eyes might be stretched as wide as one should like. The space which opens up between the eyes embraces a set of techniques of spatial dilation. Thus, two conceptions of space, one of closed and one of open space, come face to face in this kind of practice. For a post-modern geographer such as David Harvey, these two conceptions effectively challenge the belief that there is a time and a place for everything. [25] In this sense, Perejaume has disentangled the extreme localization of the system of art. It was for this reason that he and a group of students carried a Miró to the top of a mountain (*Un miró al Planell d'Uja* [A Miró Painting at the Uja Plain], 1990; p. 20), and that he led a Hodler, a Lorca and a Picabia through a series of urban and natural itineraries (1996); the effect produced, on both occasions, was exotic. The natural oppositions of space were subjected to a productive friction. Thus, unbound from that discursive apparatus which protects them, these paintings came to be adapted to a kind of writing based orography, on the fact and study of relief in the land and the contour lines which represent it. This gives rise to a kind of expanded writing which, in the end, has come to form the base of Perejaume's most recently formulated methods: oism [26] (*L'autor encebant la tinta en un vessant del Montnegre* [The Artist Priming Ink on the Slopes of Montnegre], 1998; p. 148). [27]

11. Autonomous Landscape

The publication of *Oïsme: Una escriptura natural a partir del croquis pirinencs de Jacint Verdaguer* (1998) has marked the reinvention of Perejaume's career. The fiction which had constituted the setting of his work thus takes on yet another layer. Perejaume's alter ego, the plenairist, appears in this fiction, his body covered with branches (p. 151) The landscape and its observer are fused, just as painting cloaked the body of the soprano with gestures.

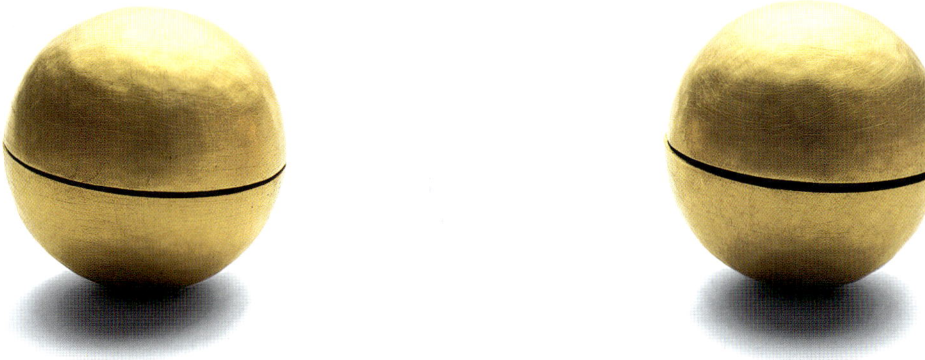

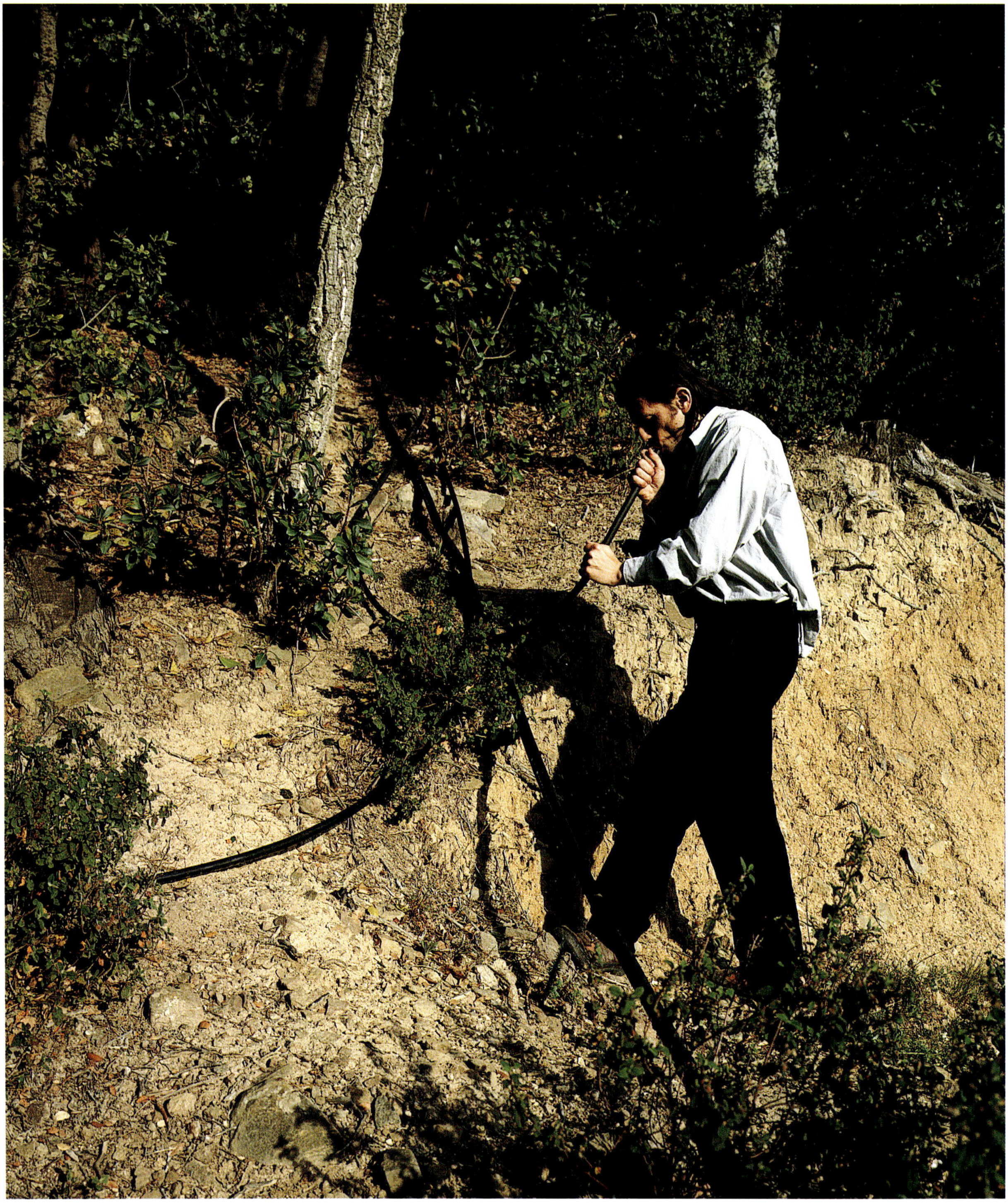

L'autor encebant la tinta en un vessant del Montnegre 1998
(The Artist Priming Ink on the Slopes of Montnegre)
Photograph

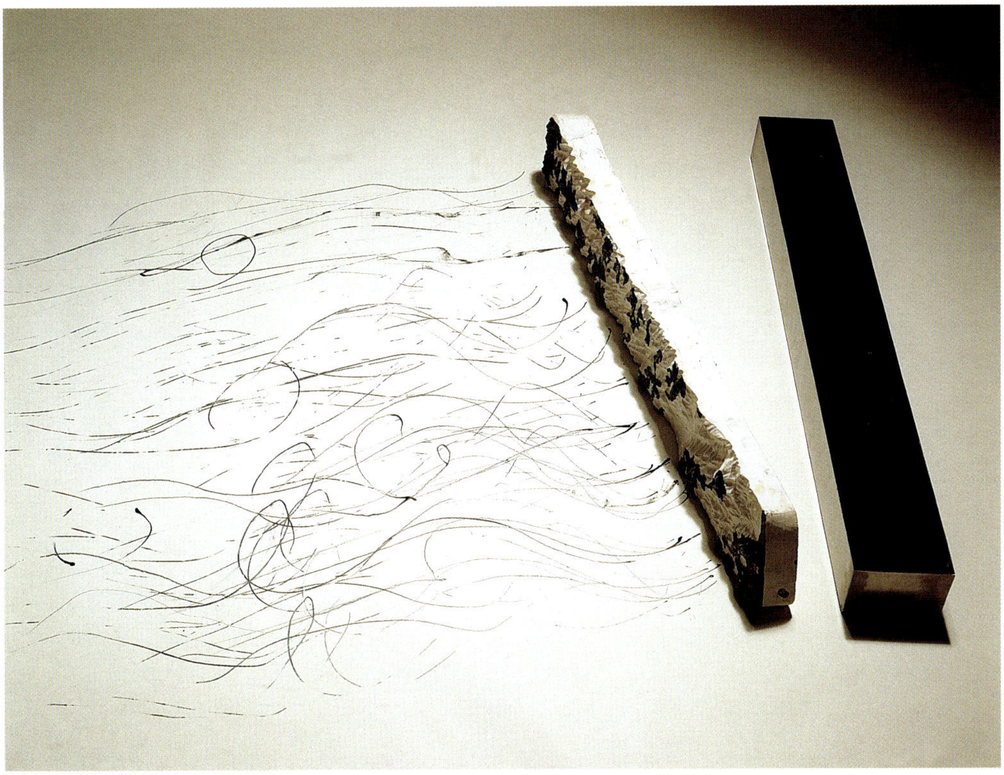

Entintar els pics, escriure amb el Pirineu 1998
(Ink the Peaks, Write with the Pyrenees)
Chalk, ink and paper. 131 x 270 x 15 cm.

Apart from the formulation, visualization and demonstration which these methods comprise, there exists another component, which forms part of the method itself. By this I mean an illusion of passivity which is nonetheless productive, as when Perejaume set out "to dis-exhibit". The artist thus gave up his own capacity to produce. Perejaume surrendered modern artists' much-vaunted autonomy to the landscape. In fact, he returned a statute of autonomy which modern art — when it mirrored itself in Romanticism's understanding of landscape as creative — had believed to be its own. From that moment on, Perejaume became a spectator subjugated to the independent life of the territory.
By means of this concession, the artist has achieved an inversion of the process of production. Unpainting is, together with its variants, doubtless the method best able to foster this. The reversibility of process (*Desescultura* [Unsculpture], 1991) provides the spectacle of repetition, like the instant replay of televised sports, as well as providing an ecological compensation and restitution. [28] We said earlier that 'layings-down' redeem culture; we are now able to state that repetition holds out the promise of revealing an absence, which is of an order at once material and moral. To use a cinematic model: the machine of nature may withdraw beyond the reach of any human intervention. Afterwards, this machine would take charge of repeating the landscape until it produces a second nature. It is this kind of repetition which leads to that which Perejaume has called *Tedi museogràfic* (Museographic Tedium, 1997; p. 216), a sort of calculated boredom belonging to an image factory . The model of nature's productive autonomy is thus the most appropriate model to take the place of the model of a Romantic creator. The fact that characters appearing in Caspar David Friedrich's landscapes stand with their backs to the observer is not entirely irrelevant here. They are workers in nature's factory. By contemplating nature, they produce nature.
What this entails is a shift in the locus of production, which is now set in nature. Indeed, the notion of the artist's studio has never been especially relevant for Perejaume. It is rather the plenairist, the protagonist of the fiction which sustains Perejaume's works, that marks the territory of production with his incursions. It is this character who comes and goes to the factory of nature.
The linguistic and cognitive inversion which the forming of this image of the landscape has entailed brings Perejaume face to face with a complex machine. As Toni Negri has written, "nothing would be more false than to pretend that the determinations of this machine are *natural* in the true sense of the word." [29] From this perspective, the immediate opposition between exploitative reason and nature is mitigated. The installation entitled *A imatge i semblança* (In Image and Appearance, 1988; p. 12), along with the 1984 piece *Excavadora recollint postals* (Excavator Retrieving Postcards, 1983; p. 151), could lead to a denunciation of the aggressiveness of humanity's intervention in the landscape; in fact, the purpose accomplished is quite distinct. The excavator, though an evident sign

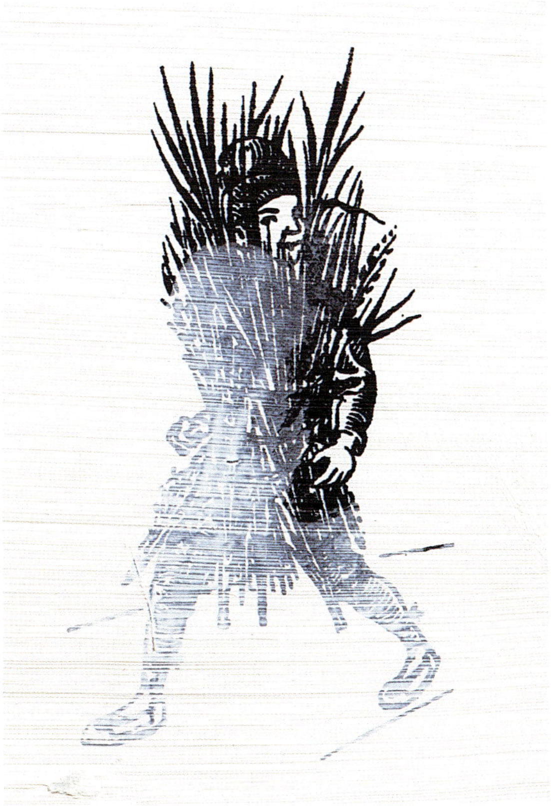

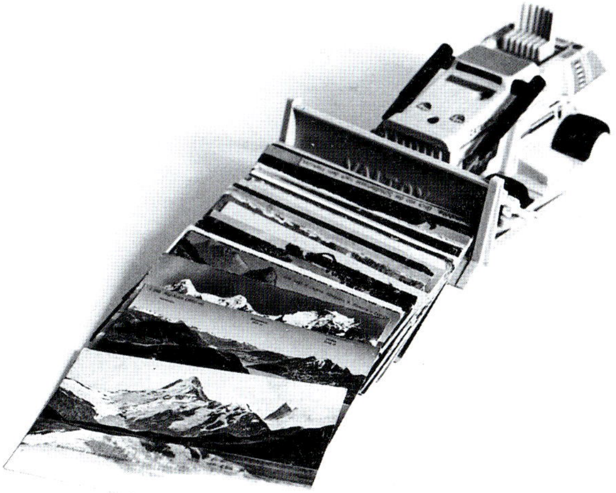

Excavadora recollint postals 1983
(Excavator Retrieving Postcards)
Toy excavator and postcards. 10 x 16 x 35 cm.

Pintor plenairista 1996
(Plenairist) Detail
Mixed media on paper. 30 x 42 cm.

of an attack on the landscape, works together with nature here as an extension of the machinery which defines and explains landscape. Landscape is not, from this perspective, outside the discourse of progress which machines symbolize.

Faced with the threatening possibility that this machinery might make him feel alienated, Perejaume has reproduced forms of emancipation. Oism entails the recovery of hearing as a sense which, given its historical marginalization, has acquired a certain degree of independence from sight. The sense of hearing's autonomy balances the acculturation of the sense of sight. Given that Perejaume's works had denied their own autonomy, though such autonomy is characteristic of modern artworks, his placing of hearing at the centre of forms of artistic production recovers the ideal of an emancipating practice. Another aspect of Perejaume's work which manifests this recovery is the appearance of homophones which, for some time now, have compensated for the lack of common logic in Perejaume's output.

For example, the term "pic-ment" (peak-ment) has appeared recently in the titles of works and brief texts by Perejaume. This neologism invokes "pigment" and the Catalan words for "peak" and "the mind", thus suggested both the lowliness of pigment and the greatest of the mind's peak. Once again, everything becomes a mountain.

Oism carries out this emancipation by criticizing sensorial naturalism. The destruction of synchrony between the signifier and the signified, between image and voice, leaves a gap in a space which seems compact. The invisibility of this fissure which Perejaume introduces is, however, a sign to us that this link is in and of itself an ideological and mental construct which must be made visible. It is only when it has been made visible that we shall realize that access to representation is denied. Just as painting had come to be seen on the body, this obstacle is experienced physically.

In dismounting the naturalism of the spectacle — which is based on illusory synchronies between voice, image, and gestures — the spaces pertaining to each of these senses initiate a process of segregation from one another. Thus, the Catalan word for a drawing, "dibuix", is deconstructed in a 1998 video entitled *Dir-buix* (Say-draw, 1998; p. 153), projected behind a glass wall. This title incorporates the verb "dir", meaning "to say". The viewer hears a voice, yet this voice emerges from the viewers side of the glass wall rather than from the space of the projection itself. At the same time, there appears in the video a mouth which moves as if to produce speech and yet it is mute. Sound and image emerge from different spaces, divided by a wall which triggers a neutralization of learnt correspondences. Shifts in point of view to the internal elements of representation, as was the case of those characters who looked upon Informalism from inside a painting (p. 51), or those appearing in *Olzinelles* (1988; p. 55), solve this problem in advance. This projection of the point of view into the interior of the space of representation nonetheless betrays the fact that this space — despite an illusion of transparency and accessibility — is impenetrable. We may only come to see through another gaze which is already anchored in the field of representation. This projection repeats the gesture Perejaume used to transfer autonomy to the landscape. Landscape will only speak from landscape, as though it were imitating the behaviour of a modern artist, reflexive and withdrawn into his or her own subjectivity (*Entintar els pics, escriure amb el Pirineu* [Ink the Peaks, Write with the Pyrenees], 1998; p. 149).

As Michael Fried has commented in a discussion of the theatricality of nineteenth-century French painting, "The Painting would be sealed in front as by an invisible wall."[30] This "invisible wall" materialised in an installation Perejaume realised at Girona's Teatre Municipal, *Retaule: Teatre Muncipal de Girona. De com posar vidre al marc d'un escenari* (Retable: Girona Municipal Theatre. How to Put Glass on a Stage Proscenium, 1997; p. 98-99). The inaccessibility of the stage of performance tells us that if a recovery is intended, it belongs to the world of fiction and of spectacle. Thus, if it is nature that is represented, it will surely be a second nature. And if we should insist on finding "nature", we will discover that it has "chosen to hide".[31] It was this that the series of layings-down discussed earlier in this essay essentially demonstrated. The advantage of recognizing this second nature comes, of course, from the consequent ability to identify a second vision, as when we re-view a film. In this second viewing will always be able to find a different meaning from that which we saw at first. It is not that our vision has gained in depth; rather, it has been corrected.

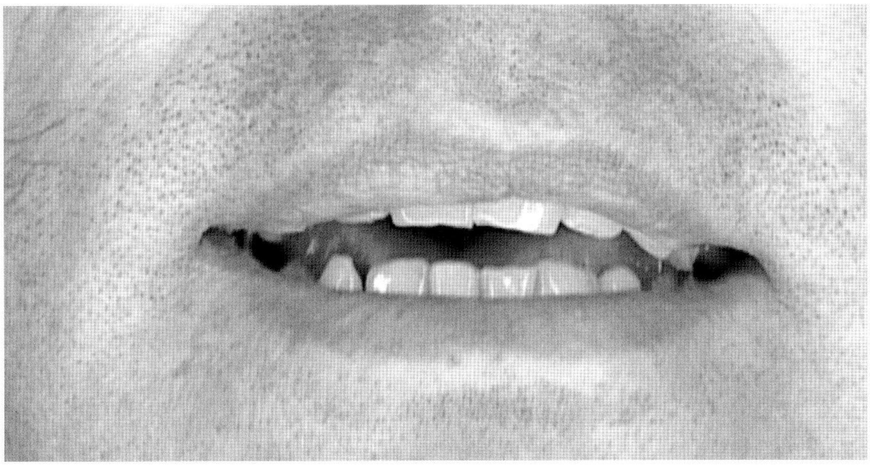

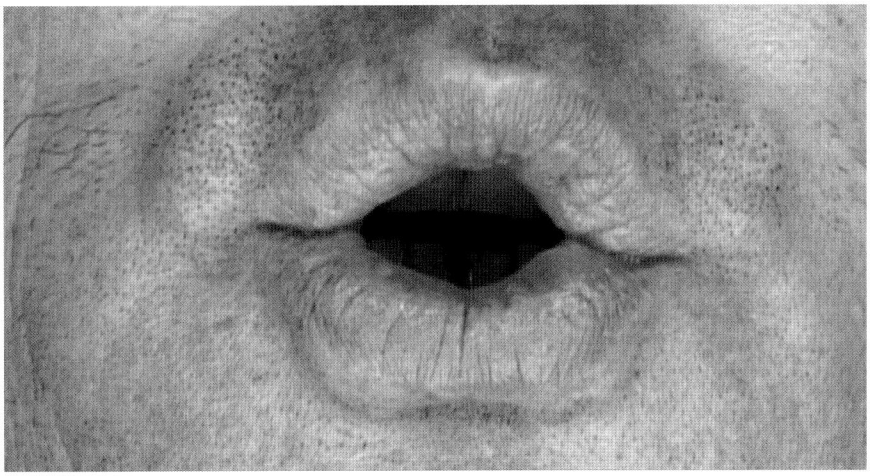

Dir-buix 1998
Say-draw
Video

1 This photograph seems to draw on another Perejaume's work, *Tres vailetes* (1993), which contains a photograph of Consol Boquera (the model appearing in Joan Miró's *Retrat d'una vaileta*) with a pile of paint on her skirt. The latter image reproduces both *La vaileta* and a fragment of *Allegory: Venus, Cupid, Folly, and Time*, a painting by Agnolo Bronzino. Plates of *Els tossals* and *Tres vailetes* are included in Perejaume's *El Pirineu de baix: Mont-roig, Miró, Mallorca.* Barcelona: Edicions Polígrafa, 1997.
2 Perejaume, *Ludwig-Jujol. Què és collage, sinó acostar soledats?* Barcelona: Edicions de la Magrana, 1989, p. 84.
3 This illustration appears in the prologue to a book by Perejaume, *El paisatge és rodó.* Vic: Eumo Editorial, 1995.
4 While it is true that we could link Perejaume to the milieu of the Catalan art group Dau al Set, we should realize that by continuing this contextualization, we would be completing the paradox. Nonetheless, we would do well to consider the situation of the political and artistic avant-gardes in Catalonia in the mid-1970s if we are to interpret Perejaume's position in that period, at the beginning of his career.

Dau al Set was one of the few attempts to renew contacts with the avant-garde on a collective level in the Barcelona of the post-Civil War years. The heterogeneity of the aesthetics which comprised Dau al Set's effort to re-animate modernity in the city's art circles had an effect which did not go beyond a strictly local level. Antoni Tàpies, who came to be well known outside Spain from the early 1950s on, constitutes the exception to this. In the absence of open communication with other countries, most of the output in the period was marked by introspection. Not surprisingly, Dau al Set produced variants of Surrealism and aesthetic derivations from Abstract Expressionism. Perejaume's early work could also be read in terms of this background.

Of course, in retrospect it seems surprising that we should have to link Perejaume to art produced immediately after the Spanish Civil War. Meanwhile, other artists such as Antoni Tàpies, Albert Ràfols Casamada, Josep Guinovart, Joan Hernández Pijuan, Pilar Palomer, and Frederic Amat, often considered to make up the "second Catalan avant-garde", fell within the traditions of Informalism or of Abstraction (see Daniel Giralt-Miracle, "L'art català de la posguerra", in *La seconda avanguardia catalana* [Vallechi, 1979]). In the mid-1970s, the somewhat surrealist tone of Perejaume's paintings combined informalist surfaces with scenes reminiscent of Max Ernst's engravings in *Une semaine de bonté* (1934). It is likewise possible to see in Perejaume's works the influence of nineteenth-century Catalan landscape painting. These two influences, the local and the international, come to be fused in these landscapes in such a way that the limits of each one cannot be discerned.

In all of these pictures there is a magical air that takes on more importance than does the equally present Informalist tendency. With the appearance of small figures incrusted on the painted surface, there also appears an element which interrupts contemplation. In paintings such as *En un racó de món* (In Some Place in the World, 1979), the narrative presence of such characters deactivates the strictly visual dimension of the painting. This aspect shows the affinity existing between Perejaume and the poet Joan Brossa, a member of Dau al Set. In this sense, Perejaume absorbed a literary vein which appears translated in both his visual works and in the books he has been putting out since 1989. This is so much so that it may seem that Perejaume's starting point is a text.

This operation consists, then, in consigning Informalism to the background of the picture in such a way that it should participate in the action, thus releasing its transcendental character. By withdrawing the textures of Informalist paintings, Perejaume caused mountains to appear in his landscapes. Whatever the case, by the end of the 1970s Informalism had ceased to be a heroic practice and had become a synonym for modern refinement. From the perspective of Perejaume's practice, Informalism would seem to have been continued literarily. Thus, it passed into the realm of fiction. Informalism began then, for Perejaume, a new life as a natural territory.
5 Alexander Cirici Pellicer, "Perejaume i la seva poesia", in *Perejaume: Olis i objectes*, exhibition catalogue; Barcelona: Galeria Joan Prats, 1980.
6 Vicenç Altaió, "Visita guiada o abans existí la impremta que l'escriptura", in *A 2000 metres de pintura sobre el nivell del mar*, exhibition catalogue; Tarragona: Tinglado 2, 1988; p. 24.
7 "[T]he Museum as a storehouse of the unique object has turned into an archive." Quoted in Maria Gough, "In the Laboratory of Constructivism: Karl Ioganson's Cold Structures", in *October* 84 (Spring 1988), p. 114.
8 Cirici Pellicer 1980.
9 Both Freud and Robinson Crusoe distribute these attribution along the two axes. The natural is associated with the horizontal axis; culture, with the vertical. To this characterisation of the axes we might add a meaning adapted to the field of vision. Indeed, Hubert Damisch has stated that the scopic drive and the drive to civilize go together (see Hubert Damisch, *The Judgment of Pâris* trans. John Goodman, Chicago: University of Chicago Press, 1996. In fact, as much is suggested in Freud's *Civilisation and its Discontents*, New York: W. W. Norton, 1962; translated from the German and edited by James Strachey.), in which he plots the process of humanization between one and the other axis. According to Freud, the conquest of verticality (and hence of culture) is followed by a 'redemption'. The most immediate parallel with the laying-down of the postcard rack in *Postaler* is, however, Rosalind Krauss's analysis of Jackson Pollock' decodifications. This analysis earmarks Eva Hesse's shapeless sculptures, Robert Morris' fallen felt, Andy Warhol's urine-rusted paintings, and Carl Andre's bricks on the ground, and classes them as successors to Pollock's gesture, which brought painting up from the ground onto the wall. According to Krauss, all these works have the effect of returning Pollock's vertical plane of painting to the plane on which it had been originally produced. If painting sublimated, then these works desublimate. In the psychoanalytical map onto which Krauss plots her thesis, this gesture should reveal the lowliness of that which would later come to be Pollock's painting when it is hung for exhibition (Rosalind Krauss. *The Optical Unconscious.* Cambridge, MA: MIT Press, 1993. p. 276).

Of course, to insist on this parallel would be to fall into an anachronism. The photograph in *Postaler* was taken in 1984, while the text in which Rosalind Krauss discussed these decodifications dates from 1993. The fallen postcard rack could, nonetheless, be added to the list which Krauss proposes. This tucking-in may be understood as a gesture shared by many practices employed in the second half of the twentieth century. Yet we must seek out the background against which *Postaler* and other works appear.

10 This Catalan term was first used in an English-language text by the art critic and translator Jeffrey Swartz in his prologue to *El grado de verdad de las representaciones* (Madrid: Galería Soledad Lorenzo, 1991; pp. 43-44). In that text, Swartz both explains Perejaume's highly individual use in his own writing of pessebrism (derived from *pessebre*, meaning 'creche' or 'nativity scene') and his own decision to naturalise it typographically by foregoing the italic typeface to which loan words are normally consigned. I have followed Swartz's practice. As for the place of pessebres in Catalan popular culture, "Such scenes include additional, often lightly irreverent representations of rural life and customs. From inside each house, then, the pessebre serves to exteriorise the onlooker's vision, setting up a miniaturised scenographic transference; a piece of cork bark becomes a mountain range; a few twigs create a forest; a chunk of moss is a pasture". (Swartz, p. 43)

Quoting Perejaume, Swartz goes on to say that "every rock or tree 'is an opening with worlds folded into it'. That is what pessebrism is all about" (43). [Translator's note.]

11 Perejaume, *Em giro a mirar*, exhibition catalogue; Sabadell: Museu d'Art, 1986. Also published in Perejaume, *La pintura i la boca*, Barcelona: Edicions de la Magrana, 1993, p. 20.

12 *Perejaume, Mont-blanc, Mont-roig, Mont-negre*, catalogue for an exhibition entitled "Perejaume"; Barcelona: Galeria Joan Prats, 1990, p. 24 (my italics).

13 Raymond Roussel, *Impressions of Africa.* London: Calder, 1983, trans. Lindy Foord and Rayner Heppenstall.

14 Robert Smithson, "A Museum of Language in the Vicinity of Art" in *The Writings of Robert Smithson*, ed. Nancy Holt, New York: New York University Press, 1979, p. 67.

15 Carles Guerra, "The Only Thing that Knows its Own Essence is the Thing Itself: An Interview with Lawrence Weiner" in *Cave Canis*, Barcelona, Spring 1996. A Catalan-language translation of this interview appears in the same issue.

16 Salvador Dalí, "Prólogo a la edición original francesa" in *El mito trágico del "Angelus" de Millet*, Tusquets Editores, Barcelona 1983, p. 15.

17 See Christoph Menke, *The Sovereignty of Art: Aesthetic Negativity in Adorno and Derrida*, trans. Neil Solomon. Cambridge, MA, and London: MIT Press, 1998.

18 Dalí 1983, pp. 15-18.

19 Terry Eagleton, *Walter Benjamin, or Towards a Revolutionary Criticism.* London and New York: Verso, 1981, p. 106.

20 "Les premiers principes doivent être hors de discussion." Isidore Ducasse, Count of Lautréamont. I encountered this in the following Spanish edition: *Poesías*, trans. Ángel Pariente. Seville: Renacimiento, 1998, pp. 17-18.

21 This disorientation might very well constitute a gloss on what we might call a tradition of lost poets. In texts such as *Nadja* (New York: Grove, 1960; translated by Richard Howard.) and *Cròniques de l'ultrason* (Barcelona: Quaderns Crema, 1996; edited by Jaume Vallcorba), both André Breton and the twentieth-century Catalan poet J. V. Foix allowed themselves to be led, eyes half-closed, by mysterious female characters, in order to reach an unknown place. The characteristically surrealist unlearning by which one is surprised anew by something familiar is thus added to the economy of representation which characterizes Perejaume.

22 Perejaume, *Oli damunt paper.* Barcelona: Edicions Empúries, 1992, p. 49.

23 "Maintenant commence la transmission de peinture télépathique, tout le monde ferme les yeux, je vais créer dans l'espace noir de mes yeux fermés, des tableaux, couleurs lumières dessins, statiques et en mouvement. Vous verrez mes travaux sur l'écran de vos yeux fermés." Michelangelo Pistoletto, *L'homme noir, le côte insupportable*, École Nationale Supérieure des Beaux-Arts, Paris, 1998, p. 35.

24 Jonathan Crary, *Techniques of the Observer: On Vision and Modernity in the Nineteenth Century.* Cambridge, MA, and London: MIT Press, 1990, p. 14.

25 David Harvey, *The Condition of Postmodernity.* Oxford: Blackwell, 1995.

26 This neologism appears to have been coined from the Catalan verb oir, meaning 'to hear'. Suggested translations include 'hearism' and 'hearingism'. As pessebrism has set a precedent, I have preferred to use oism rather than either of the English renderings suggested above. [Translator's note.]

27 This photograph appears in the appendix to Perejaume's *Oïsme: Un escriptura natural a partir dels croquis pirinencs de Jacint Verdaguer.* Barcelona: Proa, 1998.

28 "Put gold back into the earth, scatter the mountains with bronze and marble and ivory, so that they might represent just what we are missing most: the place from whence they came." Translated from Perejaume, "Torneu a posar", in *La pintura i la boca.* Barcelona: Edicions de la Magrana, 1993, p. 113.

29 Toni Negri, "De la fábrica a la máquina ecológica" in *Fin de siglo.* Barcelona: Paidós, 1992, p. 85. The English source text is *The Politics of Subversion: a Manifesto for the Twenty-First Century.* Cambridge: Polity, 1989.

30 Michael Fried, *Courbet's Realism*, Chicago and London: University of Chicago Press, 1979, p. 79.

31 Perejaume 1995, p. 13.

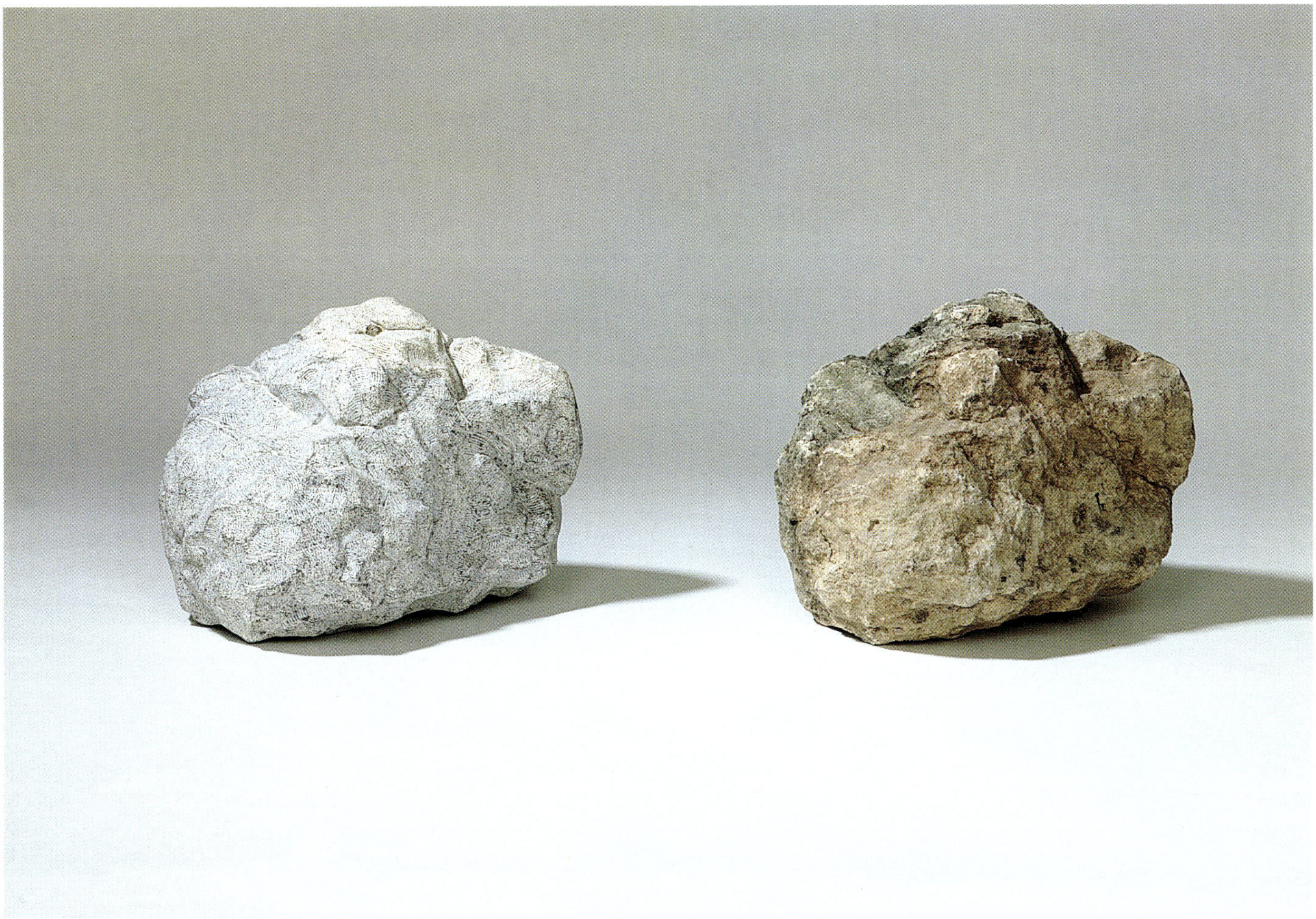

Natura i signatura 1990
(Nature and Signature)
Two stones. 32 x 32 x 35 cm. each

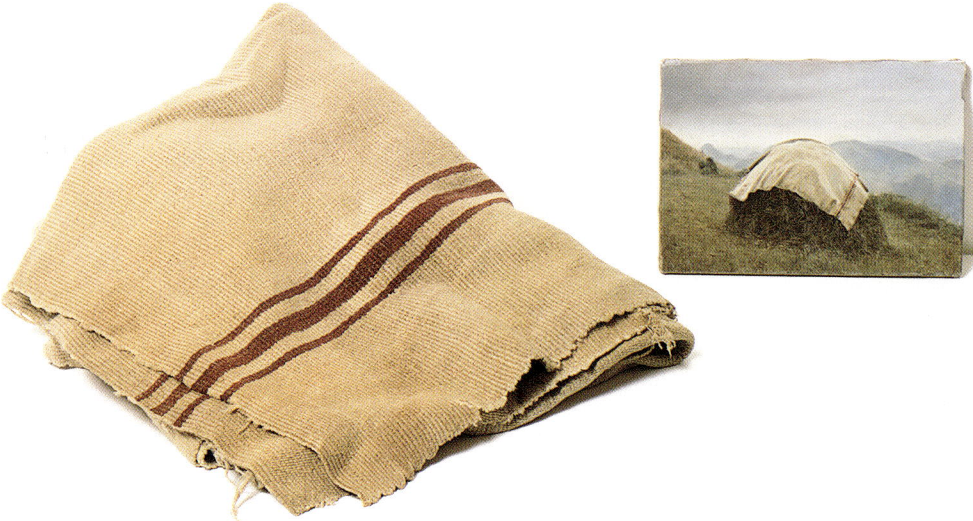

Dues teles 1988
(Two Cloths)
Oil on canvas and blanket. 24 x 35 cm.

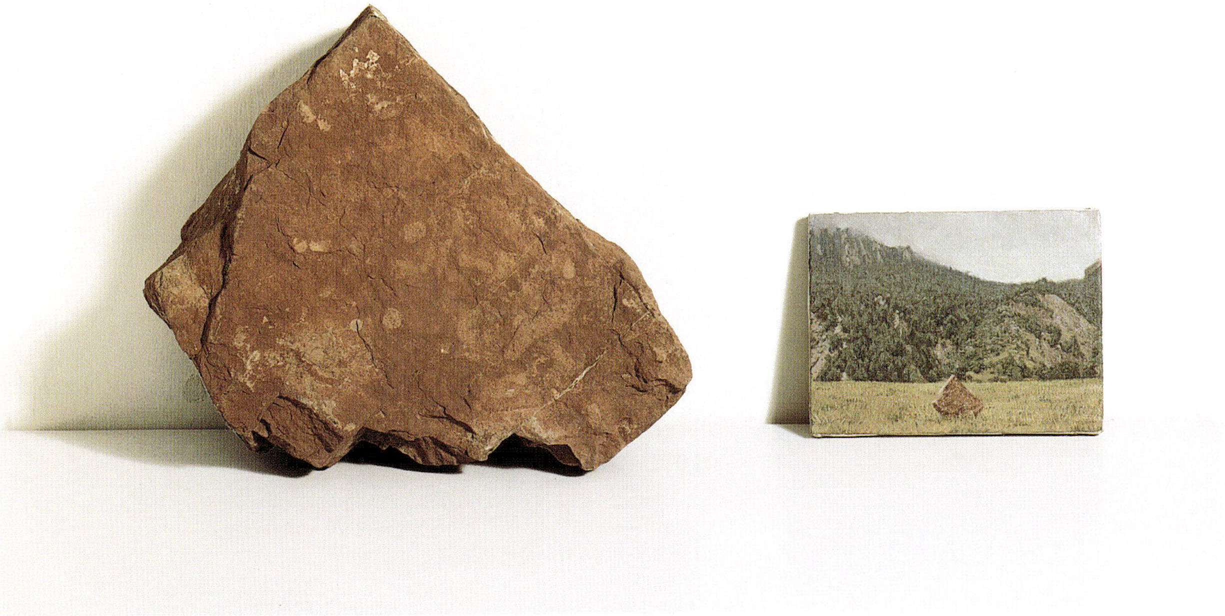

Marea II 1988
(Tide II)
Oil on canvas and stone. 24 x 32 cm.

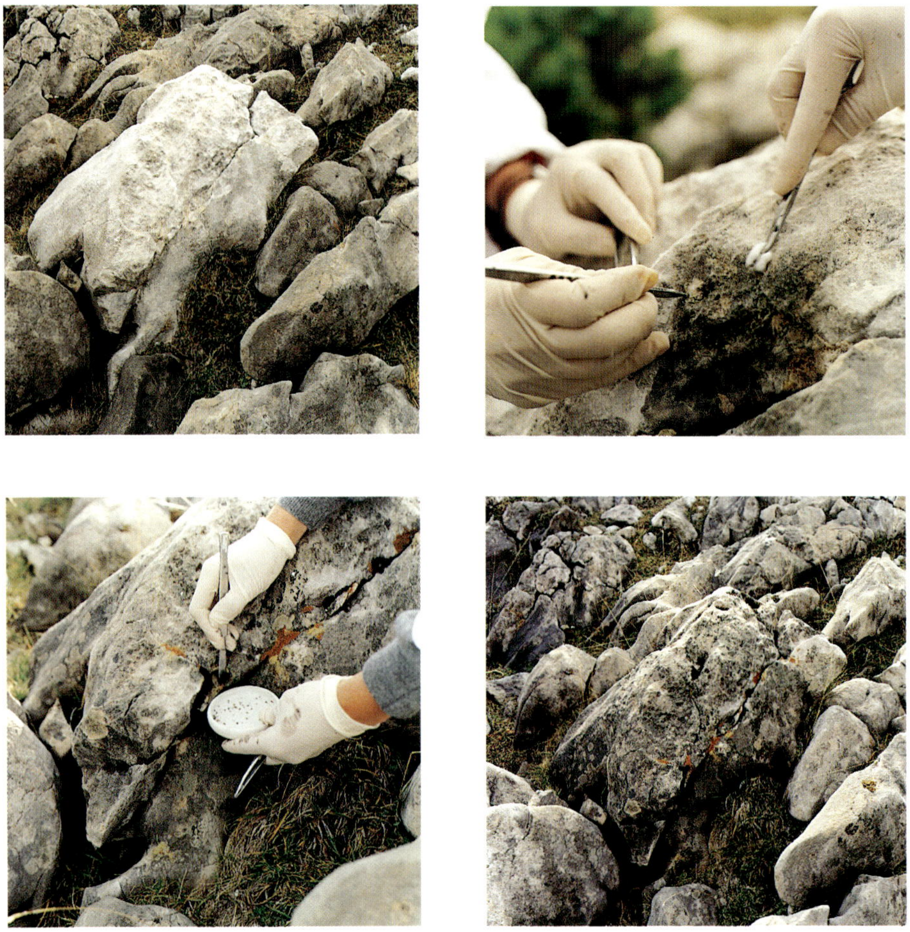

Restauració de dues pedres al Port del Comte (detall) 1995
(Restoration of Two Stones in Port del Comte (detail))
8 photographs. 50 x 50 cm. each

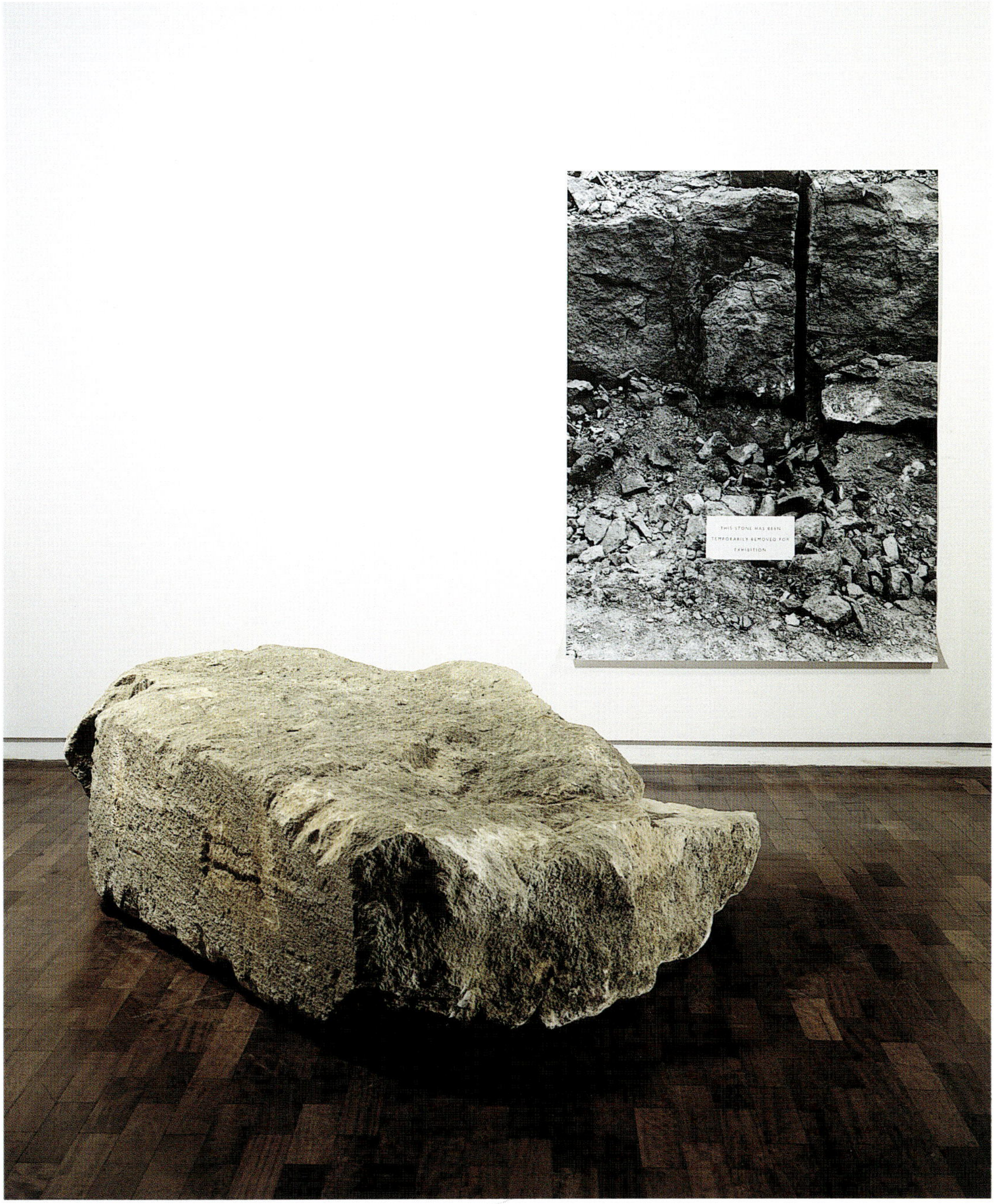

Obra en préstec 1993
(Work on Loan)
"This stone has been temporarily removed for exhibition" Arnolfini, Bristol.
stone 62 x 182 x 139 cm. and photograph 170 x 130 cm.

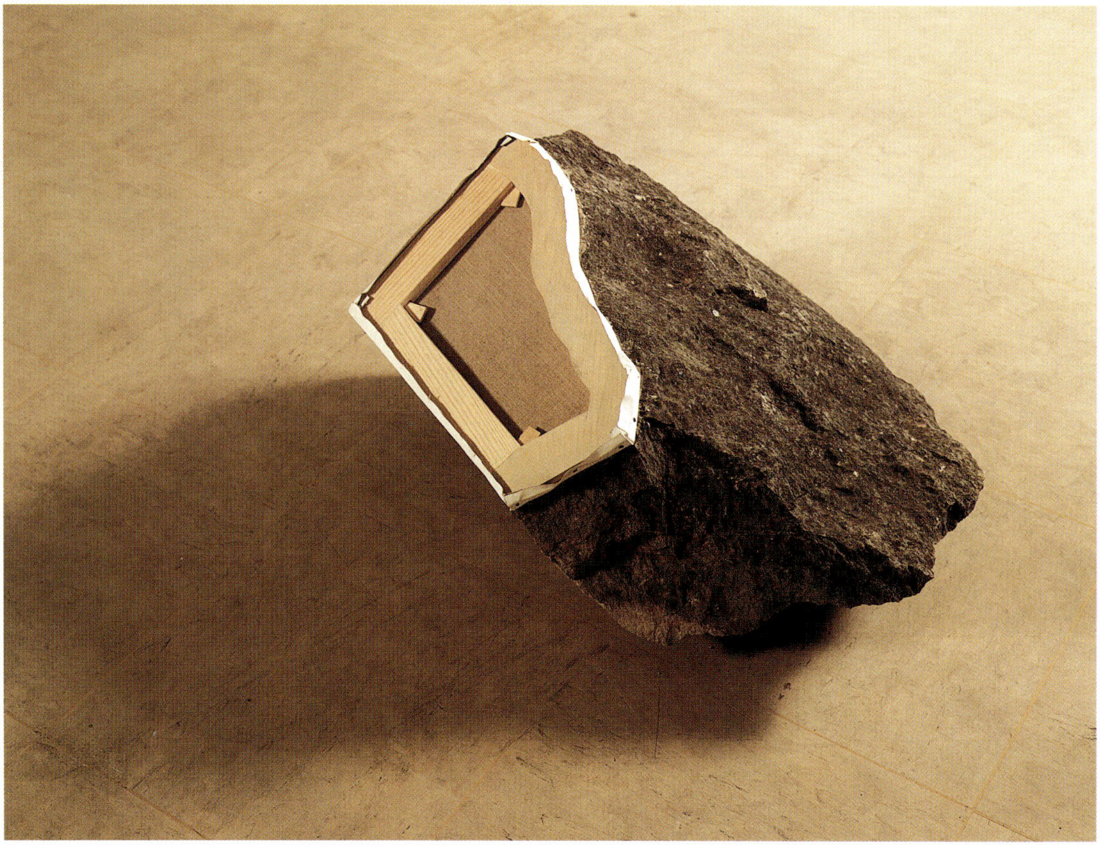

Diorama Neuschwanstein 1989
(Neuschwanstein Diorama)
Stretcher frame, canvas and stone. 50 x 70 x 90 cm.

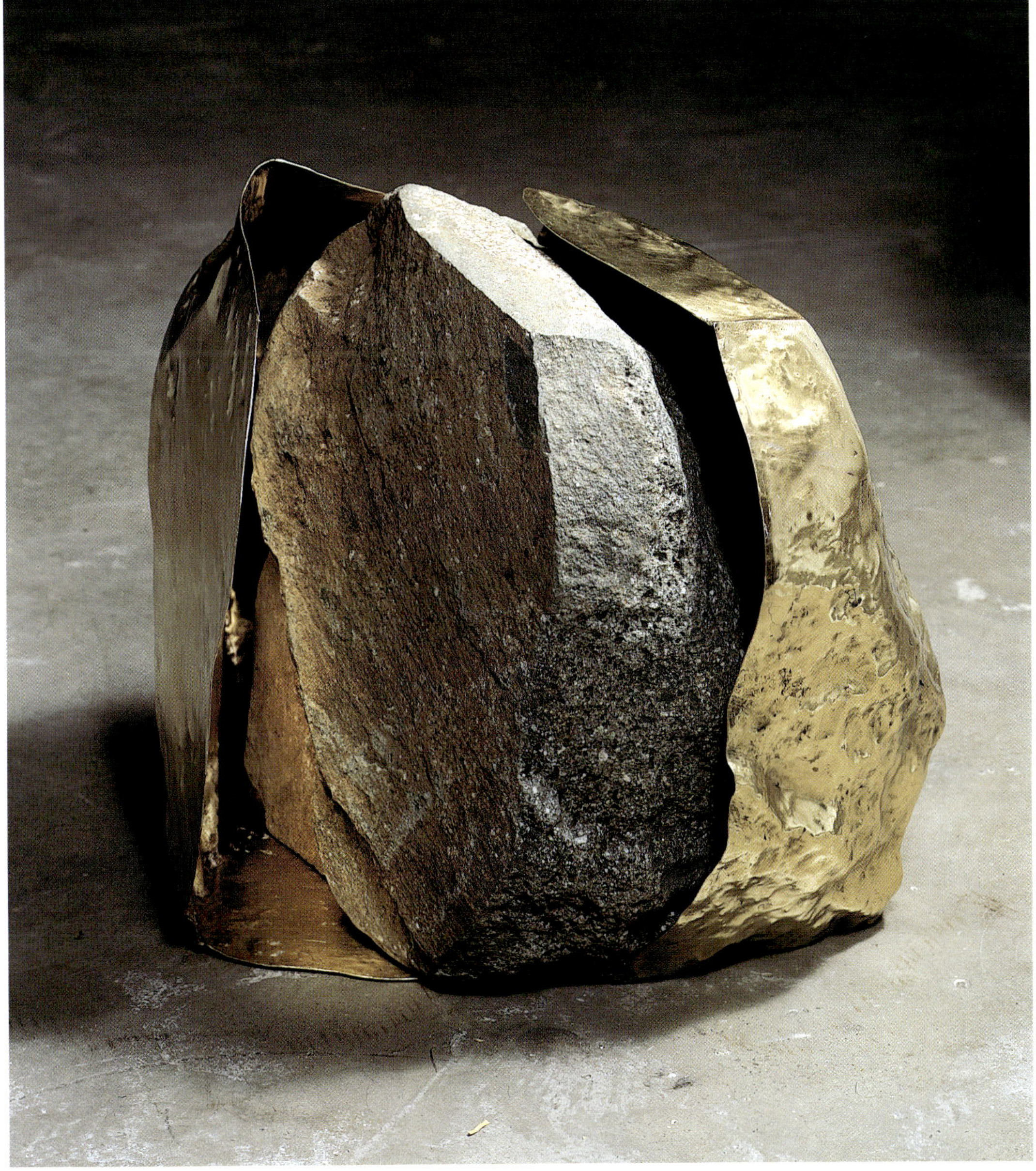

Can Poliva 1990
Stone and brass. 42 x 40 x 27 cm.

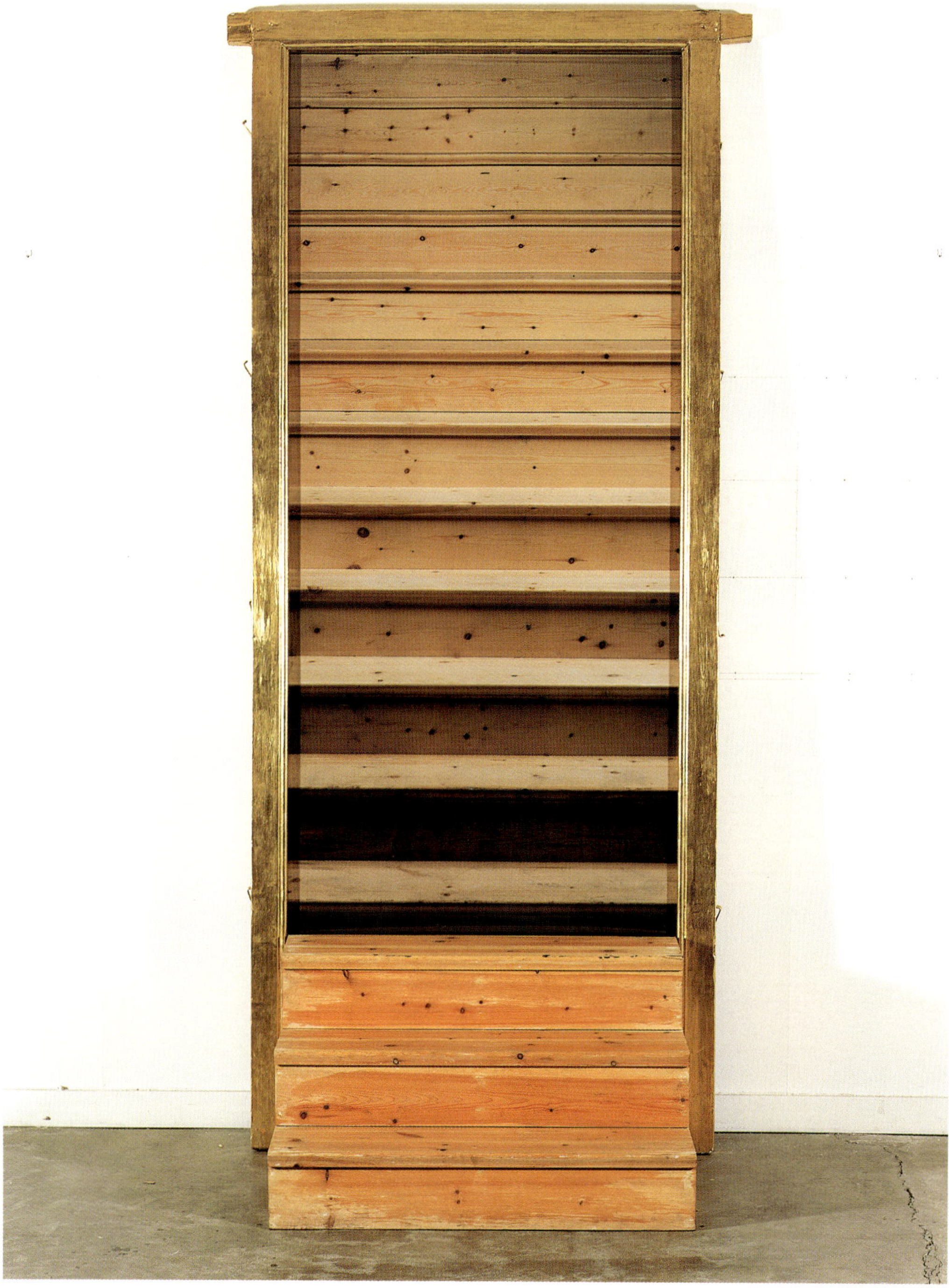

Portal amb escala 1993
(Door with Steps)
Photograph, wood, gold leaf and glass. 287 x 135 x 7 cm., 55 x 100 x 77 cm.

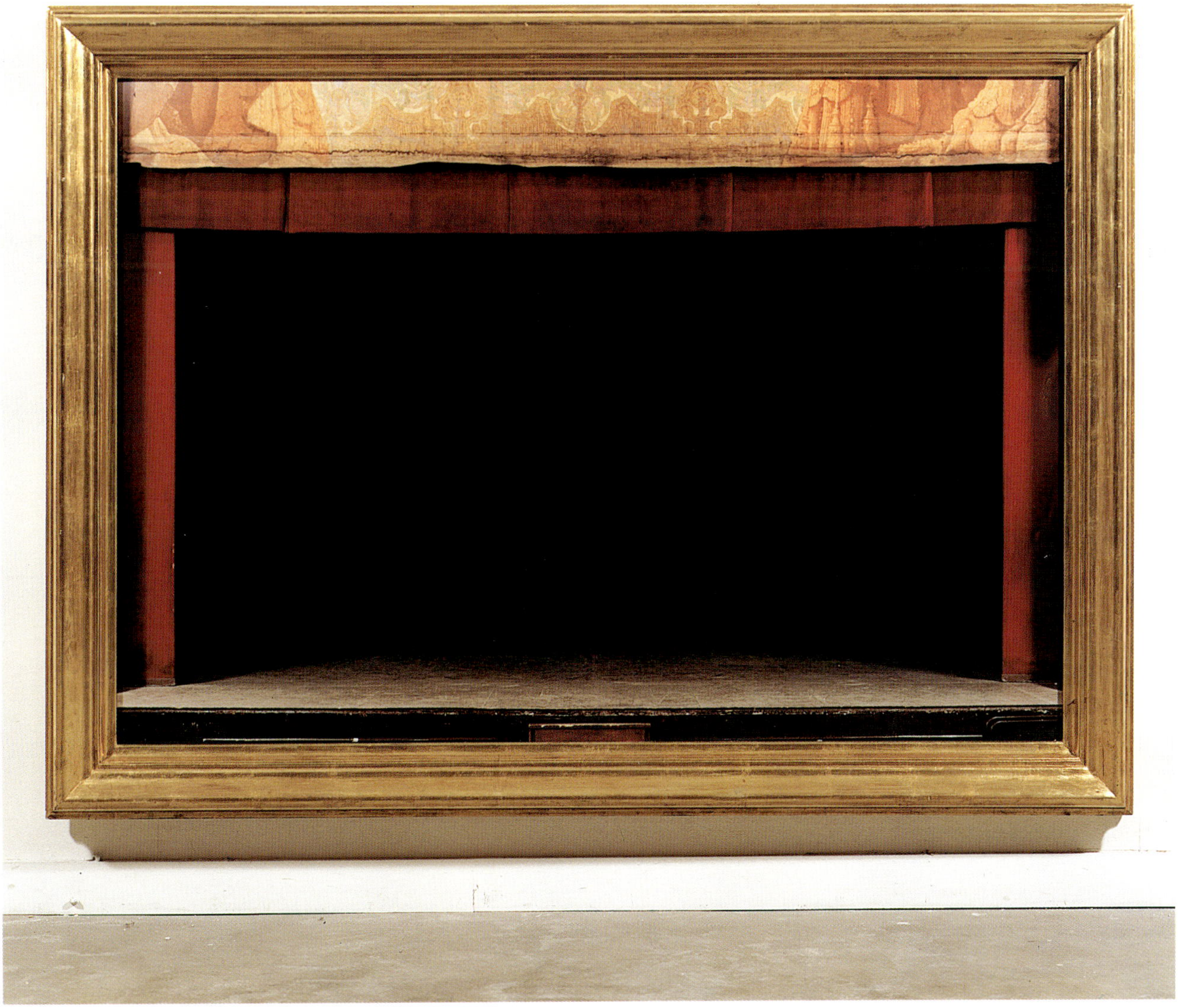

No és segur 1994
(It is not Sure)
Photograph, gilded frame and glass. 145 x 200.5 cm.

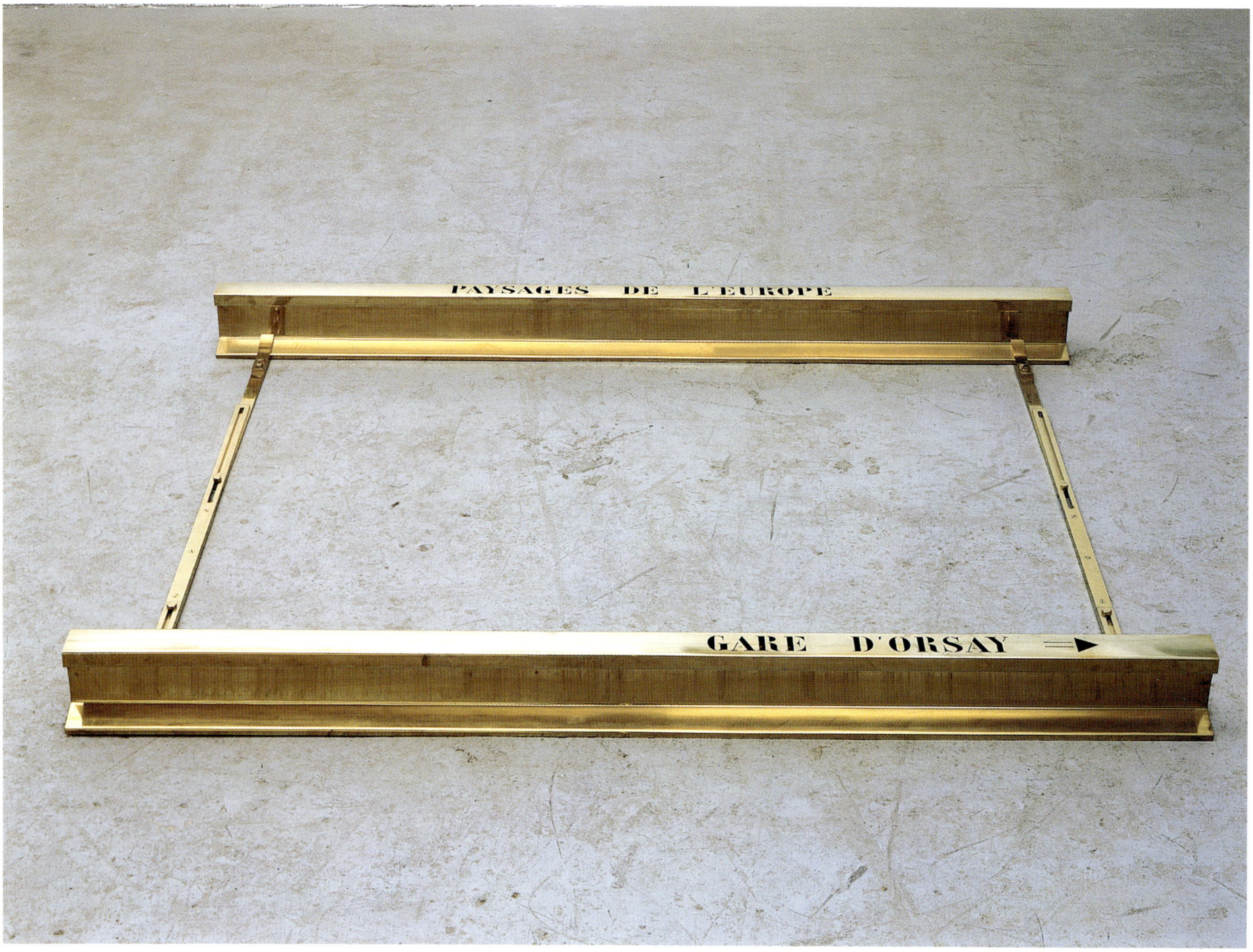

Paysages de l'Europe. Gare d'Orsay 1996
Brass. 15 x 200 x 186 cm.

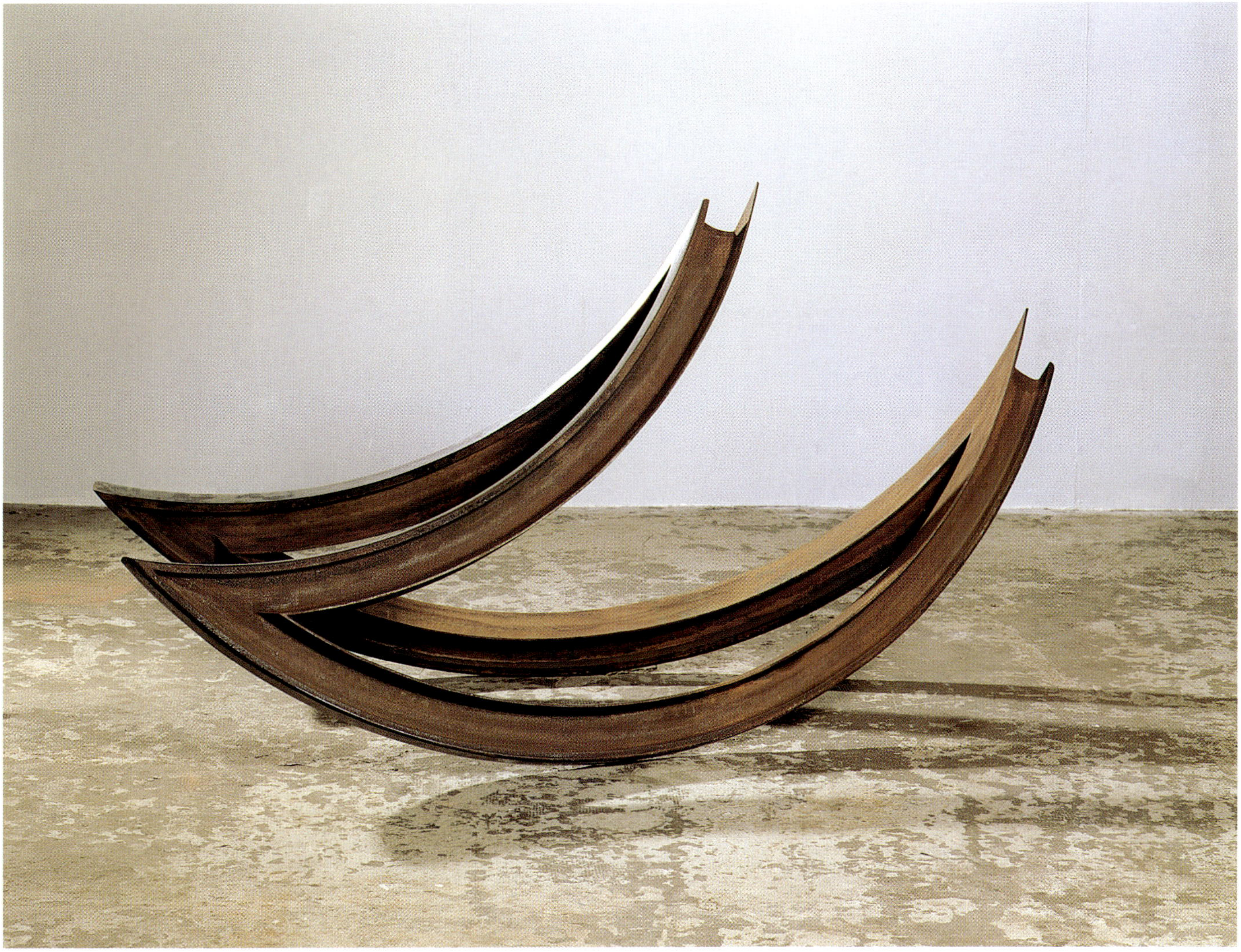

Trineu I 1989
(Sledge I)
Iron rails. 135 x 238 x 102 cm.

Perejaume's Writing

Pere Gimferrer

On the way to Ogassa we walked, in the midst of a loaf of low fog –"the soft bread of the fog", in words of J. V. Foix– enveloping the rustic nudity of the Romanesque chapel and the agrarian quietude of the livestock, just as powerful as any deep and all-absorbing lowing. The fog delivered the present-tense of an immemorial Beyond into our hands, the crystallization of a fossilized fir needle in the shape of a spontaneous poem-object, returning it to a cool and verdant clarity, set outside of time. But more than anything else on that summer afternoon in 1987 on our way to Mitjavila, it was the blinding light of the sun melting into the grass that struck our eyes and spirit most profoundly.

There we found Perejaume, painter and writer, in the middle of the field, beneath the great bluish dome of a liquid sky with its smoky dragon clouds in battle. There was a canvas on his easel that gave the entire scene the look of a landscape from the Olot school. Off to the side were a few typewritten pages, fragments from *Ludwig-Jujol*. We knew that in time the naive Olot-like landscape would become a pure concept, the ideogramme of itself, as if seen in a microscope or in the old deformed mirror in the Tibidabo amusement park. It was not thus this mutation that disturbed us, but the transitions and metamorphoses that had established a common subterranean current in the text between Ludwig II of Bavaria and Josep Maria Jujol. Perejaume does not feel the text can be excerpted, so the reader will find here only the add-on of Ogassa, which though separate from the body of the work serves as its closure. To understand Perejaume one must come to know Ludwig-Jujol, not just because along with *Oïsme* it is his most important literary work, but because the aesthetic operation it carries out characterizes Perejaume as a writer and visual artist.

The "I just paint" school or club has long since disappeared in Catalonia. Miró wrote fine poems in French and personal annotations in Catalan of clear interest. Dalí had an undeniable literary talent, though we are not quite sure in which language (perhaps not even he knew for sure). Tàpies has developed a serious and ongoing body of essays, as well as a worthwhile book of personal memoirs. In none of these cases, however, do we find the extreme degree of complementary force and interconnectedness as in Perejaume, whose theoretical work (especially in *Ludwig-Jujol* and *Oïsme*, together with slivers and margins of other books) is not just an explanation or illustration of his visual work, nor a type of parallel irradiation or projection. To a great degree it prepares it, launching it and spurring it on, much like the diary of Delacroix anticipated the canvases he wished to paint; or to be even more exact, as if Delacroix, instead of writing his own diary, had written Baudelaire's art criticism.

If he is more than just a painter who writes, is Perejaume perhaps a writer who paints, like Strindberg, or, in a certain sense, like Antonio Saura? Not quite: we cannot precisely define him as a visual artist nor as a writer. (In this he is not alone: in my view this occurred with Henri Michaux, though along different lines). What Perejaume epitomizes is the conception and realization, whether intellectual, verbal or visual, of a series of visual and ideological transmutations and interchanges between apparently different orders of both natural and artistic reality. The pursuit of unity thus defines him, and in this sense his work resembles that of the poet, an extreme intelligence in union with his instinctive capacity for preter-rational intuition. The poet tries to uncover the originary unity of the world and the word by means of metaphor or metonomy. Perejaume's writings, paintings and installations are also metaphors and metonyms. The unity they are searching for is the lost primordial paradise of poetry and painting, the territory (not a legendary one, but one that is historically real) which poet and painter naturally co-inhabited in the dawn of cultures. Yet Perejaume does not let himself be seduced by anthropological myths, knowing that unlike what Artaud legitimately (though vainly) believed, a contemporary Westerner will not do Balinese theatre, aware as well that if Picasso discovered African art, it was not in order to produce African art but to create the art of Picasso.

In Perejaume's particular case, this lost unity of the world and the word is due to a division of meaning signalled out in the moment the Catalan language lost its capacity to confect, all by itself, a total vision of the world (an ability it had to a great degree in Ramon Llull). It has been proposed that the poetry of J. V. Foix and Carles Riba, or Joan Miró's and Tàpies' painting, could be treated on the basis of this loss or division, though along different lines. In this sense it is more profound and essential that the textual and visual adventure of Perejaume might continue the task of these masters in a very personal way, taking up their legacy. All of us will in the end find ourselves facing Ramon Llull upon that shady slope where the crevice between the word and the world is meant to disappear, where the split between sign and sense has been wiped out: a most ancient territory, which is at once the most vigourous and rigourously contemporary site of all.

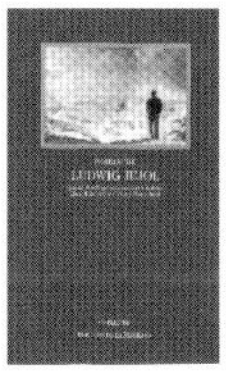

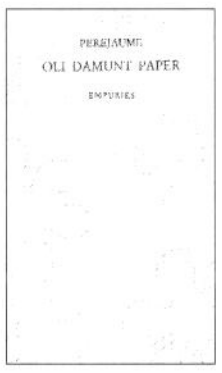

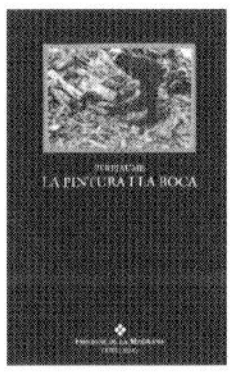

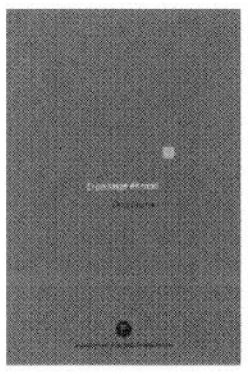

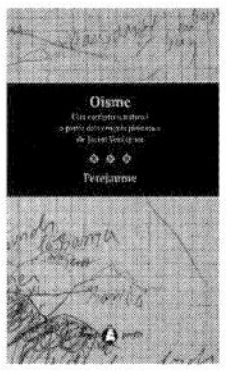

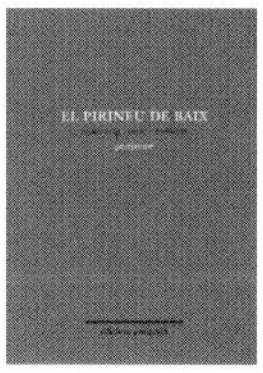

Selection of Writings*

*This selection of Perejaume's writing was made by the author himself
with the assistance of Pere Gimferrer and Carles Guerra.
The introductory notes to each section were written by Carles Guerra.
When the origin of the text is not indicated,
the text is unpublished and appears here for the first time.

A FEW TEXTS ON COLLAGE

The texts which have been gathered together under this heading deal with collage as a technique which is no longer confined to the medium of paper. Perejaume first broadened the meaning of collage in *Ludwig-Jujol. Què és el collage, sinó acostar soledats? Lluís II de Baviera, Josep Maria Jujol*: using literary means, he draws comparisons whose territorial dimension suggests a new order which goes beyond "cartographic order". Thus, metaphor becomes the chief instrument by virtue of which we may "go from place to place". By transforming this last statement into something literal, the text itself becomes a means of tranport.
Based as it is upon literary substitutes for reality, the circularity to which Perejaume's discourse has surrendered produces, according to Joaquim Sala-Sanahuja, "metaphors of double circulation". The most obvious consequence of this is that the focus of enunciation erodes. In two texts on Barcelona's Gran Teatre del Liceu opera house, we begin to see that distance is also a productive space for Perejaume.

LANDSCAPE, A POSTCARD MADE SCULPTURE

Just as the surface of a pond transforms the trees, men have learnt to flatten the earth out on a piece of paper, inventing a portable landscape, a hand-landscape, memory set out in a definitive version under a differed light. Here the gaze is fossilized on the paper, time has disappeared, the dregs of so many surfaces found on the water's bottom. This is what the printing of postcards and their copies entails: a series of mirrors, cardboard clarities upon non-existent waters. Doorways or postcards? Walls longing for windows, for one unchanging window remade on the exterior: printed trees and mountains, mountains here at hand, yet so far away! That morning was not this paper, it was everything I know about it, and all that I do not: the solitary hour of that light. This piece of paper speaks of that morning, the reflexion of that place in this hour, the seed of one place in another landscape. I conjugate that morning in the present, I rediscover it, shiny, in a turning of the postcard rack in the infinite tourism of the gaze: the water flows by, the grass grows, day breaks, it rains. That day and this day.
We live as we would have lived.
The present has become the rearview mirror of the future: a changing postcard where everything is shifted into two dimensions in some secret time, a collage being constantly dropped off and picked up, one postcard icing over into another, doubling over, being translated, something other: Sintra and Munich side by side, the sea half sea and half pond, Bulloses Lake, the Atlantic. Sintra and Sintra far away in the distance, the peak of Bassegoda reflecting the Jungfrau in the Brull gorge, in Bulloses Lake, in a previous sea, or along a cascade of retrospective waters.
A tree at Sintra, a tree in Munich, a postcard of Sintra in Munich.
I am in Barcelona a four o'clock sharp in the afternoon, on the peak of Bassegoda but also at Sintra, with a snowy landscape in my hands, and in Munich looking at the same postcard. Cars whiz by with their lights on, with sunbathed mountains in the rearview mirror, the sky above hiding the sunlight at four in the afternoon, thumbing through the postcards in the final railway car images of a long landcape. A forest of sequoias, the woods slashed by switchbacks with the railway lines nailed onto the mountain background, a snowy postcard view beneath a verdant sky, in a series of terminal points and limits set behind the same pane of glass that has now been altered by a never-ending parade of postcards. We are speaking of the climatic logic that fuses them together, the assemblage of an unfolding reality, only an amphibian gaze making it understandable as it passes by. I look at the window: *Mer de glace de Chamonix, Santa Cruz of giant sequoia, Eruzione Vesuvio.* Landscapes arising at the turn of a

leaf, moving from one place to another with the aid of a postage stamp on the vertex, in the hope that the glow of a lighthouse, the binding of an atlas, or the rising and falling curtain of the Liceu might make them reappear, here and now, in some orderly fashion. We follow the poetic order of appearances, for we have gone beyond cartographic order, and only metaphor allows us to go from one site to another without losing our sensibility for a weightless, detachable nature. Is this not the most extreme form of collage: the fragmentation of the sun, machine-reproduced landscapes, and their infinite transplantation onto the deserted surface of this *Âge de la colle*, as Max Ernst once termed it?
On the peak of postcards of Bassegoda I am in the Liceu with postcards in the private boxes, meteorite fragments of one landscape against another, contemplating the lowlands of Brull —where the postcards are still so tangible, so orderly, that they do not seem to be what they really are— beneath that mobile firmament composed by the lights of cars, upon the inner lining of postcards sent from the four corners of the world, through four o'clock rearview mirrors, under an aviation of sun and moon. It is four and five in the afternoon, under a preterite sky with its four-sided panorama. Which as yet unseen route might trace the coast of this lonely postcard? Which mobile scenic sites might it follow? Which cascade, falling from a river dam, which balcony bannister, might hold it back? Where have the volumes of so many images gone? A flat landscape is a word, but the world is a poem turning in the nocturne of a mailbox.
We have turned the world into a reiterating postcard, the only one illuminated on the surface of forgetfulness, and now, as part of our insecure existence, we require fragments unveiling fragments, rearview mirrors distinguishing and affirming each moment of this neverending postcard we live in on the front, though write upon on the back.

Bassegoda Peak, Les Tribunes.

Exhibition catalogue for *Postaler*. Barcelona: Fundació Caixa de Pensions, March, 1985. See also the French translation by Nathalie Bittoun Debruyne in the catalogue for the staging of the same exhibition at Centre Regional d'Art Contemporain Midi-Pyrénées, Toulouse, April-May 1987; and in *ALEA* 9, Paris: Christian Bourgeois Éditeur, 1989. See also *La pintura i la boca*. Barcelona: La Magrana, 1993, pp. 16-18, and Tonia Raquejo, *Land Art*. Madrid: Editorial Nerea, 1998.

THE DEATH OF ROBERT SCHUMANN

After the *Morning Songs* (Op. 133), Robert Schumann was unable to compose any more music. Whenever he would set out to write so much as a note, another even better one would come to him, and then another. Any murmour whatsoever -a door slamming, the buzz of the street, the subdued passing of a bee- would suggest an overture to him. Every sound, once freshly opened, would soon be put to the side, overcome by another sound that had just emerged, and then by yet another that would drown out the previous one, and once again by that B major assuming an independent life, suddenly pushing itself to the fore in all its solitary beauty within the dark volume of the composition. Everything thus began and nothing continued, like when we are driving in the snow at night and the carlights draw the constant appearance of the snowflakes into the centre of the gaze, melting just before reaching our eyes. The instant when everything disappears, the place where everything reappears. The fragment, and that "nothing is to be scorned". The meteoric intensity of the fragment and of that found sound, of any old sound. A precipitation of notes and blanks deliberately left in the writing. Whiffs of dawn, of the century approaching him, the one we now live in, instantaneous: I do not know if this is the emergence of everything or nothing, of ecstasy perhaps, or of death.

Exhibition catalogue. Barcelona: Galeria Joan Prats, Dec. 1986-Jan. 1987. This text also appeared in *La pintura i la boca*, p. 15.

LICEU GARAGE

The Gran Opera del Liceu (Barcelona's opera house) is a metaphorical operation: a shelter from inclement weather. Or better said: the true and tangibly sharp figuration of a metaphorical operation that with time, as with any artifice of language, has come into common use as something natural and deep-rooted. Once settled into one of the seats, we are brought to think of just how unreal these courteous Pyrenees really are, how the image they evoke has become so tactile and corpulent, supplanting and abandoning it in all its rustic weightiness, with steeply arranged seating in an interwoven ornamental style, the crimson and gold of the various strata, the wooden scenery of the veloured front curtains, the make-up, and finally the unfocussed state of everything else placed somewhere off in the distance.

Quite often there is a palace placed right in front of the landscape scenery, keeping a watchful eye on a rustic and sunny nature. At other times the palace is painted into the scenery and the seat then becomes a rough crag where one can contemplate it from. Together auditorium and stage seem to bring us nearer to a Pyrenees that one might look upon while listening to Berg or Monteverdi or Wagner or Messiaen. It would be much simpler to go to the mountain to find an oval-shaped gorge there, or better still a high ridge with a gully for the orchestra, a rich and solemn site, sometime after the thaw, where the hall might be the scenery itself. From there we would see the Gran Teatre for what it is: an enclosure for those days when it is too cold to be outside, a shelter from the rain.

Every year the same thought comes to my mind: "when the good weather comes we will all go off to hold the concerts in the Busa Range or in Ribelles Valley or at the summit of Catiu d'Or." But things just do not seem to work that way. We prefer to watch our summer theatre in stifling heat, "conditioning" it with fresh blown air and carpet scents, closing the windows and widening the aisles, who knows whether to sharpen the artifice even more, making the language even more inevitable and the distance more real, without speaking of what the distances narrate.

Or perhaps this is all meant to protect us from the natural world, when we are obliged to begin protecting ourselves from language itself, in whatever place we find ourselves.

In the theatrical opacity of the seating and decorative mouldings, with that liveliness all subtlely suggested things proclaim, the Pyrenees seem very far away. They are like some wrapping material dominating the object, suggesting only its forms. We are witness to a metaphorical pouring out of impossible longing and irredeemable distance, together with another in a body that is present, claiming for itself a certain etiquette, a lustre, even comfort: our time is spent in a highly ragged natural world where the inclemencies of the weather and overly long journeys are avoided.

Thus the Pyrenees reveal themselves to us in the moment the door is opened, though they are not exactly the Pyrenees. Instead it is an interior Pyrenees, like the exterior of a palace in the interior of a mountain, resembling even the confused agglomeration of all these elements in a garage that loses the real, concrete site in the effort to be all possible sites, even if they are not as real. It is then that we see the Liceu as what in fact it is: a gathering of frames, a garage full of moulding and velour curtains, a kind of picture gallery, the golden resting point of landscape.

Exhibition catalogue for *Coll de Pal-Cim de Costabona*. Barcelona: Galeria Joan Prats, June-July 1990. This text also appeared in *La pintura i la boca*, pp. 27-28

LICEU. MAP OF CATALUNYA PRINTED WITH ASHES OF THE GRAN TEATRE DEL LICEU

In the hope that the Mountain might be theatre FRANCESC MARÉS

The burning of the Liceu opera house allowed us to perceive the enormous format of a collapsing painting. The *mise en nature* of the Gran Teatre was a demonstrable fact in those fragments of the building falling upon all kinds of objects and places over a radius of various kilometres.
The very chemical make-up of the theatre had given the blaze the appearance of a volcanic eruption. A confined air, layered thick with performances, broke out amidst a tempestuous explosion.
The inconsistency of that abrupt density of images in the interior of the premises made such a reaction predictable. Audaciously piled up over various floors, the maleability of the golds, velours and rigid decorative reliefs was submitted to extraordinarily spectacular contorsions and folds.
The steep contours rose dramatically, full of images and assorted appearances, reaching saturation; above the stage a wooden structure held back a second tier of curtains which entered the repertoire in every new production. It was thus not strange to see the Liceu fall in a completely different figurative sense, shifting towards a new resting place.
After the fire of 1861 the official architect of the theatre, Josep Oriol Mestres, imagined the building to be soaring high in the sky, its golden features and velour curtains spreading out so as to encompass all things, representing everything. Now that the theatre had decided to extend itself outwards: the pigments flew far, from one end of the country to another, only coming to rest when they were so far away from each other that they had come to fear that the link between them could get lost, deciding then to fall upon the ground, like stitches applied to the earth.
The gloomy night sky carried all the specks of the theatre in suspension, letting them fall as they would. A fleck of velour came to rest on a three thousand metre peak; another bit of moulding reverently and obligingly dropped on the slopes of Costuix or on the beach at Llançà; meanwhile tiny particles of the seats settled upon the town of Noedes or upon the holm oak at Mas de Borbó. Indeed, the Liceu had become all told an enormous painting set for landing, after flying across the earth in decomposition, tracing the contours of the surface in the air, its pigments later coming to rest in a most imperceptible way. The theatre remained, to a certain point, intact –there in the facade, the staircase, the hall of mirrors, Ferrera Valley, the Busa Range, Garrigues County– and the ash flakes did nothing but respond to that idea of musée éclaté with which the new museography might encompass an entire region in a permanent collection.
It is in this way that figuration only becomes suspicious behind these images that we so love to feed and let ourselves be fooled by. Like a reddish air set in a great dark space, the cirque at Gorgutes beneath the Mall Pintrat, now has turned into a theatrical architecture of the 18th century. Things become simply whatever we contemplate; figuration makes them ostentatious, yet hard to get a handle on. It is not so much that figuration makes this or that image real, but that it is able to make itself even more real, more decisive, more peaceful and discreet, than any other image. In this way the theatre that houses everything inside itself, is the theatre which represents all things outwardly.
I see the theatre that falls here beside me, my breath pushing at the stank air, because this is happening inside a theatre, just as it might occur at the Gorgutes cirque. In ruined grandeur, nature seems to have grown by placing a theatre of our day within the sets of a theatre that once was.
A half sunk pillar testifies to this, like the deep though tiny cracks that painting has formed in submission to climactic trials. In fact, the configuration of theatres is indebted to a geological model –a soft slope curving upon a rising surface– just as it responds to the attentive form of a head with the stage

placed inside the eyes. All posterior velveting and upholstering went about transforming this empty form of a head into a heart: a majestic and intimite heart, drifting from one point of reference to another. I could go on for pages and pages trying to convince you that the Liceu is all this, that its walls are drawn to each other and dilate like a heart, that it has now become a theatre without limits leaving nothing on the outside. The curtain is as red as the day as it rises and sets, or like the red of the sun when we close our eyes, or simply red, for the curtains are enough to make the images "bleed" for us along with each duration, each framing; or just as well as red as fire, with a golden fringe on the bottom and the flames shooting up the folds. Leave the painter's palette where you wish, wherever you feel, loaded or not, it does not matter! Theatre has expanded. This irrepressible capacity of paint to be something else has been passed on to the earth, to our eyes, and to our hearts, so that we no longer can pick out a trace of theatre anywhere, all we see is the pigmentation of a velour curtain. Some saw a luxurious redemption, an unexpected luxurious rusticity in all of this. Others in turn have emphasized the return of all things to their separate models, while others still have perceived a threatening turbidity of agreements carved out between the real and the represented, on the basis of an immense pictorial reforestation of nature. It is true in fact that this embered Liceu, now using real objects for its scenery, inscribes the most genuinely representative mechanisms onto an experience of the natural, leading to a light and malignant phosphorescence for many. It is no less true, though, that this has been a common perception of the majority of Romantic travellers who have seen nature as a spectacle precisely in its most savage formations, those that are found furthest away from human influence. We might imagine that simulation is a sincere tendency of things, and that sites, in the course of offering us a fable, make them manifest to us more realistically than they would do without such fictional pretexts. The spectators for their part are always placed right in front of the paradox that all flight from pictorial reality implies, while insisting on some great figurative acceleration, without ever knowing if a viable —now we would say sustainable— agreement exists between one thing and another.

It is here where the velour curtains and mouldings offer a magnificent geologic, botanical, natural presence, with decorative quadrants, mirrors and columns. The high golden reliefs, with busts of compositors and fantasic animals, image rockpiles, bottom valleys and recesses of all types and sizes with all of the elements we have mentioned, as if the Liceu had changed its address and had gone off to those spots in the Pyrenees that so many scenographers have longed for, an upside-down Liceu, purer and less reducible, the origin and final buffer of an enormous cleft of stages.

Beneath Mall Pintrat in the Gorgutes cirque, there is an enormous amphitheatre gully with damask sphagnum moss and craggy tapestries: a cushioned Pyrenees with high backs and snowy embroideries, with the private boxes and slopes similar to those found in that high valley in Comalada, near Canigó, which according to Josep Sebastià Pons "draws itself out and widens like an amphitheatre made especially for the epic of Saint William". Once in the Gorgutes cirque, in the middle of the valley along a low ridge with ironwork like in a found Liceu, we see how easy it is to configure one thing in another. Strictly speaking we are dealing with more than just anything; we are speaking of the real exhibited object which becomes the illusory structure exhibiting them, connecting them from below and from within. Instead of seeing the Liceu or the rocky crags, we try to see the figuration that they carry with them. Yet not so much the figurative image as figuration itself, this thing that must be figuration, its very density: the ceiling so high that the theatre comes to comprise everything to be found therein.

Cave Canis n. 1, Barcelona, October 1995

ADDENDA ON THE WAY TO OGASSA

We do not discover new relationships between things until we have moved far away from them. Catalonia is a morning land, the waterways flow towards noon, with its farmhouses, quaint sites and little villages set along a slight slope to the east. I see this from Sant Arranç, or from Mount Taga, or from Estela Peak in the Cavallera range, far from Bavaria and the Tarragona countryside, but with Bavaria and the Tarragona countryside in the distance regardless. They are present in the extremes of the Pyrenees as well, closer to Bavaria in appearance though in real space closer to the Tarragona countryside. In the end, Linderhof and Casa Bofarull move into alignment: an architecture set diagonally across an intersection of words and the gaze. Everything we have said about them has been in vain –except for the way we might approach that hidden point they are based upon, relating and distinguishing them; except for the way we move around this point whose existence we only sense, though remaining latent, unrevealed. In fact neither art nor knowledge –faithful as they are to a definitively uneasy and incomprehensible cosmos– have ever aspired to eliminate the mystery. Just the contrary, they have strived to heighten it.

We know that the creator of Casa Bofarull, Casa Negre and Vistabella was Josep Maria Jujol. But who was the creator of Ludwig II: Lohengrin? Bavaria? Louis the 14th? He himself? His biographers? His castles? What –to continue– is Ludwig II really the author of? Did he create *Die Meistersinger*, composed by Wagner under his protection at Berg castle? Was he the creator of the winter sleighs he ordered carpenters and machinists of the royal theatre to construct? Was he the author of Neuschwanstein, designed by Jank and carried out successively by Riedl, Von Dollman and Hofmann? Or of Lindehof, whose architect was Von Dollmann, with its Quoglio decorations and Effer gardens? Or perhaps he made the Herrenchiemsee, designed by Von Dollman and later completed by Julius Hofmann? Even in his most intimate diary there are jottings in someone else's handwriting. Nor can we be sure whether his many extravagant habits were real or had been attributed to him by his enemies. Ludwig is all of these things; or to be even more precise, he is what all of these things wanted to be, the victim and driving force behind all these elements, which all told are the monarch's creators and creative destinations.

We return to look upon the plains, slashed by cuts and incisions, as if contemplating from the summit of an ornamental letter an extensive codex rivetted with toponyms. We believe, along with Bofill i Ferro, that "a Gaudi-like construction in the mountain would be a redundancy, it would be senseless", admiring the contrasting locations of Ludwig's castles, their isolation heightening artifice, set in imposing natural sites with their artificial-natural grottos and internal gardens. The afternoon is an aging though sumptuous tapestry, courteous and intensely rural, the golden thread running along the ridges which divide Bavarias from sunnier climes. There in the background, the wide curvature of the sea is retained along an embroidered line of snow. Catalonia, as I once remarked, is a unique Pyrenees set in the confluence of waterways. Metaphor reaches its zero point when Joan Miró points at a tool in his studio and says "that" without naming it. In the mountains, in turn, faced with an excessive accumulation of exposed elements, with a primitive, unarguable language -the box shrub that is the language of box, the spring that is the beginning of water, the stone which is itself in the moment it is abandonned- this zero point, this "that", is made overly manifest. The only metaphor that fits responds to a traditional shifting of senses, the saying of "that" or "the other thing", or just as well pointing to the nearest stone to say "there". I imagine a landscape whose foreground shows a vague and spinning ground of distant, misty mountains, with the background distinguished by the sea represented in great detail, in a close-up view that clearly shows each blue ripple and each rising wave, concise and sharp like a precise line dilineating the dark fir-green tone of a Turkish sky in the paintings of Lucas Cranach. It is a landscape I have not seen anywhere, nor has anyone ever seen it, though we might make it comprehensible and almost visible through language. It is in vain, however, that we try to represent all of this with the landscaping elements of the traditional cork bark nativity scene. If we take the piece of cork bark that represents the mountain range and we put it in the foreground, it is no longer a range, becoming instead a nearby stubble field, the stony edge of a edge, a rough rock, and finally the bark of a cork oak. If I push the moss further away from this bark, it does not maintain figurative illusion either; it is no longer a field, but returns to the state of a small woods, a lush hill, or a distant forest again.

It is almost dark. It is not hard to construe figurative qualities in the grass at Ogassa, with its northern firs as tall as the mountains themselves. If we keep the illusion up, we will see that it half invites us to lose ourselves in the patches of new greenery sketched out by tender birch groves, dotted with winter oaks, resting upon the stems of dry grass. In the film *Parsifal* H. J. Syberberg brings pessebrism into play: the winter, the mountains, the temple, the gorge, all of this is suggested by Wagner's death mask placed flat upon the earth, face up upon the expanse of the stage. Just as years earlier Antoni Tàpies had added a photo of a mask in profile in a similar position into a painting done in homage to Wagner, like a rocky monticule or a maquette of the Alps.

Captivated by these lost limits between the "that" and "there" of all metaphorical shifting, we once again think of that mountain range that dissipates when the cork bark is brought closer than the grass, which becomes gigantic as the moss is placed further off. We do not understand how we can verbally express a background placed in the foreground, but cannot so express a traditional piece of cork bark. The two limits of language –words and what they designate– correspond to the two distances that separate cork bark and the observer: bark and mountain range. One of them is supposedly formless in the language of words, unlike objectual metaphor. The biblical man was formed out of clay, but the clay had no concrete figure, deciding to adopt the form of man. If I make a nativity scene out of plaster, I might represent a distant mountain range; upon bringing it closer to place behind it the sea, where the water can be touched, it continues to be a distant range. Language is thus in fact a plaster nativity scene which, in certain cases –such as when I made *La tarda és un tapís* (Afternoon is a tapestry) or just as well when I said "Language is thus in fact a plaster nativity scene"– we set out like a cork bark nativity scene, though made in plaster. I thus hike down this plaster path that hardly modifies the path it represents at all, comfortable and completely natural, until I make it to Mitjavila.

And now in the darkness I contemplate Linderhof and Casa Bofarull: Ludwig makes a nativity scene out of plaster or ice, while Jujol dreams up an architecture made of cork bark, moss and tin foil.

Mitjavila, June-October 1987

Ludwig-Jujol. Què és collage sinó acostar soledats? Lluís II de Baviera, Josep Maria Jujol. Barcelona: La Magrana, 1989, p. 91-95.

PESSEBRISM

The word "pessebrism"[1] alludes to a creche or nativity scene showing the figures traditionally associated with the birth of Jesus in a rural landscape. Cork has normally been used in such scenes to simulate mountains. While collage consists in transporting something to something else, pessebrism is a matter of "seeing something in something else". Thus, pessebrism is doubly realistic: it is an effort to represent with material that is readily available; furthermore these materials are taken from the very landscape which they represent. The illusionism which triggers a burst of vision and the fleetingness of these depictions serve to place these images in a spectacular scale, as *El suro de Sils*. (The Sils Cork). For the first time, Perejaume considers pessebrism to be a method applied and repeated. Yet by designating pessebrism as a method, he means to liberate the resulting vision from the very subjectivity of the viewer, with the caveat that "the method that commands us is the method we command."

1 For the rendering of the English version of this and related terms, see p. 155, note 10, of this volume. (Translator's note)

PESSEBRISM

"To look at ice without thinking it is water"

RAMANA MAHARHI

We remain in uncertainty, and whoever claims to understand perhaps is only making things up. They pretend to understand by seeing in one thing some other thing, but in the act of seeing it, they merely invent it. Any reading seems to provide us with a certain experience of invention, the same situation that makes it possible, when writing, for language to preceed what we are about to say. Certain creations fit perfectly into these sites of connections and artifice where the relation between facts is never proven anyways. It is just as illusive to wish to capture reality whole, as to resign oneself to its ups and downs. Understanding and invention are only with difficulty discernible to those who try to follow that certain reality where form serves to block out distance, articulate connections, take hold of facts and legitimate fiction. This is a reality where we can comment upon the rupture while at the same time eluding it, in this unexpected solidity that the most discordant facts seem to give rise to, in pessebristic fashion. We have commented on this elsewhere: just as if we had gone from a paternal and agrarian painting to a service sector painting, it is not so much the pigments that we must figurate but that which binds them together. More than the simulation of a territory, we long for an extended and sustained territory of simulation. As if painting would permit us to perform an operation around painting, standing upright on grooves in the earth, like someone who moves along the ridge where no ridge exists, following those little peaks that someone or something has, with connections of so many figures that we can make our way across. Ridges then, and aligned watercourses, followed and written, where the the word reads whatever the world does not tell it, and painting gives the world the meaning it cannot encounter. We could go by foot along a straight ruler of what I have written, or hold onto the line as if it were a bannister set before a delicate exhibit of ivory objects, of cool and cloudy sites. With *Pessebrisme* I do not wish to offer up a pseudo-scientific code of cork bark perceptions. Away with gratuity! What method has not failed in such a wild land? What building? It is good to improvise as well. Let the figure come, let it be the figure that comes. There are no failproof strategies. The cork bark is the co-writer. We do not see the idea coming, it turns us over and there it is, like in the studio. Later it wonders whether it has really turned you over, if it was justified in doing so. How can we be confounded by an idea that comes as a given, though we do not know where from? How can its direction be shifted so that it might go elsewhere carrying something that is ours, something we have ever so lightly put our mark upon? The method that commands us is the method we command.

We are three thousand metres up above embers from the 1800s, on planks of wood, right on the spot we must see from. Wherever there is path on each side, all we need to do is make use of bridges set over the canyon. With the bricks laid out longways along the archway, defining its trajectory in an inexorable flight, pessebrism creations a real sundrenched example of these intermediate passages. Its domain is thus not just the cork bark nor the resulting pessebre, but a fuller, straighter and more refined pessebrism that connects them, basking in a rustic air.

With brusque uneven steps we often obtain a kind of Pyrenees that is sharper than that normally depicted, in the very flight path of creation. It is there that the mountains surge and disappear. They pass by like a seismograph wave, the scenic apparatus that is everything to the eye, covered with shrubs just like the models that bring them closer to us. So that with oil paint and words, with bronze and light —and leaping over the rhetoric of appearances— we observe, as mountainous as a pessebre, as concrete as the bark, pessebrism itself: a painting wrapped in theatre, padded with nature, lined in velvet.

This term must be difficult to understand for those who have never lived the pessebristic experience in a traditional, everyday way. Joan Amades says that the word pessebrista appears for the first time in 1805, applied to the Barcelona cutler Ramon Beguer. In fact, the tradition of making scenes with figures depicting the birth of Jesus is age-old and widespread throughout many countries. But in 19th Century Catalonia the stable where Jesus was born was reduced to a kind of miniaturized cave tucked into massive wooded mountains, with rivers and cultivated fields representing the rural areas of the land in great detail, with all kinds of additional references to specific local customs. This localism was reenforced by the inclusion of elements from the immediate surroundings, which hinted at a greater reality: a piece of bark could be an entire mountain range; a twig could become a tree; a chunk of moss, a pasture. And with all this they were still able to give a sense of the isolated deserts of Judea united with those woody surroundings of their own day.

"The principal idea of of a pessebre is the landscape". So ran the first prescription that Josep Oriol Mestres wrote for the Barcelona Pessebrist Association in 1863. This too is the trait that undoubtably defines the Catalan pessebre: a creation lying somewhere between the Baroque and Romanticism, where the figures seem to obey the style of a retable, with its union of sublime and profane, with the site and the figures depicted taking on an even more markedly Romantic air, with a rural tone and homey feel.

J.V. Foix is the first to use the word "pessebrista" in a figurative sense. He does so in a text on Dalí where he speaks of "astral pessebrism", and again in another text called *Miró, el pessebrista astral* (Miró, the Astral Pessebrist). In a later text the poet Foix is more explicit, recalling the case of an Italian professor, Giuseppe Sansone, who after reading a poem that he wanted to translate from *Gertrudis* (also dedicated to Miró), commented to him: "C'è un originale presepio". "Like us", added Foix, "the Italians have transferred the name of the pessebre from that of the visual representation of the Nativity scene to mountain landscapes with houses and huts scattered about amongst pine forests and cool springs."

Set on the table is the world or a piece of the world pursued by so many authors, authors who could convert the term "pessebrism" into a highly extensive style. The shrunken world of Noah floating on the water is the precedent, Zen gardens the period of splendour, the Tuscan *Thebaides* of the 14th and 15th centuries the most faithful depiction in paint, with those Miró's where Montroig can be seen in the carob trees or in a few blades of grass one of its most intimate manifestations. Is it not a pessebre to place time in a watch, or to see, along with whomever might turn to look, certain things far away in time captured in the bluish hues of distance? All of these changes in scale take place along a dividing line halfway between consciousness and automatism, which arranges along the same line the art of cork bark displays, latent images of Dalí, Foix's rocks set on plinths, the stained and unexpected sonorities of John Cage's prepared piano, the stone disease of the entrance arch at Ripoll monastery, the smudged walls of Leonardo, Alexander Cozen's landscape studies begun with just a stain, Max Ernst's *frottage,* or that "living vegetation from the trunk of a tree" stamped upon a closet door that Pere Gimferrer has observed "as if he were a medium". These pictorial effects are set against an imposed figuration, maintaining indecision and inexactitude at all costs, searching for a miniaturized Alps in a piece of cork bark, then to be liberated by poets, children and painters.

Just as with no intervention on our part the effects of time, humidity, and a general wear and tear deteriorate the walls, paint often pretends to be unaware of the image it represents, presenting sites and figures as a careless act. Sometimes we are confronted by a figuration that has been patiently stored up over the years. Other times we are faced with a surface that has cracked from drying too fast, full of pocks, ridges and plateaus. Just as well we find ourselves in mid-air between pigments and their limits, with the signposts partially hidden in the bushes. And still other times we come up against something concrete and real, looking carefully until we are able to surprise a figure in the painting, as if the site had come to us without our hardly intervening. Just like that image now coming to find us, catching our eye and dragging us along from a longstanding obsession to put a name and a face onto the official report, this image, with its highly illusionary spectacularity and exceptional relief work, and with its well-doted theatricality —however encrusted by time— reveals to us a new visual overlapping of mountains and theatre stages.

Now among the statues that give rise to a reading, we contemplate how the gaze itself has been gathered into a pile of cork bark. How much bark is necessary in the land of words to explode our vision, so that the rise of these words might allow us to forget the letters and take hold of an alpine world in the purity of its primary materials? We find ourselves before the gaze and its related parts, in a place that is happy to assume any form at all, as if it had felt an incredibly strong attraction for the very precariousness of things. These is a closed off horizon, an interior horizon with the light of a table lamp there on the horizon. And then we hear the images fall with a crash in the closing of the book.

Exhibition catalogue for *El grado de verdad de las representaciones*. Madrid: Galeria Soledad Lorenzo, October-November 1991. The catalogue includes a Spanish and English translations by Ángel Crespo and Jeffrey Swartz, respectively.
This text also appeared in *La pintura i la boca,* p. 282.

CORK BARK AT BATH

Observe amidst the woods, a theatre curtain before the cork bark harvest, when the bark is peeled back and the velour begins to bleed! All wild thicknesses have originally been a velour curtain like this one, with a rusty copper tone, the colour of grape juice later rusting, rusting until the landscape begins. You might say that the cork bark sap seeps out to take a peek and goes rusty, though not as murky as sap itself, more celestial and airy. Once done, year after year, the curtain folds in upon itself in a falling orography and –sprouting elevations, acrobatics in the rocks, final raisings of the earth– never stops growing and moving. The more image is derived (offering us as a gift more territories it does not own) the further the final cut, separating it completely from the trunk. It is then that only in seeing the cork bark laid flat, we begin to search for a high rocky place. Everything –ravines, fields, hills– is set upon a pattern of clearly perceptible intercuts. After we have observed the process, the bark cries to the harvester who puts another piece of cork bark to the task.

William Beckford learnt the art of staining from Alexander Cozens: the ability to see one thing in another just as Cozens did, with his clean landscapes born out of messy tinctures. Joan Miró, who surely did not know Cozen's method, offers an exemplary and just as systematic application (or more) in his collage-based paintings, like Cozens attaining a concrete reality from an unpredictable sketch, though accomplishing an even more remote and intimate degree of associative suggestion. William Beckford's application of the method is in turn more free-roaming. The sketch or the stain –in a literal sense as well, applied to smoky England, dirtied by nascent industrialization– is the surrounding reality upon which Beckford dresses up and illuminates a parallel life. More than a discovery of that stain's suggestive capacity, we are dealing with a total invention, a flight towards external figurations extracted from his travels and diverse readings. Travels, we must say, where the landscapes interpret remote realities, found even further afar. Places, like books, are a support for other places. The materials are positioned so that the gaze might capture them, cork oak groves, stand-in characters. As his last biographer Didier Girard said, "before the itinerant poetry of Henri Michaux, Beckford used places as a veritable support for vision."

This glimpse in some sites of more and more other sites –remember that the so-called "Caliph of Fonthill" did not ever set his feet in the Orient except via a multitude of texts (the first of them being the *Thousand and One Nights* that Cozens gave him when he was only thirteen years old), or recall the oriental aura he discovered in Venice or Andalusia– brings us to Joseph Wright of Derby, the painter of light. Wright of Derby, Cozens and even Beckford were linked to the city of Bath in one or another period of their lives. They were practically contemporaries (with twenty odd years of difference in age between them), all slightly marginal, all nevertheless associated with official art. Of them it is Wright of Derby who was known to have elaborated all sort of risky endeavours around the picturesque nature of night illumination. His is the smallest light of that enlightened, defenseless century which in his day already languished, surrounded by darkness. I am thinking of those paintings with lanterns, lamps, heated forges and planetariums illuminating the characters and the things lying closest to the centre of each painting, while the rest of the scene is left in darkness; or just the opposite, of that other painting where the skeleton of death walks across a placid and serene scene in the middle of the day.

Wright of Derby made his voyage to Italy as well (February 1774 to July 1775). Various drawings from his stay in Rome have come down to us, along with two oils of a grotto in Naples, as well as a painting in tempera (of uncertain authenticity) of Vesuvius erupting, apparently done on the spot. The rest of the works of Italian subject matter were painted in Bath (some of them were later finished in Derby) or just as well, around Bath. Nocturnes continued to be frequent, though those tiny focal points of light that are familiar to us from the previous period grow and expand, like pessebres, in a most unusual way: first –on winged rays of light– in the great fire castles done in Rome; and later –in a definitively corky light– in his views of Vesuvius burning in a total re-creation –Wright never really coincided with a real eruption of the volcano– of lanterns, planetariums and forges, accumulated and resplendent, conserving in spite of everything an equally or even more extensive wrapping of gloom.

One thing recognizes itself in another, putting on the cork we have taken to it, looking at us with it on. The fact that the bark changes trunks like an actor changes roles aligns and unites everything, though at risk of confusion, without hardly distinguishing the cork where the mountain begins from the cork where the peak ends it. We know of a Wright of Derby drawing in Cozen's landscape style, starting out from a previously observed stain. After much walking, I found a place in Bath that reminded me of it. It is not so much that Bath and the drawing are trying to resemble each other, however; I made this discovery, we might say, in spite of them both. In reference to the method of Cozens, the cork as used by Catalan nativity scene makers has the advantage of being natural, the woody botanical expression of pigments that the landscape already holds within; unlike the *New Method*, which suggests a lack of interest in the actual presence of the site, preferring to fabricate stains in the dominion of language, the cork bark nativity scene maker discovers his stains in the very model. It is thus profoundly realist; it does not turn its back on the world nor disdainfully flee from immediate reality, unlike the pessebrists of Bath.

Let the ascendent growth of cork bark, with its ruts and ruddy stains, its scratches and serrated surfaces like those in Wright of Derby's paintings that take us from the lantern to the hill, from the light to the lava, bring us back again to Beckford. Once, on the occasion of a stay in Switzerland where he met Henri Benedict de Saussure –one of the founders of meteorology and a great lover of mountain climbing– he came into contact with the rough and aged cork bark of the Alps. His first novel, *The Vision*, takes place in a intensely fictitious alpine setting, much like the world of lonely lights and solitary moons portrayed by Wright. "The rays of this glorious planet", he wrote, "gave the crusty stone pinnacles a strange, fantastic air, sometimes like giant idols, others like obelisks or even mysteriously formed pyramids, great sculptures which seem to stand as if confessing." Later, a few lines further on, the cork bark is liberated: "It is with serenity that I now observe the rocky pinnacles, nothing but pinnacles."

Everything rises and falls, a piece of cork bark gives account of itself in the order of something which seems something else; the larger it gets the sharper it seems, the higher it gets the more broken up it becomes. Beckford carries out these enlarging ascents outside of the text. Aware of his rejection of the world as it is, he has another sort of elevation available, another type of writing; already at the age of seventeen in a letter addressed to Cozens, he swears that he will raise "a Tower with which to escape from the earth of men towards another place where the air will not be corrupted by the breath of those miserable folk who are the object of our disdain and rejection." Years later, when he writes *Vathek*, he constructs a verbal palace for the caliph: the palace of Alkorremi, in the city of Samarah. A palace, as Beckford explains, which Vathek has inherited from his father, though he expands it, adding on five more palaces, one for each sense:

Eternal Festival or the Unsatiable; the Temple of Melody or the Nectar of the Soul; Delight of the Eyes or Support of Memory; Palace of Perfumes or the Spire of Voluptuousness; and the Jewel's Retreat, or the Perillous One. To finish Vathek invokes the aid of the genies and with great speed a tower of eleven thousand stones is raised, "not so much to save us from the flood, but out of the insolent curiosity to penetrate into the secrets of the Heavens."
At Fonthill Beckford plans to bring the Palace of Alkorremi to life. He raises this piece of cork bark on the top of a hill, on the airiest spot in the region, in a pointy Gothic which flees from the more austere English Gothic. The architect hired is James Wyatt. The first tower raised collapses just after it is built in October of 1793. But by 1807 Fonthill Abbey can finally be inhabited, its main tower climbing to the extravagant height of 84 metres. Unlike the exoticism of Splendens —the palace at Fonthill inherited from his parents, which behind a Palladian facade enclosed an exotic array of curios from Egypt, Turkey, Holland, or China— the interiors of Fonthill Abbey were furnished with highly valuable pieces from as far away or more, never failing to demonstrate a great erudition in taste: precious porcelain, ostrich eggs, a six-thousand book library -essentially literary and biographical works, but also medieval manuscripts, ocult tracts, spiritual texts, Blake illustrations- as well as exotic fruits, perfumes, paintings by Raphael, Watteau, Velázquez, Bellini, silverworks, reptiles, all told creating a multitude of exquisite, unpredictable references constituting a pre-spotting or sketch of the type of ambience which Huysmans insinuated in *À rebours*. Meanwhile, once set up in Fonthill Abbey, Beckford demolished Splendens, the mansion at Fonthill where he had spent most of his life, Beckford's Hohenswangau, his inheritance at the edge of a lake which had become the workshop for the latter construction.
In 1810, as a consequence of the falling prices of Jamaican sugar —there is always some far-off cause, distant and remote— his fortune is considerably reduced. In 1822 Fonthill Abbey appears in a Christie's auction catalogue. Three years later, James Wyatt calls Beckford to his death bed to plead forgiveness, confessing that the foundations of the structure had not been laid according to his instructions, so that the building was bound to tumble some day. Suddenly the cork bark cedes and that very year the tower falls, the entrance way and cloister also collapsing. Beckford decides to move to Bath to live, where from 1826 to 1828 he erects another tower, the Lansdown Tower, raised on a hill at the highest spot in the town. Henry Goodridge, the architect hired for the project, designs a cemetery at the foot of the tower two years after Beckford's death where the latter's sarcophagus, designed by Beckford himself, was laid. Still today Beckford Tower can be seen climbing above the red granite sarcophagus set flat upon the earth.
Cork bark imitating copper, in a parody of dark etchings, allows Ludwig the Bavarian king to wander into these lines. He buries a view of the Edward III gallery at Fonthill (Beckford believed himself to be descended from the king), giving rise to a never-ending, ever-flowing collectionism, convoking styles and latitudes in a story, like that of Ludwig, of centuries and kings in corresponding degree.
Now the cork bark cracks with the sound of badly burning wood, tree trunks or fishing sinkers, as if a name had been revealed to its memory: Hohenswangau? Fonthill? Falkenstein? A whole series of towers are raised and then collapse. Whatever they may be, golden tones shut off all apparitions with goldleafed cork bark and wooden mouldings. Time has softened some creators with a carpet of moss, while the cork bark leaves other, fatally capricious creators exposed to the elements.
The corkers of Bath, unlike the Catalans, tend irresistibly towards the shadow, with a certain disdain for the immediate world. We have not mentioned that what Vathek accomplished with his eleven thousand stone tower was, finally, the Citadel of Infernal Fire, "the first truly atrocious hell in litera-

ture", as Borges would say. There is a painting by Wright of Derby that narrates such a pompous discovery. It is called *Miravan Forcing Open the Entrance of the Tomb of his Ancesters*.
The very author described it as thus: "Miravan, a young Hungarian noble, orders a tomb to be opened which is headed by an inscription that reads: Within this tomb is found the greatest treasure that Cressus could ever possess. Once inside the tomb we find only filth and another inscription: Here reigns repose. Miserable sacrilege commits he who searches for gold among the dead! Go, son of lucre, you will never find this repose." In the painting reproducing this scene there is a central light as well, a lantern hung with a small bronze figure which, as Judy Egerton remarks in the catalogue text, "spins unperturbed, turned eternally away from the world to keep its feeble light over the tomb".

La pintura i la boca, pp. 150-157

THE SILS CORK

All this turns into a stage at Sils. Then a nativity scene maker, dressed in a three piece velvet suit, shows the auditorium a piece of cork. First he shows the back with its admirable, velvety reddish colour that cork bark typically acquires a year after harvest. Next, he holds the cork with all its wrinkles and pocks in his open hands, as a kind of ceremonial offering to the public. Within a few seconds, the cork begins to grow until it reaches the size of the stage itself. Then —even more impressive— it doubles and then triples its size, though its immense optical field never diminishes the true dimensions of the stage. There comes a moment when the audience is surprised to see the expanse of the entire town in real size, like a nativity scene in cork bark, full of all kinds of details. The expectation is extraordinary.
The performance lasts until the nativity scene maker suddenly turns the cork bark back around and everything disappears. He waves to the audience and the applause rings out, a delayed noise surging from out of those very extensions which in a flash have shrunk in size as if the spectators were squeezing what they had just witnessed with their hands. It has been said that some spectators, after leaving the show, went off to their own cork oak groves to pick up chunks of bark in their hands, in the hope of playing out their curiosity.

EXERCISES IN WRITTEN PAINTING

In this series of texts, the illusion that one can journey across painting undergoes an elaborate process which begins with the statement that "the canvas and nature are one and the same". Once this has been accepted, writing, painting, and walking take place in the same territory. The animism which emanates from this is an effect of Perejaume's having removed the traditional medium from painting, which is now placed in the landscape. To reach completion, this process requires a moment of forgetting, such as that in which Perejaume writes, "Mondrian, Mondrian, Mondrian — on and on until the name becomes odd to your ears."
The tone of these texts, and especially of the briefest among them, is typical of the impersonal propositions of Conceptual Art. In this case, it is practically impossible that the conditions needed to accomplish such propositions should be met, despite Perejaume's suggestion that the reader check them — as his choice of verbal moods reveals. The indirect function of these texts is, therefore, one of indicating the imbalance between the conditions of enunciation and the real conditions with which we live.

PAINTING ON A WALK

Do I love –you'll say– this landscape,
so beautiful, green and covered with waves!
How I delight in going beyond with it
on to the canvas, with a few brush-strokes

at night! And to let the brush open pathways,
as though I willed myself to vanishment, and at times,
between painting and umbrage, edgeways,
to sit on a frame under golden oak-trees.

Landscape and I are set free through the painting,
we go deeper into the woods again:
Montalt, Montnegre, the sea, nothing halts us.

I return weary when I think, happily enough,
that picture and nature are the same thing.
Walking along, the paintings keep growing.

Translated by J. L. Gili
Nova antologia de poetes del Maresme, Vilassar de Mar: quaderns de la font del cargol, 1983. *Traç*, 21, Mataró 1988.
This text also appeared in *Perejaume, Oli damunt paper*. Barcelona: Empúries, 1991 p. 11

PICTURE GALLERIES

Painting is probably living out one of the most rebellious moments of its history. On one hand, the cession of part of its repertoire to photographic or cinematographic supports has grown to such a degree that these photographic images can be composed, invented and virtually processed with technological pigmentation and sophisticated post-pictorial methodologies. On the other hand, painting has become more and more a territorial reality, spacious and independent, a legacy that is not so different from the earth, the forests, or from our language. The very name "Picture Galleries" corroborates this ever so expansive legacy, with Louvres trapped in nature and autonomous Himalayas aligning themselves in a museological ordering of time. Here the creator employs other creators, along with walls and frames, as the support for monochromatic fields; here painting, thick and obscure, exposes its own opacity onto the image of the photographic support: covering and concealing what until now it had attempted to represent. Thus leaving the pigments to the side in what was a much wider possibility of meaning and silence, using real, accessible pigments instead, as if in the end paint were not considered for painting, but simply for its own existence.

Exhibition invitation for *Pinacoteques*. Barcelona: Galeria Joan Prats/Artgràfic, February 1992. This text also appeared in *La pintura i la boca*, p. 166.

THE PAINTER

The painter has surprised us while he was working, uncovering us in a chance combination of brushstrokes; we have watched him search us out, and in a most familiar way put his signature upon what he has seen.

La pintura i la boca, p. 85.

EVERYTHING EVOLVES

Everything evolves in pairs like in a spacious dance hall. Sometimes the painter does not come back, he takes the path of painting and never returns.

La pintura i la boca p. 86.

ANAPHORAS, SYNECDOCHES, AND ASYNDETONA

to Saint Luke

They say that the Virgin Mary took visible form, in mystical fashion, on a picture surface when Saint Luke attempted to paint upon it. As if Saint Luke would now try to paint something that had already appeared, untouched, that Saint Luke had already painted.

La pintura i la boca, p. 101.

DETOUR A WILD CREEK

Detour a wild creek home, or send a whiff of the sea into the theatre pit. Build picture galleries at the foot of the mountains, with avalanches rushing in.

La pintura i la boca, p 90.

DRAPE THE PYRENEES

Drape the Pyrenees in canvas, from a certain height up.

La pintura i la boca, p. 91.

GRIND

Azurite blue, malachite green
reds and yellows of cinnabar
vermilion, realgar, and orpiment
minium orange, gypsum white.
In a small mortar grind up the entire world.

THE WHITENING

The whitening of the Pedrera facade by sandblasting.
The whitening, by sandblasting, of the crags of les Agudes, on Montseny.

TAKE ELEVEN STILL LIFES

Take eleven still lifes by Zurbarán to the main field at Can Tarrades. You arrive by lorry on a rough road and, once there, unload the paintings one by one in the middle of the field. Make sure that the paintings are laid out evenly side by side so as to form a flat retable upon the ground. Exhibit the paintings right where the field lightly rolls, so that the retable might gently curve with it.

THE PLENAIRIST

The pleinairist makes up his eyes and lips and then, before the dressing mirror, a terrible commotion is raised. Right there, with a twist in the air, another room appears: on a promotory he sees an old woman carrying a bunch of broom. Behind her, great clouds drift through the walls. At the far end of the room a buzz of surprise and admiration is heard. Then the vision slips away and the air is once again shut off, like a curtain falling on the stage.

PAINT FIVE BRUSHSTROKES

Paint five brushstrokes in oil on a piece of ice as if the painting were the future, able to return to the earth in just a few hours. As if the paint, in clock-like fashion, were to join time; as if it had incorporated itself into time so as to separate itself from its necessary support. As if the support itself were time.

La pintura i la boca, p. 96.

FLY IN A SMALL PLANE

Fly in a small plane at eight or nine hundred metres above sea level, picking up enough speed so that a brush placed outside, loaded with heavy paint, might run as soon as it touched the air, turning the air into a rigid base. In this way the paint flows out from the brush as if spread upon a wall, with the air holding the brushstroke flat and long for a metre or so, before letting it fall.

La Pintura i la boca, p. 95.

MONDRIAN, MONDRIAN

Mondrian, Mondrian, Mondrian – on and on until the name becomes odd to your ears, until you are sure it is the site of an inevitable, preemptory reality. Who has never been to Mondrian, to the toponymic Mondrian, to the ever so indigenous Mondrian?

La Pintura i la boca, p. 100.

SOME WORKS HAVE PUNCHED HOLES

Some works have punched holes and dented my thought, making my head spin. Some have been made and done, and I have not been able to get rid of them, as they strike my forehead, bruise the nape of my neck. Works made from that paint we carry in our mouths, never able to find the words to get it out.

A MAN

A man sits on a rock. He holds a long brush as if it were a spear. He reaches out his hand and points to another man, off in the distance, who is approaching with a brush as well. Nearby eight men are speaking, each with an enormous brush in his hands. Right in front of us, a lump that we had taken for a rock stands upright: it is another man with yet another brush.

NOTION OF THE ARTWORK

Pulverize all notion of the artwork. Make pigmentation out of such a notion. Aglutinate, with linseed oil, the pigmentation of the notion of the artwork.

UNPAINTING

As subgenres of late Modernity, the abstraction-induced elimination of representation, monochrome, and demateralization are radicalized by unpainting. Premised on a view of painting as 'predatory', unpainting is meant to methodically restore the materials which have been given over to the representation in which we are immersed. The phrase "to stop making", which appears repeatedly in these texts, is conceived of as a way of allowing things to appear already made. This is effectively an ironic comment on Duchamp's readymades. The activities which are suggested after the interruption of representation are of such a rich range that there is no room to speak of an ultimatum: "we half-discover an active will in stopping making". Unpainting is, rather, a point of inflection which assumes that images and representations are to be treated in accord with sustainable principles.
Parcs Interiors: l'obra de set despintors (Inner Parks: The Work of Seven Unpainters) affirms the co-occurence of painting and unpainting and ultimately develops unpainting as a paradox. The range of attitudes for which these seven painters stand suggests a number of possible ways out of a hypothetical crisis which threatens to deplete our natural resources.Yet this text may also be read as a history of art in the future, in which 'chosen' artists will react to what is at present unquestionable.

OH PAINTERS

Oh painters, here where we stand, is there or is there not painting? Must it be or must it not? Should we lay some down, add some on, or should we not?

ART AND ARCHEOLOGY

Art and Archeology seem to fulfill each other somewhere.
Perhaps one day, in a dig, we will find the art of what is to come.

SCULPTURE OF BUSA

Do no sculpture on the Busa mountain range. See the range as the sculpture it already resembles. Be aware that there is something of Foix written in the margin and signed upon it. And what is more, another part that we now sign, upon reading the sculpture I am speaking of.

La pintura i la boca, p. 105.

POSTNATURALISM 1

Spread out a Giacometti, straighten out a Soutine, fill the fauves with greys, curve a Mondrian.

La pintura i la boca, p. 98

ERASE EVERYTHING

Erase everything and blur the erasures! Eagerly seek out new delays! We do not have to know whether paintings hinder us from getting where we are going, or whether they lead us there. An avenging site drives us on, headstrong, and it is with this irrepressible desire to paint that we conjure up Lutheran whites, the erosion of impediments, open formats – and with paint fixer on a rubber eraser, we half discover an active will by stopping doing things.

La pintura i la boca, p. 112. A Spanish translation of this text by Ana Romero appeared in the exhibition catalogue for *Espacios públicos: Sueños privados*. Madrid: Government of the Autonomous Community of Madrid, 1994, pp. 156-157.

POSTNATURALISM 2

By real genetic transformations in a rose, obtain the very scarlet that Emil Nolde used to paint a rose.

La pintura i la boca, p. 99

TURPENTINERS

Not a precipice, not a torrent, not a cliff,
but pregnant with religion and poetry.
THOMAS GRAY

Oh painters, all too bold, we who make pictures out of anything! Just try some day to go to the peaks. If they are real, if there are any left – can't you hear their laughter as they watch you climb them? Can't you hear the peak's guffaws on seeing you with your canvases? Can't you see them, high above us, laughing and laughing?

La pintura i la boca p. 110. This text also appeared in *Espacios públicos. Sueños privados*, pp. 156-157.

PUT GOLD BACK

Put gold back into the earth, scatter the mountains with bronze and marble and ivory, so that they might represent just what we are missing most: the place from whence they came.

La pintura i la boca, p. 113. This text also appeared in *Espacios públicos. Sueños privados*, pp. 156-157.

INDOOR PARKS: THE WORK OF SEVEN UNPAINTERS

Sweep away these footsteps on high /
I will not be a bother any more.

J. VERDAGUER

To the end and effect that painting as such be banned from painting.

CODEX OF THE CROWN OF ARAGON

Unpainting is an upside down formula, where painting questions some of its very own foundations. It is difficult to imagine the painters of our day not being tuned into this budding point of concern and illusion, where everything seems painterly. It is in this way that, in as much part of the craft repels today's painters and the other attracts us, painting has become a vibrant centre of reflection and controversy.

All told, we do not yet know how to clearly discern if unpainting is a new craft or if it is still a pure simulacrum of the painter's craft, or just as well a subterfuge that has chosen painting itself in order to keep on painting, simply using (or at least seeming to use) the very pigments that have come up against it.

The examples of unpainters that we have united here are, as we will see, greatly varied in intention. What really brings them together is the starting point, which is the same for all unpainters: the search for a higher myth where painting and anti-painting might come together. It is in this search that unpainters unfold all the ambiguity of their position, vaguely conscious of the fact that they paint to not paint. Trying to chose the exact dissolvent, the adequate anti-colour... Even though, when you think of it, they could just as easily search for some place to hide away artist, painting and art itself, in fact they try to continue practicing their craft, even when united in the rhetorical licence that the term 'unpainters' grants them.

If unpainting rose again, if such a moment came, if it were to be a fundamental trait of the art of the future, then the trajectory of its language would have had three well-differentiated phases: the use of expressive materials in the traditional period; the cheapening of expressive materials in the modern period; and the staged suffering of materials, their effective elimination, or the attempt to eliminate them, in the current period. But this remains to be seen; for now we can only refer to the artful question concerning the painting some artists seem to be doing, among whom we have chosen the seven that follow.

The first unpainter we must turn to has become an archer. For him, colours are put into the world just right, so full of oil that in the simple act of opening the paint pot the point of the shot has been fulfilled; to add more paint or to copy colours would be redundant. Thus this unpainter travels towards the sites he wishes to unpaint prepared with a bow and quiver, with long brushes as arrows. He chooses the most picturesque sites and, grabbing his polished wood bow, is the first to get his colours right, each according to the exact tone it already has.

It is difficult not to find a medieval, legendary air in his exercises, where with each tone he seeks he lets go an unerring shot, battling with the landscape like a knight with a dragon until no more brushes are left in the quiver, so that these brushes, within this archer's reality, cause the landscape to fall flat, with turpentine streaming from its wounds.

The second unpainter also shuns his craft with the idea that the world is beginning to break apart. A long time ago he observed the chemically poisoned turpentines and the grime of the earth, carried from one place to another in great abundance, along with the successive paintedness shining from within things, piled up in glowing layers. He then decided to close himself off in the studio for days on end, in the hope that he might find a paint so porous as to be transparent, vanishing once it had been used.
His investigations into a paint that leaves no traces apart from a miraculous effect on the observer, have lead him to imagine a painting that might appear before a small public through the action of a few images shown by projection, though always by a secretly guarded mechanism. Our unpainter believes that this kind of technological pigment marvellously suits the overall sense of creation. With the dissolution it allows, very soon we might employ an opalescent and thinly luminous paint kept in small flasks, which we could make appear in expanded form in the most unexpected of places, all thanks to a technology so well prepared that it lightens the excesses of its very processes. In this task it remains absorbed, searching for a painting that sparkles, one that is full of holes, an emminently porous painting with an extreme mediatic cleanliness, thanks to which the frame that supports it need not be soiled, nor bear any contagious substance other than the pure miracle of its appearance.

Another unpainter —the third as we go— proposes repairing a secular grievance, trying to turn paintings into those places they have been taken from, returning images someone had tried to take away to the places they had come from. In order to do this, he travels to those motifs and places which he knows have inspired these paintings, and, when finding them, lifts all the paint off of them, using strippers and dissolvents. The flakes of paint he then obtains are carefully guarded in a box, and box in hand he goes to the places which inspired the pictorial content of these pigments. Once there, he digs a hole in the ground, a forearm deep or more, and deposits the paint crusts like someone making a votive offering. When done, he covers them up with earth so that they can never be found again.

The following unpainter, driven by intense conviction, has taken it upon himself to persuade his fellow painters to stop painting. He is, thus, an activist, accustomed to verbal discourse, defending a nature free of unctions and paints, like a fresh face, lacking make-up. Eloquent and articulated, he travels through studios and the other places where he knows artists gather, especially going to those places frequented by those who paint in the open air; and once there, he speaks to them like this: "Stop reproducing things, and stop inventing things to reproduce as well! Observe the grove as the grove really is, what other could better it! Take pleasure in each thing just as it appears to us. And if literary or pictorial activity is an obligation, take the very grove as an infinitely unfolding literary or pictorial activity, just needing to be captured. You should not take more pleasure in anything, nor in anything should you be more spellbound, nor in any way should you feel you are before a more realistic and true art, than in the art of painting that the sky performs on things, which things do between themselves, which each thing does to itself. Believe me, artist friends, whoever continues to paint things should not put more paint on them than the paint they already have on them; better even to take off a layer, if in this way we could learn more than in painting them again." We can see here how this unpainter loves to speak to other painters he encounters, doing everything possible to seek them out and tell this to them, urging them to renounce the world of images, of banal, flighty layerings: 'Make yourselves a hole inside', he tells them, 'so that the world might turn inward, because the world thus returns to its origin as unique and original; and the world rests, once again, within itself, and vision is not just exterior but interior as well'. The work of this unpainter is anyone who will listen to him. And this comes to mind because some of his most ardent followers have come together under the name 'The Gazers'. We do not as yet have conclusive enough data to really say how many of them there are, nor to what degree their attitude will last, nor whether it is a pure emmanation of the doctrines of the master.

'The Gazers' —as far as we know— are those who practice gazing and try to maintain it without having need of anything else, trying to make sure that the gaze, so carefully protected, may be translated through them in their way of living, seeing and speaking. For their part, with their eyes they signal out what they only know, thus letting things speak out in favour of themselves, without holding anything back.

Painting for them is a pure source of light. Rather than going out to see, the gazing author travels to places to ask himself what there is of him that these places draw, watching the sites observing him, as they make light sketchings in the air that only he can see and admire. Here we see that 'The Gazers' practice the act of painting or watch it being carried out in their very selves, while at the same time they themselves are the work of this unpainter we have just met, whose enthusiasm seems to have converted them.

The fifth unpainter is, for his part, quiet by nature, fleeing from overly crowded places. Perhaps it was due to his timidity and gentleness that he loved to go walking for hours on end, his painting implements around his neck. It relieved him tremendously to wear himself out. It was an act of restoration and pleasure for him to celebrate the fact that things stayed in their places, that it was not necessary to reproduce or paint them, but rather just pass them by, materials in hand.

He knew no painting as reverent and erasable as that which carried him past the roughest of places with his painter's utensils. Later on, thinking of the strictly graphic activity of his hikes across the land, he determined which landscapes would not be drawn, as well as all the pictures that are constantly moved across the world to be shown. It pleased him then to imagine the enormous quantity of paintings that every day go from here to there, how these paintings were able to outline the natural reliefs with their own landscapes, or draw their destinations in the air, with the help of all kinds of transportation vehicles.

Seeing how the paintings generally chose routes that were not very safe, but rather too straight and slippery, he thought of having a few paintings made by authors he especially admired, to be done along surer, more intercut paths. In this way he wore a painting around his neck, just as previously he had carried his painting utensils, directing himself towards a craggy spot outlined by the painting itself, so that little by little the painting would come to obey the real relief he was carrying it across. While he was doing this, he noticed a third dimension in painting, a sculptural aspect in finished canvases that their creators certainly had never imagined. Thanks to these sort of imaginings, he has carried a small Giotto through the mountain ranges of Wales, a Rodchenko monochrome along the east coast of Corsica, and is thinking of tackling the peaks of the Atlas Mountains accompanied by a Ferdinand Hodler landscape.

As with those who have come before, the sixth unpainter venerates the landscape as the most fundamental thing of all, for like them he believes that the landscape is all-encompassing, that it is everything. For this unpainter, however, painting may no longer sidetrack us, nor can it be played around with. The great physical and human transformations that the land has undergone have made him takes sides in favour of those activities that strengthen places, in detriment of those others, whether painterly or sporting, that ravenously consume the land's reality and presence. This unpainter would find it distasteful if we were to speak of him for much longer. He has simply decided to stop painting to work within the landscape in the profession that, according to him, most benefits it, whether farming the earth, working in the woods, tending livestock, or simply being friendly to those who still live in it in the way he thinks is right. His is an exercise in disappearance: to become a farmer, woodcutter, or shepherd, to enter fully into the landscape and directly avoid any popularizing derivation of his art.

There is still a seventh unpainter, even though the landscape is so round and nature so concave that this unpainter goes back to being a painter. According to him, Duchamp had already tempted unpainting, as the ready-made was already, as he observed, a subterfuge, the attempt to make a clean, alert painting. For this reason we can now affirm that the painting of the ready-made has not been any less predatory than traditional painting, since it has ended up capturing things in a more invisible fashion and in greater number. The unpainter-become-painter likes to note how even though at first we believed that it was pleasant enough to take art as anything that came our way, it has not taken long to see that, as a consequence, our surroundings have become even more artified, painterly, excessively reworked. From this he thought that perhaps it was painting itself and not any other thing that had to take us away from hateful painting, and it was our fault for not knowing how to make use of it adequately, for having overwhelmed it through misuse. From here we see that he has directed all his efforts to find out if there is a painting that has kept its innocence, with a style that feeds representation, a style that more than covering it over, takes root; an art so arid and ingenious that it overcomes all expectations, so that a ready-eemed painting might remain after having senselessly tumbled all over the place. The great fidelity with which this artist lives out his vocation allows him, so he says, to discern to what degree paint is pure and to what degree is it soiled, and once this has been established, to go on from there.

El paisaje, collection "Arte y naturaleza", n. 2, Huesca, 1996, pp. 163-167. Republished in *Perejaume, Tres dibujos*, Santiago de Compostela: Centro Galego de Arte Contemporánea, 1997, pp. 40-45.

OISM: VOICE EXERCISES OF A PAINTER

Oism [1] concentrates the perception of landscape in the sense of hearing. Perejaume has consistently addressed the question of phonetics in his writings. (Indeed, *El puig* [The Peak] appeared in 1993's *La pintura i la boca*) The figure of the place-namer, which first appeared in *El paisatge és rodó* (1995) refers to the technique of naming. In a later book, *Oïsme: Una escriptura natural a partir del croquis pirinencs de Jacint Verdaguer* (1998), Perejaume enlarges his hypothesis of sound which is liberated from writing and discerned from vision. Nonetheless, oism gets underway with a poetics based on latent writing and linked to territory, *La bardissa* (The Bramble Patch). Writing thus behaves just as painting does when granted its independence from the canvas.

Oism allows landscape to be reformulated as a "field of transmission". Although based on sound, the texts in this series visualize connections which fill apparently empty space. Thus, despite their old-fangled rhetoric, these texts address a very contemporary problem by alluding to the invasion of physical space by communication technology.
Texts such as *El suro sorollós* (The Noisy Cork Bark) make it evident that the essayistic spirit present throughout these writings manifests itself in shapes and genres as different as the short tale.

1 From the Catalan "Oir" which means "hear". Oism could be understood as "hearism". (Translator's note)

THE BRAMBLE PATCH

More than once, while out walking somewhere, I have come to see a most marvellous rubric in a bramble patch. That web of lines, floating and twisted, is perhaps nature's way of putting its signature on everything, there where it can be seen, with each bush sprinkled with various names in an entangled and interwoven handwriting. Not in vain, clearing the woods or a field consists above all in pulling out blackberry bushes, honeysuckle and saddle trees, so that the remaining trees and the ground below might be freed of that graphology the land expresses itself with, that writing which serves as its shade and protection.
I have always thought that instead of personal and unchanging autographs, we would do better to bring into our written modes those odd, easy-going, tree-like traces that nature seems to be woven with. Such brambly flourishes are in fact beautiful writing models. It seems at times as if reality operates as these bushes do, proceeding in a similarly mangled prose, closing in on the certainty and measure of a definitive version in a never-ending series of loops and leaps.
We must admit that any notion of interlacing tends, in our thought, to respond to an unruly and capricous graphology. Rarely are we able to comprehend where what we say begins, or where it ends, or where it might take us: we always pick it up somewhere in the middle, in the midst of speaking, just letting it happen. This is the mystery that makes things real, happy to abandon us half way down the road, slipping us up, showing us again and again how all connectedness is extended and widened, how it lives amidst the missing links. Disorder is thus an interlocutor we have requested to enable us to move on to wherever he might take us, with that natural spontaneity that disorder seems to instinctively carry out everything with, like a mute and cunning guide we are left to follow.

It is quite probable that a profound and hidden order does exist, though we can rarely transmit this order with common language or intellectual concepts. It is rare that we can even conceive of it. Instead we insistently perceive it as something certain, copious, vast, even tutelary, though it can never be followed up. If it does appear it does so like a lightning strike, shaking us out of our habits and logic, dynamiting the rule of order we carry with us. It is in this way that we might observe how the course of events is shifted, how it changes direction, like a kind of fold which ends up being the most abrupt way this profound order —this apparent disorder— has to emerge.
Sometimes it is as if we were unable to think at all, as if we were unable to concentrate enough. All vertebrate peacelessness is hopeless. We know that this or that other is fundamental, though we cannot quite distinguish it clearly, nor give it all the attention it deserves. First off we abstain from writing until the subject is made fully manifest. Finally, however, we annote the instructions that have come to us out of fear of losing them, out of fear that in spite of all indications, they will be forgotten to us, slip away from us, and depart.
Words are not able to fully write themselves out either, their foliage thinning out and getting lost within the shadows and twists of a bramble patch. They look like they are going to speak about a fact or thought just as we have ordered them to, but they stop half way as another word comes along to distract them, as if obeying an even vaster order than the one we tried to impose.
It is then that you get the impression that, as if sitting upon a white swan, everything moves back and forth without stopping to rest. It is then too that the stable and changing worlds coincide, coming to pertain to a single order, tracing its phosphorescent signature through all we have just written. [...]

Oïsme, pp. 17-19.

THE NOISY CORK BARK

The toponymist went about with his ears covered, no sound distracting him; there he was all right, listening to himself. The very site he was in was making the sound within him. The sound would always ring out in his head after staying still and silent on the spot for a while. It was a dry sound that did not repeat itself, made in each site only upon entering for the first time; the sound in each place was different, completely genuine, the buzz of each site that settled inside of him.

Another toponymist tried to read in the sites the eurythmics of the surrounding horizons, a harmonious arrangement of relief lines. "Perhaps the relief is in fact a wave shape", he thought, "the oscillograph of a sound someone has emitted." This toponymist wandered about the cliffs, as carefully as someone walking across the roof of his mouth, speaking the sites out loud in the conviction that they were mere sounding devices. He saw the voices, or tried to see them; and then, in front of some name he had suddenly discovered he would exclaim: "Learn, oh poets, to write. Observe Mount Carlit or the Valley of Oo or the Rosal lowlands, it does not matter.

No word has ever been written so splendidly!"

It might also occur that the name is listening to us, like it does on the Montsant range: a gigantic range which, as Joan Coromines wrote, looks from the town of Cabdella "like a series of small heads on top of an near-impenetrable wall". Great attention must always be paid. In the majority of cases the breaths escape so timidly that noone is afraid of them. All of those who move through toponymistic territories are aware to what degree a sound, even the most deafening sound, is nothing more than a quality of silence. It is precisely with such conviction that they might go to the mountain pass at l'Oreller –at twenty minutes from Espinalbet– to the deep pools of Fumanya –in the Lluçanès river gorge– or over Tambor ridge –on the way to Oris near Pont de Suert– to carry out their investigations. Apart from whether the air is more or less lively, the earth for these oists, as if set in an outdoor kiln, often carries the air as if trapped in clay letters. If we want to guess what they are, we would have to do so in complete silence. It has been told in this regard that some oists made deep wells in the earth for the sole purpose of discovering the hidden depths of a name.

None of this contradicts what has been a widely held belief about all kinds of sounding stones: stones which keep sound closed off and recorded within. As with the case of a stone from Gallicant, near Gallecs in the Vallès district, where it is said a rooster crow is heard. In the rock of Polls on Montserrat, on the path from Collbató up to the monastery, the chirping of a brood of baby chicks is heard, while at Àngels rock, within the ancient walled compound of Pedralbes, you can hear the song of birds in spinning flight. It seems that the harvesters at Hortsavinyà who discovered the Virgen Mary of Erola in a bale in the middle of a muddy field just as they were undoing for threshing, heard a voice which clearly pronounced each one of their names.

We have also been told the story of those who named the Busa flats. It seems that three men had climbed up the Ora Valley through the mountain passes at Ordigues and Arques, until reaching the The Cross, when none of these places yet had names. Upon arriving they mutually decided that the name they would give to the place would encompass all that they could see before them. Soon enough they all agreed that the site, though itself quite large, required a short name. After all, what good would it do to draw out the name when they knew that the marvellous variety of forms, colours and textures that lay before them was undescribable? Instead of a bunch of letters put together to describe the place, they were required to think of a group of letters that would contain all they could see.

Together they came across the form of an "s" in the scrub grass that pleased them enormously, so much so that they were then able to see it in the hills as well, and along a long curved ridge.
So they had the "s", but it was not easy for them to find other letters. One of the climbers noticed that the changing light and the splendour of the view had distracted them from carrying out their appointed task, so they all decided to close their eyes for a moment and put their hands on the earth to see what sound could be felt. It was in this way, as if they were the sounding boxes of the site they were at, that they discovered the sounds of the "u" and the "a".
The three of them then set about to combine these letters, writing the combinations they felt were more appropriate down on a piece of paper: "Sasu", "Assusa" and even "Asussa". They became aware that the name had grown all too emphatically, deciding that such sounds were not right for a place of that altitude. The discussion continued, and with it a rising uncertainty. Some say that the "b" was dictated to them by a bubbly creek nearby. Others say that the clouds wrote it out for them, like an ornate initial letter on Capolat Peak. They are not even sure what lead them to the name Busa. The fact is that they would have been hard pushed to analyze how they came to the Busa name. But the truth is that not one of them came to it first; they all saw it at once, and it frightened them to witness the enormous breath of truth that the name seemed to expire from within when they pronounced it. It was as if the name had always been there, established on those heights, and that all they had done was flush it out into the light.
Perhaps all names were here first. It is possible that in each site there was a name written on a label before anything else, and that all the landscapes had to do was settle into the thrones of honour and other armchairs set across that great amphitheatre of names. Perhaps all sites, all things and our lives themselves are nothing but the ornamentation of names. Or perhaps the mountains and all other things have taken the place of such naming, with their names held within them. This sound within invites us to find such places, to go out to them, correcting our hearing so that we might distinguish the sounds which best suit them. Or perhaps each site is little more than a thickening residue accumulated around the word that names it.
[...]

Oïsme, pp. 47-51.

A BOX OF VELVET

[...]

In vain you attempt to smooth the cork bark of your tongue out on a piece of paper. You take pen and paper and go to the tongue to make a copy; exhausted, you see that it is impossible to follow the voice the tongue articulates, and how the tongue is too high and wide for the voice, with an empassioned will bringing forth a great flow of words, sinking the world into the words and printing them in volumes and volumes so that no word may be forgotten. In the volumes of the tongue the words are pleated and pressed, pushed up in even newer folds and altitudes by the weight of the tongue.

Oh landscaped voice! Great sonorous compression of airs and geological reliefs! Whoever speaks has the landscape itself as a discursive field! A pure crack setting apart the voice, and the path the voice takes as it passes by. Observe this dark mass of respirating trees nearby: all the woods has been unfolded to receive the warm, rising breeze, the lively winds search for a brave chest that might make them even more sonorous; they would blow down some site along the straightest of routes into the darkest reaches of the woody hill, and having arrived, hack their way through the wall of undergrowth, throwing their sketching voices into the void of the air.

Oratory of winds and of the vernacular! Local character of the breezes! The oral use of geological reliefs in the moment the wind comes to squeeze them. Sound out (for you will sound out); we move from field to field with the wind blowing us onward through names which appear in infinite quantities and variety. Mutual soundings of air and elements! "Cacaphony of noises pursuing their adventure through the valleys" (Lezama Lima). All things stretched out along the places they sound out, the wide channel of the voice agitating the forests with names of yet other forests.

The windy valley has become a twisted muzzle, the brambles offering a fitting pose for the sound they wish to emit. Certain rocks retain air so they might make a lighter sound, a sound coming from deeper within, ventilated, as if drawn from a well. Wide channel of the voice! Long-winded landscape of the air! Gaze upon a huge exhalation within this grand physionomy.

"Ora" is the synonym of "oratjol", a "soft wind". The rocks at Busa, seen from the Valley of Ora, have the shape of a great snorting mouth, with sharp teeth and a spiky oak tree tongue. A few rock juttings hold off the wind, while small acoustic masses condense and fall due to the gravity or air conditions, with others in turn taking to the air, gravity-less, or just as well floating through it. Everything responds to the forms and measures of the voice: a leafy speech with windy characters and silent vowels set beneath unfinished peaks along an all too thin finger of stone. The river of the Valley of Ora begins as a stream between the Upper Berguedà and the Cardener. It then cuts through the gigantic ranges of Busa and Bastets. Each one of these names is inflated and respectively deflates in the puff of a flat ridge; sometimes the wind stops suddenly with an almost animal sigh, while other names are placed upon the sites in an arid lexicon that once again envigorates the wind, and the stream continues to move downwards through silences and heavy exhalations. There is another Busa sounding out at Serralbo in Upper Aragon. It does so, in fact, indirectly, all alone. We refer to a small isolated church called Saint John of Busa whose origin is unknown, as not the least bit of documentation has been found in reference to it. And even further away, in Portugal, we are lead to the paronym "Buçaco", a rough mountain range to the north of Coïmbra from where we can just make out the waters of the Atlantic. [...]

Oïsme, pp. 85-88.

OF GREAT LANDOWNING AIRS

[...]

In the same way that the site goes forth to tell us its name, or to speak of itself tucked away in a creator's name, so on the site we often note the passing of a voice that does not belong to it.

This fact especially intrigues us. We are often dealing with unspeakable phrases, murmoured and confused, which cross the air, cooling it down as they leave it cracked and out of breath, lingering for a good two or three minutes. They are phrases that go on their own, without any external support. The air brakes the letters as they leave a whistling sound behind them.

It is hard not to be surprised by these eagle-like phrases that estrange both the air and the sense of all they move across. We have always thought that a turning and twisting ribboning was the representative form painting gave to these phrases in antiquity. We are dealing, after all, with sound's links to revelation, to godsend. They are phrases that the poet Hölderlin knew how to gather, the hidden meanings that Blake deciphered, the never-expiring god of the great writers of the air, the sonourous and transparent territories of the ether. Curiously enough, technology has provided us with an enormous proliferation of errant and annoying words and images that move invisibly in electronic formats. An enormous volume of language that draws the territory in, modelling it without even trying to, like no descriptive language has ever done.

We would hear voices everywhere if this type of incessant technological telepathy, traversed by dark waves and materials, would only reveal its trajectories to us. We would then see how the voices of the lowlands make it to the peaks, how once there they are thrown across to another ridge or just as well bounced off a satellite to be immediately heard in some other lowland, only to be tossed about again, depending on the case. Today a silent mass of voices compresses the air, circumscribing geological reliefs, cabling peaks, linking plains and mountain passes together with a copyist's wanton spirit.

Each historical moment lays out certain basic questions about the landscape; nowadays one of these questions is the idea of landscape as a transmitting field. If until now we have spoken of an idiomatic nature that the earth prescribes and the currents describe, from now on we have to add this fattened air to earthly diction, stuffed as it is with codes and paperwork.

It turns out that air makes sites ring out. The vernacular of the site makes a sound, but the air that moves through the site carries all kinds of phrases printed in the deepest and darkest reaches.

It is a great composition that cannot be followed. You would say that everything is calculated with the view towards some final result, which seen from here cannot be guessed at. This new sonorous enviroment gives off an overall sensation of connectedness and erasure, speaking to us of an ecumenical world, porous and polycentric. The multiple layers of electronic media provide a new but undefinable pantheon of legends. All sounds and images move across each point indiscriminately and the air stirs the old toponyms with a shock that is noisier than the imprints it carries, more so than those it may find.

This foreign ambience has given rise to an unavoidable, uniform, atmospheric presence. It is not odd to view, on a lonely highland, the wide murmour of the circuitry or the buffetting blows of high frequency, or even the silent mechanisms of a security camera. Nor is it strange to be found interpreting an ordinary and anodine message in the most sublime of spots. It seems as if all we had to do was plant paper in channels and on mountain passes, for it to end up being printed from top to bottom (considering the general state of baseless reason, the connectedness of electronic space, so misplaced, as if rolled into a ball and adorned with ribbons and a bow). It turns out that

all words and no word at all are the same thing in the end, and that in this gluttony of language, amidst so much naming, the earth becomes uncultured and wild once again. It is perhaps for this reason that we need to convince ourselves that some names are fictitious, that they are more real because a place gives them subtance, with the toponyms ringing out in sweet firmness, appearing to us as the most ostensible of all words, so that upon reading them the visual cone of the reader is framed by a writing so real we could go there by foot, with stains so high and us standing below.
In a space that is more and more pocked with words, nothing is so well spoken of as a bramble patch, undoing itself in spirals or buttoning itself up even higher up, like bindweed pulling at itself amongst the branches, waiting to be grabbed at, like water whose rush has become so deafening that it cannot be read. No more careful solution is applied —the drawing appropriate for the sound it wants to emit— as with those characters rooted to their originary supports in the moment that mountain springs, brambles and serpents are ostensibly darkened, and the site where each name emerges entertains panting zephyrs and four heads huffing with misty breaths, reading the entire earth. It is then that a sigh of names is spread out, hovering widely over us, as if torn from the natural world, even though each one of them has the limits of it reign well marked: the concrete site where each site aligns the letters of its name, where in each angle the air puffs cheeks with sonourously inspired air, firmly held in place by the four corners of the earth.
It is quite pleasant to observe each site in the sculptural immobility of its letters, and even more agreeable to perceive the great fluidity of space through the solid walls of those letters, as it is precisely this specific firmness of the letters that advances our gaze upon reading them.

Oïsme, p. 94-97.

THE PEAK

In an extreme of language, in an inhospitable cranny of language, rough and wild, prepare a concert. Carry up the instruments and chairs, but once there, do not play a thing. Let the instruments listen too, there on high, to the extreme volume of language.

La pintura i la boca, p. 104. Also published in *Espacios públicos. Sueños privados*, pp. 156-157.

ON HIS LIPS

On his lips, like on the rim of a well, a cord and bucket. On setting out to write, the bucket reached slowly into the darkness, the sound of his voice growing dimmer and dimmer, searching out inky, phreatic depths.

ELOQUENCE

Touch your lips with a drawing by Raphael.

THE TONGUED SITE

As if in a land of bewilderment and ruin, like the air fluttering in a mouth pronouncing "Comoloforno" or "Maragall". Single breaths are filtered into view, bathing themselves in ink; shadows shut out names, spying out caves where onomatopoeia guides the dripping: Tring-tring rock, Trington corner, Ting-a-ting spring, in a dark auditorium, awaiting an opening to the sky.

BIBLIOGRAPHY

BOOKS BY PEREJAUME

Ludwig-Jujol. Què és el collage, sinó acostar soledats? Lluís II de Baviera, Josep Maria Jujol. Barcelona: La Magrana, 1989. (Cotlliure; 10)

Fragmente der Monarchie. Texts by Perejaume, Andrea Tschechow, Erik Mosel and Joan Tarrida. Munich: Mosel und Tschechow, 1989.

Oli damunt paper. Barcelona: Empúries, 1992.

La Pintura i la boca. Barcelona: La Magrana, 1993. (Cotlliure; 19).

El Paisatge és rodó. Vic: H. Associació per a les Arts Contemporànies; Eumo, 1995.

Nocturn: Miquel Campeny, Nicolau Raurich, Joaquim Pou, Benet Martorell. Texts by Perejaume and Jordi Pomés. Sant Pol de Mar: Museu de Pintura, 1995.

El Pirineu de Baix. Mont-roig, Miró, Mallorca. With texts by Vicenç Altaió, William Jeffett, Michael Pennie and Perejaume. Barcelona: Polígrafa, 1997.

Diürn: Ignasi Mas, Avi Vila. Texts by Perejaume and Juan José Lahuerta. Sant Pol de Mar: Museu de Pintura, 1998.

Oïsme. Prologue by Josep Palau and Fabre. Barcelona: Proa, 1998.

Oleoducte. Barcelona: Polígrafa, 1999.

ARTICLES BY PEREJAUME

"Alexandre Cirici", *Avui*, 16 January 1983.

"Nocturn per a J.V. Foix", *Àrtics*, n. 2, December 1985-January 1986, pp. 35-39.

"Catalunya", *Àrtics*, n. 8, June-August 1987.

"Marià Manent i l'indret", "El Paó", *L'Avenç*, n. 120, Novembre 1988

"Paisatge interrogat" dins *Arts escrits.* Lleida: Institut d'Estudis Ilerdencs, 1988.

"Descripció d'un vers", *El Guía*, October 1988.

"Sis sonets", *Reduccions*, n. 39, Vic, 1988

"Tres sonets", *Traç*, n. 21, 1988

"Justificació del tiratge", *Àrtics*, n.3, December 1988 - February de 1989, pp. 30-31.

"Un paisatge és una postal feta escultura", *Alea*, n. 9, 1989.

"Perejaume X Perejaume", *Balcón*, n. 4, summer 1989, pp. 230-235.

"Fragments de monarquia", *Lletra de Canvi*, September 1989, pp. 25-28.

"Assaig de llums sobre l'origen i l'inacabament" dins *Gaudí*. París: Centre d'Estudis Catalans; Tenerife: Cabildo de Tenerife, 1990.

"Montblanc, Mont-roig, Montnegre", *Arts Magazine*, vol. 65, n. 11, 1991-1992.

"Les terres de Foix", *Avui*, 16 March 1991.

"El camí del dial", *Avui*, 17 August 1991.

"Avantguardistes pairals" dins *Catalonia 92.* Barcelona: Llibres de l'Índex, 1992.

"Rondalla de Costuix", *Vèrtex*, n. 18, 1992.

"Trois îles", *Antigone*, n. 16, 1992.

"Algunes pintures d'esborrar", *El Observador*, 7 June 1992.

"La llum", *Avui*, 27 June 1992.

"Algunas pinturas de borrar", *Creación*, n.6, October 1992.

"L'heretat dels pigments", *Avui*, 11 October 1992.

"Els aspectes", *Papers d'art*, n. 50, December 1992.

"Museografia de Can Pau-Foguera", *Papers d'art*, n. 50, December 1992.

"Inesquivable presència", *Butlletí dels mestres*, n. 233, January 1993

"Un segle", *Cultura*, n. 41, January 1993, pp. 47-50.

"Els terrabuits de dalt", *Avui*, 7 October 1993.

"Somiers i Polinèsies" dins *Escriptura i combinatòria.* Barcelona: Generalitat de Departament de Cultura, 1994.

"El cofre", *Antigone*, n. 19, 1994.

"No pas com un paisatge circular", in Albert Roig, *Vedat*, editorial Proa, 1994

"Vuit artistes al «Cim Pintrat»" in *L'escola invisible. Tallers de la QUAM, 1988-1994.* Barcelona: Diputació de Barcelona. Servei de Cultura; H. Associació per a les Arts Contemporànies, 1995. (Llibres de la Quinzena; 7)

"Una terra sonora", in *Joan Coromines 90 anys*, Barcelona, 1995

"Visions" i "V. M." dins *Nicolau Raurich: 1871-1945, visions Mediterrànies.* Barcelona: Museu Nacional d'Art de Catalunya, 1996.

"Aparició de Nicolau Raurich", *Avui*, 23 November 1996.

"Parques interiores: la obra de siete despintores", a *El Paisaje, arte y naturaleza*, Huesca, 1996

"Borrells", A *Alfons Borrell o l'aura de la pintura*, Eumo Gràfic, 1996

"El Pelele: segon mètode pessebrístic de lectura", *Urc*, n. 10, primavera 1996

"Dels 'des' i dels 'dis'", *Reduccions*, n. 67, Vic, 1996

"Les fissures", *Avui*, 27-28 de March 1997.

"Els retaules de Fuirosos", *La sitja del llop*, n. 15, December 1997

"Epíleg" a Vicenç Altaió, *La desconeguda*, València, 1997

"Nivell freàtic. Nivel freático", *Zehar*, n. 33, primavera de 1997, pp. 44-48.

"Cada arbre un mot", *Avui*, 15 de May de 1997.

"Breu semblança del Pirineu de Baix", *Transversal. Revista de cultura contemporània*, n. 6, 1998.

"Oïsme", *Extra del 9 Nou*, 22 May 1998

"El cant de les relacions", *Avui*, 27 November 1998.

"Sota els vessants pairals d'una a brossiana", *Avui*, 7 de January 1999

"Lectura", *El Temps*, n. 761, January 1999

ARTIST BOOKS

PEREJAUME. *Bola nocturna: poema aerostàtic.* Sabadell: Èczema, 1980.

PEREJAUME. *La muntanya del firmament.* Barcelona: Ed. Les Edicions, 1985.

PEREJAUME. *La matèria de les visions.* Barcelona: Les Tribunes, 1986.

PEREJAUME; BROSSA, Joan. *El bosc a casa.* Barcelona: Polígrafa, 1986-1989.

COLINAS, Antonio; PEREJAUME. *Diapasón infinito.* Barcelona: Les Edicions, 1986.

BORRELL, Alfons; PEREJAUME. *Pintors.* Barcelona: Les Edicions, 1987.

Diorames: Joan Brossa, Alfons Borrell, Jordi Alcaraz, Perejaume, Jordi Rosés. Calella: Centre Internacional de Recerca Gràfica, 1988.

PEREJAUME. *Il·lustració.* Barcelona: Les Edicions, 1988.

PEREJAUME; GIMFERRER, Pere. *Llegenda. Tres Perejaumes. Monòleg d'un poeta i un pintor.* Barcelona: Les Edicions, 1988.

PEREJAUME. *Paisatges catalans.* Barcelona: Galeria Joan Prats, 1989.

PEREJAUME; MESTRES QUADRENY, Josep Maria. *Lied.* Barcelona: Les Edicions, 1990-1992.

PEREJAUME. *Perejaume.* Madrid: Torre de Babel, 1992.

L'Art pot morir: homenatge a Joan Miró. Text by Vicenç Altaió and works by Brossa, Guinovart, Llena, Perejaume, Ràfols-Casamada, Saura and Zush. Arenys de Munt: Murtra Edicions, 1993.

PEREJAUME. *Pla de la morera*, Granada, Ediciones Originales, 1997

PEREJAUME; PALAU I FABRE, Josep. *Cant Espiritual.* Barcelona: Boza Edicions, 1999.

SOLO CATALOGUES

Perejaume, pintures. Text by Joan Brossa. Barcelona: Galeria Ciento, 1978.

Perejaume. Text by M. Mercè Marçal. Mallorca: Galeria Sa Pleta Freda, 1979.

Perejaume: olis i objectes. Text by Alexandre Cirici. Barcelona: Galeria Joan Prats, 1980.

Exposició al bosc de can Montells. Guió-itinerari de Perejaume. Text by Jordi Coca. Cardedeu, 1983.
Perejaume. Text by Perejaume. Barcelona: Galeria Joan Prats, 1983.
Perejaume. Text by Marià Manent. Mataró: Can Xammar, 1984.
Perejaume. Text by Pere Gimferrer. Figueres: Galeria Massanet, 1985.
Postaler. Text by Perejaume. Barcelona: Fundació Caixa de Pensions. Sala Montcada, 1985.
Marcs. Text by Perejaume. Sabadell: Museu d'Art. Espai 83, 1986.
Perejaume: pintures, escultures, instal·lacions, vídeos. Text by Perejaume; traducció del text a l'anglès Jamey Gambrell and text by Jamey Gambrell; traducció del text al català Josep Sala. Barcelona: Galeria Joan Prats, 1986.
Perejaume. Text d'Àngel Crespo. Madrid: Galería Montenegro, 1987.
Perejaume. Texts by Perejaume and Vicenç Altaió. Toulouse: Centre Régional d'Art Contemporain Midi-Pyrénées, 1987.
Perejaume. A 2000 metres de pintura sobre el nivell del mar. Texts by Vicenç Altaió and Dan Cameron. Tarragona: Tinglado 2, 1988.
Perejaume: Pintura y representación. Madrid: Galería Montenegro, 1988.
Perejaume: L'ombra. Text d'Annemieke Van De Pas. Barcelona: Col·legi Oficial d'Aparelladors i Arquitectes Tècnics de Barcelona. Anar i Tornar, 1989.
Perejaume: Marea-Tide. Text by Perejaume. Nova York: Galeria Joan Prats; Milford Gallery, 1989.
Viatge. Text by Perejaume. Barcelona: Fundació Joan Miró, 1989.
Escala. Text by Helmut Friedel. Munic: Städtische Galerie im Lenbachhaus, 1990.
Perejaume: Coll de Pal - Cim del Costabona. Text by Perejaume. Barcelona: Galeria Joan Prats, 1990.
Broadway Window Installation. Text d'Alice Yang. Nova York: The New Museum of Contemporary Art, 1991.
Perejaume: Dos geografías. Texts by Pere Gimferrer and Manel Guerrero. Bilbao: Windsor Kulturgintza, 1991.
Perejaume: Dues Geografies. Texts by Pere Gimferrer and Manel Guerrero. Lisboa: Galeria Graça Fonseca, 1991.
Perejaume: El grado de la verdad de las representaciones. Text by Perejaume and pròleg by Àngel Crespo. Madrid: Galería Soledad Lorenzo, 1991.
Perejaume. Künstler. Kritisches Lexikon der Gegenwartskunst. Munic: Weltkunst und Bruckmann, 1991.
Perejaume: Pintura per a exteriors. Text by Miquel Molins. Barcelona: Fundació Miró. Espai 13, 1991.
Perejaume. Text by Josep M. Llompart. Sevilla: Expo 92, 1992.
Perejaume: Pinacoteques. Text by Perejaume. Barcelona: Galeria Joan Prats-Artgràfic, 1992.
Perejaume: landscapes and long distances. Texts d'Adrian Searle and Tessa Jackson. Bristol: Arnolfini Gallery; London: Anderson O'Day Gallery, 1993.
Perejaume: Mont-Roig. Text by Perejaume. Mont-Roig: Església Vella; Ajuntament de Mont-Roig, 1993.
Perejaume. Text by Perejaume. Gant: Museum van Hedendaagse Kunst, 1994.
Perejaume. Pintures. Barcelona: Galeria Joan Prats, 1994.
Perejaume: Terra de suro. Texts by Perejaume, Vicenç Altaió and Jean-Christophe Bailly. Céret: Musée d'Art Moderne de Ceret, 1994.
Perejaume: diciembre, enero, Febrero, marzo. Burgos: Caja de Burgos, 1995.
Perejaume: Girona, Sant Pol, Pineda i la Vall d'Oo. Texts by Perejaume and Joaquim Sala-Sanahuja. Girona: Ajuntament de Girona; Pineda de Mar: Ajuntament de Pineda de Mar; Sant Pol de Mar: Ajuntament de Sant Pol de Mar, 1997.
Perejaume: Tres dibujos. Texts by Perejaume, Carles Guerra and Jaume Trabal. Santiago de Compostel·la: Centro Galego de Arte Contemporánea, 1997.

BOOKS AND GROUP CATALOGUES

La seconda vanguardia catalana. Viareggio: Palazzo Paolina, 1979.
Casino. Sabadell: Èczema; Perpinyà: Symptômes; Montpellier: MEDaMOTHI, 1983.
Nits. Barcelona: Fundació Caixa de Pensions, 1984.
Actitudes: diez proyectos de jóvenes creadores. Madrid: Ministerio de Cultura. Instituto de la Juventud, 1986.
Extra! Barcelona: Departament de Cultura de la Generalitat de Catalunya, 1987.
Naturalezas españolas: 1940-1987. Madrid: Ministerio de Cultura. Centro de Arte Reina Sofía, 1987.
10. Barcelona: Galeria Joan Prats, 1988.
Acta 88. Madrid: Palacio de Velázquez, 1988.
Arts escrits: Joan Brossa, Perejaume, Benet Rossell, Antonio Saura, Antoni Tàpies. Lleida: Institut d'Estudis Ilerdencs, 1988.
Le Défi catalan: Picasso et Miro à la nouvelle génération. Barcelona: Département d'Éditions et Publications de la Mairie de Barcelone, 1988.
Todo fluye. Madrid: Comunidad de Madrid, 1988.
Àngels de la Mota Galeria: temporada 88-89. Barcelona: Àngels de la Mota Galeria, 1989.
Die Spanische Kunst in der Sammlung der Fundació "la Caixa de Pensions". Mannheim: Städtische Kunsthalle; Düsseldorf: Kunstmuseum, 1989.
L'avantguarda de l'escultura catalana. Barcelona: Generalitat de Catalunya. Departament de Cultura, 1989.
Les grâces de la nature, sixièmes ateliers internationaux des Pays de la Loire. Garenne Lemot: Le Parc de la Garenne Lemot, 1989.
Mediterraneo per l'arte contemporanea. Bari: Regione Puglia Assessorato alla Cultura, 1989.
Nuits blanches. Barcelona: Generalitat de Catalunya. Departament de Cultura, 1989.
What is contemporary art? Malmö: Rooseum Center for Contemporary Art, 1989.
6 Katalanische Künstler. Ludwigsburg: Kunstverein Ludwigsburg, 1990.
Art espagnol des années 80 dans la collection de la Fundació Caixa de Pensions. Labege: Centre Régional d'Art Contemporain Midi-Pyrenées, 1990.
Confrontaciones: comentarios a la década. Madrid: Instituto de la Juventud, 1990.
CORTÉS, José Miguel G. (ed.). *La creación artística como cuestionamiento.* Valencia: IVAM, 1990.
Imágenes líricas. New Spanish visions. Long Beach: University Art Museum; California State University, 1990.
La Biennale di Venezia. Venècia: Biennale di Venezia, 1990.
Sculpture contemporaine espagnole. París: Ministère de la Culture, de la Communication, des Grands travaux et du Bicentenaire, 1990.
To be and not to be. Barcelona: Centre d'Art Santa Mònica, 1990.
2ª Biennal Martínez Guerricabeitia. València: Patronat Martínez Guerricabeitia; Universitat de València, 1991.
Das Goldene Zeitalter. Stuttgart: Wüttembergischer Kunstverein, 1991.
Formes de la dissensió. Barcelona: Fundació Joan Miró. Espai 13, 1991.
Kunst, Europa: 63 deutsche Kunstvereine zeigen Kunst aus 20 Ländern. Mainz: Hermann Schmidt, 1991.
L'Exposition de l'École du Magasin. Grenoble: Centre national d'art contemporain de Grenoble, 1991.
Literatures submergides. Barcelona: Generalitat de Catalunya. Departament de Cultura, 1991.

Onze escultures. Granollers: Museu de Granollers, 1991.
5. Triennale Fellbach 1992: Kleinplastik in Mexiko, Spanien, Italien, Deutschland. Stuttgart: Cantz, 1992.
BALCELLS, J.; ROIG, A. *Dels trobadors a la poesia actual.* Barcelona: Laertes, 1992.
Barcelona abroad: Pep Agut, Jordi Colomer, Ramon Parramon, Perejaume. Ipswich: European Visual Arts, 1992.
Ceci n'est pas une sculpture: I und II. Munic: Musel und Tschechow, 1992.
Constants de l'art català actual: pintura-escultura. Barcelona: Generalitat de Catalunya. Departament de Cultura, 1992.
Escultures: col·lecció Museu de Granollers. Mataró: Patronat Municipal de Cultura; Museu Comarcal, 1992.
Espagne 23 artistes pour l'an 2000: peintures et sculptures. París: Artcurial, 1992.
Izoztea/Helada. San Sebastián: Diputación Foral de Guipuzcoa, 1992.
Los 80 en la colección de la Fundación "la Caixa". Sevilla: Ayuntamiento, 1992.
Na Miró, Keuwerkeen van de Hendendaagse Catalaanse Kunst. Amsterdam, 1992.
Pasajes: actualidad del arte español. Sevilla: Pabellón de España, 1992.
The boundary rider: 9th Biennale of Sydney. Sydney: Biennale of Sydney, 1992.
Tropismes: col·lecció d'art contemporani Fundació "la Caixa". L'Hospitalet: Tecla Sala, 1992.
Différentes natures: visions de l'art contemporain. Torí: Lindau; La Défense: Etablissement public pour l'amenagement de la Region de la Défense, 1993.
Escultura española do seculo vinte: pequeno formato. Santiago de Compostela: Consorcio da cidade de Santiago de Compostela, 1993.
Impulsos i expressions: pintura espanyola dels anys 80 a la col·lecció de la Fundació "la Caixa". Granollers: Fundació "la Caixa", 1993.
IV Bienal de pintura "Ciudad de Pamplona". Pamplona: Ayuntamiento de Pamplona, 1993.
Museo Marugame Hirai. Arte español contemporáneo. Marugame: Museo Marugame Hirai, 1993.
Partitures plàstiques. Barcelona: Balmes 21, 1993.
Veure Miró: la irradiació de Miró en l'art espanyol. Barcelona: Fundació "la Caixa", 1993. (ed. cast.: *Ver a Miró: la irradiación de Miró en el arte español.* Las Palmas de Gran Canaria: Centro Atlántico de Arte Moderno, 1993).
Espacios públicos: sueños privados. Madrid: Comunidad de Madrid. Consejería de Educación y Cultura. Dirección General de Patrimonio Cultural, 1994.
J.V. Foix. Investigador en poesia i amic de les arts. Barcelona: Fundació "la Caixa". Sala St. Jaume, 1994.
La llum. Vilafranca del Penedès: Palma Dotze, 1994.
La Màgia de la ciutat. Barcelona: Fundació "la Caixa", 1994.
OLIVEIRA, Nicolas de; OXLEY, Nicola; PETRY, Michael. *Installation art.* With texts by Michael Archer. London: Thames and Hudson, 1994.
Züge Züge-die Eisenbahn in der Zetgenössichen Kunst. Esslingen: Galerie der Stadt; Goppingen: Märklin Museum, 1994.
Fundación Coca-Cola España. Madrid: Fundación Coca-Cola España, 1995.
Art espanyol per a la fi de segle. L'Hospitalet: Ajuntament; Barcelona: Àmbit, 1996. (ed. cast: *Arte español para el fin de siglo*).
Essències: col·lecció Ernesto Ventós Omedes. Pintura i escultura contemporània. Barcelona: Ajuntament, 1996.
Mirades (sobre el museu). Barcelona: Museu d'Art Contemporani, 1996.
Thinking of you: a selection of contemporary Spanish art. Göteborg: Konsthallen Göteborg, 1996.
ABELDA, José; SABORIT, José. *La construcción de la naturaleza.* València: Generalitat Valenciana, 1997.
ALTAIÓ, Vicenç. "Visites guiades", "Breu nota biogràfica", "A 2.000 m. de pintura", "Mont-roig i Mallorca, Miró i Perejaume", "El diluent i l'aglutinant", *Escriptura sense llançadora,* Barcelona: edicions Parsifal, 1997
Llibre de les meravelles. Libro de las maravillas. València: Generalitat Valenciana. Direcció General de Promoció Cultural, Museus i Belles Arts, 1997.
ADLAN i el Circ Frediani, Mataró, Can Palauet, 1997
RAQUEJO, Tonia. *Land art.* Madrid: Nerea, 1998.
Viva Wagner! Bayreuth: Richard Wagner Museum, 1998.

SELECTED ARTICLES

PERMANYER, Lluís. "Perejaume del Montnegre", *Hoja del Lunes,* 29 de December 1980.
SUÀREZ, Alícia; VILA, Mercè. "Perejaume", *Serra d'or,* n. 187, 1981.
GIRALT-MIRACLE, Daniel. "Perejaume, la lluna, el bosc i el misteri de la pintura", *Avui,* 4 de January 1981.
PERMANYER, Lluís. "La poesía, por los aires", *La Vanguardia,* 21 de January 1981.
SALA-SANAHUJA, Joaquim. "Somnis d'aigua", *El Correo catalán,* 4 de March 1981.
PARCERISAS, Francesc. "Poesia i celístia", *El Món,* 19 November 1982.
COCA, Jordi. "La postal, text i imatge per a un art possible", *El País,* 16 October1983.
BARÓN, Javier. "Perejaume", *Lápiz,* n. 22, Januaryde 1985, pp. 8-9.
CAMERON, Dan. "Report from Spain", *Art in America,* vol. 73, February 1985, pp. 25-35.
SAN AGUSTÍN, Arturo. "Perejaume, pintor: «El mediterraneísmo es un tópico»", *El Periódico,* 24 July 1986.
CAMPBELL, Lawrence. "Perejaume at Galeria Joan Prats", *Art in America,* vol. 74, November 1986, pp. 170-171.
CALVO SERRALLER, Francisco. "Protocolos nocturnos de Perejaume", *El País,* 16 de Januaryde 1987
VENRIES, Patrick. "Perejaume, Musée Khombol. Centre d'Art Contemporain de Labège-Innopôle, 2 avril-10 mai 1987", *Art Press,* n. 115, June 1987, p. 74.
GAMBRELL, Jamey. "Five from Spain", *Art in America,* vol. 75, September 1987, pp. 160-171.
CLOT, Manel. "En pos de las huellas de lo indecible", *El País,* 10 November 1987.
MOURE, Glòria. "Perejaume. Barcelona. Galeria Joan Prats", *Artforum,* vol. 26, January 1988, p. 126.
BROS, T. "Perejaume. The world in the third person", *Flash Art International,* n. 138, January-February de 1988, p. 94.
PICAZO, Glòria. "Barcelona. Perejaume. Galeria Joan Prats", *Sur Expres,* n. 7, February de 1988, p. 27.
PICAZO, Glòria. "Àrtics: Amat, Navarro, Pazos and Perejaume", *Artefactum,* vol. 5, n. 22, February-March 1988, pp. 29-31.
ALTAIÓ, Vicenç and Perejaume, "Homenatge a Josep M. Jujol", Josep M. Jujol, arquitecte, *Quaderns,* núm 179-180, Barcelona, 1988
"Perejaume. Künstlerporträts", *Kunstforum,* vol. 94, abril-May de 1988, pp. 144-147.
LEBRERO STALS, José. "Bezünge und Identitäten", *Kunstforum,* vol. 94, Abril-May de 1988, pp. 94-95.
BREA, José Luis. "Perejaume. Montenegro, Madrid", *Flash Art International,* núm. 140, May-June 1988, p. 115.
SIMONS, Riki. "Kunstenaar Perejaume. Verenigt Verschillen", *Avenue,* October 1988, pp. 108-110.
PARCERISAS, Pilar. "La metàfora de Perejaume", *Avui,* 4 December 1988.
GUERRERO, Manel. "Perejaume", *Tema Celeste,* 1989.

CAMERON, Dan. "Perejaume, l'art de la métaphore", *Art Press*, n. 144, February 1989, pp. 31-33.
CLOT, Manel. "Las ensoñaciones del paseante solitario", *Lápiz,* n. 56, February 1989, pp. 65-71.
CLOT, Manel. "Perejaume. The hard vindication of the spirit's presence", *Flash Art International,* n. 145, March-April 1989, pp. 108-109.
CAMERON, Dan. "De vuelta a lo español", *Flash Art* (ed. española), n. 2, spring 1989, pp. 68-71.
COMADIRA, Narcís. "Fertilitat. Ludwig Jujol", *El País*, 4 de May 1989.
"The Peripatetic artist: 14 statements", *Art in America*, July 1989, pp. 130-137.
MAHONEY, Robert. "Milford Gallery ; Joan Prats Gallery, Nova York ; exhibits", *Arts Magazine,* vol. 64, September 1989, p. 98.
TARRIDA, Joan. "El rei i l'arquitecte: la construcció d'un univers", *Lletra de Canvi*, September 1989, pp. 23-25
PRESTELE, Karl H. "Die Utopie, der König und die Kunst. Perejaume bei Mosel & Tschechow", *Applaus*, n. 11, 1989.
CZÖPPAN, Gabi. "Perejaume", *Kunstforum*, Bd. 104, novembre-December 1989.
ZAHM, Olivier. "Les grâces de la nature. Sixièmes ateliers internationaux des Pays de la Loire. Parc de la Garenne-Lemot", *Art Press*, n. 143, January 1990.
BLANCH, Teresa. "Esculturas de la entropía", *New Art International*, February-March 1990, pp. 62-63.
CALVO SERRALLER, Francisco. "El espectáculo está servido", *El País*, 2 June 1990.
CLOTHIER, Peter. "Perejaume. Phenomenology of the painting", *Artspace*, July 1990, p. 31.
MARZO, Jorge Luis. "El lugar imposible", *Lápiz,* n. 73, December 1990, pp. 48-55.
VANAUTGAERDEN, Alexandre. "Perejaume. L'oeil ne perçoit rien de certain", *Artefactum*, n. 38, April-May de 1991, pp. 2-4.
GUILLAMON, Julià. "Perejaume, els genis del lloc. Entrevista a dos mil metres de pintura sobre el nivell del mar", *Revista Cultura,* n. 25, juliol-August 1991, pp. 51-58.
SALA-SANAHUJA, Joaquim. "El «reialme de l'aura», paisatge de Perejaume", *Revista Cultura,* n. 25, juliol-August 1991, pp. 59-62.
MELO, Alexandre. "Arte e/ou natureza", *Expresso*, 19 October 1991.
CALVO SERRALLER, Francisco. "Perejaume: el grado artístico de la verdad", *El País*, 4 November 1991.
CLOT, Manel. "Perejaume: poéticas de la representación, alegorías de la salvación", *Revista de Occidente,* n. 129, 1992, pp. 57-64.
SWARTZ, Jeffrey. "Perejaume. Soledad Lorenzo, Madrid ", *Flash Art International,* n. 162, January-February 1992, p.162.
GUERRERO, Manel. "Geografies de Perejaume", *Avui*, 28 March 1992.
ZABALBEASCOA, Anatxu. "Perejaume. Galerie Joan Prats, 4 février-15 mars 1992", *Art Press*, n. 169, May 1992, pp. 97-98.
MELO, Alexandre. "Perejaume. Graça Fonseca, Lisbon", *Artforum*, September 1992, p. 106.
GARTSIDE, Mike. "Perejaume. Arnolfini, Bristol", *Venue*, 20 August 1993.
ROIG, Albert. "De la poesia, encara", *Avui*, 12 September 1993.
HALL, James. "The art of nature", *The Guardian*, 27 September 1993.
KASTNER, Jeffrey. "Perejaume", *Art Monthly*, n. 170, October 1993, pp. 21-22.
JEFFETT, William. "Perejaume. Bristol, Arnolfini 24.7-12.9.1993; London, Anderson O'Day Gallery 23.9-4.11.1993", *Artefactum*, December 1993-January 1994, pp. 56-57.
PUJAS, Philippe. "Céret s'ancre dans l'art moderne", *Le Monde*, 19-20 December 1993.
GUERRA, Carles. "Perejaume. La pintura i la boca", *Kalías*, n. 12, 1994, pp. 144-145.
USLÉ, Juan; PEREJAUME. "Juan Uslé; Perejaume", *Lápiz*, n. 99-101, January-March 1994, pp. 64-67.
LORÉS, Maite. "Contemporary Spanish Art", *Contemporary Art*, primavera de 1994, pp. 16-19.
GRAS BALAGUER, Menene. "Perejaume. Galeria Joan Prats, Barcelona", *Artforum*, octubre de 1994, pp. 110-111.
GUERRA, Carles. "Pintat amb la boca", *Avui*, 22 December 1994.
OLIVARES, Rosa. "Perejaume. A plein air", *Lápiz*, n. 125, October 1996
GUILLAMON, Julià. "El trabajo con el lenguaje", *La Vanguardia*, 24 May 1996.
ALTAIÓ, Vicenç. "A la recerca del plenairista ideal", *Transversal. Revista de cultura contemporània*, n. 1, November 1996.
MONTOLÍO, Celia. "Entrevista con Perejaume", *Lápiz*, n. 128-129, February de 1997, pp. 59-67.
MURRÍA, Alicia. "Juego de ojos", *Lápiz*, n. 128, February de 1997, pp. 138-139.
SERRA, Catalina. "Perejaume: Cuando una metáfora funciona es tan firme como la tierra", *El País*, 31 July 1997.
SPIEGEL, Olga. "Perejaume inaugura una exposición en cuatro lugares distintos con el retablo como motivo", *La Vanguardia*, 31 July 1997.
GUERRERO, Manuel. "Perejaume o l'experiència de l'art", *El Punt*, 1 September 1997.
BADIA, Montse. "Orografies escrites", *Avui*, 30 October 1997.
LAHUERTA, Juan José. "Homenatge al lloc Miró", *Transversal. Revista de cultura contemporània*, n. 6, 1998.
SWARTZ, Jeffrey. "Perejaume. Joan Prats", *ArtNews*, vol. 97, n. 2, February 1998, p. 144.
MEDINA, Jesús. "Perejaume. Entrevista", *L'extra del 9 Nou*, 22 May 1998.
SERRA, Màrius. "Perejaume onomàntic", *Avui*, 2 July 1998.
ALTAIÓ, Vicenç. "Oïsme", *El Mundo*, 12 de July 1998.
GUERRERO, Manuel. "Perejaume, assaig i ficció", *Avui*, 24 September 1998.
GUERRA, Carles. "Un so emancipat de l'escriptura", *Transversal. Revista de cultura contemporània*, n. 7, December 1998, p. 127.
OLMO, Santiago B. Desde el paisaje, *Lapiz*, n. 145, July 1998

BIOGRAPHICAL NOTES

Perejaume (1957)
Lives and works in Sant Pol de Mar. In Perejaume's work literary and visual practices come together. In the mid 1970's, when he began to exhibit, his work linked the historical avant-garde to certain ultralocal phenomena of Catalan culture. Painting, writing and hiking, as well as other activities, have contributed in his art to a redefinition of the landscape, which becomes a type of absolute reality where even authorship appears and disappears with a clear territorial meaning. Exhibits like *Postaler* (1984), *A 2000 metres de pintura sobre el nivell del mar* (1988), *Fragments de Monarquia* (1989), *Galeria Joan Prats, Coll de Pal-Cim del Costabona* (1990), *Girona, Pineda, Sant Pol i la Vall d'Oo* (1997) are witness to this process. Rather than an evolution of form and concept, over the years Perejaume's work has constituted a complex corpus, combining theoretical proposals with artistic production. This is particularly notable in his written creations, where the discourse is elaborated in a rich and authentic language, both object and instrument, as seen in books like *Ludwig-Jujol. Què és el collage sinó acostar soledats?* (1989), *La pintura i la boca* (1993), *El paisatge és rodó* (1995) i *Oïsme* (1998).

Pere Gimferrer (1945)
Writer. Member of the Royal Spanish Academy, of the European Academy of Poetry (Luxemburg) and elected member of the Royal Academy of Lettres of Barcelona. He has received some of the most important literary prizes, both in Catalan and in Spanish, the most recent being the Spanish National Poetry Prize. He is currently publishing his *Obra Catalana Completa* (Complete Catalan Works), five volumes of which have been published since 1995. His most recent publications are *Mascarada* (1996) and *L'agent provocador* (1998).

Boris Groys (1947)
Doctor of Philosophy, Professor for Aesthetics and Media Theory at the Zentrum für Kunst und Medientechnologie (ZKM) in Karlsruhe, Germany. He is the author of numerous publications on art and art theory of the 20th Century.

Carles Guerra (1965)
Artist, art critic and independent curator. His work brings together research on visual culture in the context of disciplines such as contemporary art and mass media. He is a member of the editorial committee of the journal *Acción Paralela*, and is associated with the research group on televisuality of the Media Studies Department of The New School University, New York.

Marcia Tucker (1940)
Founding Director of the New Museum of Contemporary Art, New York, where she organized numerous exhibitions, among them "Bad Girls" (1994), "A Labor of Love" (1996), and "The Time of Our Lives," which opens in July 1999. She has lectured and published extensively in the United States and abroad, and is the series editor of Documentary Sources in Contemporary Art, five volumes of theory and criticism published by the New Museum.

THE WORLD AS ART GALLERY

The sketchy nature of the work of art inscribes the world with traces of a painterly museology. An extenuated, excessive and geographical museology, as if we had made upon the ground a plaster image of the path each artwork had followed. It is as if each painting were just a single pigment and both new and old paintings had to be ordered about to create a new one, combining them with each other in exhibits and travelling shows, allowing the pictorial absolute of each of them to stand out, or at least attempting to do so.

Naturally, as much as I have carried certain paintings through unfamiliar lands —like a Hodler in the Atlas Mountains of Morrocco, a Lorca in the Ports de Besseit near the Ebro, or a Picabia taken by foot from Valencia to Sagunt— the sketchings of this museology go beyond any kind of personal authorship, instead using authorship the way the owner of a work of art employs his possessions, abandoning them to the mercy of loans, sales and temporary transfers. The museology I speak of is thus delicately picturesque, infernally picturesque. Its consequence is an unquestionable figuration, sketchy lines which have ordered us to elaborate them, in spite of our belief that we have created them by ourselves, however misleading they may be, as we sign them with our very own names.

Perejaume

Glossari 1991
(Glossary)
Earth and gilded label. 30 x 50 x 12 cm.

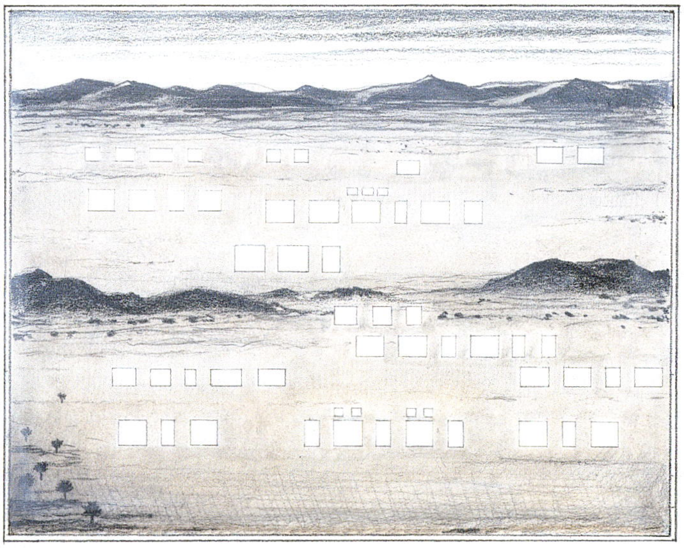

El món com a sala d'exposicions 1997
(The World as an Art Gallery)
Mixed media on paper. 30 x 42 cm.

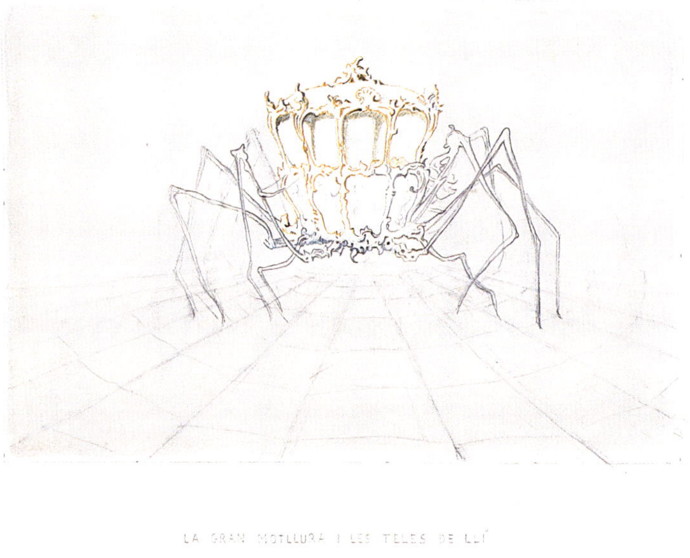

La gran motllura i les teles de lli 1997
(The Great Frame and Linen)
Mixed media on paper. 30 x 42 cm.

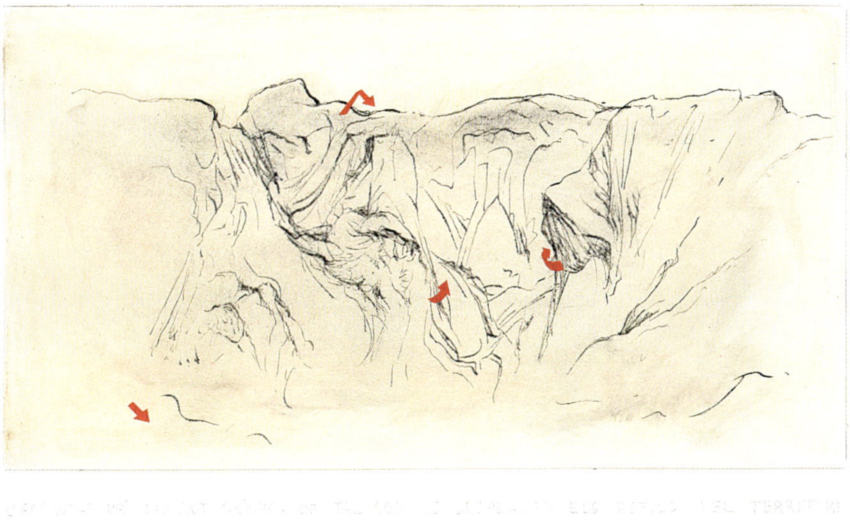

L'activitat pròpiament gràfica de tal com es desplacen els estils pel territori 1995
(The Intrinsically Graphic Way in Which Styles Move Through the Territory)
Mixed media on paper. 30 x 42 cm.

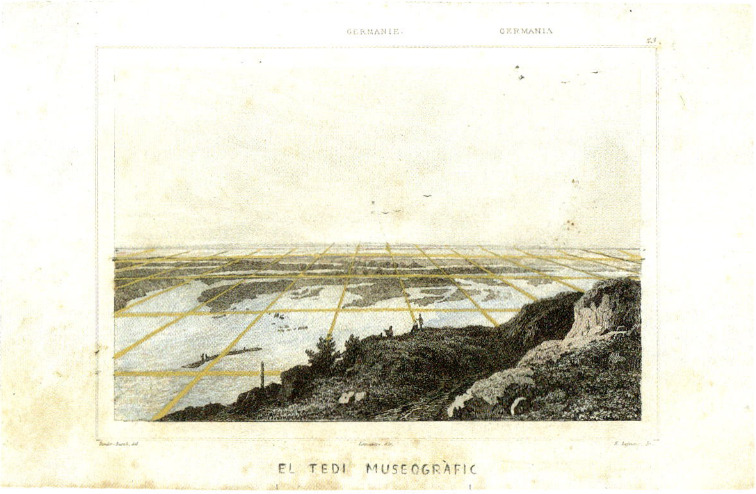

El tedi museogràfic 1997
(Museographic Tedium)
Mixed media on paper. 12.5 x 19.5 cm.

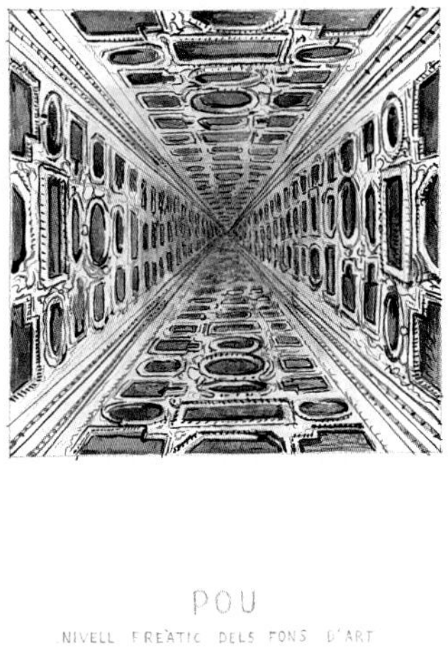

Pou. Nivell freàtic dels fons d'art 1996
(Well. Phreatic Level of the Art Collection)
Ink on paper. 42 x 30 cm.

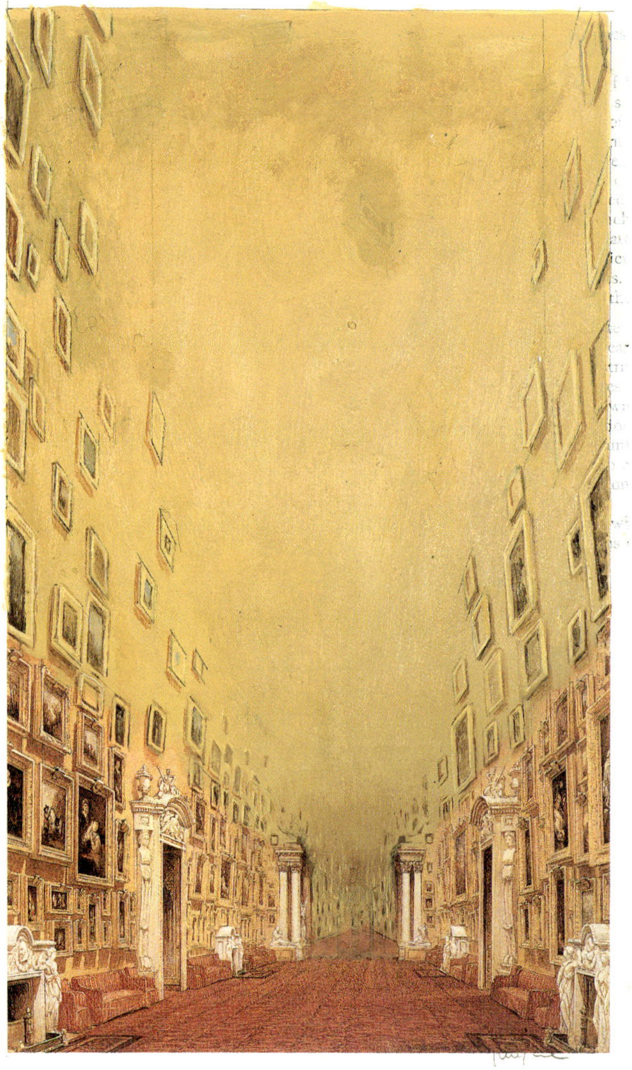

Gran pinacoteca 1996
(Great Picture Gallery)
Mixed media on paper. 23.5 x 14.5 cm.

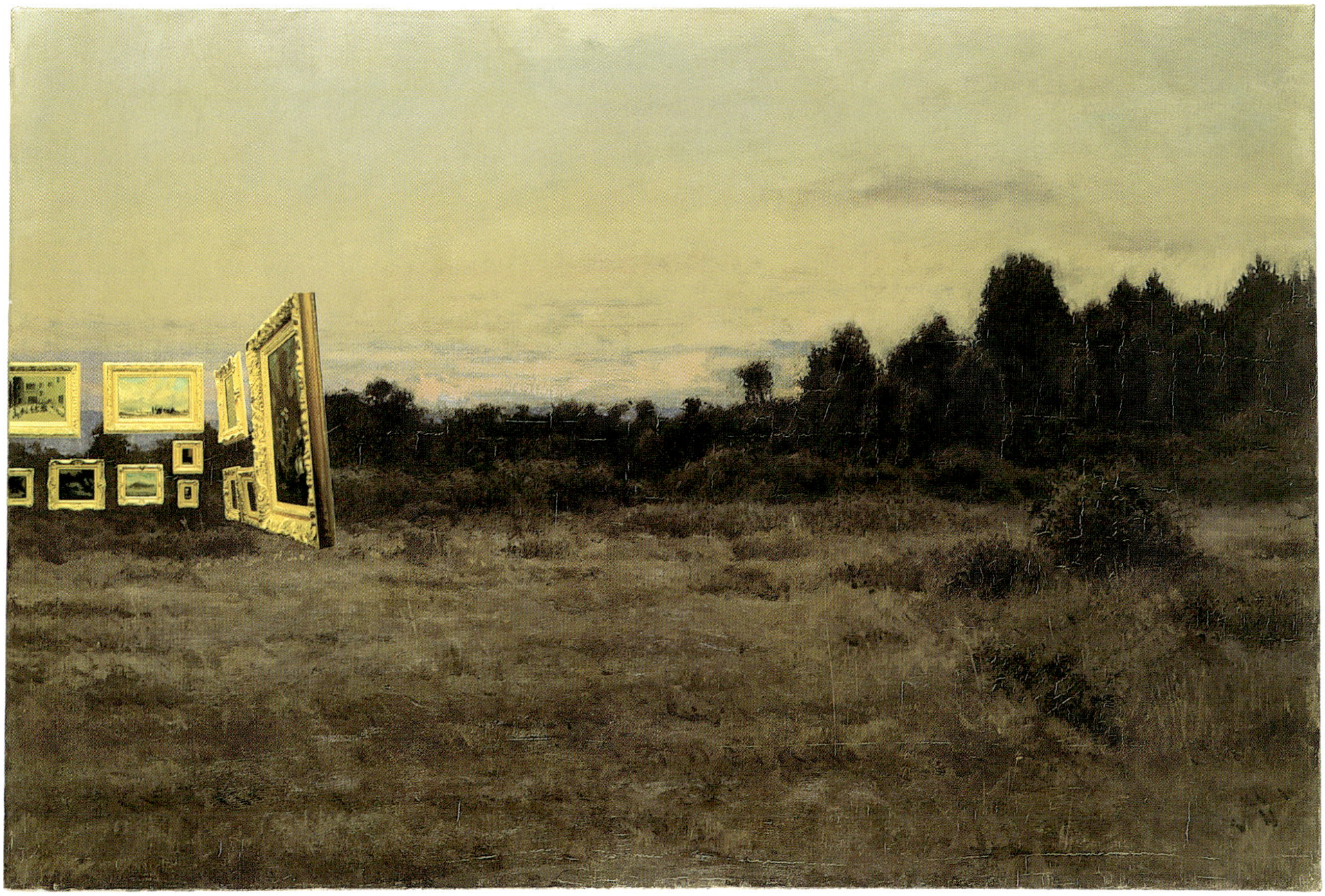

Cal Peraire 1993
Oil on canvas. 65 x 92 cm.

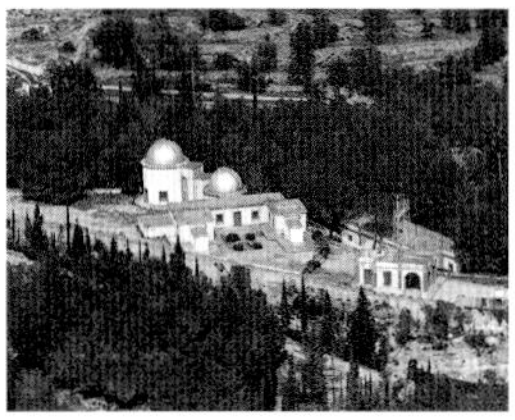

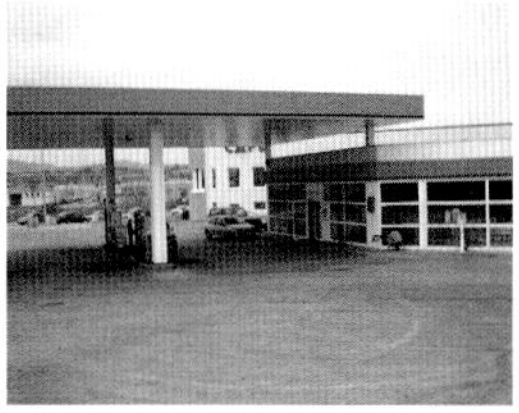

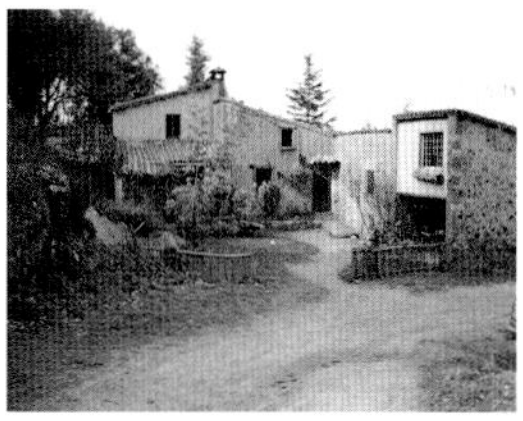

So as to abandon the museum walls, the artist has placed three works in different sites throughout the land. *Paisatges sotmesos a un far* at the Ebro Observatori
Pintors! at the Manlleu Service Station
Pinzellada at Parral del Sobirà, Santa Creu d'Horta, Osor

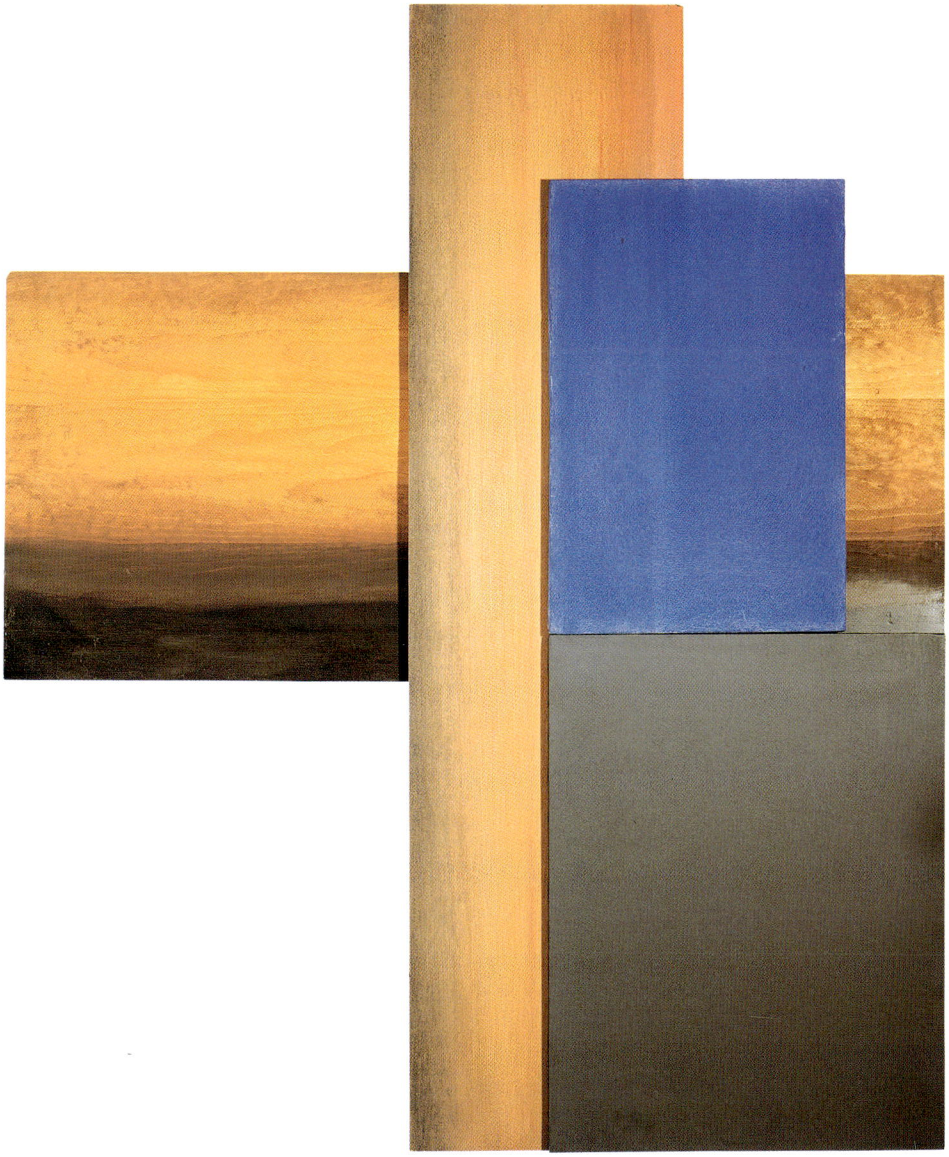

Paisatges sotmesos a un far 1987
(Landscapes Attached to a Lighthouse)
Collage of wood and canvas. 206 x 175 cm.

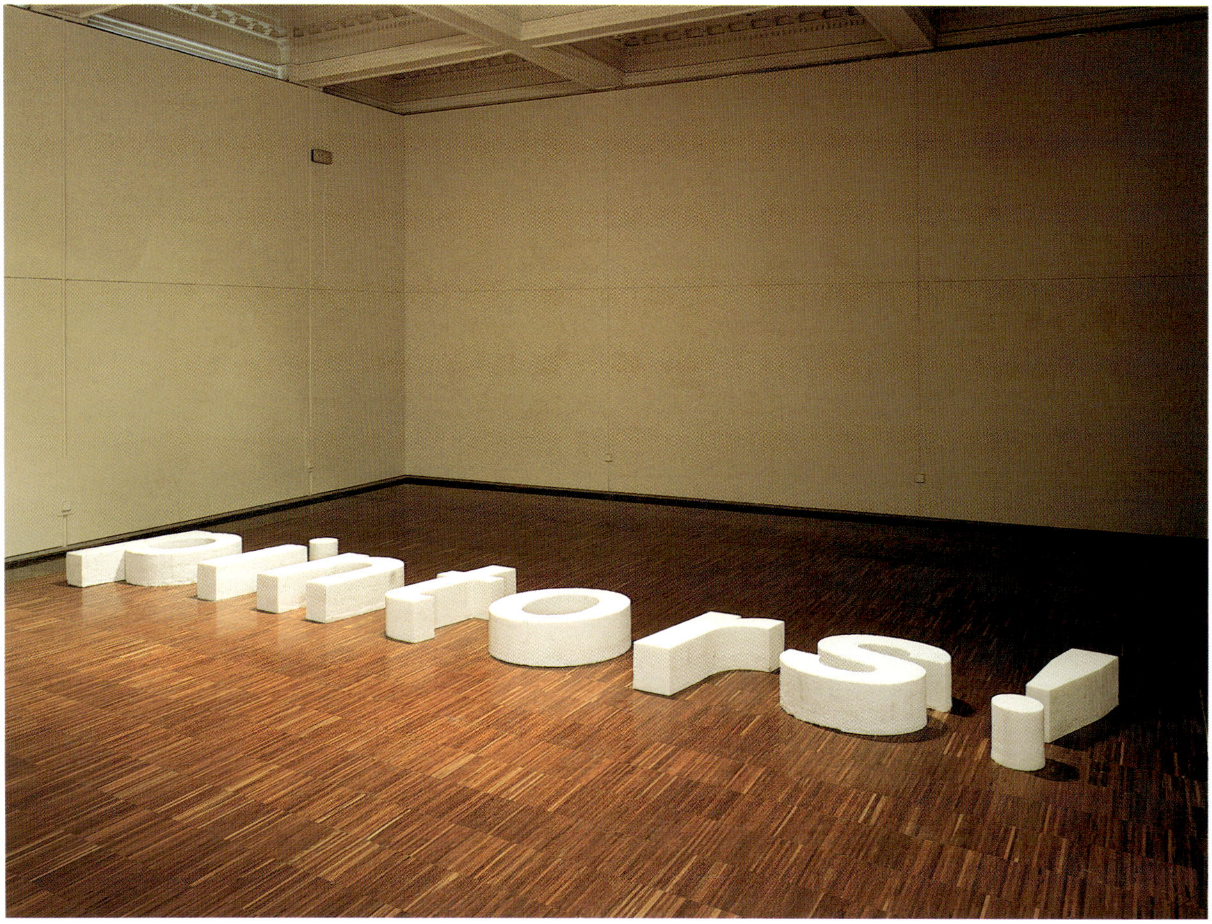

Pintors! 1997
(Painters!)
Alternating letters of salt and sugar. 630 x 130 cm.

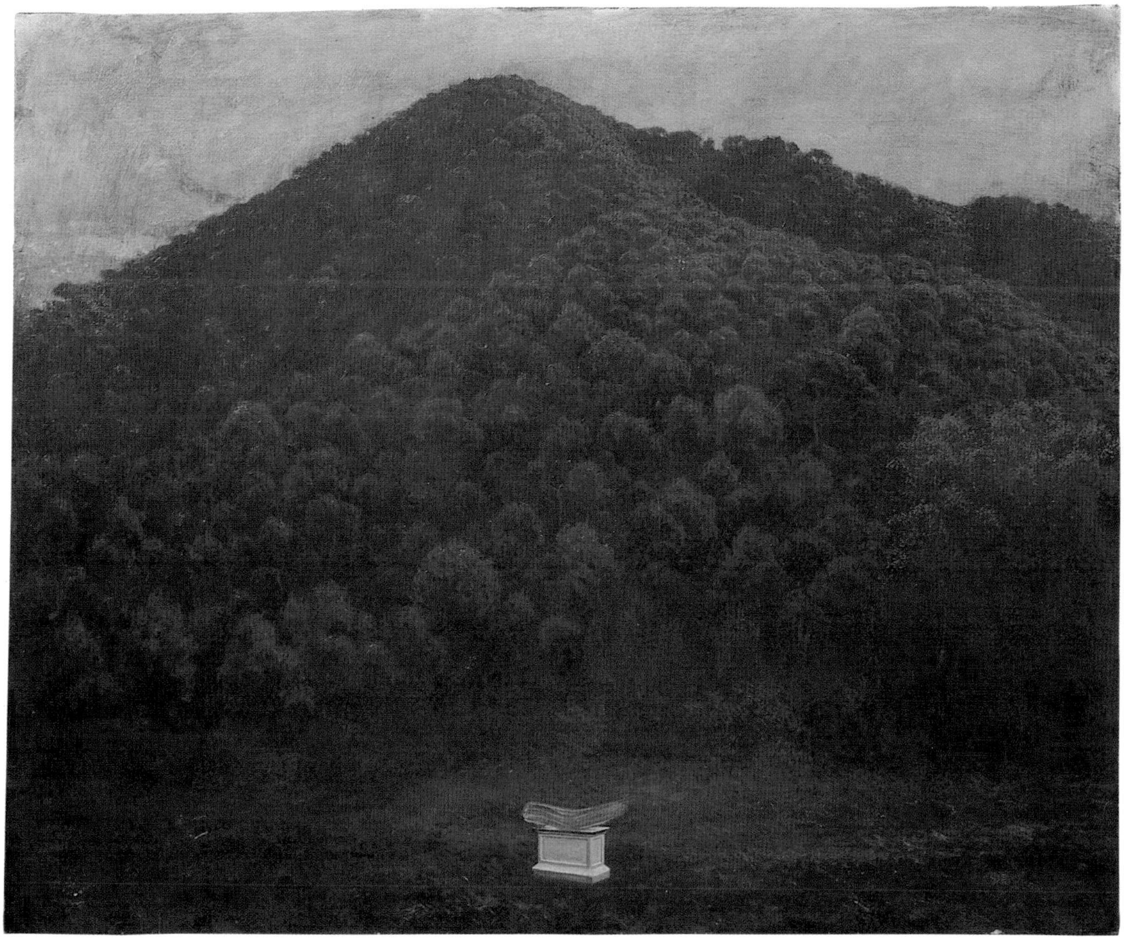

Pinzellada 1991
(Brushstroke)
Oil on canvas. 65 x 81 cm.

Intempèrie. Exposició del Garraf (1993-1999) ►
(Open Air. Exhibition of Garraf)
Gilded frames. 300 x 300 x 420 cm.

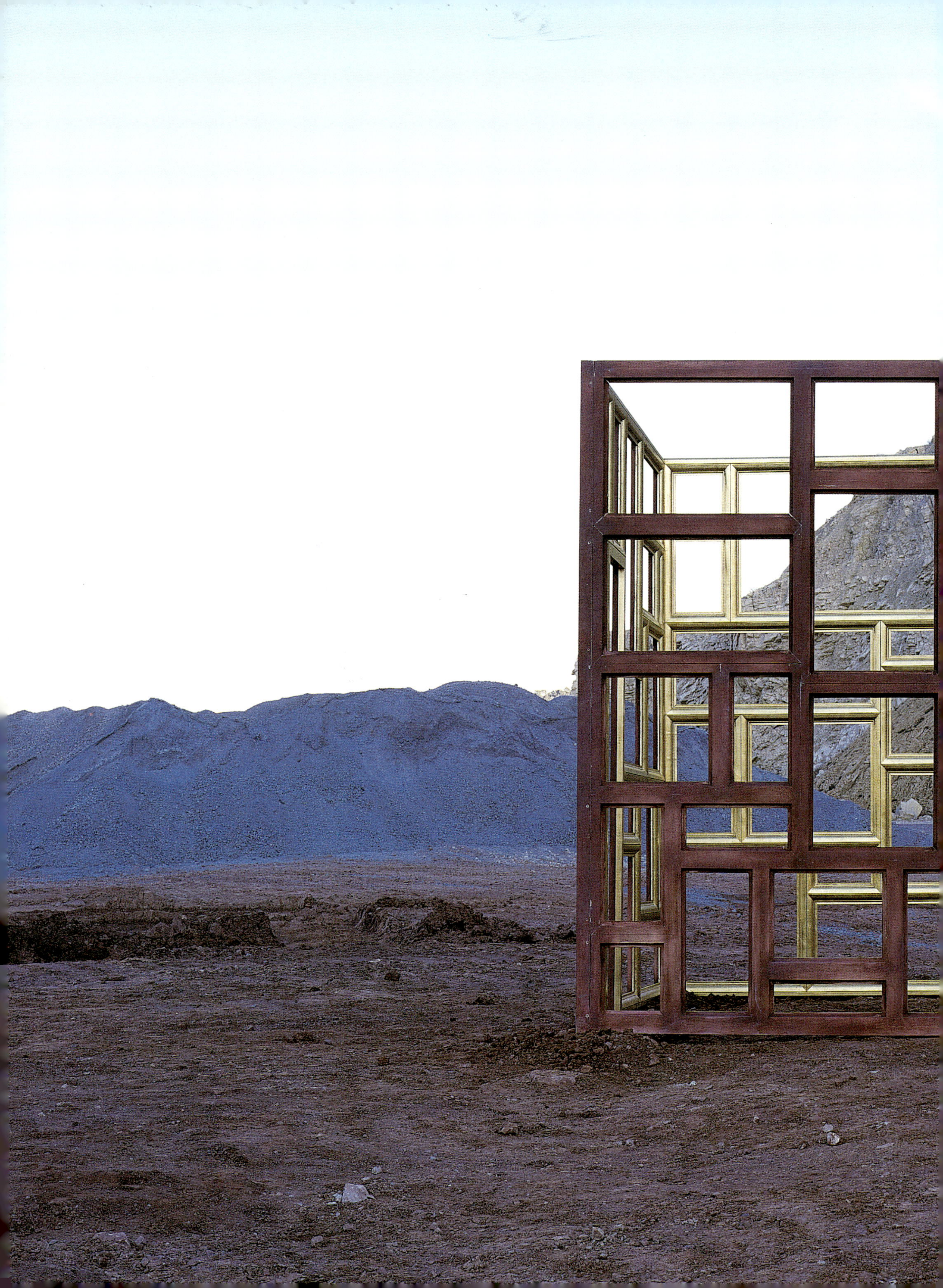

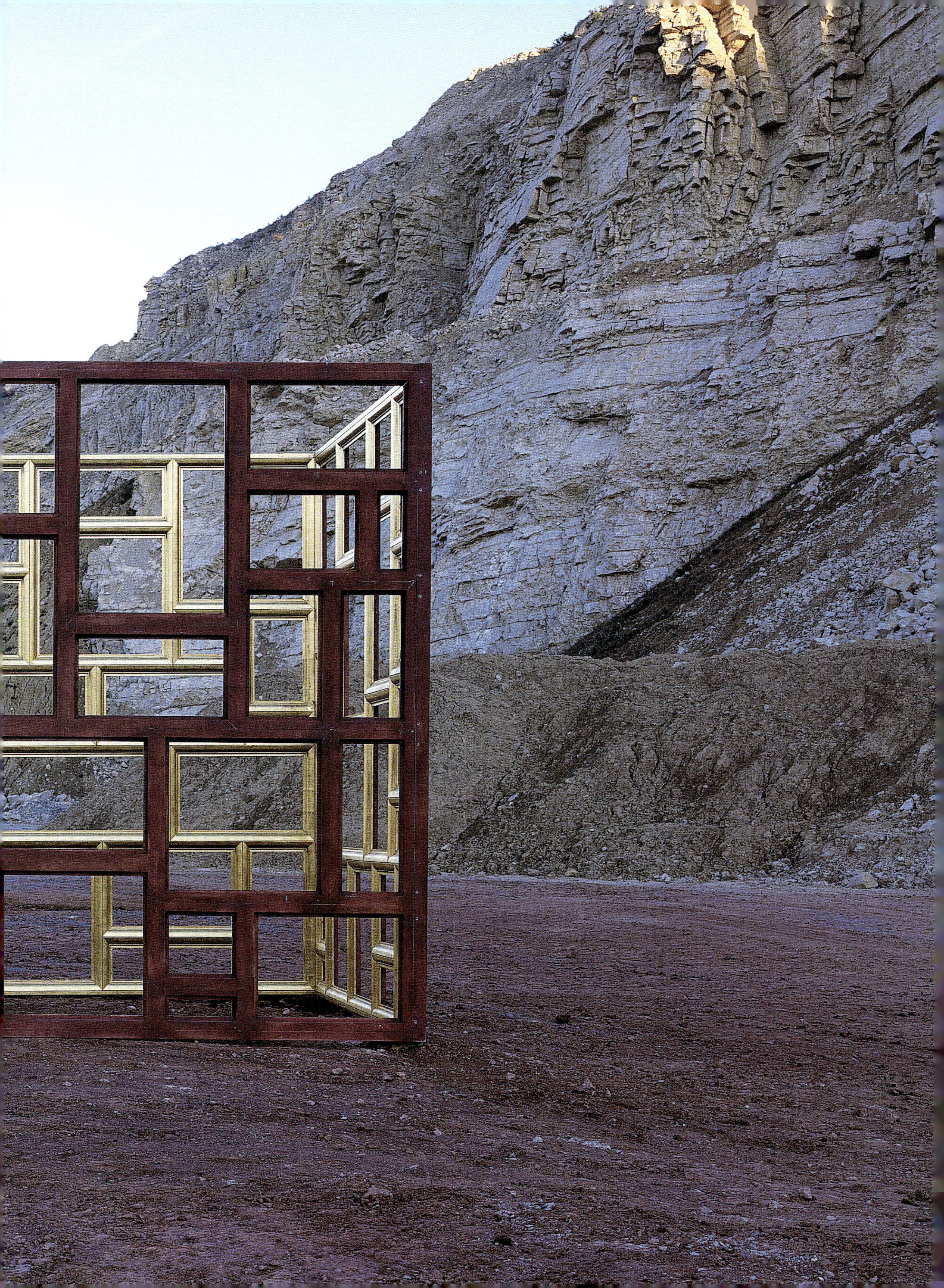

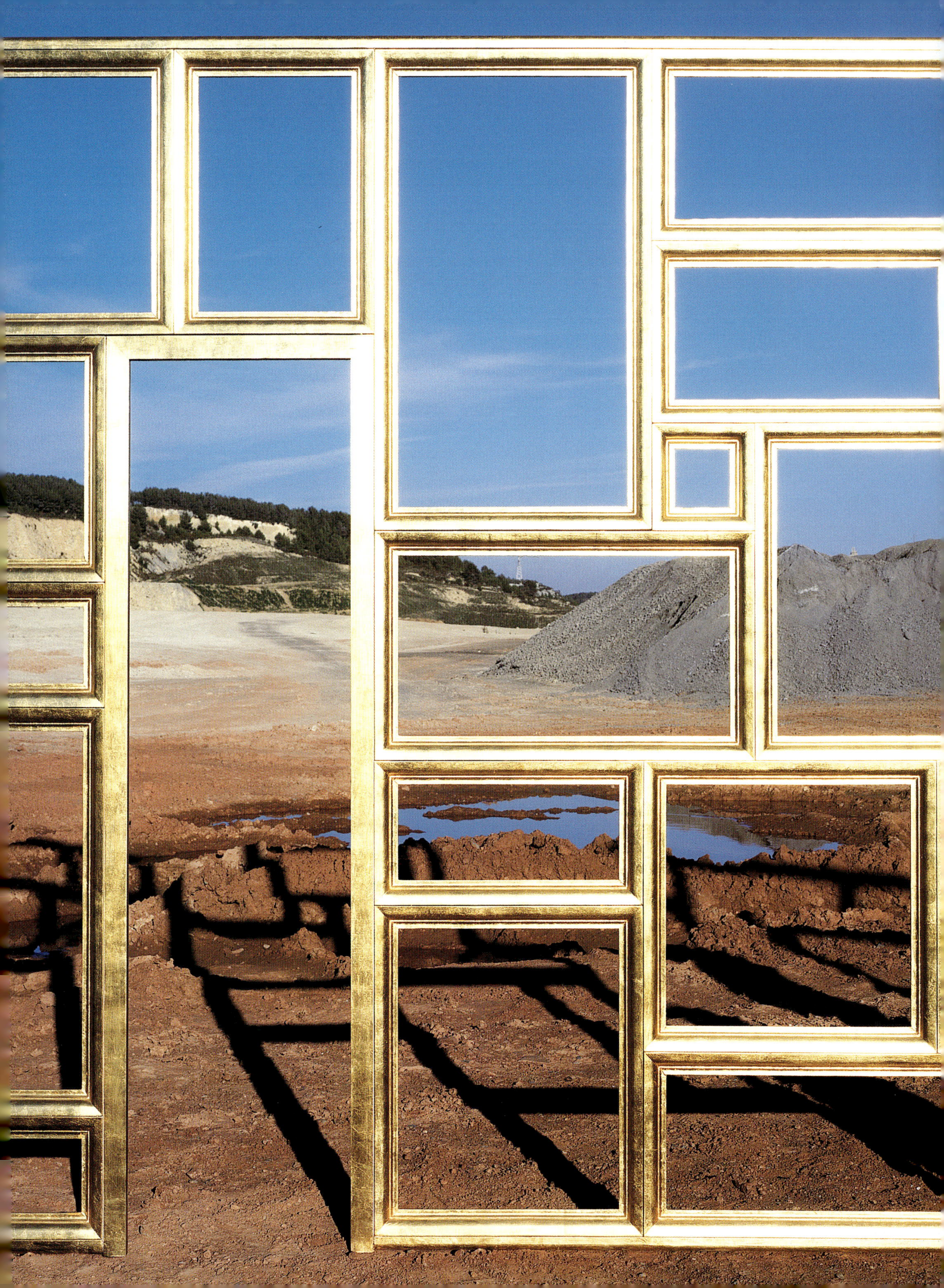

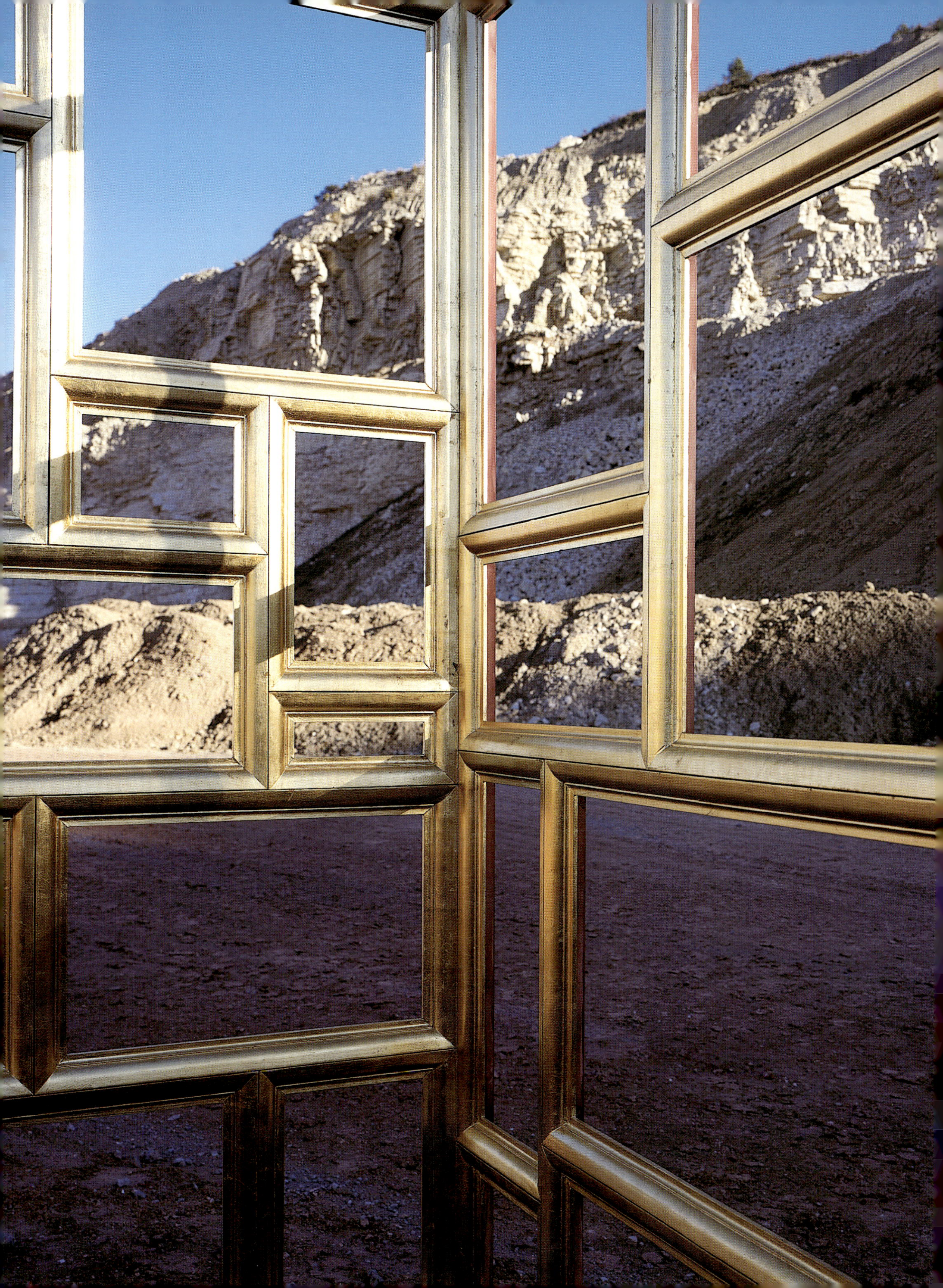

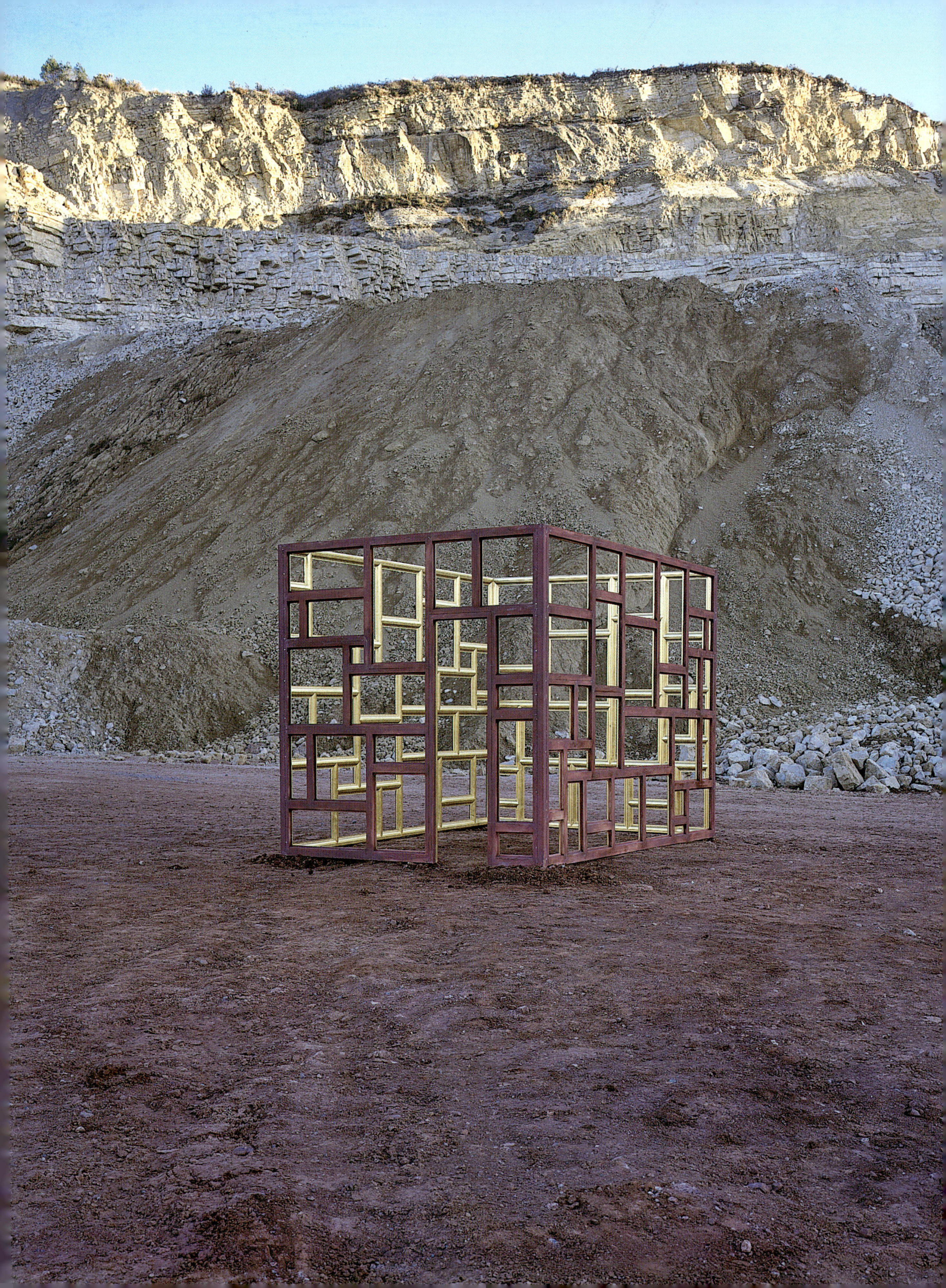